An Introduction to Television Studies

In this comprehensive textbook, now updated for its third edition, Jonathan Bignell provides students with a framework for understanding the key concepts and main approaches to Television Studies, including audience research, television history and broadcasting policy, and the analytical study of individual programmes.

Features include:

- a glossary of key terms
- key terms defined in margins
- suggestions for further reading
- activities for use in class or as assignments.

New and updated case studies include:

- 'Every Home Needs a Harvey' ad
- approaches to news reporting
- television scheduling
- *CSI: Crime Scene Investigation*
- animated cartoon series.

Individual chapters address: studying television, television histories, television cultures, television texts and narratives, television genres and formats, television production, television and quality, television realities, television you can't see, television audiences, beyond television.

This book is accompanied by a companion website featuring activities and case studies, flashcards, a glossary of key terms and links to useful websites, available at www.routledge.com/bignell.

Jonathan Bignell is Professor of Television and Film at the University of Reading, UK. He is the author of *Beckett on Screen: The Television Plays, Media Semiotics: An Introduction, Big Brother: Reality TV in the Twenty-first Century* and *Postmodern Media Culture,* and co-author of *The Television Handbook, 2nd edition.* He is the editor of *Writing and Cinema,* and joint editor of *Popular Television Drama* and *British Television Drama: Past, Present and Future.*

'At a time when the question of what constitutes "television" is being ever more keenly debated and as the medium continues to be reimagined, I can think of no other book to so adroitly meet the needs of students new to Television Studies. Engaging, accessible, and with a diverse series of activities and case studies that capture both the history and dynamism of this subject, Bignell's invaluable new edition provides a comprehensive entry into the most significant debates in the field.'
Dr Deborah Jermyn, *Reader in Film and Television, Roehampton University*

'In covering key areas of Television Studies, ranging across history, aesthetics, genre, production and reception, this book remains a key touchstone for students entering and studying the field. Accessibly written and well-illustrated with the addition of up-to-date examples, Bignell manages to span the core concepts and concerns of the discipline in an engaging and stimulating manner. At a time when the very idea of 'television' as an object of study is undergoing significant shifts, *An Introduction to Television Studies* succeeds in taking us on a journey which maps out longstanding aspects of television (and Television Studies), whilst embracing the "new" context of television's dispersed screens and digital culture.'
Su Holmes, *Reader in Television Studies, University of East Anglia*

An Introduction to Television Studies

Third edition

Jonathan Bignell

Routledge
Taylor & Francis Group

LONDON AND NEW YORK

Third edition published 2013
by Routledge
2 Park Square, Milton Park, Abingdon, Oxon OX14 4RN

Simultaneously published in the USA and Canada
by Routledge
711 Third Avenue, New York, NY 10017

Routledge is an imprint of the Taylor & Francis Group, an informa business

First edition published by Routledge 2004
Second edition published by Routledge 2008

LEEDS TRINITY UNIVERSITY

British Library Cataloguing in Publication Data
A catalogue record for this book is available from the British Library

Library of Congress Cataloging-in-Publication Data
Bignell, Jonathan.
An introduction to television studies / Jonathan Bignell. – 3rd ed.
p. cm.
Includes bibliographical references and index.
1. Television broadcasting. 2. Television. I. Title.
PN1992.5.B48 2012
791.45–dc23
2012018128

ISBN: 978–0–415–59816–3 (hbk)
ISBN: 978–0–415–59817–0 (pbk)
ISBN: 978–0–203–13495–5 (ebk)

Typeset in Janson and Akzidenz Grotesk
by Keystroke, Station Road, Codsall, Wolverhampton

MIX
Paper from
responsible sources
FSC® C004839
www.fsc.org

Printed and bound by CPI Group (UK) Ltd, Croydon, CR0 4YY

Contents

Illustrations

Acknowledgements

I would like to thank my colleagues at the University of Reading and, in former times, at Royal Holloway University of London who have assisted in shaping my approach to Television Studies, and whose expertise has suggested material, activities and further reading in some of the chapters of the book. The wider community of scholars in Television Studies also deserve my thanks, not only for the work explicitly acknowledged and referenced in the text but also for the wealth of ideas that I have encountered over the past two decades of studying and writing about television. I am grateful to the undergraduate and postgraduate students I have worked with over the years, because discussions with them have often prompted new ways of thinking and new problems to grapple with. During the preparation of the first, second and now the third edition of this book I received invaluable feedback from anonymous readers of draft material, and I have benefited from the expertise and enthusiasm of the editorial staff at Routledge. Finally, as always, I acknowledge the support and love of Lib Taylor, to whom the book is dedicated.

Introduction

Using this book

This book is an introduction to Television Studies, aimed especially at those who are new to the study of the medium at college and university level. It describes some of the critical approaches to television that have become widely accepted in the subject. It also explains and makes use of key concepts in Television Studies that every student needs to know about. The book re-evaluates the terms and ideas that have been significant in studying television, and tests out their limits, drawing attention to the strengths and weaknesses in the ways that television has been studied up to now. So the book draws together a collection of concepts and critical languages that are sometimes quite diverse, or even contradictory, and suggests how there are some ways of thinking about television that are more fruitful than others. Television Studies is a recent, dynamic and rapidly changing field of work, as the next section explains. This makes the task of the student of television an open-ended and exciting one, and the book also aims to convey some of this energy and diversity in its organisation and layout.

This book outlines significant strands of critical work in the field, and provides worked-though case study examples of how critical approaches can be applied to actual problems, programmes and issues. It encourages active learning by including many activities that can form the basis of classroom discussion or written assignments.

The book is organised into chapters that are suitable for use as preparatory reading for class study, or as follow-up reading to support classroom debate. Significant terms are highlighted in **bold** in the text when they are doing important work in the discussion. A definition of the highlighted term appears in the margin next to its first appearance in a chapter, and these definitions can also be found in alphabetical order in the glossary of key terms at the end of the book. The terms I have highlighted in this way are those that seem to require a specific definition. Some of them are part of the critical terminology of the academic discipline of Television Studies or one of the areas of research that has fed into the field. Some of them are terms used in the television industry in Britain or the USA to describe an aspect of how television technology works, or how programme-making and broadcasting are carried out. Some terms are more widely known and are part of non-professional language, but seem to me to need a precise definition so that they can be understood and used accurately by readers and students of television. Readers of this book will already know some terms, will have heard but not understood others, and will be introduced to some completely new vocabulary that I hope will enrich their capacity to talk and write about television.

Each chapter ends with a short list of suggested further reading. The books, essays and articles chosen are often those I have quoted from, but there are also some other books listed that deal with the topics covered in the chapter. Some of the sources are available only online, and in those cases the URL (the internet address) of the source is provided. I have created my own online materials to support this book, where extra material can be read, some of it from earlier editions of this book. There is great insight to be gained from noting how other voices have expressed ideas that I have written about here, and especially so if another writer has an alternative or even opposed attitude to a subject. Like any academic subject, Television Studies is diverse and evolving, and there are strongly held and articulately presented points of view within it that differ greatly in aims, assumptions, emphases and conclusions. Approaches to Television Studies are not a set of tools, but more like a group of different languages. They do not translate neatly one into another, and each defines its world in rather different ways. This book is concerned with the most commonly studied theoretical issues in television courses. The major differences between courses of study are in their focus on one or two of the following areas:

- analytical study of television programmes as texts
- the television industry as an institution and its production practices and organisation
- television in contemporary culture and the sociological study of audiences
- television history and developments in broadcasting policy.

This book provides introductory explanation, evaluation and routes for further study in each of these areas. I aim to show why these approaches have a significant role in Television Studies, to encourage students to participate in debates within and between these approaches, and to gain an understanding of the strengths and weaknesses of particular theoretical models for studying television.

In each chapter the reader will discover references to work by others who have contributed to Television Studies, and these references can be followed up in the Select Bibliography at the end of the book. Indeed, the Select Bibliography can itself be a useful tool for looking at the range of the subject, and exploring sources for independent work. In a single volume it is impossible for me to note all of the significant ideas in the sources I have used, and readers have many opportunities to build on the brief discussions of existing research that I have included here by reading the source texts that I have cited. Indeed, the many directions that such further work can take indicate the comparative newness and potential of Television Studies, and I hope that readers of this book will be encouraged to make their own contributions to the subject by identifying the gaps, new directions and even contradictions opened up in these pages.

Television Studies

Television Studies has tried to define how the medium communicates, and this has involved distinguishing between television communication and the media of cinema or radio, for example. But it has used methodologies for describing and analysing television texts that come from disciplines including Film Studies, methods of discussing audiences and television institutions that come from sociology, and ways of describing the development of television that amount to different histories of the medium. Charlotte Brunsdon (1998b: 96) has summarised this by explaining that:

much of the literature of television studies could be characterised as attempting to formulate accounts of the specificity of television, often using comparison with, on the one hand, radio (broadcast, liveness, civic address), and on the other, cinema (moving pictures, fantasy), with particular attention . . . to debate about the nature of the television text and the television audience.

Because television includes so many different programmes, channels and ways of addressing its audiences even at one point in time in a single geographical region, it has proved very difficult for critics and commentators to produce useful general insights into the medium. This is even more the case once the history of the medium and its regional variations across countries and regions of the world are considered.

Early predictions (in the 1930s, for instance) of what television would be emphasised its liveness, its ability to present to a mass audience images of what was happening in the real world. Commentators remarked on television's inability to compete with cinema as entertainment and therefore expected the medium to focus on information and actuality. These early thoughts conditioned the ways in which realism, connection to the contemporary and uneasiness about bringing controversial visions into the home were played out. The connection of television technology to immediacy (television as a means of relaying something that would have happened anyway) predisposes it to linear real-time progress, and the claim to report the real world. Film has been theorised in terms of space (what can be seen on the space of the screen), and this has led to theories about how individual film spectators identify with the usually fictional characters and points of view offered for spectators to see. Some of these ways of thinking from studying film have been deployed in Television Studies to explain how viewers make sense of the television medium. On the other hand, television has also been theorised in terms of time. Television consists of a flow of audio-visual material that, although divided up into programmes, runs on across a period of time without empty gaps in between. Brunsdon has noted that:

> Television is, for the most part, made as programmes or runs of programmes: series, serials and mini-series. However this is not necessarily how television is watched . . . It is precisely this possible 'drifting' through an evening's viewing that has come to seem . . . one of the unique features of television watching.
>
> (1998b: 105–6)

Rather than anticipating and wishing for the end of an individual film narrative, the television viewer is usually drawn into and out of a flow of material that does not come to a decisive end.

The experience of watching television occurs in a dimension of time where little end-points (like the ends of programmes) keep occurring, but where viewers are always aware that something new is about to take the place of what they have just been watching. Television Studies has tried to address this situation by looking not only at individual programmes but also at the ways they link together. These links might be in terms of the similarities of one programme with another, where shared features of a genre tell us something about the persistence of some kinds of storytelling, sets of issues or ideas being explored or the conventions to which the makers of programmes adhere. The links might also be in the planning and organisation of a period of viewing, for example an evening's television schedule on a certain channel. Planning a schedule to include variety, yet also a continuity of interest that can keep a viewer tuned to a single channel, can tell us a lot about how an idea of the viewing audience and its interests drives the organisation of television and assumptions about how television is used and enjoyed. The links between programmes in a schedule are the responsibility of the institutions that broadcast them, and looking at how television institutions work has been important to Television Studies' understanding of the medium's role as an industrial product, made and organised in different ways in different parts of the world.

Even though television programmes and formats are distributed globally, its local forms are different. This can be seen immediately in the difference between commercial television in the USA and the British tradition, which has a strong civic, 'public service' character. In Britain there has always been a tension between taking television's responsibility to society seriously and regarding television as entertainment for a consumer. So although television has been regarded as the medium most appropriate to the way we live now in Western societies, it is not the same everywhere across the world; nor does it lack a history that has shaped its present form in each society. The contexts that the organisation of television in particular places offers to Television Studies are important because they draw attention to the fact that television does not have to take the form that it does in the places with which we might be familiar. There is no necessity about the fact that in Britain, for example, there are television channels funded by advertising and sponsorship, and others funded by a licence fee that is in effect a tax on the ownership of television sets.

The ways in which television connects with the character of the society where it is watched raise the issue of the social significance of what television represents. The questions of what is represented, in what ways and with what possible effects have been considered in Television Studies with particular attention to the representation of groups who are relatively lacking in social power. This kind of study can illuminate the active contribution of television to the ways that viewers understand and experience their social environments, as well as how television reflects that environment to them. As well as looking at what can be seen and heard in the medium of television, how it is organised in different parts of the world and its relationship with the ways of thinking and experiencing the world in social contexts, Television Studies pays attention to the audiences of television and how they interact with the medium. This involves noting which programmes and kinds of programme are watched the most, using information that television institutions themselves collect in statistical form. But it also involves undertaking independent studies where groups of viewers are asked by Television Studies researchers about their attitudes to what they watch, and how their television viewing fits into their life experience and their sense of who they are. Research on audiences attempts to engage with how viewers make sense of television, and how it is important (or perhaps unimportant) to them. In this way Television Studies aims to break down the boundaries between the academic agendas that it has developed for specialised work on the medium and the place of watching television in the lives of non-specialist viewers for whom television can function in a range of ways among other routines and everyday experiences.

The first edition of this book was published in 2004 and the second edition in 2008. The new relationships between television and other electronic media are the most significant change that has occurred in British television in the interval preceding the completion of this new third edition of the book in 2012. All television broadcasting to home viewers is now done by means of digital signals received by a **set-top box**. Many viewers watch television programmes on computer screens as well as on home television sets, accessing programmes to watch them live at the time of their first broadcast or accessing previously broadcast programmes on catch-up services like the BBC's iPlayer. Programmes and television channels have accompanying websites, and some of them also offer social networking and other internet-based services. Television can be watched on mobile phones and portable computers. So the relationship of television to other media technologies is now much closer than ever before, and television is increasingly part of a convergence culture. Television can be accessed over the internet in a wide range of places (on a train, or in a café, as well as inside the home), and programmes are available for a longer period (for a week after broadcast in the case of iPlayer) rather than being broadcast at a set time. These changes to the production, distribution and reception of television are the reason for many of the changes to the content of the new edition of this book.

set-top box the electronic decoding equipment connected to home television sets that allows access to digital television signals.

The organisation of chapters

Studying Television

The first chapter sketches out the topics of study and critical approaches which can be found in academic Television Studies, noting its significant emphases and exclusions. Television Studies in Britain and the USA, for example, is dominated by work on television in the English-speaking world. One dominant strand is the detailed textual analysis of programmes, with a preference for popular programmes in serial and series form, concentrating on drama, documentary and news programmes. This derives from the tradition in academic work of studying content and form in detail. It also reflects the dominance of English-language programmes in the world television market. There are other kinds of television to mention, however, which stimulate thinking about what television can include: trailers, commercials and channel idents, for instance. As mentioned, television can now be viewed on computer screens, and is viewed in a different position and often in a different room from the traditional household television set. This chapter considers different understandings of what television is, and how Television Studies approaches are based on assumptions about the television text, the form of its transmission and who is watching where and when. The chapter includes a case study comparing and contrasting representations of television viewing in the 1950s and the 2000s, showing how the medium has been thought about in different ways at different times.

Television Histories

Chapter 2 describes and analyses the different approaches to the evolution of television from the 1930s to the 1990s in Britain, comparing and contrasting these with historical approaches to television in other countries, especially the USA. This involves discussion of state regulation of television, the increasing proliferation of channels and the introduction of cable and satellite broadcasting systems, competition and commerce. Part of the different historical shape of television around the world comes from distinct and different understandings of the television audience, perceived as a market of consumers or as a public whose needs television should serve. The chapter aims to introduce the subject of television history, with regard to the changing social place of television in society, changes in television institutions and changing conceptions of the television audience and the nature of television viewing. The range of approaches to television history in the chapter provides different selections of landmark developments and landmark programmes, for example according to whether the focus is on technology, institutions or audience issues. The chapter explains a range of historical approaches, in order to show how television history can be written in many different ways. The case study at the end of the chapter explores one aspect of television's likely future, as new technologies allow viewers to compose their own viewing schedules and selections of programmes from huge databases from which viewers can download their choices, or have their personal video recorders make choices for them.

Television Cultures

Chapter 3 looks at the competing ways of analysing television institutions, and the significance of national and international cultures of television broadcasting. It explains and discusses patterns of commercial and public service broadcasting, and debates about whether television contributes to media imperialism. This leads to a discussion of television globalisation, comparing and contrasting ways of thinking about television as a market and an industry with political implications. Television in the developed world is still largely organised on national lines, but the increasing significance of international flows from West to East and North to South has been hotly debated. The chapter refers to inequalities in production funding and the role of imported programming in national television cultures. The focus of the chapter is on theories arguing that television institutions both embody and transmit ideologies because of their ownership, and their relationships with national broadcasting cultures. The chapter finishes with a case study on the ways in which talent shows and reality TV formats have been adopted outside the UK, and how they can be understood in the context of debates about the politics of global television.

Television Texts and Narratives

Chapter 4 evaluates the theoretical approaches that have considered television programmes as 'texts' that can be studied in close detail to reveal how their meanings are made. The techniques for undertaking this kind of close analysis, deriving from the methodologies of semiotics, are explained. This includes methodologies for analysing narrative, the relationships between programmes across a period of television viewing, and ways of thinking about the relations between image and sound. While this way of working can be very powerful, the chapter also considers what it leaves out, such as television's institutional context and history, and the relationships between actual viewers and programmes. The question of who or what is the maker of television's meanings, in other words the question of authorship, is also considered in the chapter, and it explores different genres of television and how they can be studied. The case study in this chapter takes a single television commercial and conducts a close analysis of its images and sounds, showing how textual and narrative approaches to television can be used in practice.

Television Genres and Formats

Chapter 5 focuses on the significance of genre in television, showing how genres are relatively stable, but also how genres mix and change over time. It addresses the distinctions made by academics and broadcasting companies between, for example, fact and fiction, drama and documentary, series and serial. The chapter explains theories of genre, and tests them out in relation to a range of programmes, some of which have mixed or uncertain genre. The effects of the flow of television viewing for audiences, and channel hopping, are introduced since understandings of genre depend not only on how programmes themselves work but also on how they are watched. The chapter explains the concept of a television programme format, suggesting that formats display much less variability than genres. The case study at the end of the chapter looks at American animated series, analysing how they draw from a range of television genres and combine them in interesting ways to address different audiences.

Television Production

Chapter 6 discusses the production practices and technologies that are used in bringing programmes to the screen, including the pitching, production planning, production scheduling, shooting and post-production of programmes. It gives an account of the professional culture of television production in different kinds of broadcasting environments and in different genres and forms of programme. The chapter aims to provide a critical understanding of the television industry as a profession. This includes such issues as the conventions of lighting, camerawork and editing, and the significance of sound, music and graphics. Attention is paid to developments in technology such as digital editing by means of computer software programmes, and the different kinds of equipment used in programme-making. The chapter discusses the institutional organisation and technology of television, and encourages readers to gain an understanding of the production process. The chapter includes a case study of the Avid editing system, noting how the design and operation of the system carries assumptions about the role of the programme-maker, and discussing the opportunities and constraints which the system allows or imposes.

Television and Quality

Chapter 7 discusses the social and cultural frameworks that enable some kinds of television to carry value, and for some programmes or kinds of television to be labelled as 'quality TV'. Deciding on what counts as quality TV has a relationship with genre, since it works as a way of separating 'good' television from everything else. Attaching the label 'quality' involves assigning cultural importance to programmes or kinds of television that have acquired a valued position in culture, rather like theatre's distinctions between serious theatre and musicals or pantomime. The debates about what constitutes quality TV are also ways of engaging with the common criticism in the press, and sometimes in the television industry itself, that some television is unimportant and lacking in artistic value. The chapter explains how understandings of quality may be different in the different contexts of the television industry, in academic studies, or in the reactions of audiences. Quality can mean different things, depending on what is being discussed and by whom. The majority of programmes discussed in the chapter are American drama programmes, since recent discussions of quality have claimed that US television has overtaken British programmes in achieving quality. The chapter's case study addresses *The Wire*, an American series that exemplifies this argument.

Television Realities

Chapter 8 focuses on the ways that questions of realism can be addressed in Television Studies. This includes looking at what realism might mean in different programme genres, and the conventions used in various kinds of documentary and factual programmes. Television has a strong tradition of showing its viewers images of reality, using live footage and actuality in such diverse forms as news, documentary, docusoap and reality TV. The chapter debates the different understandings of reality and realism in television, and how kinds of realism are achieved. This chapter also looks at how television criticism has dealt with the representation of certain groups in society. The chapter outlines the different methods adopted in Television Studies for approaching these issues, including content analysis, and debates over fair and accurate representations of different groups of people. In this context television has participated in setting up and also changing the cultural norms that underlie how members of society think about themselves and about people who seem different to them. As well as dealing with television forms that are centred on representations of reality, the chapter considers the realist conventions in fictional programmes, and the crossovers between documentary modes and other television forms. The chapter ends with a case study on dramatisations of real events in drama-documentary, also known as docudrama.

Television You Can't See

Chapter 9 is about television regulation, with particular attention paid to broadcasters' assumptions about the audience and what viewers should not see or would like not to see on television. This includes an account of the main principles of broadcasting regulation in Britain and the role of Ofcom, the official body that deals with this. The chapter discusses the assumptions about the protection of vulnerable groups (such as children) that are embedded in broadcasting regulations. A significant aspect of the issue of what can and cannot be shown is the way that television institutions and programme-makers censor themselves, and why and how they do this. The chapter also explains the regulation of programme content at moments of political and military tension, and the effect of a perception by broadcasters of public concern. The chapter ends with a case study on television coverage of war and conflict in the Middle East, where, as this edition was completed in 2012, coverage included showing video shot by unofficial observers and participants in political protests. When television institutions were unable to get access to events themselves, they made use of amateur footage of events that otherwise viewers would be unable to see.

Television Audiences

Chapter 10 analyses the methods of understanding audiences, and of seeking to control their television viewing behaviour, which are used by television institutions. The methods used by British and US broadcasters to gather information about television viewers are explained in the context of a discussion of the underlying assumptions about viewers and the television medium that accompany them. The chapter introduces the different industry and academic approaches to audiences, and their implications. The identification of niche audiences in today's multichannel environment, and the ever-increasing drive for reliable information in order to predict audience behaviour, have led to a greater interest by broadcasters in fragmented, specific viewing groups and viewing practices. This mirrors the emphasis in academic audience research on highly specific studies of audience behaviour and people's responses to television. The chapter addresses issues connected with the activity or 'agency' of viewers, the role of academic television audience researchers and the ways that audiences make and resist the meanings of television programmes. The discussion of understandings of audience is placed in the context of how broadcasters try to attract and hold audiences, especially through the ways they schedule programmes. The chapter concludes with a case study on television scheduling which develops these issues in more specific detail.

Beyond Television

Chapter 11 discusses the ways that television has recently changed and is likely to change in the future, because of the medium's convergence with related audio-visual media like the World Wide Web and social networking. Some commentators have clamed that in the first decades of the twenty-first century, television in its previous forms is ceasing to exist, and is being absorbed into a digital media culture that takes distinctively new forms. The delivery of audio-visual content to viewers changes when programmes are available on computers or mobile phones, as well as on television sets, and when viewers can choose where and when to watch. Viewers can also interact with programmes in new ways, by accessing web resources or engaging with programme makers and other viewers over the internet. The chapter explores how these changes came about, and what their implications are for how television can be defined and understood. It analyses the continuities and ruptures in the evolution of television, and argues that the critical approaches and vocabularies of Television Studies are still useful.

Further reading

Allen, R. (ed.), *Channels of Discourse, Reassembled: Television and Contemporary Criticism* (London: Routledge, 1992).

Bennett, J., and N. Strange (eds), *Television as Digital Media* (Durham, NC: Duke University Press, 2011).

Brunsdon, C., 'Is Television Studies history?', *Cinema Journal*, 47:3 (2008), pp. 127–37.

—— 'What is the television of television studies?', in C. Geraghty and D. Lusted (eds), *The Television Studies Book* (London: Arnold, 1998), pp. 95–113.

Corner, J., *Critical Ideas in Television Studies* (Oxford: Clarendon, 1999).

Fiske, J., *Television Culture* (London: Routledge, 1992).

Geraghty, C. and D. Lusted (eds), *The Television Studies Book* (London: Arnold, 1998).

Gillan, J., *Television and New Media* (London: Routledge, 2011).

Goodwin, A. and G. Whannel (eds), *Understanding Television* (London: Routledge, 1990).

Jenkins, H., *Convergence Culture: Where Old and New Media Collide* (Cambridge, Mass.: MIT Press, 2006).

McQueen, D., *Television: A Media Student's Guide* (London: Arnold, 1998).

Mullan, B., *Consuming Television* (Oxford: Blackwell, 1997).

Newcomb, H., 'The development of television studies', in J. Wasko (ed.), *A Companion to Television* (Malden, Mass. and Oxford: Blackwell, 2005), pp. 15–28.

Turner, G., and J. Tay (eds), *Television Studies after TV: Understanding Television in the Post-Broadcast Era* (London: Routledge, 2009).

Wasko, J., 'Introduction', in J. Wasko (ed.), *A Companion to Television* (Malden, Mass. and Oxford: Blackwell, 2005), pp. 1–8.

Studying Television

Studying Television

Introduction

This chapter briefly maps out the topics of study and introduces some of the critical approaches that are central to academic Television Studies today, with emphasis on the approaches used in Britain and the United States. By doing this the chapter aims to provide an overview of the kinds of questions which students of television should carry with them as they use this book. Each of the chapters in the remainder of this book focuses on a particular aspect of the study of television, picking up the concerns and ways of thinking about television that are introduced here. The discipline of Television Studies is a relatively new academic subject, and in its short history the questions that have been asked about television, and the answers which researchers have discovered, have changed in interesting ways. Television Studies, like all academic subjects, is in a continual process of development. This is partly because researchers discover new information and respond to changes in what is happening in television in the present. Television Studies also changes because, as ways of thinking about television are discussed and their strengths and weaknesses discovered, new questions and problems in understanding television are found. One of the aims of this book is to involve readers in the debates and disagreements about television that animate Television Studies.

The study of television emerged out of the larger field of media education. Media education began in the 1930s on the assumption that mass media had negative effects on society, and that educating citizens about how media products are made would help to protect them from their impact. Television, beginning its history as a medium at about the same time, has long been regarded as a medium that has a special relationship with its viewers' everyday lives. Television is very familiar to most people and often taken for granted, so the scholarly study of television tries to examine familiar programmes in new ways, introduces unfamiliar programmes and aims to attain critical distance from television as a medium. The premise that underpins media education is that academic studies should engage with everyday media experiences that are understood as an aspect of everyday popular culture. Television and media studies encourage the questioning of media by means of the analysis of media products, media institutions and media technologies. The work of the literary and cultural critic Raymond Williams (1974) was crucial in establishing this breadth in the field, as a result of his interest in evaluating television as an aspect of contemporary culture. In Europe, media education is often referred to as **media literacy** and it was in the United Kingdom that the idea was first put into practice in the context of school and university teaching. Key issues that structure this curriculum include:

media literacy
the skills and competence that viewers learn in order to understand easily the audio-visual 'languages' of media texts.

■ Institutions and ownership: the patterns of ownership of media organisations, where the national and global holdings of corporations such as News

Corporation, Disney or Time Warner are assessed in terms of the concentration of media power in the hands of a few main players.

■ The laws and **regulation** of media industries: in relation to censorship, bias and assumptions about their influence.

■ Texts and their conventions: in addressing specific media texts like television programmes, films or magazine advertisements, media education asks what audience the text is addressed to, and how the conventions of a certain **genre** or form are used to target an audience.

■ Audiences: the study of media audiences is interested in how different groups of viewers or readers interpret media content in different ways according to (for example) age, sex, gender or economic status. Scholars of television have conducted studies of individual media users or audience groups, to provide a more finely textured understanding of how and why television and other media are used in the context of ordinary life.

Television Studies draws on each of these approaches, with different scholars adopting them to differing extents. In this book, aspects of each way of studying media are examined specifically in relation to television.

regulation the control of television institutions by laws, codes of practice or guidelines.

genre a kind or type of programme. Programmes of the same genre have shared characteristics.

Beyond broadcasting

Clearly, an important place to start is to consider how wide or how narrow television might be as an object of study. Television Studies has until recently focused on **broadcast** television, where programmes are watched at the time they are transmitted, in the home on a television set. The transmission signals for broadcast television have been received by rooftop aerials or receiving dishes, or along cables embedded in the ground. Many different broadcast signals may be available to be received at any one time, but all the television receivers tuned into a specific channel would receive the same broadcast programme at the same time. But in 2012 all British television transferred to digital, and the former system for broadcasting to the rooftop aerial was switched off. For several years it has already been possible to watch television digitally, on devices like computers, mobile phones or games consoles that do not rely on rooftop aerials and are instead connected to the internet. In the home, rooftop aerials still work after 2012 and receive digital signals that need to be decoded by a **set-top box** or by television sets with digital receivers built into them. Television sets with built-in internet connectivity provide a much fuller watching experience, and viewers are able to download programmes and films, browse the World Wide Web, or connect to social networking sites via their televisions. There is already some convergence between television and digital networked technologies, but shortly this is going to be the norm. This raises the question of whether what viewers do in the post-broadcasting world can still be called watching television. This question comes back in many ways throughout this book, and the case study at the end of this chapter addresses the issue directly. But the short answer at this point is yes, since traditional ways of watching will continue and television will adapt to them. Television has always borrowed from other media around it, and been a hybrid medium – one that does some of the same things as newspapers, radio, magazines, advertisements or films while adapting what they do into its own distinctive form.

broadcasting the transmission of signals from a central source which can be received by dispersed receivers over a large geographical area.

set-top box the electronic decoding equipment connected to home television sets that allows access to digital television signals.

Television is a hungry medium that borrows audio-visual content from a range of other places. For instance, *Crimewatch* might broadcast extracts from surveillance video in order to show a crime being committed and to identify the perpetrator so that television viewers can provide information to help catch the offender. Wedding videos and videos of family holidays, sometimes posted onto the web on YouTube or other internet sites, appear in television programmes especially for comic purposes (in *America's Funniest Home Videos*, for example). Mobile phone footage appears in news programmes, when people in an accident or in a war provide footage of news events. In the case of both surveillance video and domestic video, the footage changes its meaning once it is put in a broadcast context. What was private becomes public. The fascination of **reality TV** programmes such as *Big Brother* derives partly from this contrast between the usually private material caught by surveillance or amateur cameras and the very public broadcasting of the material on television. Since the 1960s visual artists have incorporated live or recorded video into artworks, to be seen in a gallery space, in a different location of viewing from conventional television and designed for different ways of watching (standing up rather than sitting down, in a gallery rather than in the home). Occasionally these art videos might be screened in a late-night compilation of **avant-garde** works, or as part of a television **documentary**, but like wedding videos these films change their meaning once they are transmitted to a different kind of audience. At some large public events, such as football matches or rock concerts, live video is shown on big screens. One of the conventions of pop videos such as those shown on the MTV or VH1 television channels is to recreate the kinds of images that are projected at concerts, by using mist and lighting effects, and footage of the band apparently playing their instruments on a stage. For a long time, television has borrowed the conventions of non-broadcast video in order to communicate the excitement of being at a live performance. Some of the distinguishing features of music television (e.g. MTV), or reality TV, for example, come from the ways in which they draw on non-broadcast television or video and make use of the **connotations** which they carry, such as

- privacy (in reality TV, where private behaviour becomes public)
- performance (on MTV or in talent shows, where television borrows the conventions of a live show), or
- evidence (where surveillance video or mobile phone footage confirms that something shocking or controversial has happened).

reality TV programmes where the unscripted behaviour of 'ordinary people' is the focus of interest.

avant-garde work aiming to challenge the norms and conventions of its medium, and the group of people making such work.

documentary a form aiming to record actual events, often with an explanatory purpose or to analyse and debate an issue.

connotations the term used in semiotic analysis for the meanings that are associated with a particular sign or combination of signs.

ACTIVITY 1.1

What is it about television that might make it seem unworthy of serious study? How would you respond to such criticisms?

---

digital television television pictures and sound encoded into the ones and zeros of electronic data. Digital signals can also be sent back down cables by viewers, making possible interaction with television programmes.

The hybridity of television becomes more visible when **digital television** permits viewers to do more than just watch programmes as they are transmitted. Updating your Facebook page on the same piece of technology that you use to watch *Doctor Who* makes it obvious that television has become one among several interconnected

Figure 1.1 Metropolitan Police CCTV still handout of an assault on Wayne Miller, who was sleeping rough in a doorway in Leake Street, London, 29 October 2004. © EMPICS/Metropolitan Police.

aspects of digital media culture. But television has always looked outwards beyond the domestic living room to borrow and adapt aspects of social life. Popular entertainment programmes such as *Strictly Come Dancing* or *The X Factor* work by connecting the private sphere of television viewership with the public world of celebrity performance. Television is a medium that is predominantly experienced in the home, but it has both adopted and transformed existing forms of popular entertainment that come from public, collective experiences. Light entertainment television negotiates between a 'here' and 'there' of home and public spaces of entertainment, between ordinariness and spectacle, between ordinary people ('us') and performers and stars ('them') (Dyer 1973). Each of these terms can blur into the other. *The X Factor* has star performers acting as judges, but the television audience is also invited to judge by voting for their favourite contestant. Amateur 'ordinary' contestants perform as if they were stars, and seek to become one. So talent shows recognise how the television medium sits between domestic familiarity and a spectacular world of celebrity. The effect is to frame the programme as a mediating format, and the content of singing, comedy routines and entertainment acts in light entertainment comes originally from earlier forms of popular enter-tainment, such as vaudeville or music hall, which have been adapted into television for domestic and private consumption. Like music hall variety performances, talent shows are either really or apparently live, take place in an auditorium setting and are made up of a mix of types of content. But at the same time, on television their domesticity is signified by the placement of the programme within the routines of a schedule designed to match the rhythms of domestic life (mealtimes, work versus leisure time, etc.), modes of address that assume a home audience, and the use of multi-camera shooting techniques to edit the material into an event for television rather than a relayed performance. Television's hybridity is evident in how some genres of programme borrow and adapt cultural forms.

Television Studies is now developing theoretical approaches to the distribution of programmes to different kinds of screen and to locations other than the home. Downloading episodes of programmes has become like downloading music from the iTunes website, and users are now familiar with the principle that watching television streamed over the internet or downloaded from YouTube is as normal as watching broadcast programmes. These developments are questioning the assumptions that television is watched on a television set rather than a computer, and that programmes are broadcast at a set time in a schedule. The traditional broadcasters have until recently seen YouTube as a threat, because users have posted copies of programmes illegally onto the YouTube website. Broadcasters commission programmes and show them as the basis of their business, and have legal ownership of the copyright on the programmes that they show. So uploading programmes to YouTube is breaking the law and threatening the revenue of conventional television channels and programme makers. YouTube is owned by Google, the internet search technology company, and it has responded to these concerns in two ways. It created a computer programme called Content ID that automatically searches the internet to find illegally uploaded content. Google then informs the owners of the uploaded material, for example the BBC, and offers the choice of having Google delete the content or allow Google to place advertising on the page where the content is displayed. BBC, Channel 4 and Independent Television News (ITN) agreed in 2009 that where their content appeared on YouTube, advertising could appear around it and the broadcasters owning the material would receive all of the income paid to Google by those advertisers. Broadcasters are gradually finding ways of adapting to the new media landscape where control over content is hard to police, and where the boundaries of television are expanding to include these new ways of delivering and experiencing audio-visual content.

Television nations

subtitle written text appearing on the television screen, normally to translate speech in a foreign language.

dubbing replacing the original speech in a programme, advertisement, etc. with speech added later, often to translate speech in a foreign language.

Almost all the examples of television that are discussed in this book were made and shown in the English-speaking world, and most of the books which are used in courses in Television Studies in Britain refer to British and American television. One of the reasons for this is that English-language television programmes are exported around the world to many other countries whose national language is not English, where they are shown either with **subtitled** dialogue or with a **dubbed** soundtrack in another language, spoken by actors from the country in which the programme is broadcast. This issue is discussed further in Chapter 3, where television around the world is considered. Television advertisements are also sometimes shown in several different countries, with the same visual images but with a soundtrack made in another language. People in Britain are notoriously resistant to watching television programmes in languages other than English, and are unwilling to read subtitles translating foreign-language dialogue. But this is relatively unusual:

■ In Poland imported foreign-language programmes have the dialogue of all the speakers (whether young or old, male or female) read in Polish by a single actor.
■ In France, British and American programmes are usually shown with dubbed dialogue in French.
■ In the Netherlands, British and American programmes are shown with Dutch subtitles.

The experience of watching television in Britain is relatively unusual, in that almost all programmes are in English, originating either in Britain or in America or Australia, countries with which Britain has had an historical 'special relationship'. The situation is different in other countries, where imported television from Britain or America is immediately marked as different because of its dubbed or subtitled dialogue. There are also countries where there are several commonly spoken languages and which broadcast television in each of these languages:

■ In Singapore there are television channels in English, Chinese and Malay.
■ In the United States there are channels in English and Spanish.

The sense of what a national television culture might be is different in these countries, and the experience of familiarity would be different from the experience in Britain.

Television has aimed to represent a relatively unified **culture** in Britain, though its division into the nations of England and Scotland, together with the principality of Wales and the province of Northern Ireland, means that television also has a regional character. The further, related division of terrestrial television broadcasting into regional areas (the south-west of England, the Midlands or East Anglia, for example) where there are distinct programmes aimed at local audiences, makes this situation more marked. The issue of belonging to a region, nation or country complicates the assumption that British television can be referred to as a national television culture. Furthermore, since Britain is a multi-cultural society, there are channels aimed at people from an overseas background and in languages other than English, such as channels in Chinese and the languages of the Indian sub-continent. The proliferation of channels in recent years has permitted the development of new television services aimed at British people from specific ethnic backgrounds. Zee TV began broadcasting in 1995 and targets its programmes at British Asian viewers, as does the B4Utv channel which screens Bollywood films from the Indian sub-continent and several other channels that specialise in Asian celebrity features and sports reports. Greek Cypriots in Britain are the target audience for Hellenic TV, and households equipped with cable television or a satellite dish are able to receive programmes from broadcasters transmitting from Cyprus and Greece. The Phoenix Chinese Channel was launched in 1999 and shows programmes for Chinese communities around the world on five different channels which are themed around different kinds of content such as entertainment, news and films. The unity and diversity of contemporary television matches the co-existing forces of unification and diversification that are at work in 'our' society, and raise questions about who this 'we' might be.

Television has regional, national and transnational aspects, and is thus implicated in the concept of globalisation. As with other media at the present time, television

culture the shared attitudes, ways of life and assumptions of a group of people.

is transnational but takes nationally specific forms. British television draws primarily on programmes by British programme-makers, but that consciousness of national identity in and through television is also constituted against imported programmes and those that are modelled on formats associated with other cultures. The better-funded production cultures of the USA, UK, France and Germany produce programmes designed partly for export as well as for their national domestic audiences, and thus their national specificity exists in tension with conceptions of transnational marketability. For the UK in particular, the global spread of the English language offers opportunities for British television to be internationally popular and to rival US programmes in international trading.

Studying programmes

An important component of many courses in Television Studies is the study of particular television programmes. Particular programmes might be chosen for study in each week of a course, and there are several reasons for this. Television Studies emerged in the 1970s and 1980s out of three ways of writing about television:

- the reviewing of programmes in newspapers and magazines (Caughie 1984, Rixon 2011)
- the criticism of programmes as works of art (like literature texts)
- and the **sociology** of culture (see Brunsdon 1998b).

sociology the academic study of society, aiming to describe and explain aspects of life in that society.

text an object such as a television programme, film or poem, considered as a network of meaningful signs that can be analysed and interpreted.

Journalists' reviews and literary criticism focus on television programmes as **texts**, where the method of discussing them is to study closely their structure, characters and themes, in ways similar to the study of literature and drama. The advantage for the students and teachers who adopt this way of studying television is that there is an example accessible to the class, who can watch and rewatch the programme, and focus on selected moments in it. By closely analysing a programme it can be discovered how the programme is structured and how it creates its meanings by using images and sound in certain ways; critical arguments about the programme can be tested out and proved by referring back to a concrete example. Chapter 4 of this book explores this method of study in detail, and introduces some of the methodologies that it uses.

Studying television by analysing programmes is useful for setting up categories and making distinctions between programmes. Making distinctions is a good way of discovering the rules and **conventions** which the makers of programmes use, and which television viewers learn to recognise, in order to make meaning in the television medium. As well as complete programmes, television also includes trailers, advertisements and channel **idents**. It can often happen that several minutes in each hour of broadcasting are taken up by these kinds of television, but they are not programmes and are not often studied. Nevertheless, it could be argued that trailers for forthcoming programmes have important functions:

conventions the frameworks and procedures used to make or interpret texts.

idents the symbols representing production companies, television channels, etc., often comprising graphics or animations.

- They inform the audience about what will be available to watch in the future.
- They shape the viewer's expectations about what a future programme will be like.
- They offer suggestions why it might be interesting and enjoyable.

Since television advertisements are the means of gaining income for many television broadcasters, who charge fees to advertisers to screen them, it could be argued that they are more significant to what television is than the programmes that they interrupt. Television advertisements cost much more per minute of screen-time to make than programmes, and they are often innovative, memorable and amusing. The density and speed of information and meaning in television commercials make them rewarding objects of study, and show the conventions by which images and sounds can be put together in the television medium. Since our society is one where desiring, buying and owning products is important to our sense of identity and our place in society, it is also illuminating to see how products are brought to our attention in television advertisements, so studying them may also tell us much about how our society works. Channel idents are also moments of television that are frequently repeated and familiar, giving a **brand** identity to television broadcasters, like advertisements for the broadcaster, and they too are worthy of study. So it is not only programmes that can be analysed in Television Studies, though programmes have been the core of syllabuses in the subject for many years.

Studying programmes closely as single texts also has the disadvantage of separating a programme from its place in the schedule of the day in which it was broadcast. There are some television programmes which viewers might select and view with special attention ('must see' programmes), and this kind of viewing is becoming more common with the availability of catch-up and downloading services where programmes can be selected for watching and re-watching at any time. At present, television is most often watched as a sequence of programmes, ads, trailers, etc., and of course viewers also switch channels, sometimes part-way through a programme, and their level of attention may vary considerably from moment to moment and programme to programme. Indeed, within programmes, high-points or turning-points are included by programme-makers where breaks for advertisements are to be included. This is done to encourage viewers to stay on the same channel to find out what the consequences or developments will be once the programme returns after the break. The two consequences of studying programmes as individual units relate to the important Television Studies concept of '**flow**' (Williams 1974). Selecting individual programmes for study means extracting them from the flow of material of which they are a part, and which might have important effects on their meaning. For example, a news programme including items about rising petrol prices might be followed by a commercial break including ads for new cars, and then the programme *Fifth Gear*, where new cars are reviewed and motoring issues are discussed. While each programme or ad might be interesting to analyse in itself, more meanings relating to speed, pollution, road safety or **masculine** bravado might arise because of the connections between the programmes and ads in this television flow.

Part of the textual study of television is an interest in **authorship**, in who the authors of television programmes are and what the intended meanings of their work might be. In Britain television was established in the 1930s by the same broadcaster, the BBC, which operated all the radio broadcasting. Both radio and television have been required by their legal constitutions to fulfil a **public service** role. Public service television aims to:

brand recognition the ability of audiences to recognise the distinctive identity of a product, service or institution and the values and meanings associated with it.

flow the ways in which programmes, advertisements, etc. follow one another in an unbroken sequence across the day or part of the day, and the experience of watching the sequence of programmes, advertisements, trailers, etc.

masculine having characteristics associated with the cultural role of men and not women.

authorship the question of who an author is, the role of the author as creator and the significance of the author's input into the material being studied.

public service in television, the provision of a mix of programmes that inform, educate and entertain in ways that encourage the betterment of audiences and society in general.

■ provide programmes which are educative or improving
■ offer a range of different kinds of programme at different levels of accessibility
■ engage audiences in the significant events and issues occurring in the present.

Since literature and drama are also considered to be educative and improving, it is authored dramatic television work which has often featured as the ground for debates about the quality of television in Britain and whether the public service commitment is being fulfilled. Graham Murdoch (1980: 25) wrote, in an early theoretical essay on this subject, 'The promotion of authorship and creativity lies at the heart of the broadcasters' presentation of themselves as guarantors of cultural diversity and patrons of the contemporary arts, elements which are central to their claims to responsibility and public service.' Television drama has been regarded as the most culturally prestigious part of broadcast output, and it is expensive, and often prominently scheduled, trailed and advertised. Its high profile has made it the subject of hype and controversy, orchestrated by the broadcasters themselves, the press, or concerned groups such as MediaWatch that represent viewers' interests.

Authored drama has also been one of the main forms of television exported to other countries (for example the *Masterpiece Theatre* slot on US **public television**). There were and still are debates about public service television, seen either as:

■ an old-fashioned and monolithic system which prevents change, or as
■ a space in which television that challenges commercial values and aspires to artistic **quality** might find an audience.

In this context, the analysis of television programmes provides the grounds for valuing one programme over another, as more or less conducive of social change, or more or less worthy of consideration as a creative statement. A further reason for this focus on authored television drama and its connection to literary and drama studies is that in the early years of television broadcasting in Britain, in the years before and after the Second World War, many television plays were adaptations of theatre plays or extracts from them, sometimes using the same cast as productions being staged in London's West End playhouses. But a drawback of this concern for television drama as if it were literature or written drama is a neglect of the importance of performers and performances in television. Although Film Studies has for many years had a critical interest in stardom and stars, Television Studies has not often remembered the significance of how actors and television **personalities** affect the meanings that television programmes may have (Caughie 2000).

The fact that a television play or **serial** can be considered a self-contained text, written by an author, made this television form especially significant for researchers studying television from this perspective. Although there were some early studies of television (Williams 1968, Newcomb 1974) that discussed popular programmes such as **soap opera**, writing about television focused on the high-profile programmes regarded as 'quality television' (an idea discussed in Chapter 7). But Television Studies has in the past couple of decades or so moved away from the close study of fictional programmes (although this is still an important part of the subject) and

public television television funded by government or by private supporters, rather than solely by advertising.

quality in television, kinds of programmes that are perceived as more expensively produced and, especially, more culturally worthwhile than other programmes.

personalities people appearing on television who are recognised by audiences as celebrities with a media image and public status beyond the role they play in a particular programme.

serial a television form where a developing narrative unfolds across a sequence of separate episodes.

soap opera a continuing drama serial involving a large number of characters in a specific location, focusing on relationships, emotions and reversals of fortune.

considered other problems. Part of the reason for this is that Television Studies has established itself by breaking away from the study of literature and drama, so that the methods of textual criticism increasingly appear to be drawn from subjects outside of Television Studies itself. Rather than studying high-profile television fiction by authors whose names become nationally known (such as Stephen Poliakoff or Andrew Davies), Television Studies academics have discussed programmes which fall solidly into **genres** (such as soap opera or police fiction) and whose authors work in teams or groups and are little known outside the television industry. These are also the programmes which attract the largest audiences, and which can be described as '**popular**' rather than 'elite' culture.

popular culture the texts created by ordinary people (as opposed to an elite group) or created for them, and the ways these are used.

ACTIVITY 1.2

Look at the articles in current listings magazines. Are any of the articles about the authors of television programmes? If so, what kinds of programmes are these? If not, which personalities are associated with programmes, and why?

Television and society

Unlike cinema, television has always placed emphasis on the witnessing of events in the real world. When television began, all of its programmes were live, because the technology to record television signals had not been invented. The thrill of watching television in its early days, and still occasionally now, is to see and hear representations of events, people and places distant from the viewer. Indeed, the word television literally means 'seeing from afar'. On one hand, television gives viewers access to the world with immediacy and credibility, because television technology appears to transcribe or reproduce faithfully what is seen and heard. The ability of television to disseminate information widely, beyond the local and personal experience of its viewers, can be argued to broaden the experience and awareness of the television audience. The political effects of this might be for television to assist national institutions in involving citizens in social and political debate, so that television enhances public debate and participation in democratic decision-making.

Television broadcasting might therefore contribute to the '**public sphere**': to discussion and thought about issues which concern the direction of society as a whole, and have bearing on the lives of most people. Figure 1.2 is an image from the television coverage of the wedding of Prince William to Kate Middleton, at Westminster Abbey in April 2011. As this image shows, the main purpose of the coverage was to give access to an event of public importance that only a small number of selected guests had been invited to see in person. The tightly framed close up that is evident in Figure 1.2 offers a privileged kind of view. This notion of access underpinned a different use of television in Channel 4's 2010 series *Tower Block of Commons*, in which four Members of Parliament each spent a week living on a

public sphere the world of politics, economic affairs and national and international events, as opposed to the 'private sphere' of domestic life.

Figure 1.2 The wedding of Prince William to Kate Middleton, 29 April 2011.
Photo © George Pimentel/WireImage/Getty.

different council estate. The aim was to give the MPs (who were Austin Mitchell, Ian Duncan Smith, Tim Loughton and Mark Oten) an insight into the lives of ordinary people, and to let the television audience see how they reacted to this experience. Whereas the Royal Wedding gave access to an event centred on Britain's social elite, *Tower Block of Commons* placed members of Britain's political elite in an ordinary situation. The series gave the television audience access both to the lives of the MPs' less privileged hosts and to the ways that the MPs were educated about the lives of people affected by their political decisions. Note the way that framing and composition are used in Figure 1.3 to place Austin Mitchell's concerned face next to the image of a tower block that represents the harsh social conditions experienced by the people he met in the programme. Figure 1.4 is from the television debate in May 2010 between the leaders of Britain's three main political parties, ahead of the General Election that year. Framing and composition here are tightly controlled to give equal space in the frame to each party leader, and to position them as if they were directly addressing the viewer. Amid a concern that British people were sceptical about the value of parliamentary politics, and might not bother to vote in the election, the political leaders agreed for the first time to stage the debate for the cameras. The aim was to inform potential voters about the parties' policies and to encourage participation in the election and the political process more generally. So again, television was being used to provide access for the audience to people, events and political issues that broadcasters considered important to the citizens of the nation.

Figure 1.3 Austin Mitchell in *Tower Block of Commons*, when four members of
Parliament spent a week living on a council housing estate. Channel 4,
2010.

Figure 1.4 In May 2010, British television showed the live *First Election Debate* between
party leaders, preceding the General Election of that year.

The role of television in Britain has been, and still is, to offer a public service by
informing and educating its audience, as well as entertaining viewers. But television
can present only selected images and sounds, chosen by someone else, and present
them according to the conventions of storytelling and reporting which are
established by television institutions and by legal regulations. In a sense, television
takes over the job of relating the viewer to the world around him or her, and

separates the viewer from his or her experience of reality. The political consequences of television from this point of view are negative. If television experiences the world on its audience's behalf, and substitutes mediated and partial versions of information and understanding for the authentic experience of people, then its effect is to dissuade people from involvement in discussion and debate. The television viewer might be disempowered and alone, with discussion and participation simulated by television rather than enabled by it. Watching the political question-and-answer programme *Question Time* or the commentaries by experts in current affairs programmes might allow viewers to feel involved in debates when they are not. From this point of view, television viewing reproduces the apparent passivity of consumers and spectators, turning its audience into '**couch potatoes**', and encourages it to continue. A key advantage of interactive television and its convergence with the internet is the possibility for viewers to respond to programmes, to criticise what they see on television, and occasionally to contribute ideas and audio-visual content that become part of the television experience.

Social science research in Television Studies considers how television has a role in reproducing the patterns of values and the divisions between groups and **classes** of people in society, in other words how television represents and affects the social order. Part of this research concerns how television adopts the 'public speech' of institutions such as:

- Parliament
- academia
- the judicial system.

Social science is concerned with how this contrasts with adoptions of 'private speech' such as:

- gossip
- everyday talk
- the language of subcultural groups such as football fans or youth subcultures.

By investigating these aspects of television, it can be seen how television gives different kinds of value and legitimacy to different facets of social life, and separates out or unifies people with each other. Since television is controlled by institutions, and governed by laws, questions of the regulation and ownership of television are also addressed by this strand of research. Social science research considers television as a form of mass communication, in relation to sociological and political issues rather than studies of textuality or the form of programmes. Because of their interest in the relations of social groups to each other, and the place of television in communicating social values and attitudes, researchers tend to discuss popular genres such as television sports programmes, or kinds of content (especially violence and social disorder) represented in different kinds of programmes.

The ways in which broadcasting is organised in different nations are surprisingly different, and it is important to study broadcasting cultures in comparison and in contrast to each other. Although it might seem that American television is the dominant norm because of the worldwide export of such programmes as the American drama *CSI*, about police forensic scientists, the conventions, laws and

couch potatoes a derogatory term for television viewers supposedly sitting motionless at home watching television passively and indiscriminately.

class a section of society defined by their relationship to economic activity, whether as workers (the working class) or possessors of economic power (the bourgeoisie), for example.

assumptions about television differ in different countries because of the different evolution of television broadcasting and different conceptions of the nature and function of television. In Britain, for instance, broadcasting (first on radio) began as a monopoly business entrusted in 1922 to the British Broadcasting Company (a commercial organisation), paralleling the monopoly control over the supply of water or electricity in the Victorian period. Radio, and television when it appeared in the 1930s, was considered as if it were drinking water, on tap, which could be run by a national company as long as it was kept clean and available to everyone equally (Caughie 2000). Only later did commercial television and competition appear, and even now there is a strong body of opinion in Britain that television must be taken seriously and must fulfil its moral responsibility to an audience of citizens. In America, by contrast, television quickly developed as a form of commercial business, where the requirements of advertisers and the need for local relay stations to make profits from the programmes supplied by programme-makers have driven the development of television. To put this distinction crudely, there is a debate between two sets of assumptions about television:

- television should provide resources to answer people's needs and raise cultural standards, or
- television should give people what the majority seem to want and what makes the most profit.

Television Studies has engaged frequently in this debate, most often by taking the perhaps impossible compromise position that broadcasting should be a public service but that it should not impose the cultural standards of the few upon a majority whose 'popular' tastes should not be denigrated.

The background to this position in Television Studies is closely bound up with the changes in how broadcasters have conceived of their audiences. The BBC shifted its conception of its role from an initial aim to train its audience to understand and enjoy more and more 'quality' programmes, with 'worthwhile' levels of intellectual content and sophistication, requiring sustained and attentive viewing (Ang 1991). When the arrival of ITV introduced **commercial television** to Britain in 1955, the high **ratings** for the new channel forced the BBC to compete against popular **formats** such as imported American drama series and quizzes. From the 1950s onwards, the conception of the audience as consumers able to exercise a free choice has become increasingly dominant in British broadcasting, and this both reflects and supports the view of society which has come to be familiar and natural today. Rather than thinking of British society as if it were a pyramid with a small cultural elite at the top, with sophisticated tastes, and a broad base of ordinary viewers underneath preferring undemanding entertainment, the image of society has changed to one of overlapping and scattered sets of viewers, or **niche audiences**, who have changing and diverse preferences across many genres, forms and levels of complexity. Broadcasters no longer attempt to lead the nation to the top of the cultural pyramid, but instead reflect what they believe to be the demands of contemporary society. The audience is conceived as a collection of diverse and autonomous individuals whose viewing habits and interests are hard to discover and predict, and who can be as fickle as any other kind of consumer.

commercial television television funded by the sale of advertising time or sponsorship of programmes.

ratings the number of viewers estimated to have watched certain programmes, as compared to the numbers watching other programmes.

format the blueprint for a programme, including its setting, main characters, genre, form and main themes.

niche audiences particular groups of viewers defined by age group, gender or economic status, for example, who may be the target audience for a programme.

The role of the academic discipline of Television Studies in political debates about the direction of television in Britain has always been rather peripheral. When the subject focused on making distinctions between progressive or conservative texts in the 1960s and 1970s, and valuing the progressive ones, the highly theoretical arguments about the form and meanings of programmes were largely inaccessible to readerships outside the lecturers and students who engaged in them. Despite the often-repeated claim that programmes could empower audiences to think in challenging and radical ways about their own lives and cultures, Television Studies had little engagement with programme-makers and policy-makers. The discipline of **Cultural Studies**, pioneered in Britain in the 1970s at the University of Birmingham, recognises the significance of popular television and studies how television contributes to the assumptions and attitudes of sectors of society, a set of ideas and emotions described as a '**structure of feeling**'. Key work in this field includes the books by Raymond Williams (1974) and John Ellis (1982), whose interest was in the flow of programmes in the television schedule, and how viewers rarely watch programmes singly but instead as part of flow of programmes and commercials over a period of hours. Viewers also switch from one programme or channel to another, composing their own 'text' of television from these segments, which does not exhibit the bounded and unified qualities which derive from thinking of television as a series of whole individual texts to be analysed singly. In the 1980s the issue of the progressiveness of particular television texts was overtaken by interest in audiences, and how real viewers gained pleasure from their viewing (Morley 1980). This approach began to transfer to the USA in the 1980s, and is evident in the work of Lawrence Grossberg (Grossberg *et al.* 1992). While still a political debate, because there could be progressive or conservative kinds of pleasure, this phase in Television Studies refused to identify some programmes as good and some as bad, preferring to value the different kinds of pleasure that different audience groups might gain from programmes. The **commissioners** and **producers** of programmes, let alone actors, politicians or journalists, have always made distinctions between good and bad programmes, in terms of their popularity, cost as compared to profit or the social status of their majority audience.

The sophisticated arguments which led to the refusal to judge quality in Television Studies meant that academic criticism has been largely unable to engage in the debates about television that can be seen expressed in different contexts, including:

- newspapers
- parliamentary debates
- broadcasters' policy documents.

Therefore, the issues which still concern viewers and commentators, such as the effects of violence in programmes, whether there is more or less 'quality television' than there was and the standards of **taste and decency** in television, often remain absent from the books and articles written and read by Television Studies academics and students. So although Television Studies is crucially about the relationships between television and society, the topic can often seem to be debated in a vacuum.

Cultural Studies the academic discipline devoted to studying culture, involving work on texts, institutions, audiences and economic contexts.

structure of feeling the assumptions, attitudes and ideas prevalent in a society, arising from the ideologies underpinning that society.

commissioning the process by which an idea for a programme is selected to go into production.

producer the person working for a television institution who is responsible for the budget, planning and making of a television programme or series of programmes.

taste and decency conformity to the standards of good taste and acceptable language and behaviour represented on television, as required by regulations.

ACTIVITY 1.3

Which kinds of television programmes, on which channels, do you think are aimed at a family audience? How do you know?

Figure 1.5 Watching the television. © Mark Bowden/istockphoto.

Television audiences

Because of the variety of the different kinds of programmes and advertisements on television, as a medium it appears to offer an almost unlimited range of information and entertainment. The different genres of programme, and the range of factual and fictional output on television channels, appear to offer vast choice and to address the needs and desires of different viewers. This is even more evident in recent years with the emergence of themed channels on digital television, which focus, for example, on:

■ sport
■ films
■ science
■ drama
■ comedy
■ shopping
■ lifestyle.

licence fee an annual payment by all owners of television sets, which is the main source of income for the BBC.

subscription payment to a television broadcaster in exchange for the opportunity to view programmes on certain channels that are otherwise blocked.

audience share the percentage of viewers estimated to have watched one channel as opposed to another channel broadcasting at the same time.

anthropology the study of humankind, including the evolution of humans and the different kinds of human society existing in different times and places.

focus groups small groups of selected people representing larger social groupings such as people of a certain age group, gender or economic status, who take part in discussions about a topic chosen for investigation.

uses and gratifications a theoretical approach that assumes people engage in an activity because it provides them with a benefit of some kind.

effects measurable outcomes produced by watching television, such as becoming more violent or adopting a certain opinion.

feminism the political and theoretical thinking which in different ways considers the roles of women and femininity in society and culture, often with the aim of critiquing current roles and changing them for the better.

Television companies are especially interested in who is watching which kinds of programme, when and why. Television broadcasters have always referred to audiences in order to back up their claims to give the public what it seems to want, to set the level of fees charged to advertisers and as an indication of which forms and genres of programme seem to 'work'. The BBC's channels are funded by a **licence fee** that must be paid by all owners of television sets. The ITV channel, and the newer terrestrial channels Channel 4 and Five gain their income from charges made to advertisers to screen their advertisements. The various non-BBC digital channels are funded either by **subscription** charges or by advertising, and often a combination of both. In all cases, information about audience size and composition is highly significant to television institutions.

Channels funded by commercial advertising need to attract audiences for their advertisers, and BBC channels funded by the licence fee need to justify the compulsory payment of the licence fee by attracting substantial audiences. The competition between channels is measured by audience size (the ratings, calculated by multiplying the audience sizes in a representative sample of viewers), and by the proportion of the total available audience watching one channel rather than another (**audience share**). The methods of audience research used in the television industry derive from the methods used to identify new markets for consumer products, to survey current users of products and to measure the sales and reactions to products of all kinds, from washing powder to brands of lager. Television Studies researchers working with methods deriving from the academic disciplines of the social sciences, such as **sociology** and **anthropology**, have a related interest in television audiences. But rather than finding out about audiences in order to target or maximise audiences in the interests of increasing profits for broadcasters, academic audience researchers seek to understand how television viewing fits into people's cultural life, and how pleasure, knowledge and opportunities for social interaction (but also boredom, anger and dissatisfaction) in television arise. The methods used to gain this information include:

- questionnaires
- interviews
- **focus groups**.

The strand of work in Television Studies called '**uses and gratifications**' research describes the uses and pleasures which audiences derive from television, by focusing on how and why people use television. This approach is in contrast to the study of television's **effects** on its viewers (such as making them more violent, or more informed about science, for example) in that studies of effects regard audiences as passive vessels waiting to be filled up by television messages. Uses and gratifications research shows how television is used as an information source, as entertainment and as a resource for constructing the viewer's sense of identity, often by identifying himself or herself as a member of a group. The drawback of this kind of work, however, is that it can neglect the specificity of the television programmes which viewers actually watch.

Academic audience researchers have been especially interested in understanding the ways television fits into the lives of people whose relatively unequal social position has led the programmes they watch to be denigrated, and their reactions to television belittled. When Television Studies researchers sought to analyse the politics of programme texts, they tended to mean how programmes dealt with 'national issues' such as law and order, work and political viewpoints, associated with the predominantly male spokespersons and leaders in party politics, trade unions and business. The feminist movement started to focus on television in the 1980s, and argued that 'the personal is political', meaning that people's private concerns with family life, shopping or relationships also had political implications, and these areas of life were associated with women. Feminist Television Studies took an interest both in programmes which represented the '**private sphere**' of life, meaning the usually private goings on in the home, and in the place of television in the lives of ordinary people, especially women. In particular, feminist academics studying television audiences directed attention to the often despised genre of soap opera, and have explored in detail the ways that women viewers watched television in the real circumstances of their own homes (Brunsdon *et al.* 1997). Indeed the home is an important site of audience research in Television Studies, since television is usually watched there and it has been associated with domesticity.

private sphere the domestic world of the home, family and personal life.

ACTIVITY 1.4

Feminist television theorists conducted important work on soap opera as a 'women's genre'. Which other television forms might be of interest to feminist television theorists, and why?

One of the shifts that has taken place in television culture over the twentieth and twenty-first centuries has been the massive expansion of television ownership. Just a small proportion of homes in a few areas of the country had television in the 1930–50 period, but the present situation is one in which households may own several televisions, as well as computers, phones or games consoles which can show television. From being a collective experience shared with family, friends and neighbours, watching television may take place simultaneously in different rooms in the same household, individually by members of the same family. How people of different age groups, genders and daily routines use television in the home is a subject of interest to audience researchers seeking to discover how television integrates into the fabric of present-day life. Television Studies' interest in audiences and the programmes which most ordinary viewers watch attempts to understand the processes of how television engages its audiences in ways that the audience finds satisfying and valuable, rather than simply dismissing ordinary viewers' apparently shallow enthusiasms. With the pendulum of critical interest shifting in the direction of audience studies, popular programmes and relatively inattentive viewing, however, Television Studies unfortunately lost sight of the programmes that are watched with concentration and intensity (such as 'quality drama') until quite recently.

A particular strand of audience research that places special emphasis on what viewers have to say about their relationships with television is the approach called television **ethnography**. Ethnographic studies draw on the methods of the discipline of anthropology, in gathering information through close and often lengthy

ethnography the detailed study of how people live, conducted by observing behaviour and talking to selected individuals about their attitudes and activities.

interactions with small samples of viewers (Lull 1988b). Whereas both mass communications research in Television Studies and the television industry have thought of audiences as homogeneous masses whose reactions and interests are broadly the same, and have investigated them by quantitative methods such as counting audience sizes, ethnographic audience research focuses on smaller-scale groupings, selected by factors such as locality, gender, age group or social class. The problem which ethnography faces is the challenge of selecting some information relevant to the research question while leaving out most of the responses that viewers give to the researcher's questions, and rearranging or 'translating' research information into a wider context that illuminates how television works as a medium (Geraghty 1998). The political project of granting legitimacy to ordinary viewers, their interests and pleasures, as well as involving them directly in Television Studies research as respondents to ethnographic researchers' questions, leads to the claim that audiences are active makers of meaning and negotiators with the television they watch. This celebration of the active audience is most associated with the work of John Fiske (1992a, 1994) and with a body of research on television **fan culture**. Television fans (such as *Star Trek* fans, or *Doctor Who* fans) use programmes as the central resource for activities including:

fan culture the activities of groups of fans, as distinct from 'ordinary' viewers.

- constructing social networks
- setting up social and commercial events (such as conventions)
- creating new texts (such as songs, fanzines or websites).

So studies of fan audiences show how some television viewers take hold of television and transform it into their own cultural text, and it is argued that all television viewers, though to a lesser extent than fans, make their own meanings and social relationships out of television. Fans and audiences in general appear to resist swallowing whole the meanings which television programmes may have, and instead they take and reshape the aspects of television programmes that make sense to them and offer them opportunities. Fans, and indeed all viewers to some extent, are **resistant** and **active audiences**.

resistance the ways in which audiences make meaning from television programmes that are counter to the meanings that are thought to be intended, or that are discovered by close analysis.

active audience television audiences regarded not as passive consumers of meanings but as negotiating meanings for themselves that are often resistant to those meanings that are intended or that are discovered by close analysis.

ACTIVITY 1.5

In what ways do particular television forms lend themselves to some approaches in Television Studies more than others, for example television news to sociological study? What kinds of television have not appeared in your list of television forms and approaches to them?

ACTIVITY 1.6

List methods of study which Television Studies might involve. How many of these might appear in studies of another medium? Why is this?

ACTIVITY 1.7

What problems might be associated with ethnographic study of television audience groups different from those that you belong to (for example, children)? How might you deal with these problems?

Case study: television past and present

Analogue television transmission finished in 2012, as all of the different parts of Britain became digital-only. Digital television became very widespread before the analogue switch-off, due to the success of the Freeview transmission system that offers the mainstream television channels (BBC1, BBC2, ITV1, Channel 4 and Five), and also about fifty other channels, via a roof aerial. The media regulator **Ofcom** publishes a regular report on the communications market, and in 2006 it announced that 73 per cent of homes in the UK had digital television. Freeview is free, apart from the modest cost of a set-top decoder box. Satellite and cable services like Sky also offer multi-channel digital viewing for a small monthly charge. The BBC has been at the forefront of this digital revolution, offering all its existing radio and television channels, plus the more recent BBC3 and BBC4, to Freeview viewers. The BBC has said that it is part of its role to offer 'public value' by enabling everyone in Britain to receive its services without direct payment, reflecting the traditional public service broadcasting principles of offering a wide range of different kinds of programmes to as many people as possible, to suit the needs and desires of the whole nation. It is important to the survival of the concept of public service broadcasting that the BBC has appealing programme content, and a trusted brand as Britain becomes a fully digital TV nation. The rising popularity of High Definition (HD) television sets was supported by the BBC's launch of a free HD channel, and Ofcom's annual report on the communications market in 2010 revealed that 22 per cent of people surveyed had bought an HD television set in the previous year. The prospect of the convergence of television with the internet means that viewers will not only watch television as transmitted but can also access programmes to download at any time, browse the web and use social networks all from the same device. Television is at a turning-point where it becomes a hybrid of several technologies and a resource for accessing a whole range of content and experiences at the time of the viewer's choosing.

> **Ofcom** the Office of Communications, a government body responsible for regulating television and other communications media in Britain.

    This case study contrasts the beginnings of television as a mass medium with its development today. In order to see and evaluate the present, it is necessary to understand the history of how television arrived at where it is now. Early predictions in the 1930s of what television would be emphasised its liveness, and its consequent ability to present images of what was happening in the real world to a mass audience. There was little sense that the new medium would compete with cinema as an entertainment medium, because of:

- the small size of early television screens
- their poor definition of pictures and sound, and
- the location of the television set in the home.

It seemed that the role of television would be similar to radio. Television would bring information to its audience, and relay images and sounds of events actually happening in distant places.

realism the aim for representations to reproduce reality faithfully, and the ways this is done.

These early thoughts conditioned the makers of television to think of the medium in terms of **realism**, since television would reflect society to itself. Television would focus on the contemporary, and as a new technology, having a television was associated with being modern and engaged in the growing technological sophistication of Britain's industrial society. At the same time there were concerns about television's intrusiveness, because of the uneasiness or even shock which viewers might feel when the box in the corner invaded their private domestic space.

The emphasis on liveness, on seeing things as they happen, made drama and performance important to the first television schedules (Caughie 2000). Plays performed live were fixed points in the BBC's evening television schedules and were very popular, as was a television version of the variety show, where singers, comedians, magicians and other performers from the stage music hall and radio shows of the time did their acts. There were some films on television, but very few because the film studios would not allow television broadcasters to screen them, for fear of competition with the cinema as a dominant medium for entertainment. Plays were performed live in the television studio, and could also be relayed live from a London theatre. So the function of television seemed to be to relay the live occasion of a performance (including one made for television) rather than to find programme forms which were different from what audiences might experience in other media such as radio, music hall or theatre. British television began broadcasting in 1936 to tiny audiences, but even in 1950 the television audience for the only broadcast channel in Britain, the BBC, was only about 300,000. Television was available only in London and the Midlands, and viewers paid a £2 licence fee

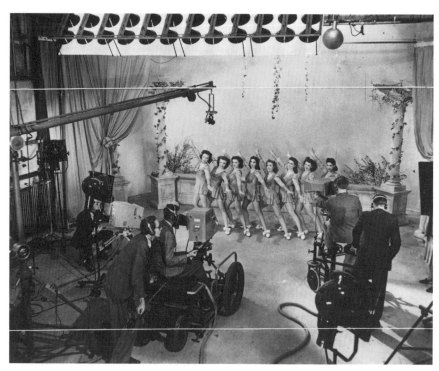

Figure 1.6 Television rehearsals at Alexandra Palace, 1946. Photograph courtesy of the National Museum of Photography, Film & Television/Science and Society Picture Library.

covering both television and radio sets. Programmes were broadcast each weekday morning and every afternoon, but stopped in the early evening so that children could be put to bed. Programmes began again at 8.00 p.m. (after the closedown period known as 'the toddler's truce' was over) and there was no set closedown time, since **outside broadcasts** of sporting events, for instance, could extend the day's viewing hours. On a typical day in 1950, nine hours of television were broadcast altogether.

There was a widespread anxiety that watching television might disrupt family routines and waste people's time, especially if it was too entertaining. Writing in the *BBC Year Book 1951* (an annual collection of reports and essays about the doings of the BBC over the year), Ivor Brown responded to this concern by arguing that

> People who view do not stop going to the play or the films or the cricket-match. Television, at two pounds a year for a whole household and friends, does not, after the initial purchase, seriously affect the family's allotment of cash to fun and games.
>
> (1951: 17)

Brown was somewhat on the defensive, protecting television from the accusation that people had to make a choice between staying in to watch their expensive new television sets or going out and doing something healthier instead. It is important to notice too that Brown considers the television audience to be 'household and friends', a collective audience rather than a lone viewer in front of the screen. For most people the experience of watching television was collective, and they gathered in friends' and neighbours' houses to watch television as an event in itself. So rather than being a distraction from other ways of spending time, or a means of filling in dead time, the television set could be a magnet around which social interaction could take place.

In the years following the end of the Second World War in 1945 a relatively prosperous middle class was living in the expanding suburbs around Britain's major cities, and it was these people who could most easily afford the time and expense of watching television. On one hand, the new suburban semi-detached houses offered people more private space than they had ever had before (larger rooms, more bedrooms and big gardens, for example), but also potential loneliness in the recently created suburban estates populated by people who were strangers to each other, and intensely conscious of the social status they and those around them possessed. Ivor Brown (1951: 17) saw television as a remedy for these problems: 'In the suburb, television is plainly acting as a cohesive force'. Owners of television sets invited people round to watch their televisions, to show them off, to make friends, and to enjoy being an audience for programmes:

> That friends and neighbours should come in to watch makes for better audiences, especially in the case of comedy and light shows . . . The more viewers, in the case of comedy, the more they enjoy themselves, since to be a member of an audience is quite a different thing from sitting aloof at a dress-rehearsal, as all theatre people know. So my guess is that, as television expands, it will begin to collect little group-audiences. So it will become a new factor in social life.
>
> (1951: 17)

The television of the 1950s was aimed at community and family. Television sets were placed near the fire in the family living room, and being warm and cosy together suited the communal experience of watching television as a family group. Families with television sets engaged in

outside broadcast the television transmission of outdoor events such as sport or ceremonial occasions, using equipment set up in advance for the purpose. Abbreviated as OB.

social talk that was given new interest by the television programmes they could watch together. This has to be seen in the context of the BBC's public service ideals, which were to encourage people to expose themselves to a range of programmes, some of them requiring concentration and an aim of self-improvement.

Ivor Brown considered television watching to be a rather special event, and thought that television would support the raising of cultural standards among viewers:

> The BBC has long advocated, I think, selective listening to sound radio, instead of the vague tap-running which is destructive of taste and leaves its public wayward instead of critical. Television curtails the tap, and makes of viewing a planned and intelligent exercise.
>
> (1951: 19)

This conception of television is probably very different from the ways most people think of television viewing now. Brown was concerned about the directions that viewing might take:

> What I most dread for the future is television available at all hours and the coming of the portable plug-in T.V. set which will destroy the isolation and concentration now imposed by the fixing of the mechanism in one corner of the room.
>
> (ibid.: 19)

His worries about the invention of the portable television were not only that it would lead to more distracted viewing but also that the television would follow viewers around the house to different rooms, breaking up the collectivity and sociability which television involved.

The proliferation of televisions in contemporary homes means that it is common for different age groups and genders within the home to view different programmes in different rooms in different ways. The other domestic technologies such as video games, uses of computers for surfing the web and email and leisure communication by text messaging and telephone rival the television as the centre of home leisure and the collective experience of television viewing. The explosion in the number of available channels also means that different individuals or groupings in the household can watch entirely different programmes from each other, on different television sets in different rooms or on other devices than television such as laptops and phones. A major question for broadcasters, for Television Studies researchers and for all kinds of commentators on the British media is how digital television will change television culture.

British digital multi-channel television began to develop slowly. In the first six months of 2000 the rate of increase in digital subscribers was 53 per cent, but in 2001 the increase fell to 10 per cent, suggesting that the 30 per cent of British households who were connected at that time were those who were keen on the new technology, and that the mass of the British audience were not attracted by digital services. In a government survey only 25 per cent of British households said they expected to connect to digital television by 2006, the earliest date that the government said it would cease **terrestrial** broadcasts using the existing **analogue** transmission system. In homes connected to digital television, average viewers watch only eight to twelve of the dozens of channels available, and the **interactive** services and email through the television set which digital connection offers seemed less attractive to households than home computers that run these services more quickly and more cheaply. Now that dozens or hundreds of channels are available, the size of the audience watching

terrestrial broadcasting from a ground-based transmission system, as opposed to broadcasting via satellite.

analogue broadcasting signals in waves of varying frequency. Analogue signals require greater space or 'bandwidth' than digital signals, and do not allow interactive response from viewers.

interactive offering the opportunity for viewers to respond to what is broadcast, by sending signals back to the broadcaster (along a cable or phone line, for example).

each channel can potentially be a very small fraction of the total. It was unclear how channels would support the cost of producing programmes watched by such small audiences. Some income was clawed back by the paid channels offering films and sport, but the prospect of paying for content was the main reason why the majority of households had not connected to digital television. However, the government committed itself to digital television, primarily so that it could sell the unused analogue frequency spectrums then left over to communications companies who use them for mobile telephone services. In September 2001 the Minister for Culture, Media and Sport approved BBC plans for two new digital channels, BBC3 and BBC4. BBC3 is targeted at under-twenty-fives, while BBC4 is based around the content provided on BBC2 and also BBC Radios 3 and 4, featuring arts, music and culture programmes. Channel 4 launched its digital channels E4 and More4, and ITV launched a suite of channels, ITV2, 3 and 4, followed by Channel Five's own digital channels. The existing broadcasters moved into the digital arena, where they competed with Sky and a wide range of channels from the USA like Discovery, FX and Universal, and channels offering specific genres of programme like sport, films and children's programmes.

Despite all these changes, the distinguishing features of past television are still evident today. Live programmes on BBC, ITV, Channel 4 and Five are still made, long-running programmes still appear especially in the soap opera genre, and occasionally programmes gain the significance of a 'TV event'. Earlier in this chapter the live broadcast of the Royal Wedding of 2011 and the General Election debate of 2010 were mentioned, each of which could claim to be 'TV events'. When the soap opera *Coronation Street* celebrated its fiftieth anniversary in 2010, a special hour-long episode was broadcast live on ITV1, with a dramatic rail crash that threatened the lives of the main characters. A tram fell from a bridge onto the street at night, causing a power cut. In Figure 1.7, we can see how the chaos and terror of the event are represented visually by the low light on the shocked characters' faces, contrasting

Figure 1.7 The fiftieth anniversary of ITV's *Coronation Street* was marked by an hour-long live episode in December 2010.

with the flashing blue and white light of emergency service vehicles. This dramatic lighting in exterior scenes was paralleled by candle-light used in the interiors of houses.

Television in Britain seems to be at a turning-point which is interestingly similar to that in the early 1950s, when the small audiences and single broadcaster of the time were about to be transformed by new channels, much greater television set ownership and new ways of thinking about audiences. The issues of how television is delivered, how it is watched, financed and organised into schedules and channels are matters of major concern to broadcasters, government and cultural commentators. Delivering programmes over the internet, mobile phones and other devices requires viewers and television institutions to think in new ways about producing programmes, scheduling them, addressing audiences and financing the making of television. The television landscape has changed enormously in the past fifty years, and important changes are happening right now. Studying television in the early twenty-first century is a demanding but important part of understanding culture and society in the past, present and future.

SUMMARY OF KEY POINTS

- Television Studies focuses on broadcast television, but new ways of delivering television to viewers pose questions about television's place in society.
- Television has aimed to represent relatively unified cultures, though it also has regional and ethnic characteristics.
- British television has an important emphasis on public service functions, and representing society to itself.
- Television Studies has emphasised the study of particular programmes.
- The flow of programming, and audiences' experience of this flow, is a way of distinguishing television viewing from that of other media such as cinema.
- The study of audiences and their responses to television has become increasingly significant, both to television institutions and to theorists of television.

Further reading

Ang, I., *Desperately Seeking the Audience* (London: Routledge, 1991).

Bennett, J., and N. Strange (eds), *Television as Digital Media* (Durham, NC: Duke University Press, 2011).

Brunsdon, C., J. D'Acci and L. Spigel, 'Introduction', in C. Brunsdon, J. D'Acci, and L. Spigel (eds), *Feminist Television Criticism: A Reader* (Oxford: Oxford University Press, 1997), pp. 1–16.

Caughie, J., *Television Drama: Realism, Modernism, and British Culture* (Oxford: Oxford University Press, 2000).

—— 'Television criticism: a discourse in search of an object', *Screen*, 25:4–5 (1984), pp. 109–20.

Corner, J., *Critical Ideas in Television Studies* (Oxford: Clarendon, 1999).

Dyer, R., *Light Entertainment* (London: BFI, 1973).

Ellis, J., *Visible Fictions: Cinema, Television, Video* (London: Routledge & Kegan Paul, 1982).

Fiske, J., *Media Matters* (Minneapolis Minn.: University of Minnesota Press, 1994).

—— *Television Culture* (London: Routledge, 1992a).

Franklin, B. (ed.), *British Television Policy: A Reader* (London: Routledge, 2001).

Geraghty, C., 'Audiences and "ethnography": questions of practice', in C. Geraghty and D. Lusted (eds), *The Television Studies Book* (London: Arnold, 1998), pp. 141–57.

Grossberg, L., C. Nelson and P. Treichler, with L. Baughman and J. Macgregor Wise (eds), *Cultural Studies* (New York: Routledge, 1992).

Jancovich, M. and J. Lyons (eds), *Quality Popular Television: Cult TV, the Industry and the Fans* (London: BFI, 2005).

Jermyn, D. and S. Holmes, 'The audience is dead; long live the audience!: Interactivity, "telephilia", and the contemporary television audience', *Critical Studies in Television*, 1:1 (2006), pp. 49–57.

Lull, J., 'Critical response: the audience as nuisance', *Critical Studies in Mass Communication*, 5 (1988b), pp. 239–43.

Morley, D., *Television, Audiences and Cultural Studies* (London: Routledge, 1992).

—— *The 'Nationwide' Audience* (London: BFI, 1980).

Murdoch, G., 'Authorship and organization', *Screen Education*, 35 (1980), pp. 19–34.

Newcomb, H., *TV: The Most Popular Art* (New York: Anchor, 1974).

Rixon, P., *TV Critics and Popular Culture* (London: I. B. Tauris, 2011).

Turner, G., and J. Tay (eds), *Television Studies after TV: Understanding Television in the Post-Broadcast Era* (London: Routledge, 2009).

Wasko, J. (ed.), *A Companion to Television* (Malden, Mass. and Oxford: Blackwell, 2005).

Williams, R., *Television, Technology and Cultural Form* (London: Collins, 1974).

—— *Drama in Performance* (London: C. A. Watts, 1968).

Television Histories

2

Television Histories

Introduction

This chapter discusses ways of approaching the history of television, focusing on Britain but with comparison with and contrast to other countries. Television Studies has historically focused on television in national contexts. But the assumption that programmes would be viewed and discussed by a significant proportion of a national population is now proving less secure than before. The three factors that have given rise to this change in the nature of television are:

- the proliferation of channels
- the presence of several television sets in a single household
- the increasing control of television production and distribution by corporations and institutions whose activities cross national boundaries.

So it is important in thinking about television now to understand that many of the theoretical and critical approaches to the medium derive from a television history that is undergoing significant change. While the methods of analysis proposed by Television Studies in the past remain significant and useful, it is important to pay attention to the present and the possibilities for television that are being shaped for the future. Although this chapter aims to provide information about some moments in the development and change in television across the period from the 1930s to now, it is concerned less with providing a consistent story and a set of key facts, than with how the history of television can be approached critically. This is because the historical study of any subject involves making assumptions and value judgements about what is important, how links between events and processes are explained, and what the implications of a history might be. History is always a process of narration, which makes sense by including some information and excluding other information, by linking causes and effects and by implying a direction to the ways that events unfold. So this chapter does tell parts of several stories, but tries to suggest that the history of television can be told in many alternative ways.

Collecting the evidence

Histories of television face numerous problems in relation to the evidence on which they are based. Relatively inexpensive videocassette recording became available only in the early 1980s. Until that time, studying television from the past relied on gaining access to the archives of material held by television broadcasting institutions themselves. Only in the past two decades or so could students and academics study-ing television collect examples to work on easily. Even today, when massive libraries of DVDs or digital files can be assembled by interested individuals, by academic institutions or in national archives, it is not easy to know how these resources should be used. When there is plenty of stored television from the past to look at, what principles should be brought to bear in order to decide what to study? Perhaps whole days or even weeks of the output of a particular channel or channels should be studied. Perhaps programmes of a similar **genre** broadcast on different channels should be collected, having decided how the boundaries of a genre should be defined. Perhaps the most popular programmes in a given month or a year should be analysed, on the basis of the audience **ratings** that show which programmes were watched by the most people. Perhaps all the programmes shown by all the channels at a certain time, such as on Friday evenings for example, should be compared and contrasted with each other. Perhaps it is not programmes at all that should be a focus of interest, but instead the different television advertisements, links and trailers that connect them together, since these are the stitches which hold a **flow** of television together as an object for study.

Writing a history of television over the past twenty years or so looks easy, since it is not so difficult to gather evidence, but paradoxically this produces the problem that there is simply too much that could be investigated. To write the history of earlier decades of television is difficult in other ways. Some broadcasting organisations such as the BBC or Granada Television in Britain maintained archives of programmes on tape or film. But these are far from complete. A few programmes were recorded on film from the 1930s, and more programmes were recorded on videotape after its invention in the late 1950s. But the purpose of recording programmes was not primarily to preserve them for future television students and scholars, but instead:

- to train staff in how to produce, direct and shoot television
- to make recorded repeats possible
- to make programmes available for export.

Often, such practical difficulties as lack of storage space meant that institutions such as the BBC found it too expensive and difficult to keep sizeable programme archives. Tapes and film copies were simply thrown away, or expensive videotape was used again for recording a newer programme. The technologies to record programmes on film or videotape were attractive to television institutions because they made it easier to make programmes. Film inserts could be used during live broadcasts, and videotape made special effects much easier to achieve than during a live recording. So the copies of programmes that can be found in broadcasters' archives represent a fragmentary patchwork that was not intended as an objective record or even as a collection of television programmes that could sum up a decade or a channel's output. A further difficulty is that where programmes were preserved they were usually those that had acquired some status and importance. There are few existing copies of light entertainment programmes made before the 1960s, since news programmes, documentaries and some high-profile drama were the kinds of television thought useful to preserve.

genre a kind or type of programme. Programmes of the same genre have shared characteristics.

ratings the number of viewers estimated to have watched certain programmes, as compared to the numbers watching other programmes.

flow the ways that programmes, advertisements, etc. follow one another in an unbroken sequence across the day or part of the day, and the experience of watching the sequence of programmes, advertisements, trailers, etc.

ACTIVITY 2.1

Consider what the following terms might mean in the writing of a history (you could use this chapter and the further reading at the end of the chapter to research how the terms could apply to television history, or simply think about the meanings of these terms themselves):

Evolution   Invention
Turning-points   Cultural history
Evidence   National history
Progress   International history

Contemporary Television Studies has focused on the study of programmes in their original audio-visual form. So this section has so far considered the writing of television history in terms of the possibilities of watching television programmes as they were broadcast in some earlier time. Other kinds of history writing can be undertaken by using other kinds of evidence, and some of the recent historical work on television uses written sources to gain an understanding of the television of the past. For example, looking back at the pages of the BBC's listings magazine *Radio Times*, or ITV's *TV Times*, can be instructive in understanding how programmes and programme **schedules** were offered and advertised to their audiences. These magazines also contain features such as interviews with actors and **producers**, and articles by journalistic commentators. They can reveal much about the attitudes to television that were assumed, and the balance between information, education and entertainment in the television of particular periods. These listings publications also contain letters pages with viewers' questions, comments and evaluations of programmes. Although they are hardly representative, these sources give a partial snapshot of the ways that viewers established a relationship with broadcasters, and reveal some of the attitudes to programmes that might have been significant in a particular period.

The archives of broadcasting institutions, especially the BBC, also contain some records of viewer responses to programmes. Some producers kept the letters that viewers wrote to them about programmes, and broadcasters have always engaged in various kinds of audience research. The BBC had an Audience Research department, doing similar things to what **focus groups** do now by gathering information by questionnaire and interview in order to gauge what viewers like or dislike, and what they approve of or do not approve of about programmes. As well as raw numerical information about audience sizes, these sources provide another glimpse of how people responded to the television they watched in the past. In broadcasters' archives there are also numerous paper records about the making of programmes. The BBC in particular has maintained extensive archives of letters, memos, reports and policy documents that give insight into how and why programmes were made. So the issue of evidence in television history is a complex one, since it involves these questions:

schedule the arrangement of programmes, advertisements and other material into a sequential order within a certain period of time, such as an evening, day or week.

producer the person working for a television institution who is responsible for the budget, planning and making of a television programme or series of programmes.

focus groups small groups of selected people representing larger social groupings such as people of a certain age group, gender or economic status, who take part in discussions about a topic chosen for investigation.

- What are the different kinds of evidence available about television in the past?
- How does the selection of evidence make some kinds of history writing possible, and others extremely difficult?
- How does one kind of evidence (such as recordings of programmes) relate to other kinds (such as broadcasters' archives or commercial printed publications)?
- How can the attitudes and responses of audiences be reconstructed, and what do they tell us?
- How have television institutions' attitudes to their programmes shaped the evidence available?

As John Caughie (2000) has argued, the inability to record early television encourages the view that television is ephemeral by nature. Until the recent growth of multi-channel digital television, the versions of television's own past that were aired from time to time (in re-runs of old black-and-white programmes, compilation programmes of old television advertisements or brief clips from old programmes in quiz shows) were almost always presented in a humorous context. Television from the past was used like a family photo album, which invited the audience to be amazed, embarrassed and amused by what television was. Until recently, television from the past has been something to make fun of rather than to appreciate in its own terms. British television and its audiences are sophisticated and complex, and their awareness of growing up with television can be seen in the programmes that celebrate and deride that history. Programmes such as Channel 4's *Hundred Greatest TV Moments* represented television's memory of itself, and the audience's fondness for programmes of the past. But the history of television that appeared on television was almost exclusively told in terms of memorable programmes, and was often derided

Figure 2.1 *Porridge*. Fulton Mackay, Ronnie Barker and Richard Beckinsale. Courtesy of BBC Photograph Library.

and made the subject of comedy. Television in Britain seemed unable to take its history seriously (in comparison to television coverage of other histories such as those of architecture or cinema). But now, the increased demand for programme content on the increased number of contemporary channels makes the repeating of past programmes a notable feature of the schedules. With the proliferation of new channels, there is some economic value in the archives of old programmes that broadcasters have preserved. The BBC gained income from its vast library of old programmes, by making business deals with the American cable and satellite company Flextech and the media corporation Pearson in 1995, for example, to screen programmes from its archives. The export of new BBC programmes, another source of revenue, was also made possible by links with the American Discovery Channel in 1996 and the start of BBC World transmitting programmes internationally. The pay channel UK Gold, showing repeated programmes, is now joined by a range of BBC cable and satellite channels (BBC3 and BBC4) offering themed types of programmes aimed at certain kinds of audience. BBC4 is unusual in having a special team of producers who make the *Time Shift* series of documentaries about television history and also screen examples of 'classic' programmes on the channel. The BBC4 channel has also screened newly made dramas that are set at landmark moments in British television history or around the careers of important television stars and programme-makers. Figure 2.2 is an image from *The Road to Coronation Street*, a 2010 drama written by Daran Little about the creation of the longest-running British television soap opera. First broadcast in 1960 on ITV and still running today, *Coronation Street* was an innovative programme in its time. Daran Little's play lovingly recreates the efforts of the soap opera's creator, Tony Warren, to get the programme made and the shooting techniques used to make its first episodes. In Figure 2.2 we see a detailed creation of a 1960 television studio, with Warren in the centre as he learns the techniques of production. Presenting television from the past and programmes about television's past shows how important television is

Figure 2.2 In 2010, *The Road to Coronation Street* dramatised the creation of the ITV soap opera at the beginning of the 1960s.

to the shared memories and experiences of generations of viewers, and for **culture** in general. While television as a medium has always placed great emphasis on the moment of 'now', partly because live broadcasting has been so significant throughout the development of the medium, both the television industry and the discipline of Television Studies have an awareness of the significance of television history.

culture the shared attitudes, ways of life and assumptions of a group of people.

Cathy Come Home: the most repeated television play

Cathy Come Home was written by Jeremy Sandford (a journalist and radio and television dramatist), directed by Ken Loach, and produced by Tony Garnett. It was broadcast on BBC1 in the *Wednesday Play* series on 16 November 1966, with an audience of ten million. It is the most frequently repeated television drama ever, having been shown again in 1967, 1968, 1976, 1993 and its fortieth anniversary in 2006, for example. Rather than aiming for the well-formed studio drama whose conventions derived from the theatre, Garnett and Loach adopted the apparent untidiness and immediacy of documentary. Plays such as *Cathy Come Home* told fictional stories, but used them to make sense of the realistically observed world. Rather than maintaining a consistent relationship of the viewer to the drama, the documentary techniques in *Cathy Come Home* offer the viewer a range of points of view on her story. The drama follows her as she arrives in London from the provinces, meets her husband and starts a family. But things go wrong when her husband is injured at work, and the greater part

Figure 2.3
Cathy Come Home, 1966. Sean King as Sean, Ray Brooks as Reg, Stephen King as Stephen and Carol White as Cathy. Courtesy of BBC Photograph Library.

of the play concerns the family's slide into homelessness, the break-up of the marriage and the inability of welfare services to provide for their needs. Sometimes the camera observes Cathy in a distanced way, or a voice-over will contextualise her situation and provide information. But in other sequences a hand-held camera is close up with Cathy and encourages the viewer to share her experience in emotional terms. The overall effect of the play is to dramatise the separation between officials or institutions and the human experience of being homeless, poor and powerless.

ACTIVITY 2.2

Analyse the pages of a television listings publication for one day or one week, to find programmes that were made more than a decade ago. On which channels do you find these? What kinds of programmes are they? When are they screened? Who do you think is expected to watch them?

Inventing television technologies

The history of television can be thought of in terms of the progressive improvement of technology. From the earliest mechanical devices for broadcasting pictures, through the invention of magnetic tape to transmit pre-recorded material, to the invention of **cable television**, **satellite** transmission and now catch-up screenings on iPlayer or 4OD and the streaming of programmes over broadband internet, it might seem that the history of television is driven by technological innovation. But technical innovations require the resources of large organisations, and the will to implement technologies in applications that can be sold to a public. They require the stimulation of demand for the technologies, and a framework of **regulation** and law to govern their implementation. So technologies cannot be seen as in themselves the drivers of the development of television. For example, the level of satellite dish ownership rose to five million homes in 1996, largely because of the exclusive rights to football matches which Sky Television had bought using money gained from its majority shareholder Rupert Murdoch's non-television media interests. The recognition of a potential market, and programme content that can be sold to this market, is a precondition for the successful introduction of a new television technology.

The idea of television goes back to the late nineteenth century, when after radio had been invented it seemed a natural next step to transmit pictures to accompany sound. Scientists across the developed world were aware that the way to transmit pictures would be to find a way of breaking down a camera's visual image into tiny areas of black, white or shades of grey. These tiny areas could be reassembled on a television screen in order to reproduce the original image as a series of tiny dots. The principle is the same as the way that newspaper photographs had been transmitted by telephone wires since the beginning of the 1900s, by decomposing an image into

cable television originally called Community Antenna Television (CATV). Transmission of television signals along cables in the ground.

satellite television television signals beamed from a ground transmitter to a stationary satellite that broadcasts the signal to a specific area (called the 'footprint') below it.

regulation the control of television institutions by laws, codes of practice or guidelines.

clusters of larger or smaller black dots, producing areas of darker or lighter space which together added up to the shades and outlines of a photograph. The discovery of the chemical element selenium enabled this vision of television to seem closer, since a bank of selenium sensors in an electronic camera would turn the different amounts of light falling on them into different strengths of electrical current. If the changing signals for each tiny selenium receptor were sent to a receiver, the changing light and dark of a television picture would result. Inventors in Britain, Russia and Germany worked on different methods of scanning images with selenium sensors in the years before and after 1900, but without perfecting a workable system. The British inventor John Logie Baird, and engineers at the Marconi EMI company, worked separately on competing systems of television broadcasting in the 1920s, with government and BBC support given to Baird. British television formally began on 2 November 1936, trying out both the Baird and Marconi systems and broadcasting to only about three hundred receivers in the London area.

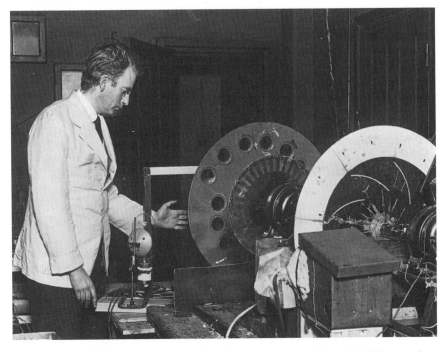

Figure 2.4   John Logie Baird with his experimental television receiver, 1926. Photograph courtesy of the National Museum of Photography, Film & Television/Science and Society Picture Library.

ACTIVITY 2.3

Do some research into what happened when John Logie Baird's and Marconi EMI's television systems were tried out in Britain. What were the strengths and weaknesses of each system? If you think the best system 'won', what made it the best, and for whom?

Television institutions

Television today is a centralised business. Large corporations and institutions own the equipment and facilities to make television programmes, and these are distributed from central transmission sources to the huge number of receiving aerials, cable television ports and internet connections that serve the homes of the television audience. So production and distribution involve a small number of powerful and centralised organisations, whereas reception is differentiated and distributed across a very broad and relatively powerless constituency of viewers. Television did not need to develop in this way. In the late nineteenth century, commentators speculated about television technologies that would be more like telephone systems (Gripsrud 1998: 20–1). People equipped with small and convenient television recording devices were imagined making and sending pictures and sound to domestic receivers. Television might have been much more personal, unregulated and cheaper to make, and services such as YouTube have realised this dream on the internet, but not in conventional television broadcasting. Another way of putting this alternative development of television would be to say that television could have been a popular medium, in the sense that it could have been made and received by people themselves, and the making of television could have been embedded within their own lives. Instead, television became big business, where national governments co-operated to set up technical standards to control the mass-production of television equipment. A professional community of highly trained technicians and production staff undertook the making of programmes.

The government and BBC gave no serious consideration to advertising as a means of support when the work of John Logie Baird was being completed in Britain, and plans for a television service were actively developed. The thinking behind the organisation of the BBC as a semi-autonomous public corporation was inherited from the late Victorian corporations that had **monopolies** to provide services such as gas, electricity and water. Their control of supply and freedom from competition was granted in exchange for a remit to operate for the public good. The BBC took seriously its aims to raise the standards of the entire national audience in terms of sophistication of taste, intellectual appetite and levels of knowledge: television as **public service** broadcasting. In the United States big corporations such as RCA and General Electric took over the work there on the development of television equipment during the 1920s. This was an important development, in that it was not the government, the Hollywood film studios or individual entrepreneurs who took television forward but the industrial combines behind the production of radio equipment. Television in the USA would be modelled on the organisation of radio broadcasting, rather than the cinema industry or the public services, and in the late 1920s experimental television broadcasts were made in New York, Boston and Chicago, backed by electronics manufacturers hoping to sell the television sets to receive them. The radio broadcasters NBC and CBS were promoting television and could supply programmes to broadcast. American television, like radio, would use national **networks** supplying programmes to local stations that paid to broadcast them, gaining income from commercials and the **sponsorship** of programmes. By the time America entered the Second World War in 1941, the regulator, the **Federal Communications Commission** (FCC), had licensed thirty-two commercial television stations, broadcasting to the few thousand owners of television sets in America's largest cities.

monopoly control over the provision of a service or product by one institution or business.

public service in television, the provision of a mix of programmes that inform, educate and entertain in ways that encourage the betterment of audiences and society in general.

network a television institution that transmits programmes through local or regional broadcasting stations that are owned by or affiliated to that institution.

sponsorship the funding of programmes or channels by businesses, whose name is usually prominently displayed in the programme or channel as a means of advertising.

Federal Communications Commission (FCC) the government body in the USA which regulates the operations and output of television companies and other broadcasters.

In the very different television culture of China, the history, purposes and institutions of television are interesting to compare and contrast with those of the United States and European countries mentioned in this chapter. Broadcasting in China was established by the ruling Communist Party that took power in 1949, as a means to disseminate government policy, news and entertainment sanctioned by the state. Television began in 1958 with one television station in Beijing, the capital city, but expanded slowly, with only thirty stations in operation by 1970, based in cities and reaching only part of the population. After 1976 television grew faster than any other communications medium in the country, with over six hundred transmitting stations by 1995. In addition to these terrestrial transmitters, eleven million Chinese people could receive satellite television signals, and 1,800 cable systems were operating. The institutions of television in China have been closely controlled by government, so that the prospect of Chinese people watching programmes and channels made abroad or beamed to them by satellites operated by foreign corporations has led to the licensing of cable television systems and largely unsuccessful attempts to ban the use of satellite dishes. Access to the internet is also restricted in China, so that viewing programmes over the web is difficult. The historical basis of this suspicion of commercial and foreign television in China comes from the principles set out by the revolutionary leader Mao Zedong, who argued that the purposes of broadcasting were:

■ to publicise the decisions made by the ruling Communist Party
■ to educate the population
■ to establish a channel of communication between the Party and the people.

In practice, however, ownership of satellite dishes is common, and services beamed by satellite, notably StarTV, carry channels such as MTV and CNN. The history of television in China can be framed as a gradual movement from state control, with an emphasis on information, political programming and entertainment programmes based in state-approved national values, to increasing commercialisation and diversity. This historical narrative is explored further in Chapter 3, where the current state of television around the world in national and international contexts is discussed. But here this brief reference to China shows how the political and cultural histories of a country can take widely different forms as they affect the establishment and development of television.

In Britain the **Annan Committee** report of 1977 put into question the role of television broadcasters as moral and intellectual leaders of society. Instead, television was increasingly considered as a market in which providers of programmes would give their publics what they seemed to want. With three channels and the prospect of a fourth, it no longer seemed necessary for each channel to expose the audience to the full range of both 'accessible' and 'difficult' programmes. The 1970s marked the beginnings of the notion that some channels would direct their resources to some types of programme more than others, leaving viewers to choose for themselves the programmes that catered for their existing tastes. Thus the role of television institutions underwent gradual change across the decades, and conceptions of the purposes of television and its relationship with its audiences developed with different emphases. The history of television involves placing the production and distribution of television in a context informed by the cultural pressures on

Annan Committee
a committee reporting in 1977 to government on the future of broadcasting. It supported public service broadcasting, the funding of the BBC by licence fee, and the planned introduction of a fourth television channel.

terrestrial broadcasting from a ground-based transmission system, as opposed to broadcasting via satellite.

governments, television institutions and audiences, all of which affect each other. The setting-up in 1982 of Britain's fourth **terrestrial** channel, Channel 4, was the result of a combination of inherited and traditional views of broadcasting with the new imperatives of the 1979 Conservative government and its allies. From the past came a commitment to public service, to educational and cultural programmes, and to programmes for minority audiences. But Conservative policies in the 1980s attempted to introduce the principles of the market into all aspects of British life. So Channel 4 bought programmes from independent programme-makers, who had to compete with each other for commissions, and Channel 4 itself made no significant investment in production facilities or training. The channel's funding derived from advertising revenue through a levy on the ITV companies, which sold advertising time on Channel 4 in their regions, and was therefore reliant on the buoyancy of the British economy. The Broadcasting Act of 1980 that established Channel 4 required it to 'encourage innovation and experiment in the form and content of programmes'. The first Chief Executive was Jeremy Isaacs, who led the channel's investment in films for domestic and foreign television screening and cinema release. There were programmes for British Asian viewers, and members of trade unions, while in Wales the companion channel S4C (Sianel Pedwar Cymru) broadcast Welsh-language programmes. Channel 4 was required by the Broadcasting Act to provide 'a distinctive service', but attracted criticism for its 'bad language' and apparent left-wing political bias.

soap opera a continuing drama serial involving a large number of characters in a specific location, focusing on relationships, emotions and reversals of fortune.

independent production companies businesses making television programmes which can be sold to television networks that transmit and distribute them.

The first night of Channel 4 was on Tuesday, 2 November 1982. The programme schedule ran from 4.45 p.m. to 11.50 p.m., with the two most popular programmes being its new **soap opera**, *Brookside* (4.1 million viewers), and the first specially commissioned television film for the channel, *Film on Four: Walter* (3.75 million viewers), directed by Stephen Frears. These audiences were low by comparison with the traditional channels, with the highest-rated programme in November 1982 being *Coronation Street* on ITV, with 15.7 million viewers. But Channel 4 introduced significant changes to several programme forms, as well as opening up the **independent production** sector in Britain. *Brookside* was the first British soap opera to be made entirely on location, on a new estate in Liverpool. *Channel 4 News* (made by ITN) was Britain's first hour-long news programme, and set standards for news analysis. One of Channel 4's aims was to export programmes in order to maximise revenue, and financing film-length dramas for television that could be sold to foreign broadcasters was one way of achieving this. In the 1980s Channel 4 began to release its films in cinemas, as a way of raising their profile and creating publicity before their television transmission. Channel 4 entered the art cinema market with these films, and the distinction between the television film and the cinema film became increasingly blurred. With the increased cost of making films to cinematic standards (of length, star quality, production value), fewer films could be made.

ACTIVITY 2.4

Examine the programme schedules on Channel 4 today. Which programmes do you find that seem to be aimed at minority audiences? Which audiences, and why?

Professional cultures in a 'Golden Age'

The technology to record television pictures and sound was introduced in Britain slowly in the 1950s and both BBC and ITV made use of it for training purposes, but rarely for transmitting programmes made and recorded on tape. Instead, the medium of film was the preferred method of recording programmes for preservation, for foreign sale or for brief sequences (such as film shot in exterior locations) that would be played into programmes recorded live in a television studio. It was expensive to transfer programmes shot on film to tape, to buy the tape itself, to store it and to buy and maintain the machines that transcribed from film to tape. This meant that television programmes that used tape were more expensive to make. The people working in television were also required to become expert and professional in new ways once tape and film became as significant as live broadcasting. The mastery of these technologies led to the development of highly trained and specialist personnel with specific tasks to perform in the production process, with fewer of the attitudes of the enthusiastic upper-middle-class amateur which had previously marked many of the personnel in television.

By the 1960s the increase in broadcasting hours and the presence of three television channels in Britain changed the culture of television production, by moving away from the pioneering amateurism that characterised the early years. The first **producers** and **directors** in the 1930s and 1940s had some of the open-mindedness, but also some of the blinkered cosiness of a public school or university drama society, making up television as they went along. The professionalism and large scale of television production in the 1960s and after encouraged programmes to be made more like an industrial product. Professional writers and directors, most of whose working time was spent in television, worked according to consistent schedules and guidelines, and developed skills, professional codes of conduct and shared expectations. In the 1960s and 1970s the producer commissioned programmes, ran the production process, including selecting the directors and technical staff, and oversaw projects to completion. The producer came to have an authorial role, and was also relatively free from the interference of department heads and television executives.

Television's Golden Age in Britain in the period from the late 1950s to the 1970s has gained this label because it was a period when the **status quo** changed. New values were being put in place, and inherited traditions were confronted by new forms and new pressures. It is important to recognise that professional workers in the television industry do not live in a separate cultural world from the rest of their society, and currents of ideas circulating among people of similar interests, social class and educational background have influences on the ways these people conceive of their role. In Britain popular books of the 1950s and 1960s by left-wing intellectuals such as Richard Hoggart, Raymond Williams, Stuart Hall and E. P. Thompson encouraged the belief that **culture** (television, radio, popular music, home decoration or sport, for example) was significant in shaping people's **class** position and personal identity, and that these cultural activities were connected to the economics of British society. These theories derived in part from **Marxist** thinking, which argues that the forms of everyday life derive from the ways people are positioned as workers in, or owners of, the industries and businesses that produce the wealth of the nation. For these writers the improvement of social structures and

director the person responsible for the creative process of turning a script or idea into a finished programme, by working with a technical crew, performers and an editor.

status quo a Latin term meaning the ways that culture and society are currently organised.

class a section of society defined by their relationship to economic activity, whether as workers (the working class) or possessors of economic power (the bourgeoisie), for example.

Marxism the political and economic theories associated with the German nineteenth-century theorist Karl Marx, who described and critiqued capitalist societies and proposed Communism as a revolutionary alternative.

people's everyday conditions of existence could come about through changing people's relationships to work and wealth, but also through debate and struggles for change in culture itself. To change television might also change society, and the influence of this view was seen in **realistic** and often pessimistic drama series such as *Z Cars* (a police series), and controversial **satire** programmes such as *That Was the Week that Was*, which challenged conventions of television and also the representations of British society.

These ideas were familiar to the new generation of school leavers and university graduates emerging in the late 1950s and early 1960s, often people from working-class backgrounds who had been given the opportunity to gain a good education through scholarships and the expansion of universities. These people were often resistant to the elitism, conservatism and traditionalism that had dominated the Establishment (the civil service, the BBC, the institutions of the churches, universities and the law) in the past. Television was a young medium, and some of these people saw opportunities to carry forward their radical ideas in the television industry. Vigorous and authentic television seemed to entail the bringing on to the screen and into the television business of people from working-class backgrounds, from outside the stodgy south-east of England. In drama a new kind of realism was needed to reflect the lives of ordinary people beyond London and the Home Counties, and television documentary could present the different regions and social classes of the nation to the television audience. Television producers, directors and writers were often resistant to the bureaucracy of the television companies, and rejected the stoical and submissive attitudes to authority which characterised the older generation which had lived through the Second World War.

The attitudes of these people committed to changing society by changing its culture were evident in the programmes being made, but also in ways of thinking and writing about television that would inform the beginnings of Television Studies. In what became known as 'committed criticism', writers condemned the status quo and sought both to praise radical television (or film or literary works) and to find ways of representing which critiqued the present and offered new and **progressive** ways of thinking. For committed critics it was important to take the **popular culture** enjoyed by ordinary people seriously, but also to discriminate wisely between what was valuable and what was deadening or worthless. One effect of this was to continue the suspicion of American popular culture (rock 'n' roll music, Hollywood cinema or comics, for instance), which had been gaining audiences and making money with the recognition of a new social group – the teenager. In many television fictions of the 1950s and 1960s isolated young outsider figures, often moving between social classes, struggle to find authentic personal meaning in their apparently absurd and empty lives. The independent outsider and rebel was always male, however, and the heroic vigour of the 1960s hero is often opposed to the entrapping seductiveness of marriage and family represented by women.

In more recent times the culture of television professionals in Britain has changed because of the structural changes made to the television industry as a result of new broadcasting regulations imposed by government, and new working practices introduced by television executives. The BBC reduced its staff by seven thousand between 1986 and 1990, for example, and since the 1980s the use of temporary contracts and the **outsourcing** of production to independent producers, and the introduction of an internal market at the BBC, have shifted decision-making powers

realism the aim for representations to reproduce reality faithfully, and the ways this is done.

satire a mode of critical commentary about society or an aspect of it, using humour to attack people or ideas.

committed a term used in the study of the politics of culture, implying that a person or a text has a commitment to positive and progressive social change.

progressive encouraging positive change or progress, usually implying progress towards fairer and more equal ways of organising society.

popular culture the texts created by ordinary people (as opposed to an elite group) or created for them, and the ways these are used.

outsourcing obtaining services from an independent business rather than from within a television institution, usually as a means of cutting costs.

from programme-makers to schedulers and commissioners and made the career paths of programme-makers much more unstable. The effect of this market-like situation is that the producer, who commissions and oversees the making of television programmes, becomes a powerful figure, to the exclusion of the writer or the director, because the producer is answerable to the demands of the television institution for audiences and cost-effectiveness. When John Birt led the BBC in the 1990s, the sweeping changes he introduced weakened the independence of the producer by centralising power in London and giving more control to commissioners, schedulers and controllers. The same process affected the commercial channels. The BBC sold off many of its programme production and technical facilities in the early 1990s, and increased the proportion of programmes commissioned from **independent producers** rather than made in-house. It increasingly resembles Channel 4 as a commissioning rather than programme-making organisation.

Reception contexts

Television is still most often watched in the private space of the home, but in the early days of British broadcasting this was by no means the dominant way that viewers experienced the new medium. Philip Corrigan (1990) has discovered that in 1937, the year after BBC television broadcasting started, there were more than a hundred public venues for watching television. These included railway stations, restaurants and department stores. Audiences sometimes as large as a hundred people could gather to watch television pictures collectively. In the United States a similar situation was evident in the 1930s, and for a short time television looked like a possible competitor with cinema as a medium of public entertainment experienced in buildings set aside for watching (J. Allen 1983). The Nazi government in Germany in the 1930s was interested partly in the propaganda value of television broadcasting, and partly in competing with the large American corporations that were investing in television production and television sets. The fact that the Olympic Games of 1936 took place in Berlin was a stimulus to German television, and broadcasts were received not in individual homes but in viewing rooms established in cities. Once again, television was being thought of as a medium for collective viewing of pictures and sound relayed live from major public events. Some of the buildings in which German television broadcasts were watched could hold audiences as large as four hundred people. But industrial corporations in Germany had considerable political influence during the Nazi era. So the corporations' plans to develop domestic television sets to be watched in individual homes, and thus to develop a consumer market for television sets, meant that these public screenings were to give way to domestic viewing when the Second World War began in 1939 (Uricchio 1989).

When the pattern of centralised production and dispersed individual reception of television stabilised as the norm after the Second World War, the form of television that we know in Western countries today had been established. There are two different and sometimes conflicting results of this pattern. First, central control of production and private individual reception set up a structure that matches the democratic organisation of the developed societies such as those of Europe and the United States. When governments have a direct role in broadcasting, or set up a legal framework of ownership and **regulation** for private autonomous institutions to make television, there is a basis for universal access to information and culture that might promote a fairer society. Mass populations, watching television in their own homes and with members of their families, could be supplied with the information and ideas they need to participate in a national or regional society. Informed viewers would be given the resources to take part in political and social debates, to vote in elections on the basis of a level playing field of information about the issues at stake. The centralised production of television and its dispersed reception suit the concept of **public service** broadcasting quite well as it has developed in Britain and other European countries. Although there is a more questionable side to this, since government propaganda and the manipulation of audiences could also be a part of this broadcasting landscape, the structure of broadcasting as we know it is associated with attempts to raise the cultural, educational and social standards of societies.

The second result of centralised production and dispersed reception of television is its connection with the culture of the home. Standards of living and proportions of surplus income available for investment in leisure and entertainment rose steadily through the twentieth century in the industrial nations of the Western world. People's houses were not only places to live but also places where consumer goods could be accumulated, and new patterns of domestic leisure could develop. Commentators in the 1940s and 1950s in Britain were concerned about how television might prove a disruptive force in the home, disturbing the family routines of eating, conversation and children's bedtimes. To watch could be regarded as a waste of time (compared to reading, doing jobs around the house or engaging in conversation), especially if television was focused on entertainment. However, for most viewers the experience of watching was not the solitary experience it often is today. Because only a small proportion of homes had invested in the new and expensive technology, most viewing was collective as people gathered in friends' and neighbours' houses to watch. Watching television was a social event in its own right, and in some respects helped to form communities. This was especially the case in the newly built suburbs of the major cities where people had chosen to uproot themselves from the close-knit but overcrowded Victorian housing of older towns and city centres. Separated by the hedges and front gardens of their new semi-detached houses, people were able to socialise and display their relative wealth and status to their neighbours by holding informal gatherings around their televisions. The television set became an important part of the culture of the home, as the prices of television sets fell through the 1950s and they could be acquired not only by the affluent middle class but increasingly by everyone. Television sets became a central feature of the household living room, often positioned next to the fireplace, where families would gather in the evening together both to keep warm (in the age before central heating) and to share the entertainment experiences offered to them by television. As well as experiencing entertainment outside the home, at the cinema for example, or at the pub, television enabled people to take their leisure indoors with their friends and their families. Radio had already fulfilled a similar function, and as the mass ownership of television sets extended in the 1950s in Europe and the United States this continued the drive to make the home the primary site of leisure and consumerism. Overall, then, the pattern of television broadcasting that dominated the twentieth and early twenty-first century was neither natural nor necessary. But it suited the developing forms of society characterised by these key features:

■ the promotion of democracy and citizenship
■ participation in a modern consumer society
■ the centrality of the home as the location of private leisure and family life
■ access by government and industry to private space and private life.

The significance of this narrative of television history is that it is a cultural history: it emphasises the ways in which television became embedded in people's lives according to the places where they lived, the social classes to which they belonged and the expectations about home, work and leisure that they held.

Programmes and forms

Writing the history of television by choosing significant programmes to exemplify a year, decade or longer period clearly raises difficult problems. The shape of the narrative of television history that this produces is strongly determined by the choice of the examples used to back it up. Since television in Britain has a public service function, one of the ways of demonstrating this historical tradition is to note the events that television has covered in order to bring a national audience together as members of a common **culture**. Ceremonies, state occasions and major sporting events are examples that support this view of television history. When the BBC was Britain's only television broadcaster (from 1936 to 1955), it emphasised the live broadcasting of these kinds of events from the start, and set up **outside broadcast** units to cover such public and ceremonial events as the coronation of King George VI in 1937, the annual Wimbledon tennis championships and the Armistice Day ceremony commemorating the end of the First World War. British writers in the 1930s who predicted the future of television emphasised its ability to relay events (such as sporting events, royal events and general elections) live across the country, thus keeping people in touch with what happened beyond their immediate experience and neighbourhood. It was felt that television would not compete with cinema as entertainment because of its domestic setting and lack of a sense of occasion, and would therefore focus on information.

It was in the 1950s that what we would now describe as mass audiences for television began in Britain. But television sets were still expensive, costing more than £80 in the early 1950s, equivalent to about eight weeks' wages for the average employed man. Between 1952 and 1959 in Britain the number of combined television and radio licences increased from 2.1 million to 10 million. The single television programme with the greatest effect on creating this wider ownership of television sets was the live coverage of the Coronation of Queen Elizabeth II in 1953. Again, a live event relayed by television suits the construction of a certain kind of history. This history regards television as a medium preoccupied with the present, and with live coverage. Furthermore, the Coronation is another example of a television event that addresses a national public (and an international one since in the 1950s Britain still had extensive contacts with and responsibilities for countries that had formed part of its empire). Televised events such as the Coronation connect television viewing with the formation of a national culture defined in part by its relationship with the royal family, heritage, tradition and ceremony. More than twenty years later, in 1974, the wedding of Princess Anne and Captain Mark Philips was broadcast live, and seen by an

outside broadcast the television transmission of outdoor events such as sport or ceremonial occasions, using equipment set up in advance for the purpose. Abbreviated as OB.

audience of around 25 million, representing about half of the UK population. Television covered the wedding of Prince Charles and Lady Diana Spencer in July 1981, showing five and a half hours of live coverage on BBC and ITV. In the UK 39 million viewers watched live, and it was broadcast live to seventy-four countries. The BBC used about sixty cameras, including twelve in St Paul's Cathedral.

ACTIVITY 2.5

Look through magazines (such as Sunday newspaper magazines, style magazines or consumer electronics magazines) to find advertisements for recent television equipment such as flat-panel television sets, DVD recorders and players, or digital television receivers. What similarities can you find in the ways these are advertised, and the potential consumers the ads seem to be addressed to?

---

commercial television television funded by the sale of advertising time or sponsorship of programmes.

Independent Television Authority (ITA) the official body set up to regulate commercial television in Britain.

Independent **commercial television** began broadcasting on 22 September 1955, available first only in the London region but expanding to nearly all of the country over the next six years. Many influential figures resisted ITV, including the BBC Director-General John Reith, who compared commercial television to bubonic plague, and concern was fuelled by the American commercial television coverage of the Coronation in 1953, when messages from programme sponsors frequently interrupted the Westminster Abbey service. But the Conservative government was keen to break the BBC monopoly and passed the Television Bill of 1954, which set up the **Independent Television Authority**, though the Bill revealed in its language the concern for the lowering of standards which commercial television might entail. It was to be

> predominantly British in tone and style and of high quality, and nothing was to be included which offended against good taste or decency or which was likely to incite to crime or to lead to disorder or to be offensive to public feeling.

The desire to preserve a national television culture and to protect it from the commercialism and triviality associated with another broadcasting culture (of the United States) can be deduced from this attitude. In a history of television, this reaction to the start of ITV is evidence of an anxiety about what British television might become.

Postmaster General the person appointed by government to regulate communications institutions such as the Post Office, radio and television.

variety programmes entertainment programmes containing a mix of material such as songs and comedy sketches.

The first night on ITV began with a gala including speeches from the Lord Mayor of London, the **Postmaster General** and Sir Kenneth Clark, chairman of the ITA. The evening was very much in the mould of the BBC: the presenter was Leslie Mitchell, who had worked for the BBC and presented its opening night in 1936. The **variety** performers on the first night, such as Harry Secombe and Billy Cotton, had regularly appeared on the BBC, and subsequent programming that night consisted of extracts from theatre plays and a boxing match, and concluded with a discussion of the latest London fashions shown at the Mayfair Hotel. Each broadcast day ended with the playing of the national anthem. Commercial television was organised in regions, with each part of the country having its own broadcasting provider. The

BBC was also divided into regions for television production and broadcasting, just as its radio services had been. Each regional company made programmes specifically for its local audience, and also offered programmes to the national network. Viewers who could receive the new commercial channel (and initially this was by no means everyone in Britain) were immediately keen on ITV, and in 1957 viewers who could get both BBC and ITV watched ITV two-thirds of the time. In December 1955, for example, 84 per cent of viewers with access to ITV watched its variety programme *Sunday Night at the London Palladium*. Both ITV and BBC channels used popular formats such as quiz shows, one-off dramas, variety and adventure series to keep their hold on their audiences, with ITV generally catering for more popular tastes. The BBC's audience fell, and it responded by increasing its broadcast hours from forty-one per week to fifty. It introduced its first **soap opera**, *The Grove Family*, in weekly fifteen-minute episodes centring on a suburban middle-class family, resulting in a deluge of approving letters and massive press coverage. Television created the new figure of the television **personality**, familiar figures such as the on-screen announcers Sylvia Peters, Mary Malcolm and McDonald Hobley on the BBC, and the hosts of popular programmes such as the television cook Philip Harben, gardener Fred Streeter, Annette Mills in the children's programme *Muffin the Mule*, and Armand and Michela Dennis in filmed wildlife programmes from around the world.

personalities people appearing on television who are recognised by audiences as celebrities with a media image and public status beyond the role they play in a particular programme.

The reasons that genres of television programmes are created and become significantly popular are varied and complex, so that looking at the selection of programmes with the largest audiences in a particular year can be misleading as well as informative. In the following boxes, the ten most popular programmes in Britain from four different years are listed, measuring popularity according to the size of audience calculated by broadcasters' audience research figures. Some of the critical points that could be made about what these lists reveal are suggested after the lists, together with some issues that complicate possible interpretations of the meaning of the figures.

The ten most popular programmes in March 1958

The ten most popular programmes in March 1958 were all on ITV. At this time audience sizes were measured in millions of homes, though of course the number of viewers in each home could vary widely. *Emergency Ward 10* appears twice in this list because two of its episodes in March made the top ten programmes.

1 *Take Your Pick* (game show, 4.1 million homes)
2 *The Army Game* (sitcom, 4.1m)
3 *Armchair Theatre* (one-off drama, 3.8m)
4 *Emergency Ward 10* (soap opera, 3.8m)
5 *Sunday Night at the London Palladium* (variety show, 3.7m)
6 *Double Your Money* (game show, 3.6m)
7 *TV Playhouse* (one-off drama, 3.6m)
8 *Emergency Ward 10* (3.5m)
9 *Shadow Squad* (thriller series, 3.1m)
10 *Play of the Week* (one-off drama, 3.1m).

The ten most popular programmes in September 1964

The ten most popular programmes in September 1964 were all shown on ITV. Audience sizes were still measured in millions of viewing homes, where of course the number of people viewing could vary considerably. *Coronation Street* and *Emergency Ward 10* appear twice in this list because two episodes from each series made the top ten programmes.

1 *Coronation Street* (soap opera, 8.1 million homes)
2 *Coronation Street* (7.8m)
3 *No Hiding Place* (drama series, 7.8m)
4 *Sunday Palladium* (variety show, 7.4m)
5 *Emergency Ward 10* (soap opera, 7.2m)
6 *Emergency Ward 10* (7.0m)
7 *Take Your Pick* (game show, 6.9m)
8 *Love Story* (drama series, 6.8m)
9 *Drama 64* (one-off drama, 6.8m)
10 *Double Your Money* (game show, 6.7m).

The ten most popular programmes in November 1974

Audience sizes were still measured in millions of homes. Both *Coronation Street* and *Crossroads* appear twice in this list because different episodes of each of them gained large audiences during the month.

1 *Bless this House* (ITV sitcom, 8.6 million homes)
2 *Coronation Street* (ITV soap opera, 7.8m)
3 *Man About the House* (ITV sitcom, 7.8m)
4 *The Generation Game* (BBC game show, 7.5m)
5 *Coronation Street* (ITV soap opera, 7.4m)
6 *Crossroads* (ITV soap opera, 7.4m)
7 *Crossroads* (ITV soap opera, 7.4m)
8 *Upstairs Downstairs* (ITV drama series, 7.3m)
9 *Jennie* (ITV drama series, 7.2m)
10 *Opportunity Knocks* (ITV game show, 7.1m).

The ten most popular programmes in November 1984

Audiences are now measured in millions of viewers.

1 *Coronation Street* (ITV soap opera, 19.0m)
2 *Give Us a Clue* (ITV game show, 15.5m)

 3 *Tenko* (BBC drama serial, 15.3m)
 4 *Just Good Friends* (BBC sitcom, 15.1m)
 5 *Crossroads* (ITV soap opera, 14.8m)
 6 *Name That Tune* (ITV game show, 14.6m)
 7 *Dallas* (BBC imported US soap opera, 14.6m)
 8 *Hi-De-Hi* (BBC sitcom, 14.5m)
 9 *Play Your Cards Right* (ITV game show, 14.5m)
10 *Surprise Surprise* (ITV light entertainment, 13.7m).

As Andrew Crisell (1997: 84) has written, 'commercial television was set up as an extension of the public service concept . . . The ITA required the contractors to inform, educate and entertain – to produce programmes of balance, quality and variety'. But, when ITV began broadcasting, the pace and style of British television changed somewhat because in order to compete with the BBC the new channel showed imported American programmes and used American **formats**, as in the action drama series *The Adventures of Robin Hood* and *The Count of Monte Cristo*. In this competitive environment research into audience sizes and preferences became more significant, and television viewers began to be seen as consumers seeking entertainment. Nevertheless, ITV followed the BBC in making **adaptations** of theatre plays, and dramas from Europe translated into English, as well as the populist quizzes and variety shows which ITV is credited with bringing to prominence. Looking at the lists, though, it seems that ITV had considerable success in attracting large audiences by broadcasting programmes in the forms that are still considered today to be popular entertainment, such as soap opera and game shows. In 1960, ITV first showed *Coronation Street*, and in Figure 2.5 a key storyline in the first episode was the tension between the youthful and ambitious, university-educated Ken Barlow (in the centre) and his working-class parents. This shot is composed to draw attention to Ken's troubled emotions, both caring for his parents but quite literally constrained by them in the restricted space at the dining table.

It is important to remember that these programme forms on ITV were designed to deliver audiences to advertisers, who had paid to screen television commercials between programme segments. The formation of large audiences for popular programmes was necessary to the profitability of the ITV companies. On its first night 170,000 sets were able to receive ITV, and, of these, 100,000 were tuned to ITV, while a quarter of households watched BBC instead. The first ITV commercial break was at 8.12 p.m. during the first evening's variety programme, and there were twenty-three commercials that night altogether. Advertisers paid about £1,500 for a slot, a 50 per cent premium above normal rates, and demand led to a ballot to select those ads that would be accommodated. The products advertised were similar to those of today: toothpaste, tyres, drinking chocolate, soap, cars and breakfast cereal. Advertisements were not allowed to concern politics or religion, and had to conform to the standards of good taste overseen by two committees. They could appear only in '**natural breaks**' of up to six minutes per hour, and there had to be a two-minute interval between an advertisement and any appearance by a member of the royal family, state occasion, church service or royal ceremony.

format the blueprint for a programme, including its setting, main characters, genre, form and main themes.

adaptation transferring a novel, theatre play, poem, etc. from its original medium into another medium such as television.

natural break a vague term meaning a point at which a programme can be interrupted without causing undue disruption to the ongoing flow of the programme.

Figure 2.5 The first episode of *Coronation Street* in 1960.

series a television form where each programme in the series has a different story or topic, though settings, main characters or performers remain the same.

serial a television form where a developing narrative unfolds across a sequence of separate episodes.

demography the study of population, and the groupings of people (demographic groups) within the whole population.

conventions the frameworks and procedures used to make or interpret texts.

docusoap a television form combining documentary's depiction of non-actors in ordinary situations with soap opera's continuing narratives about selected characters.

reflexivity a text's reflection on its own status as a text, for example drawing attention to generic conventions, or revealing the technologies used to make a programme.

The lists show that light entertainment programmes such as game shows and sitcoms, as well as long-running **series** and **serials**, had become the mainstay of the output of the channels. Costs are reduced by using the same crew, performers, sets, costumes and studios for each episode, and series and serials can be sold to overseas broadcasters in ready-made packages of programmes. One of the effects of this is to marginalise programmes that are more unconventional in form, or more challenging in social and political content. The promise that a continuing series or serial has of holding onto an audience for the duration of the programme's run offers the prospect of a consistent audience whose **demographic** appeal and/or large size may be attractive to advertisers. **Genre** television (such as soap opera, police or hospital drama, or game shows) is attractive to television executives because a popular generic programme has a brand identity. In the same way as casting a known television **personality** or performer, the recognition and familiarity of the forms and **conventions** of the programmes provide both security and appeal. Generic television also provides a sense of control and ownership to the audience, who have a stake in the programmes rather than simply being offered another new product to consume. As well as being constrained by repetition, genre allows for innovation within and between genres, and programmes gain large audiences by manipulating conventions in new ways. Generic categories are no longer separate, and such newer formats as **docusoaps**, hospital thrillers and dramedy (comedy drama) feed off the rich history and audience knowledge of television to mix **realism** with **reflexivity**.

Thus the BBC's soap opera *EastEnders* continued the British tradition of addressing contemporary social issues, while also casting Barbara Windsor as a Cockney pub landlady to draw on her associations with 1950s and 1960s saucy seaside comedy in the *Carry On* comedy films. In 1967 ITV's series *The Prisoner* had mixed an adventure story about a secret agent confined in a mysterious village with settings and costumes that referenced the Pop Art of the period, indicated in Figure 2.6 by the contrasting significance of the Prisoner's blazer, the formal garden setting, and the mysterious white bubble that has appeared behind him. In 2010 the series was reworked in a co-production between ITV and the American AMC network, setting it in a new mysterious location (this time a desert) but with a similar enigmatic style that mixed time-periods and props to confuse its audience. In Figure 2.7 the modern Prisoner sees what appear to be transparent versions of the destroyed Twin Towers of the World Trade Center that have appeared in the desert and like the 1967 version he is confronted by a mysterious white bubble. While knowledge of the original 1967 version was not necessary to understand the 2010 series, a viewer with knowledge of the original's cult status could perceive how the new version consciously drew on television history.

ACTIVITY 2.6

Look in more detail at the lists of the ten most popular programmes presented in this chapter. What are the similarities and differences you find between the lists? What might these similarities and differences contribute to a history of British television?

Figure 2.6 *The Prisoner*, screened by ITV in 1967, mixed spy adventure with surreal fantasy.

Figure 2.7 The remake of *The Prisoner* in 2010 updated the 1967 series, but kept its enigmatic tone.

Case study: 'Me TV'

Domestic television technologies cannot in themselves be regarded as the motors of change in the history or future of television, as this chapter has discussed. Technologies become marketable and attractive to purchasers because of the possibilities they offer in extending existing ways of using television, and their ability to lead practices of viewing in new directions. They also have to be integrated into the institutional and structural arrangements that shape how television is made, broadcast and financially supported. This case study considers how the technology of the digital video recorder (also known as the **personal video recorder** or PVR) changed ways of watching television and ways that television broadcasters and producers make it. The introduction of two digital video recorder products occurred in 2000, called TiVo and ReplayTV. These were **set-top boxes** which looked rather like video recorders or the decoder boxes used to bring cable and satellite television to the television screen. Both were introduced to the American market first and then became available in Britain, posing a challenge to the extrapolation of trends towards commercially supported television that the history of the medium seems to imply. The capability of TiVo and ReplayTV, and the next generation of similar recorders like the SkyPlus digital recorder, is to record digitally and store programmes under the control of the viewer (like the previous technology, the video recorder) but also to build up automatically a profile of their user on the basis of the programmes he or she has watched or recorded in the past. The machine trawls the multiple channels available through digital television broadcasting or cable, and stores them selectively according either to the user's instructions or to the machine's expectations of what the viewer might want. This capability was the beginning of 'Me TV', in other words the creation of a repertoire of programmes tailored to the desires of the individual viewer. Its implications were significant

personal video recorder (PVR) a device that records digital television onto a microchip for storage and replay, and can automatically record programmes it thinks the viewer will enjoy.

set-top box the electronic decoding equipment connected to home television sets that allows access to digital television signals.

for both television viewers and broadcasters. It became possible to time-shift any programme, in other words to watch it at a different time from its original broadcast, and to record several programmes simultaneously. It was therefore possible never to watch television as it was broadcast at all, but simply to instruct the machine to create a menu of programmes that can be seen at any time. Some of the machines could be programmed to omit commercials or to skip through them at high speed. So for channels that gained income from advertising (as almost all channels do in the USA and as the majority of non-BBC channels do in Britain) this threatened to reduce their income dramatically, because advertisers pay fees according to the numbers of viewers expected to watch their ads.

From the perspective of Television Studies and its accounts of the history of television, this development questions some of the trends identified in this chapter and supports others, changing the possible direction of the history of television in significant ways. This chapter has noted the change from a paternalistic notion of the viewer as a member of a collective national audience to the notion of the viewer as increasingly an individual consumer, offered multiple choices of television content by a proliferating number of channels. Rather than supervising the viewer's cultural education towards 'better' taste and informed citizenship, television institutions increasingly either offer mixed programme schedules which attempt to satisfy perceived desires and capture audiences through entertainment, or diversify their offerings into themed channels which offer related programme types to small **niche audiences**. Digital video recorders opened up a future in which the identities of channels, and the interest in and loyalty to the programming character of channels, has become less relevant to television viewers. From among the hundreds of digital channels available now on Sky, for example, the digital video recorder has become an agent for the viewer, taking over at least some of the work of programme selection for him or her. The channel on which a programme is broadcast, and the time at which it is broadcast, is less relevant since there is no distinction as far as the viewer is concerned between programmes being broadcast 'live' and those which are recorded. Television has moved away from the era when it consisted of must-see programmes that large audiences view live at the same time as they are broadcast, except perhaps in rare times of crisis such as the terrorist attack on the World Trade Center in New York in 2001. The heritage of liveness and the conception of the audience as a mass or series of masses is ceasing to apply. Viewer choice, along the lines of the almost infinite choice available to online internet shoppers, has been dramatically increased.

The response to the introduction of digital video recorders among American television producers was one of anxiety or even panic, since American television culture had been almost exclusively funded by the advertising which digital recorders can skip for their users. However, virtual digital advertising was one response that they tried. Rather than screening commercials separated from programme content, advertisers could buy virtual product placement. This entails the insertion of logos, products or posters created in digital form into the camera shots of programmes. For example, a scene in which characters stand in a city street might have poster hoardings, or a soft-drink dispensing machine, inserted into the background of the shot as an advertisement for the soft drink. This technique was pioneered in the American CBS News programme's coverage of the Millennium celebrations in New York's Times Square in 2000, for example, where a large logo for the rival NBC television network was digitally 'pasted out' of the television pictures broadcast by CBS. Virtual hoardings already appear inserted digitally into the images of pitch-side advertising barriers on some American sports coverage. So the distinctions between advertising and programme content, and between 'live' images and virtually enhanced ones were eroded, in order to preserve the links between programme production funding and commercial advertising in American television.

niche audiences
particular groups of viewers defined by age group, gender or economic status, for example, who may be the target audience for a programme.

In British homes equipped with a PVR, viewers watch commercial channels more than BBC, but 77 per cent of PVR users skip the advertisements in the programmes they record. Research by companies involved in selling television advertising slots showed that PVR users watch more television, enjoy it more and watch more attentively. They are less distracted because they can pause programmes during their broadcast, and return to the same point when they have finished the activity that interrupted their viewing. PVRs, audience fragmentation due to increase in the number of channels now available, and the increased take-up of subscription channels that are not funded by advertising have not led to the demise of advertising-supported **terrestrial** channels such as ITV, Channel 4 and Five. But as the expansion of digital television was accelerating in the mid-2000s, fears for the future of the older channels led to **Ofcom**'s proposal in 2004 to set up a Public Service Publisher Fund that would be used to support **public service** programming in the absence of advertising-based money to fund public service programmes that might attract few viewers. The proposal was not accepted by government, but research undertaken by the media research company PHD Group at that time (Alps 2004) suggested that there will be a decline in advertisement 'impacts' (the number of times a viewer would see a thirty-second advertisement during a period of viewing) by between 6 and 12 per cent by 2010, because PVRs and subscription channels enable viewers not to come across advertisements at all or to skip through them. The prediction was borne out by reality. However, the same research showed that viewers skip advertisements they have seen before, normally the frequently shown ones for low-value products like washing powder, but stop skipping in order to watch less frequently shown advertisements for more expensive items and for **brands** that invest a lot of money in elaborate advertisements. Viewers also praise the entertainment value of some advertisements and both choose to watch them and also remember them. The increase in programme sponsorship also enables advertisers to reach viewers during programme time rather than in commercial breaks, as does the product placement of brands and products within programmes. Advertisers want viewers who are likely to pay attention to advertisements that occur in programmes they watch intensely and to the sponsorship sequences attached to the programme.

Television is now at another turning-point as it converges with other media like the internet and social networks, but drawing on the account of television history in this chapter, which stresses the power of television institutions to shape viewing practices at the same time as being attentive in responding to apparent viewer desires, it is also important to note the continuity between past, present and future. In the past, television producers aimed not only for large audiences but also for programmes to impact their viewers and become the subject of conversation at work or at home. Now, social network communications can have a similar role, on Twitter or Facebook. For programme-makers, this network activity measures success, since it demonstrates impact and may lead to recommendations to other potential viewers via online television guides. It is likely that social media activity will affect programme scheduling, and the ways that programmes are devised. Social network users can enhance their television experience by commenting on soap opera plots, or contestants on talent shows. For example, in 2011 *The X Factor* had 2.5 million Facebook fans and generated about 250,000 tweets each episode. Programme-making staff upload images and extracts from programmes on the web and Facebook, and re-post Twitter messages, responding to audience activity. These uses of interactive social media raise the profile of programmes, and it seems that the future of television is to find new ways to connect television and its viewers with the other media technologies and experiences that are available all at the same time.

Ofcom the Office of Communications, a government body responsible for regulating television and other communications media in Britain.

brand recognition the ability of audiences to recognise the distinctive identity of a product, service or institution and the values and meanings associated with it.

ACTIVITY 2.7

How do the issues around the personal video recorder mentioned in the case study rely on ideas about the historical development of television that have been discussed earlier in this chapter and in other sources?

SUMMARY OF KEY POINTS

■ The history of television can be told in many different ways, depending on which evidence is selected and how it is approached.

■ The evidence for writing television history includes audio-visual records of programmes, and also printed sources and archival documents.

■ Television institutions have rarely preserved historical material, though new opportunities for repeating programmes of the past are changing this situation.

■ The invention of television, and the development of television institutions, need not have happened in the ways they did.

■ The political, economic and cultural conditions in which television developed affect the ways it is made, watched and organised.

■ The future of television will be affected by technologies, institutions, regulations and the expectations of audiences.

Further reading

Allen, J., 'The social matrix of television: invention in the United States', in E. A. Kaplan (ed.), *Regarding Television: Critical Approaches – An Anthology* (Los Angeles, Calif.: AFI, 1983), pp. 109–19.

Alps, T., 'Is it make or break time for TV ads?', *The Guardian*, Media section, 11 November 2004, p. 8.

Bignell, J., S. Lacey and M. Macmurraugh-Kavanagh (eds), *British Television Drama: Past, Present and Future* (Basingstoke: Palgrave, 2000).

Born, G., *Uncertain Vision: Birt, Dyke and the Reinvention of the BBC* (London: Secker & Warburg, 2004).

Brunsdon, C., 'What is the television of television studies?', in C. Geraghty and D. Lusted (eds), *The Television Studies Book* (London: Arnold, 1998b), pp. 95–113.

Bryant, S., *The Television Heritage: Television Archiving Now and in an Uncertain Future* (London: BFI, 1989).

Caughie, J., *Television Drama: Realism, Modernism, and British Culture* (Oxford: Oxford University Press, 2000).

Cooke, L., *British Television Drama: A History* (London: BFI, 2003).

Corner, J., *Critical Ideas in Television Studies* (Oxford: Clarendon, 1999).

—— (ed.), *Popular Television in Britain* (London: BFI, 1991).

Corrigan, P., 'On the difficulty of being sociological (historical materialist) in the study of television: the "moment" of English television, 1936–1939', in T. Syvertsen (ed.), *1992 and After: Nordic Television in Transition* (Bergen: University of Bergen, 1990), pp. 130–60.

Crisell, A., *An Introductory History of British Broadcasting* (London: Routledge, 1997).

Gripsrud, J. 'Television, broadcasting, flow: key metaphors in TV theory', in C. Geraghty and D. Lusted (eds), *The Television Studies Book* (London: Arnold, 1998), pp. 17–32.

Harvey, S., 'Channel 4 television from Annan to Grade', in S. Hood (ed.), *Behind the Screens* (London: Lawrence & Wishart, 1994), pp. 102–29.

Hood, S. (ed.), *Behind the Screens: The Structure of British Television in the Nineties* (London: Lawrence & Wishart, 1994).

Johnson, C. and R. Turnock (eds), *ITV Cultures: Independent Television Over Fifty Years* (London: Open University Press, 2005).

Lacey, S., *Tony Garnett* (Manchester: Manchester University Press, 2007).

Mackay, H. and T. O'Sullivan (eds), *The Media Reader: Continuity and Transformation* (London: Sage, 1999).

O'Sullivan, T., 'Television, memories and cultures of viewing 1950–65', in J. Corner (ed.), *Popular Television in Britain: Studies in Cultural History* (London: BFI, 1991), pp. 159–81.

Scannell, P., 'Television and history', in J. Wasko (ed.), *A Companion to Television* (Malden, Mass. and Oxford: Blackwell, 2005), pp. 51–66.

—— 'Public service broadcasting; the history of a concept', in A. Goodwin and G. Whannel (eds), *Understanding Television* (London: Routledge, 1990), pp. 11–29.

Smith, A., *Television: An International History*, second edition (Oxford: Oxford University Press, 1998).

Thomas, J., 'When digital was new: the advanced television technologies of the 1970s and the control of content', in J. Bennett and N. Strange (eds), *Television as Digital Media* (Durham, NC: Duke University Press, 2011), pp. 52–75.

Uricchio, W., 'Rituals of reception, patterns of neglect: Nazi television and its postwar representation', *Wide Angle*, 11:1 (1989), pp. 48–66.

Wayne, M., *Dissident Voices: The Politics of Television and Cultural Change* (London: Pluto, 1998).

Whitehouse, M., *Cleaning Up TV: From Protest to Participation* (London: Blandford, 1967).

Winston, B., *Media Technology and Society: A History* (London: Routledge, 1998).

Television Cultures

Television Cultures

public service in television, the provision of a mix of programmes that inform, educate and entertain in ways that encourage the betterment of audiences and society in general.

globalisation the process whereby ownership of television institutions in different nations and regions is concentrated in the hands of international corporations, and whereby programmes and formats are traded between institutions around the world.

genre a kind or type of programme. Programmes of the same genre have shared characteristics.

media imperialism the critical argument that powerful nations and cultures (especially the USA) exert control over other nations and cultures through the media products they export.

ideology the set of beliefs, attitudes and assumptions arising from the economic and class divisions in a culture, underlying the ways of life accepted as normal in that culture.

regulation the control of television institutions by laws, codes of practice or guidelines.

commercial television television funded by the sale of advertising time or sponsorship of programmes.

Introduction

This chapter deals with theories of television institutions that analyse how the making and distribution of programmes currently take place. It looks at British patterns of commercial and **public service** broadcasting, and places these in the context of American and European television. Television in the developed world is still largely organised on national lines, but the increasing significance of international flows from West to East and North to South has been hotly debated, so any discussion of television today needs to take account of the social and political significance of how transnational and national television cultures work in relation to each other. What is at issue is the degree to which the meanings of television are dependent on the kinds of institutions which make and distribute it, and the conclusions which can be drawn from studying television in terms of its ownership, organisation and spread around the world. There are inequalities in production funding, and different roles of domestic and imported programming in national television cultures, and this chapter refers to television in the less developed world to explain how theorists of television have understood these inequalities.

One of the most significant theories for explaining how television is organised today is that of **globalisation**. Globalisation can refer to the phenomenon whereby some programmes or **genres** of television have spread across different nations and cultures, so that the television schedules of different countries can seem surprisingly familiar. One way of explaining this is to use the concept of **media imperialism**, in which it is argued that 'world patterns of communication flow, both in density and in direction, mirror the system of domination in the economic and political order' (Sinclair *et al.* 1999: 173). A second meaning of globalisation is to refer to the power of corporations that are relatively independent of nation-states, and which broadcast by satellite or online into several countries or regions. Theorists of television have debated whether globally distributed programmes and global television corporations have brought new opportunities and freedoms, or whether they have imposed a deadening sameness on the diverse cultures of the world. An important question that underlies this debate is whether television institutions both embody and transmit **ideological** 'messages' that are the result of their ownership, their relationship to national broadcasting **regulations** and their adoption of particular cultural values. As Chris Barker (1997: 27) notes, the term 'global television' 'implies all the various configurations of public and **commercial television** which are regulated, funded and viewed within the boundaries of nation-states and/or language communities'. This chapter provides an account of the critical models that can be employed to evaluate these issues, and the divergent conclusions that can be drawn from them.

British television in global contexts

Britain is relatively unusual in global terms because its major broadcasting organisations mainly show programmes made in Britain. Some British programmes sell to many overseas countries, either subtitled or with their dialogue dubbed into a local language:

- The BBC's new *Doctor Who* has been sold to twenty-eight countries, including Australia, Canada, France, Germany, Israel, Italy, New Zealand, Sweden, Thailand and the Syfy channel in the USA.
- The natural history series *Planet Earth* has been sold to Australia, Canada, Italy, South Africa and Spain.
- The comedy series *The Office* had been broadcast in eighty countries by 2006.
- The children's programme *Peppa Pig* has been screened in over 180 countries.

BBC Worldwide is the commercial arm of the BBC that distributes both BBC and other British programmes overseas. For example, BBC Worldwide invested part of the £14.5 million cost for 100 half-hour episodes of the children's programme *In the Night Garden* because of the international export success of its predecessor, *Teletubbies*, made by the independent production company Ragdoll Productions, and *In the Night Garden* turned out to be similarly successful. Nevertheless, American television far exceeds British television or television from any other European country in export revenue and coverage, and numerous American programmes are shown in Britain (Rixon 2006). According to a feature article in the *Radio Times* listings magazine (Eden 2006), the most popular programme in the world at that time was the American drama series about police crime scene investigators *CSI: Miami*. In the list of most viewed programmes around the world, compiled by comparing charts from most of the world's countries, American programmes dominated and included *Lost*, *Desperate Housewives*, *The Simpsons*, *CSI* and *Without a Trace*. While British programmes are relatively successful as exports, partly because of the importance of the English language as a shared language for business around the world, British television is made primarily for a domestic UK audience.

ACTIVITY 3.1

Are there any programmes in this week's British television listings that will be broadcast with foreign dialogue translated in subtitles? Whom do you think these programmes are aimed at?

ACTIVITY 3.2

Which British programmes do you think are least suitable for foreign sale? Why is this?

There are nearly twenty-four million households with television in Britain, representing all but a tiny percentage of the total households in the country, and in 2011 the average British person watched about 27 hours of television per week. When this viewing is divided between channels, BBC1 and ITV1 have **audience shares** of about 22 per cent each, with BBC2 and Channel 4 gaining equal shares of about 10 per cent each and Five about 6 per cent, leaving about 30 per cent of the audience divided between the many channels available only via Freeview, cable or satellite. In comparison to the USA, where cable television has been spectacularly successful, British people seem unwilling to exchange a television culture based on **free-to-air** high-quality programmes for the promise of increased choice which both cable and satellite bring. Cable and satellite television in Britain have continued to grow in significance but at a slow rate. It is very expensive to set up cable networks because of the physical work of wiring up streets and houses across the country, and to do the work cable providers borrowed massive sums from banks on the promise of future profits. The take-up of cable television is still small, and the introduction of **digital television** has brought hundreds of channels that do not have to be delivered by that means. Satellite television has been more successful at introducing the concept of payment for television channels with mixed content (such as Sky 1) and the concept of direct payment for specific special programmes (such as championship boxing matches).

Digital television enables broadcasters to extend **pay-per-view** television because there are hundreds of channels available on which to stream programmes that viewers might pay for. However, the availability of hundreds or even thousands of television channels does not mean that there are very many channels offering mixed programme schedules like those currently offered by **terrestrial** broadcasters. One reason is that the television services are owned by a small number of large corporations that offer similar services. Owners of the transmission equipment (the satellites and cable networks on which programmes are carried) make the most profit by providing at least some of the content, so the big firms owning production facilities are also often involved in mergers or joint agreements with the companies that distribute television. The experience of multi-channel television in other countries such as the USA shows that an average viewer watches eight or ten channels with some regularity, and there is little benefit to television companies in duplicating services across more channels than this. So the remaining digital capacity can be devoted to pay-per-view movies and **subscription** channels in which a large range of films or other attractive programmes are available with staggered start times, such as on the Sky movie channels. It is possible to view a film starting at 8.00, 8.30, 9.00 and so on, with one channel devoted to each different screening. Channels are also devoted to shopping services, sports channels and particular kinds of pop music.

The availability of multi-channel television in developed countries such as Britain has the effect of diminishing audiences for the older national channels, as hundreds of new channels split up the audience. For commercial channels such as ITV1 and Five, the splitting up of the audience threatens their income from advertisements, since smaller audiences mean less revenue from advertisers unless especially valuable sections of the audience (such as employed childless people in their twenties with surplus income) can be targeted by their programmes. Falling audiences for non-commercial television channels such as Britain's BBC pose a threat to their right to

audience share the percentage of viewers estimated to have watched one channel as opposed to another channel broadcasting at the same time.

free-to-air television programming for which viewers make no direct payment.

digital television television pictures and sound encoded into the ones and zeros of electronic data. Digital signals can also be sent back down cables by viewers, making interaction with television programmes possible.

pay-per-view specific television programmes (such as sports events, or films) offered to subscribers on payment of a fixed one-off fee.

terrestrial broadcasting from a ground-based transmission system, as opposed to broadcasting via satellite.

subscription payment to a television broadcaster in exchange for the opportunity to view programmes on certain channels that are otherwise blocked.

funding, since they cannot expect viewers to pay television **licence fees** if they are rarely watching BBC programmes. But to try to grab audiences back by imitating the programme **formats** and audience address of commercial television programmes causes another problem for the BBC since duplicating the programme forms of their rivals means they have no claim to being an essential alternative to commercial television.

The sale of programmes to other national broadcasters and diversification into global channels are useful ways for broadcasters to consolidate their position in the international television marketplace, but it is also possible to sell the idea of a programme, its format, rather than the programme itself. The sale of programme formats is similar to the business of selling complete programmes to other national broadcasters. The format business involves the sale of a programme idea and its narrative structure, character relationships and setting, often including the scripts for batches of episodes. So, rather than buying copies of the original programme itself, overseas broadcasters acquire the template or set of instructions which enables them to remake the programme using their own facilities, performers and native language and locations. *Strictly Come Dancing*, for example, had been made in twenty-seven countries by 2006, using the same format as in Britain but with local contestants, judges and presenters. The overseas versions were shown in Germany, Spain, Poland and Russia, and the US version, *Dancing with the Stars*, drew the largest audience for an entertainment programme on the ABC network in 2005-6. But programmes whose format gained large audiences in one country do not always succeed in another. The comedy drama *Episodes* explored how the pressures of the US television industry gradually destroyed the creative potential of a US remake of a British series. In Figure 3.1 the awards for the British version and the happy faces of the writers feature prominently in this shot from the first part of *Episodes*. But the next scene is a first encounter with the American producers

licence fee an annual payment by all owners of television sets, which is the main source of income for the BBC.

format the blueprint for a programme, including its setting, main characters, genre, form and main themes.

Figure 3.1 The comedy drama *Episodes* charts a disastrous US remake of a British programme.

who will, over the subsequent parts of the serial, re-write, re-cast and ultimately wreck the writers' format in their attempt to transplant it into a different television culture.

The US sitcom *The Golden Girls* was tried in Britain (on ITV), using scripts from the US version with small adjustments for British viewers. The idea of remaking the programme must have seemed attractive to producers, since the US version of *The Golden Girls* had been a staple part of Channel 4's prime-time sitcom offering. Although the cast of the remake included well-known British comedy actresses, the programme was a commercial and critical failure and was cancelled after six weeks. *Married for Life* was a British version of the US sitcom *Married . . . with Children*, which ran for over two hundred episodes in America and was broadcast in Britain too in a late-evening slot, but the British ITV version ran for only one series. More recently, a British version has been made of the American crime series *Law and Order*. The format's key elements of linking police detection with subsequent prosecution of offenders was retained for the British remake, and in Figure 3.2 there is an example of the 'walk-and-talk' mobile camerawork used frequently in the series. The shot shows a conversation in a court building, and the movement towards the camera as the characters walk and talk is an effective way of providing pace during scenes with extensive information conveyed by dialogue.

In the USA, versions of the British drama series *Life on Mars* and the family history series *Who Do You Think You Are?* have been based on British formats. Figure 3.3 shows the actress Sarah Jessica Parker in the American version of the *Who Do You Think You Are?* format. As she examines library documents that give information about her ancestry, a hand-held camera moves in to show her face and reveal her emotions, since reaction to the knowledge discovered is a key dramatic

Figure 3.2 The British version of *Law and Order*.

Figure 3.3 Sarah Jessica Parker in the US version of *Who Do You Think You Are?*

emphasis of the format. The music channel MTV also made a US version of the British teen drama series *Skins*, aimed at the channel's mainly young viewers and containing storylines about sexual relationships that attracted much media coverage for the programme. Some television companies specialise in the development and sale of formats, and there have been spectacular successes. The company Action Time specialises in creating formats for quiz programmes, and has sold its formats widely in Britain and abroad, while the Dutch company Endemol developed *Big Brother*, and its vast audiences in Holland were paralleled by the commercial success of the programme when the format was subsequently sold around the world.

ACTIVITY 3.3

Look at the closing credits of a selection of current programmes to see which are co-productions with overseas companies. What are the common features of the co-productions you find?

Global television

The term 'globalisation' has several possible meanings. It can be used to refer to:

■ products of global corporations, whether these are concrete products like shoes or textual products like television programmes

■ the distribution system which circulates these products, like the global network of transmission satellites used by television broadcasters

■ the consumers of products distributed in this way, the global audiences.

Theorists of television have emphasised that at the levels of production, distribution and consumption it is possible for the significance of global television to change, and argue that globalisation is not a natural and unstoppable process. In production, global television corporations can be restrained by national or local laws and regulations which make them operate differently in different places.

Regional organisations have been developed in Europe to foster and protect its television culture (Bignell and Fickers 2008). The European Broadcasting Union (EBU) was formed in 1950 by twenty-three broadcasters across Europe and the Mediterranean, with further national members and associate members (some of them outside Europe, such as television companies from Canada, Japan, Mexico, Brazil, India and the USA), subsequently joining from the public service and commercial sectors. Based in Geneva, it promotes members' co-operation and represents their legal, technical and programming interests. The EBU runs Eurovision to pool programmes and co-ordinate joint programme purchases, exchanging news footage since 1958 and since 1993 via Euronews in English, French, German, Italian and Spanish. Eurovision also co-ordinates joint purchasing of coverage of European sports programming. A further organisation, the European Audiovisual Observatory, was set up in 1992 by media practitioners and governmental authorities including the European Commission. Its role is to improve the mechanisms for the flows of television across Europe, access to market and economic, legal and practical information, and to provide authoritative information about the television, cinema and video industries. The reason that such institutions are perceived to be required is primarily the influence of US popular television in Europe.

Global distribution networks may transmit the same television programme over a very wide area, but the ways in which the programme is received (by whom, how and the significance of receiving global television in a particular society) will be different in different contexts. John Sinclair and his fellow authors (Sinclair *et al.* 1999: 176) explain that:

> Although US programmes might lead the world in their transportability across cultural boundaries, and even manage to dominate schedules on some channels in particular countries, they are rarely the most popular programmes where viewers have a reasonable menu of locally produced programmes to choose from.

So the theory of globalisation in Television Studies is a way of addressing both processes which homogenise television and those which reduce differences, but also a way of addressing processes of differentiation. Furthermore, globalisation theory brings together approaches to television that concern economic, institutional, textual and reception practices.

One of the ways of approaching television globalisation is to consider it as part of **postmodernism**. The American theorist Fredric Jameson (1991) uses the term 'postmodernism' to refer to the ways in which cultural products (such as television

postmodernism the most recent phase of capitalist culture, the aesthetic forms and styles associated with it, and the theoretical approaches developed to understand it.

programmes) as well as physical products (such as bananas) have become part of the global **capitalist** economy. Jameson's political background is in **Marxism**, and therefore he emphasises how the economic basis of capitalism affects television and media culture, and how the production and reception of television carry on the same principles of inequality and consumerism that are found in other aspects of contemporary commerce. When we analyse television programmes, Jameson argues, they turn out to carry the political **ideologies** of contemporary capitalist culture. As an example of how this theory works, consider the background to the comedy drama series *Ugly Betty*, shown on Channel 4 in 2007, and the meanings that underlie its **narratives**. The series was made by the American production company Ventarosa in partnership with Touchstone Television, which is owned by the Disney Corporation. It was based on a telenovela made for Colombian television titled *Yo soy Betty, la fea* (which means 'I am Betty, the ugly one') in which an unattractive working-class young woman manages to get a job in a top fashion magazine, and despite being made fun of by its beautiful but bitchy employees makes herself indispensable to the magazine's success. *Ugly Betty* adapted the Colombian narrative into an American setting in New York, casting America Ferrera as Betty in heavy make-up that included braces on her teeth, thick glasses and very unfashionable clothes. Whereas the original telenovela was shot on videotape, relatively inexpensively, *Ugly Betty* was shot with the visually richer medium of film, and combined elements of drama, comedy, social comment and mystery in an ongoing storyline involving a conspiracy by the magazine's supposedly dead former editor and Betty's father's risk of being exposed as an illegal immigrant. The series was a combination of American and Latin American television forms within the same programme, and was produced by an American corporation for a Western television audience. Indeed it was a running joke in the series that Betty's family, who are Latin American, like to watch telenovelas with Spanish dialogue in which a melodramatic and ridiculous story is told about a woman working as a maid in a wealthy household who has inappropriate romantic relationships with its family members and even a priest. The woman playing the maid in the programme-within-the-programme was Selma Hayek, *Ugly Betty*'s producer, who is herself a former telenovela actress. So a product which has its origins in the culture of Colombia recycles and adds to its antecedents, with an eye to international sales. After a successful debut on the ABC network, *Ugly Betty* was sold to other countries' television channels, and in early 2007 these included:

- ■ in Europe: Britain, Ireland, Norway, Sweden, Finland, Greece and Spain
- ■ outside Europe: New Zealand, Australia, Fiji, Malaysia, Singapore, Hong Kong, Canada.

It is at this point that a **textual analysis** of the programme can illuminate the underlying subtextual meanings of the series, to show how it might resonate with current concerns and problems which might be recognised by its audience in many developed societies. It could be argued that *Ugly Betty* was successful because it responded to the current cultural concern with the roles of women in the workplace, and especially the idea that women may need to be attractive to men as well as competent at their jobs in order to gain acceptance. Among other things, *Ugly Betty* is about the pressure to be both attractive and successful in the world of work, though

capitalism the organisation of an economy around the private ownership of accumulated wealth, involving the exploitation of labour to produce profit that creates such wealth.

Marxism the political and economic theories associated with the German nineteenth-century theorist Karl Marx, who described and critiqued capitalist societies and proposed Communism as a revolutionary alternative.

narrative an ordered sequence of images and sound that tells a fictional or factual story.

textual analysis a critical approach which seeks to understand a television text's meanings by undertaking detailed analysis of its image and sound components, and the relationships between those components.

it makes this issue a subject for comedy as well as for serious comment. Indeed, when Channel 4 made trailers to prepare for the British screening of the series, they placed seemingly attractive female models around a swimming pool, but a camera movement reveals another model emerging from the pool in Betty's glasses and then as all the models smile at the camera it is clear that they are all wearing braces on their teeth. So an ideological analysis of *Ugly Betty* as a globalised cultural product would emphasise how it engages with questions of gender and identity (what are the expectations about women today, and how can women deal with a world in which these expectations might disempower them?) and tries to resolve them in a fictional form. At the end of 2006, the ABC network initiated a campaign titled 'Be Ugly 07' which aimed to draw attention to the social pressure on women to conform to images of beauty appearing in the media. The television series' potential for export to many other countries suggests that these issues are relevant to a much wider audience than the USA alone, but *Ugly Betty* addresses them by making them the subject of entertaining comedy and by staging the world of fashion and glamour in a very visually attractive way. There are numerous conventionally beautiful actresses (and actors) in the series, costumes sourced from real high fashion designers, and both designers and models appeared in the programme in minor roles, playing themselves.

Cultural imperialism

One of the problems in conducting an analysis such as that of *Ugly Betty* is that it can seem that one programme which is seen by different audiences around the world has the same meanings and significance wherever and by whomever it is watched. In the 1980s, when these questions were taken up by a number of theorists of television, it was particularly striking that American programmes were the ones most exported beyond their own borders, and seen by the largest worldwide audiences. In a famous study, television research by Tamar Liebes and Elihu Katz (1990) found that viewers of the 1980s American soap opera *Dallas* in different national cultures understood it in very different ways. They chose to study viewers of *Dallas* because it had been exported to a large number of nations, and had been seen as an indication that the future of television would be an increasing global homogeneity of programmes dominated by glossy American dramas. But, perhaps surprisingly, *Dallas*'s representation of the 'American dream' of financial success and personal happiness was understood by Jewish members of a kibbutz in Israel as proof that money does not bring happiness. By contrast, members of a North African co-operative thought that *Dallas* proved how money rescues people from everyday problems. Russian Jews who had recently arrived in Israel from the Soviet system believed that *Dallas* was a subtle critique of capitalism that unconsciously exposed its contradictions. So Liebes and Katz's study showed that, contrary to many people's expectations at the time, the meanings of television programmes are understood in relation to the cultural environment and expectations of viewers, and are not injected like a pernicious drug into the cultures where they are watched.

Sinclair and his fellow authors (Sinclair *et al.* 1999: 183) noted that 'there tends to be a more distanced realm of "pure entertainment" within which US programmes are processed – as markers of modish modernity, as a "spectacular" world – compared to more culturally specific responses made to domestic and other sources'. In the 1950s and 1960s the theory of **cultural imperialism** was developed, and versions of this theory were used to discuss the global export of Western, and especially American, television. It was this cultural imperialist model of global television that Katz and Liebes's study reacted against. Imperialism refers to the building of empires by European nations, especially during the nineteenth century in Africa and Asia. The purpose of empire was to secure natural resources and trade routes in order to feed the industrialising European nations and to provide markets for the goods produced in their factories, but by the end of the Second World War in 1945 these empires had been largely dismantled. Cultural imperialism refers to the similar process by which Western nations exercise cultural power over less developed countries, rather than exercising the military, legal and trading power which empire involved. According to this argument, the export of cut-price television pro-grammes (as well as cinema films, pop music and other cultural goods) promotes the commercial interests of Western corporations, especially American ones, and thus supports the political and military interests of the West. By means of the images of affluent Western lifestyles portrayed in television programmes, consumer culture is spread across regions and populations that increasingly aspire to the Western products and expectations that their meagre resources make it difficult for them to acquire. The crudest forms of this cultural imperialism thesis, which simply proclaim that the world is being Americanised, pay too little attention to the specifics of the local and national organisation of television consumption. They also ignore the flows of television within regions, based for instance on the legacy of the languages of the former empires, which make possible the exchange of programmes in Spanish among the countries of Latin America. There are regional television flows as well as global ones, and sometimes these regional flows allow for reversals of the more common North to South and West to East trade in television, as in the export of telenovelas from Latin America to Europe. The Colombian telenovela on which *Ugly Betty* was based, for example, was remade in many countries in which the original format of storylines and characters was retained but adjusted to the local language and setting. These versions included:

- *Jassi Jaissi Koi Nahin* ('There's No-one Like Jassi', India, 2003)
- *Sensiz Olmuyor* ('Won't Work Without You', Turkey, 2005)
- *Verleibt in Berlin* ('In Love in Berlin', Germany, 2005)
- *Ne rodis' krasivoy* ('Don't Be Born Beautiful', Russia, 2005)
- *La fea más bella* ('The Most Beautiful Ugly Girl', Mexico, 2006)
- *Lotte* ('Lotte', Netherlands, 2006)
- *Yo soy Bea* ('I am Bea', Spain, 2006)
- *Maria, i Asximi* ('Ugly Maria', Greece, 2007)
- *Sara* ('Sara', Belgium, 2007)
- *Ne daj se, Nina* ('Don't Give Up, Nina', Croatia and Serbia, 2007)
- *Cô gái xâu xí* ('Ugly Girl', Vietnam, 2008)
- *Chou Nü Wu Di* ('Ugly Invincible Wudi', China, 2008).

In the late twentieth and the early twenty-first centuries there are some inter-national corporations (such as General Electric, which owns the broadcaster NBC, and Sony) which control the manufacture of television equipment, the making of

cultural imperialism the critical argument that powerful nations and regions (especially those of the Western world) dominate less developed nations and regions by exporting values and ideologies.

vertical integration
the control by media
institutions of all levels of
a business, from the
production of products to
their distribution and
means of reception.

programmes and related media interests such as film studios and magazine publishing. This **vertical integration** represents not cultural imperialism by a nation but a form of corporate imperialism. Most of the world's largest media corporations are US owned, and have financial interests in many kinds of products. They also make deals with smaller companies (such as the makers of fast food or toys) to create interrelated promotions, advertising and sales opportunities. Although many people are aware of the importance of multinational companies and global business, the sheer extent and interconnectedness of the modern economy, and its dependence on television and other media as channels of communication and trade are often underestimated.

The big seven media corporations

This list shows some of the main holdings of seven of the world's biggest television-owning corporations in 2004, with emphasis on television operations relevant to Britain.

- **General Electric**: NBC network (USA), Telemundo network (USA), European channels including Syfy Channel UK, CNBC Europe, 13ème Rue (France), 13th Street (Germany), Calle 13 (Spain), Studio Universal (Germany, Italy), Universal Channel (Latin America), CNBC Asia, and more than 15 cable television channels in the USA.
- **Time Warner**: The WB network (USA); and television channels including HBO (Home Box Office) (USA), Court TV (USA), Cartoon Network (Europe, USA, Latin America, Asia), Turner Classic Movies (TCM) (USA, Europe, Asia, Latin America), Cable News Network (CNN) (USA, Europe, Asia, Latin America).
- **Walt Disney**: ABC network (USA); Touchstone Television, Buena Vista Television, Walt Disney Television (US television production companies); television channels in the USA and Europe including ESPN, Disney Channel, A&E, The History Channel, The Biography Channel, Lifetime and E!.
- **News Corporation**: Fox network (USA), Star TV (satellite television, Asia), Fox film, sport and news channels (USA), and channels available internationally including FX and the National Geographic Channel. Part owner of British Sky Broadcasting and its Sky channels.
- **Bertelsmann**: owns RTL Group, which operates thirty-four European television stations and produces programmes in forty countries. European television channels include Five (UK), RTL9 (France), RTL 4 and 5 (Netherlands), Yorin (Netherlands), RTL TVi, Club RTL, Plug TV (Belgium), RTL Télé Lëtzebuerg, BCE, Den 2.RTL, ENEX (Luxembourg), RTL Televizija (Croatia), Antena 3 (Spain), RTL Klub (Hungary).
- **CBS**: CBS network (USA), UPN network (USA), Showtime network (USA), and channels available internationally including Showtime and The Movie Channel.
- **Viacom**: Channels available internationally including MTV, Nickelodeon, VH1, Comedy Central, Paramount Comedy, TMF (The Music Factory).

ACTIVITY 3.4

How would you find out who owns the television networks or channels you watch?
Why is this information difficult to find by watching television?

The group of countries with the highest proportion of domestically produced
television consists of the United States, Britain, Brazil and Japan, followed by Canada
and Australia, which are able to use imports to top up a largely domestic production
base. But most of the nations of South America, Africa and Asia have small television
industries and insufficient revenue to make many programmes and depend on
imports to fill 50 per cent or more of their schedules. The national television
networks of Brazil and Mexico, for example, have the funding and facilities to make
many of their own programmes, but television broadcasters in the developing world
find it much less expensive to buy American or British television than to make their
own. Episodes of American television series from several years ago can be acquired
by broadcasters in the developing world for just a few hundred dollars, as part of a
package of programmes. The production costs of these programmes have, of course,
already been more than covered by showing them in the domestic American market,
so that the money made from the export of older series is pure profit for the
networks which sell them. The much higher production values and the aura of
sophistication that often surrounds imported television in non-Western countries
means that sectors of the television audience that are attractive to advertisers (such
as employed young people with surplus income to spend on consumer goods) may
be more likely to watch them. This not only has the effect of marginalising the
products of the domestic television industry, reducing its chances of expansion, but
also fills the most popular broadcasting slots with Western programmes in which
commercials advertising Western consumer products may often appear. Even if
crude Americanisation is not the effect of this, consumerisation and the reinforcement of Western values may be.

network a television
institution that transmits
programmes through
local or regional
broadcasting stations
that are owned by or
affiliated to that
institution.

ACTIVITY 3.5

In what ways might television programmes originating in Western television cultures
and exported to the developing world, and television advertisements for consumer
products associated with affluent Western lifestyles, share similar ideologies and ways
of addressing audiences?

News, nations and the 'New World Order'

news value the degree
of significance attributed
to a news story, where
items with high news
value are deemed most
significant to the
audience.

The ways of producing television news are similar in cultures other than Britain
because the ways in which professional broadcasters do their work, and the ways they
give **news value** to certain kinds of stories, are held in common by the journalists of

many nations and television institutions. Globalisation in television news can be regarded either positively or negatively (Gurevitch 1991). Technologies such as satellite broadcasting and distribution over the internet allow large and diverse audiences access to television news and live **actuality footage** of events such as the Olympic Games to be made available around the world. This provides possibilities for openness and democratic access to information which have never been available before. On the other hand, footage such as this has to conform to a version of news value that makes these events seem of global importance, and once they have been broadcast these events necessarily acquire global significance. Globalisation can be regarded negatively as the monopoly control of information by a few multinational broadcasters who impose Western news values across the world so that local cultures are drowned out by them. The increase in the quantity of television news which is available makes the activities of news producers in hierarchising and explaining news more significant, because, with more news, the audience is assumed to need increased guidance and support in understanding it. The effect of this is to make the form of news simpler and regularised (reports are short, story structures are simple), so that the difference between the news events reported is diminished. The conventions that are used to organise news stories predominate over the information that is communicated. But even if control of television networks is concentrated in the hands of a few providers, this does not mean that audiences will simply accept the ideological meanings carried in their news programmes. Global television news needs to be analysed also by looking at how global and international news broadcasting is organised, and how it is understood by audiences.

In the modern world the media contribute to new ways of thinking about time, space and people's relationships with the world around them. Since information circulates around the globe across the different time zones in which people live, the local time and the sense of people's familiar space can be understood as partial and local variations within a global, international time and space. The activities of people in their local area can be seen in the contexts of international and global problems and opportunities, where traditional and historic ways of understanding oneself, one's community or nation are overlaid or even replaced by globally dominant ways of thinking. Television enables its audience to witness events in different places occurring in the local times of different nations and cultures. In recent history, television has not only reflected the world but helped to change it. For example, international news broadcasts by **CNN** transmitted images of the 1991 Gulf War and the terrorist attacks on New York and Washington in 2001 around the world, preparing viewers worldwide for what became the current 'war on terror'. In the 1980s, images of the apparently comfortable lives and abundant consumer goods of the West were beamed into the countries of the Eastern bloc and aided the populations' desire for political change, and images representing Western culture such as satellite broadcasting of MTV contributed to the collapse of the Soviet Union in the late 1980s. For Chris Barker (1997: 230),

> television on a global scale has the capacity to contribute to democracy (via the principles of diversity and solidarity) through its range of representations, genres, arguments and information. However, the vision of television as a diverse and plural public sphere is seriously compromised by its almost complete penetration by the interest-based messages and images of consumerism.

actuality footage television pictures representing an event that was filmed live. The term usually refers to pictures of news events.

CNN Cable News Network, the first international satellite news channel, operating from the United States.

The international flow of television and its disruption of local cultures can be regarded as politically progressive, though the immediate impact of television has often been to intensify conflicts.

ACTIVITY 3.6

Which kinds of events have been worthy of global broadcasting? What are the common features of these events?

Complete news programmes are available over the internet and broadcast by satellite from news channels in many countries. The major players include the American institution CNN, which broadcasts to about 130 countries with content in major regional languages (such as Spanish in Latin America), and Britain's Sky News and BBC World. The selection of news stories on national television networks around the world, and the structure and form of news broadcasting there are influenced by CNN, BBC or Sky because of their global coverage, which has the effect of bringing their selection of stories to the attention of national broadcasters. International news channels can also affect the events which are being reported as news, since their coverage of events almost live can have the effect of altering the progress of a news event, for example by alerting officials to the perception of their actions abroad, or by attracting demonstrators to attend a protest which news cameras are covering. However, television's effects need to be considered within institutional, legal and cultural constraints that delimit and redirect them, and there are specific restrictions on the gathering of news and the accessibility of global television news. Attempts to manage global news by national politicians is common, in order to influence the representation of events outside a particular country where a global television news channel is gathering news. The influence of global broad-casters is limited also by the fact that their programmes are in English and/or the languages spoken by the affluent elites who are attractive to advertisers. However, the spread of internet access around the world means that in most countries (but not all, since some national governments restrict access for their citizens) the availability of news has the effect of accelerating and intensifying political change.

BBC World

BBC World was launched in 1991 as BBC World Service Television. It draws on the global recognition of the BBC's Radio World Service and uses the radio service's 250 correspondents and fifty-seven regional bureaux, as well as BBC Television's studios, technicians and reporters already stationed around the world. This scale of operation makes the BBC the world's largest news-gathering organisation. Half of BBC World's twenty-four hours of television consists of news programmes, each half an hour in length, and the other half is BBC current affairs, factual and entertainment programmes.

BBC World is the biggest rival to the American CNN network, and has a contrasting style. Rather than emphasising breaking news and live broadcast of unfolding events, BBC World is based around the journalistic comment on news which its correspondents and reporters can offer, and the very diverse international coverage that it can provide using World Service radio's expert staff.

The twenty-four-hour broadcasts began to be beamed by the AsiaSat satellite, through an agreement with Hong Kong's Star TV, and by 1992 the service reached three continents, constituting 80 per cent of the world's population. By the end of 1992 the channel was being watched in six million homes and was especially welcomed in Asian countries such as India and Taiwan where broadcasting was dominated by national government-run channels. The Star TV satellite signal also carried an entertainment channel (with mainly American programmes), sports, music video and Mandarin-language programmes, making buying satellite dishes attractive for viewers wanting not only BBC World but also the satellite's other signals. Soon deals had been negotiated for BBC World to be broadcast by satellite to the Middle East, Africa, Europe, Russia, Canada, Japan and Latin America. The channel was the first to offer simultaneous translation of its English-language news programmes into other regional languages, soon followed by its rival CNN. In 1993, however, the global media owner Rupert Murdoch bought a controlling interest in Star TV and challenged BBC World's access to the Middle East, where his own Sky News network planned to begin a news service. In the subsequent arguments China blocked all satellite signals, denying any global broadcaster access to its 4.8 million satellite television households and damaging BBC World's expansion. Nevertheless, in 2011 the BBC World News webpage stated that the channel was available in over 200 countries and regions of the world, amounting to nearly 300 million homes that can receive its programmes. In addition, BBC World News can be watched on cruise ships, in hotels, and via thirty-five different mobile phone services. It not only offers news and comment that is widely respected internationally, but also promotes the brand values of the BBC and the global significance of Britain as a world power.

iconic sign in semiotics, a sign which resembles its referent. Photographs, for example, contain iconic signs resembling the objects they represent.

simulation a representation that mirrors an aspect of reality so perfectly that it takes the place of the reality it aims to reproduce.

Sources of television news are perceived as unequal by television viewers, with some regarded as more reliable than others, and news tends to flow from North to South and from West to East. Such a situation provides fuel for arguments that global television news exacerbates the separation between the West and other regions of the world where news seems to happen, and the insulation of television news from the lives of its viewers. There is a paradox in the increasing quantity and speed of international television news. Television, with its focus on liveness, and the showing of actualities from distant places, draws on Western culture's belief in the power of photographic images to bear witness to real events (the **iconicity** of photography), so that seeing something happen on television news claims the immediacy and veracity of fact. But at the same time the proliferation of representations of realities on television news distances what the viewer sees from his or her own physical everyday experience. It was because of this sense of separation and unreality that the French theorist Jean Baudrillard (1997) proclaimed that the 1991 Gulf War was unreal, a **simulation** produced by television news because it was experienced only as images except by the few people who fought in it. Viewers who can afford access to numerous news sources (cable and satellite television channels, for example, but also internet news and email news services) will enjoy greater diversity and quantity of news, but will be further separated from the experience of news events than people who do not have access to so much information. It has often been claimed that the world is divided not only into the rich and the poor but increasingly into the information-rich and the information-poor. Television contributes to the creation of the '**information society**'. The blanket coverage of the terrorist attacks on American landmarks in September 2001, when hijacked airliners were flown into the World Trade Center in New York and the Pentagon in Washington, with great loss of life, raises questions about global news and reality. Were these events 'more real' because they were shown almost live around the world to millions of viewers, or 'less real' because the events were so quickly accommodated into the formats and routines of news broadcasting?

Television news institutions, it can be argued, contain and exchange news in a closed circuit among themselves, producing a global news market which homogenises news. Evidence for this view includes the fact that television news footage is offered to broadcasters by **news agencies** such as Eurovision and Asiavision, and is accessed by British news broadcasters through the European Broadcasting Union (EBU). Six times a day satellite links exchange news footage between Eurovision and Asiavision, for example. As well as using these mechanisms for exchanging news footage, news broadcasters have set up exchange agreements with news broadcasters in other countries. The BBC, for example, has an exchange agreement with the American ABC network. Satellite technology enables the international news agencies such as Visnews and Worldwide Television Network to operate twenty-four hours a day, sending both raw footage and complete news packages to national and regional broadcasters. Because of the different languages of television broadcasting in different nations, the news agencies mainly distribute images without commentary. This makes it more likely that their news footage will be perceived as objective by news editors, and this impression is reinforced by the neutrally phrased written material which the agencies provide with the footage to explain what their pictures denote. The agency footage can have a range of meanings attached to it by the voiceover commentaries that individual news broadcasters add to it for broadcast.

The proliferation of television channels in recent years has given rise to new channels that address audiences who have been dissatisfied with competitors and are most likely to produce **negotiated readings** of mainstream television. The international television channel Al Jazeera was launched in 1996 and initially broadcast only in the Arabic language from Qatar, funded by the country's ruling emir. Its aim was to offer a new kind of journalism to audiences in the Middle East, following Western norms by reporting opposing views instead of the official news agendas and opinions of government sources in the region. But despite this aim for objectivity and neutrality, the channel has repeatedly annoyed Western governments, especially the USA, by broadcasting videotape messages sent to it by the anti-Western Islamic organization al-Qaeda. These videotapes featured Osama Bin Laden, widely regarded as the terrorist leader behind al-Qaeda and the instigator of numerous attacks on Western targets including the destruction of the World Trade Center in 2001. During the Afghan War in 2001, two American 'smart' bombs destroyed the channel's office in Kabul, though this was said to be an accident,

information society
a contemporary highly developed culture (especially Western culture) where the production and exchange of information are more significant than conventional industrial production.

news agency a media institution that gathers news reports and distributes them to its customers (who include television news broadcasters).

negotiated reading
a viewer interpretation of a television text where the viewer understands meaning in relation to his or her own knowledge and experience, rather than simply accepting the meaning proposed by the text.

and during the invasion of Iraq in 2003, US missiles hit its office in Baghdad, killing a journalist.

Al Jazeera started a new English-language channel in 2006, Al Jazeera International. Soon renamed Al Jazeera English, the channel attracted prominent British and other non-Arab journalists to present its programmes. The former BBC news presenter Rageh Omaar, for example, presented *Witness* in which non-professional commentators (rather than academics or expert analysts) give first-hand accounts of news stories around the world. When *Witness* finished in 2006, Omaar began presenting a similar programme, *The Rageh Omaar Report*. The veteran presenter, interviewer and producer Sir David Frost hosts an hour of interviews and discussions with major world leaders and commentators. The opportunity to follow stories that have not received much coverage in existing national and international news, or have been covered from a predominantly Western point of view, is the main benefit that Al Jazeera offers to its audiences and journalists. But the perception that the channel is unlike CNN or BBC World in this respect also meant that some of its presenters and reporters were cautious about its links with political and religious movements attacking the Western powers. The controversial reputation of Al Jazeera in the West led Frost to check with British and American officials that the channel did not have links with the al-Qaeda organisation, for example (Whitaker 2006). Al Jazeera employs over two hundred staff from thirty national backgrounds in its news team, which it claims will permit reporters with local knowledge to offer new perspectives on news stories. The agenda is to avoid the categorisation of news according to the stereotypes of Western-based channels, so that items from Africa, for example, will not be driven by the narratives about famine, AIDS and war that have often dominated coverage of the region. The programme schedule of the channel is timed to match the time zones of its viewers, so that over one twenty-four-hour period, moving East to West, it broadcasts for four hours from Kuala Lumpur, eleven hours from Doha, five hours from London and four hours from Washington.

As well as offering English-speaking audiences new kinds of coverage, and a new balance of coverage that favours the developing world and non-Western nations, the channel attracts audiences from Muslim backgrounds who cannot speak Arabic but are interested in the non-Western perspectives of its journalists and may be **resistant** to coverage of news on Western channels such as CNN. There are 1.2 billion Muslims in the potential global audience, but only about 240 million speak Arabic. Some of these non-Arabic speakers will be well-educated viewers who form a core target for the advertising carried on Al Jazeera English. The channel is available free of charge to viewers via cable, satellite and broadband streaming on the internet, and in 2011 it was available in 220 million homes in over one hundred countries. In Britain, the channel is carried by Sky and Freeview, and when it launched at the end of 2006, Al Jazeera hoped to find viewers in about eight million British households. With greater resistance to the channel's brand image in the USA – because of its screening of news footage and videotape contributions associated with terrorist attacks and resistance to US military action – it seemed likely that Al Jazeera English would not penetrate widely into the American television audience. A key reason is that the channel is not available on most of the cable networks that American viewers use to watch television. However, it is of interest to the large number of US viewers who are dissatisfied with the insular and largely patriotic news

resistance the ways in which audiences make meaning from television programmes that is counter to the meanings thought to be intended, or that are discovered by close analysis.

programming offered by US-based television networks and US-owned international television services. According to Al Jazeera's own press releases, the largest number of visitors to its English-language website are from the USA. This was especially significant in early 2011 when mass protests occurred in Egypt against the country's rulers, leading to the overthrow of Hosni Mubarak, who had been Egypt's president for over thirty years. While all major news channels reported the events, Al Jazeera had perhaps the best access since its home base is in the same region. The channel claimed an increase of 2,500 per cent in viewing figures for its website where news footage of the Egyptian crisis was accessible, and explained that half of the increase derived from people in the USA seeking authoritative coverage by visiting Al Jazeera English on the internet.

The global and local interrelationship

The global dominance of Western television can easily seem to cover over local and regional differences. Western television theorists are sometimes beguiled by the presence of television familiar to them that is found outside its original cultural contexts. But the fact that Western television seems to be, or seems about to be, everywhere, and appears culturally powerful everywhere, might just reinforce the prejudice that only Western television is worth discussing in arguments about globalisation, whereas it is the interrelations of Western with local and regional cultures which need to be understood. The relationship between place and television culture is complex, and global television and global television corporations make local and regional differences more, not less, important. Local television cultures find their identities alongside or by resisting the globalisation of television, so that the dominance of global television becomes important to the production of local television. Local, in this connection, can also importantly mean regional, in that television cultures cross national boundaries to include speakers of the same language (like Spanish in much of Latin America, and in the states of the USA with large Spanish-speaking populations) or audiences which share similar cultural assumptions and ideologies (like the audiences in many nations of the Middle East who have shared Islamic beliefs).

The processes of globalisation are open to regulation by individual nations, rather than being an autonomous and unstoppable process, and global markets are regulated by contracts and by international and national laws. But the world organisations which oversee international television agreements generally support the lowering of national restrictions and **quotas**, because they seek to create a global **free market** economy in communications. The World Trade Organisation, the International Monetary Fund and regional agreements such as the North American Free Trade Agreement and the European Free Trade Association provide support for cross-border television exchanges which are based on the principles of unrestricted commercial exchange. The apparently free and uncontrollable television market is not a natural fact and depends on the taking of political decisions about deregulation and competition in television by nation-states and groupings of states. The European Parliament issued the Television Without Frontiers Directive in 1989, for example, which insists that the majority of programming in member states must originate from within that state. The Directive has been periodically updated and modified

quota a proportion of television programming, such as a proportion of programmes made in a particular nation.

free market a television marketplace where factors such as quotas and regulations do not restrict the free operation of economic 'laws' of supply and demand.

since its creation, taking account of new developments in technology, and has gradually weakened its requirements so that it allows a more commercial market approach to television in Europe.

deregulation
the removal of legal restrictions or guidelines that regulate the economics of the television industry or the standards which programmes must adhere to.

Countries and regional groupings of countries tend both to **deregulate** and to encourage globalisation, but also to introduce further regulation to protect their societies against it. However, in the global television landscape the concepts of society and nation are diminishing in usefulness. As the philosopher Anthony Giddens (1990) has argued, the concept of society as a unit bounded in time and space loses its force when, for example, live television news or sporting events confuse the sense of time and space by broadcasting across time zones. Television also brings new ways of understanding space – like the notion of a global 'war on terrorism' or a New World Order, for example, which change people's sense of their place in the world. Because television broadcasts such a range of images of culture – like versions of what youth and age, domesticity, work and gender might mean – global television provides the possibility of reflecting on local cultures. Global television provides resources for people to think about themselves and their social environment, in the same ways that local or national television does. Sinclair and his fellow authors (Sinclair *et al.* 1999: 187) give this example:

> An Egyptian immigrant in Britain, for example, might think of herself as a Glaswegian when she watches her local Scottish channel, a British resident when she switches over to the BBC, an Islamic Arab expatriate in Europe when she tunes in to the satellite service from the Middle East, and a world citizen when she channel surfs on to CNN.

People around the world negotiate their sense of place, time and community in relation to local, regional and global television cultures, and they do this by borrowing from or resisting ways of thinking and living shown on the screen.

ACTIVITY 3.7

What are the main arguments for and against the influence of television globalisation? Which side of the debate do you find most persuasive, and why?

Case study: adapting formats around the world

In 2009, despite a widespread economic recession, the export of television brought a record-breaking £1.34 billion into the British economy. The organisation representing independent television producers, PACT, commissioned an annual survey of television exports that showed a rise in sales of 9 per cent that year. The British series that were sold abroad included *Come Dine with Me*, *MasterChef*, *Spooks*, *Strictly Come Dancing* and *Wife Swap*. Australia and New Zealand were the countries where acquisition of British programmes grew most, rising 32 per cent above the previous year's total. These exports include finished programmes that are shown overseas, sales of a programme format where a local producer makes a version with their own production crew and cast, and sales of formats where an overseas company commissions a British producer to make a version for an overseas market. *MasterChef* and *Top Gear*, for example, were shown in Australia and made by Australian companies. The sale of formats rose 25 per cent in 2009, to £119 million. The largest market for British formats is the United States, where *American Idol* derives from the British *Pop Idol*, and *Dancing with the Stars* is an American version of *Strictly Come Dancing*. Finished programmes are sold in greatest volume to Europe, while the United States tends to purchase British formats that are adapted into American versions. Sales of television to the United States comprised 36 per cent of British television exports revenue in 2009, amounting to £485 million. British companies also gain revenue from overseas sales of DVDs and licences to use the names and brand images of programmes in merchandise. Elsewhere in the world, Canada, Latin America and Scandinavia also increased the amount of television bought from the UK. However, British television series tend to be made in smaller numbers of episodes than some overseas broadcasters, especially in the United States, need to fill their schedules. British drama in particular, including situation comedy, is made in series as short as six, eight or thirteen episodes, compared to the American convention of making series of over twenty episodes. The sheer quantity of programmes in British series is often too small to be attractive to American channels. But in the USA, the BBC America channel shows programmes not only from the BBC but also other British producers, providing an outlet for British television that does not depend on sales to US television networks. In 2011, about sixty million homes in the USA could receive BBC America, mostly as part of a package of channels available on cable TV services.

Cultures are of course located specifically in time and space, and reactions to television can differ in different local contexts. The remainder of this chapter comprises two case studies of formats familiar to British audiences that have been adopted elsewhere in the world. *Big Brother Africa* was an African version of the *Big Brother* reality TV format that originated in Holland and became popular in local versions over much of the world. The series ran for 106 days and was broadcast across Africa in 2003, drawing an audience of over thirty million (about two thirds of the continent's 900 million population saw the programme in total). It was accessible primarily to English-speaking Africans, and its audiences consisted not only of individual viewers but also of communal groups watching in bars or in the homes of the 4 per cent of the continent's population who owned television sets. The South Africa-based satellite television company M-Net co-produced *Big Brother Africa* and broadcast to more than forty African countries. The programme types attracting those wealthy enough to subscribe to M-Net consist of formats familiar to audiences in the developed world, such as soap operas, football and African versions of Reality TV series including *Big Brother* and *Pop Idol*. *Big Brother Africa* was also broadcast in early-evening terrestrial highlights episodes, in a similar way to the UK version's scheduling in Britain. It seems likely that for Africans the appeal of this kind of programme mix, and of *Big Brother* in particular, was that it represented an African-originated programme whose focus was not on the international news agenda's usual list of representations of the continent, which centres on war and natural disasters. *Big Brother Africa* in 2003 was the first pan-continental version, following two earlier series that contained only South African contestants and where the winners of each series were white men. *Big Brother Africa* in 2003 included contestants from Angola, Botswana, Ghana, Kenya, Malawi, Namibia, South Africa, Tanzania, Uganda, Zambia and Zimbabwe. The series began with an equal number of male and female contestants, and was won by a 24-year-old Zambian woman who collected the $100,000 prize. She met the South African president Nelson Mandela, and, like her fellow contestants, became a celebrity. As in other versions worldwide, the housemates secured contracts as endorsers of products in advertising, as actors and as television presenters.

The series achieved a significant fan base, organised in some cities into semi-formal clubs. But among the political elites of some African countries, *Big Brother Africa* raised moral and political questions:

- The parliament in Malawi banned the series for two weeks until the high court declared this unconstitutional and required the national broadcaster to carry it again.
- President Sam Nujoma of Namibia asked the state-owned Namibian Broadcasting Corporation to cease broadcasting the programme, though Namibian audiences largely ignored his opinion.
- In Uganda, religious and women's groups, members of parliament and commentators denounced the series for immorality but it continued to be shown.
- In Zambia, *Big Brother Africa* was declared immoral by a pressure-group of Zambian churches, though they failed in their attempt to have it taken off air.
- The Nigerian media regulator sought legal grounds for prosecuting the channels broadcasting *Big Brother Africa* but failed to pursue a case successfully.

These controversies were not confined to Africa, incidentally, since the Arabian version of *Big Brother* was suspended after two weeks because of its alleged un-Islamic content, and in Italy, the channel broadcasting *Big Brother*, Canale 5, was fined for infringing standards of taste and decency. In Africa, the attempts at intervention arose because of what was perceived as non-African, Western immorality among the contestants, who were as a group relatively educated and liberal. After only twenty-nine days of broadcasting two housemates had sex quite openly. *Big Brother Africa* demonstrated the shared standards of personal ethics prevalent among younger educated Africans from the participating nations, thus drawing public attention to generational differences between 'traditional' and 'liberal' social groups, and the impact of Western culture as one of the causes of that social change across the continent. Thus *Big Brother Africa* demonstrated the differences within contemporary African culture, both in terms of the mixing of different national contestants and the use of the format in itself as a Western one made specific to its region of broadcast. The visits by non-Africans to the house, notably a housemate from the British version of *Big Brother* and the exchange programme whereby one African housemate went to Britain's *Big Brother* house in return, drew attention to national, regional and global differences. Reality TV became a public space in which these similarities and differences could be played out by ordinary people, and it seems that viewers in Africa were using television in order to work through problems that they were consciously or unconsciously concerned with. Ordinary viewers and powerful interest groups were discussing and evaluating not only the issues in *Big Brother* itself but also those in their own lives.

The Western model of media culture and media use has recently begun to penetrate China, which has increasingly adopted aspects of the consumer economy that European and American people are already accustomed to. This makes China one of the newer members of a global media culture and offers support for the concept of media globalisation. In 2004, a new annual television singing competition titled *Super Voice Girl* (like Britain's *Pop Idol* and the USA's *American Idol*) began there, sponsored by the Mengniu corporation ('Mongolian Cow'), a dairy products company based in the Chinese province of Inner Mongolia. The contest declared its winner in August 2005, and in the final months of broadcast it became the programme with the largest audiences in Chinese television. Like its European and American counterparts, *Super Voice Girl* offered the chance for any woman to audition and move through stages of elimination and voting by the public with the chance to become a media celebrity. The talent competition was marketed with the slogan 'Super Girls, sing as you want!', and over 150,000 women, including a large proportion of young schoolgirls, took part in the auditions held in cities all over the nation. The final episode of *Super Voice Girl* attracted 400 million viewers, equivalent to almost one third of China's population, and the three finalists collected more than eight million votes. The winner was a twenty-one-year-old music student from the city of Chengdu, called Li Yuchun, whose performance of a mixture of traditional Chinese folk songs and American pop songs gained her 3.52 million votes. Li Yuchun's choice of songs was calculated to include some that connected her to traditional folk culture and a conception of China that is different from the global pop music culture epitomized by MTV. But the phenomenon of mass television audiences following a talent competition that promises to transform an ordinary person into a media celebrity, and does this by including the audience in the selection of the winner by means of the media interactivity of telephone voting, shows how this example of Chinese television followed Western models.

Super Voice Girl was screened on Fridays on Hunan Satellite TV, broadcast from studios in the city of Changsha. This southern industrial city was where the Chinese Communist revolutionary Mao Zedong went to college before becoming the leader of the Communist Party and the ruler who set the tone in the later twentieth century for China's anti-Western, anti-consumerist political and economic stance. The coincidence of the Western-style pop contest's production in Changsha and its association with Mao was often remarked on in the massive press coverage that accompanied *Super Voice Girl*. The major newspapers representing the views of the Chinese Communist Party, such as the *People's Daily*, described the programme as a positive example of a contemporary people's movement in which all social classes could participate, a demonstration of 'grassroots' activity along the lines of the enthusiastic mass support of Mao's Communist policies decades earlier. On the other hand, other Chinese media discussed *Super Voice Girl* as part of China's gradual Westernisation, since it is based on commercial pop music and its procedure of voting for a winner resembles the political voting characteristic of Western democratic nations. Many members of the programme's audience were active and were far from being **couch potatoes**, but the Chinese media disputed what the significance of *Super Voice Girl* was, and what its **preferred reading** might be. Chinese media coverage described the programme's fan culture as either evidence of spontaneous organisation led by ordinary people themselves, or as 'mad girl disease' (on the analogy with BSE or 'Mad Cow Disease') infecting the entire population with Western attitudes. Certainly the *Super Voice Girl* contestants exhibited Western fashions, with miniskirts, dyed hair or casual 'street style' clothes. The active fans of the programme included people of all ages, social positions and geographical locations in China, and the fans rallied in the streets holding up posters and shouting slogans supporting their favourite contestant, waving the mobile phones on which they voted, and occasionally scuffling with opposing fans supporting rival contestants. Internet chatrooms and online bulletin boards were used by fans to exchange gossip, and finalists had websites run by fans. Fan clubs were formed, each with a name and its own T-shirts showing a picture of the club's preferred Super Girl, and the largest fan clubs organised propaganda and finance to support their contestant.

Voting for the finalists of *Super Voice Girl* was done by mobile phone text message, after earlier stages in which a panel of professional judges decided on which singers would go forward to later rounds. The fans of the eventual winner Li Yuchun set up meetings in cities

couch potatoes
a derogatory term for television viewers supposedly sitting motionless at home watching television passively and indiscriminately.

preferred reading
an interpretation of a text that seems to be the one most encouraged by the text, the 'correct' interpretation.

across China to rally supporters and voters. The rules of the contest stipulated that any individual mobile phone number could only be used to send fifteen text message votes, but the more phone numbers in the possession of voters, the more votes they could send. Temporary phone cards can be bought in China, each providing a different phone number, so the organisers of Li Yuchun's fan club collected money to buy the cards, and campaigned in shopping areas and outside mobile phone shops, begging people to lend them their phones to send in votes. The voting for *Super Voice Girl* thus became very lucrative for the channel broadcasting the series, since Hunan Satellite TV charged 20,000 yuan (£1,330) for each fifteen-second advertisement in the commercial breaks during the programme. The channel also released an album of songs sung by the ten finalists in the week following the final episode and organised live Super Girl concerts in ten Chinese cities. Hunan Satellite TV began negotiations with Li Yuchun to put her under contract with the channel for further television programmes, and deals were made to market Li Yuchun dolls and to publish a book about her. Reporting on the *Super Voice Girl* phenomenon, the Chinese business newspaper *The Standard* estimated in September 2005 that Hunan Satellite TV would profit from text message voting alone by at least 30 million yuan. Further beneficiaries were China's four telecommunications companies that received income from the text message votes. Overall, the example of *Super Voice Girl* shows how Western forms of television, media culture and technology were integrated into the culture of China, and in many ways matches arguments discussed in this chapter and earlier in this book about the spread of globalisation in television:

- It promotes consumer culture.
- It integrates global and local cultural meanings.
- It draws on the audience's familiarity with media technologies (phones, the internet, print media, etc.) and integrates them.

ACTIVITY 3.8

How does the cross-cultural example of *Big Brother Africa* affect the concept of 'preferred meaning', since the meanings of television can be different in different cultures?

SUMMARY OF KEY POINTS

- Studying television today involves understanding how national and international television cultures work in relation to each other, in the context of globalisation.
- The media imperialism thesis has argued that political values are communicated when television programmes and television institutions spread around the world.
- New technologies, especially satellite transmission, have made possible greater exchange of television across the world, mainly from developed countries to less developed ones.

> ■ The effects of television globalisation can be both progressive and regressive.
>
> ■ Local audiences' understanding of global television can be different, so that the meanings of programmes change according to where they are seen.
>
> ■ Individual viewers understand their identities in relation to the television they watch, and think of themselves in different ways according to the diverse ways that television addresses them.

Further reading

Balnaves, M., J. Donald and S. Hemelryk Donald, *The Global Media Atlas* (London: BFI, 2001).

Barker, C., *Global Television: An Introduction* (Oxford: Blackwell, 1997).

Baudrillard, J., 'The reality gulf', *The Guardian*, 11 January 1991, reprinted in P. Brooker and W. Brooker (eds), *Postmodern After-images: A Reader in Film, Television and Video* (London: Arnold, 1997), pp. 165–7.

Bignell, J., *Postmodern Media Culture* (Edinburgh: Edinburgh University Press, 2000a).

Bignell, J. and A. Fickers, 'Introduction: comparative European perspectives on television history', in J. Bignell and A. Fickers (eds), *A European Television History* (New York: Blackwell, 2008), pp. 1–54.

Boyd-Barrett, O. and T. Rantanen, *The Globalization of News* (London: Sage, 1998).

Bruhn Jensen, K. (ed.), *News of the World: World Cultures Look at Television News* (London: Routledge, 1998).

Calabrese, A., 'The trade in television news', in J. Wasko (ed.), *A Companion to Television* (Malden, Mass. and Oxford: Blackwell, 2005), pp. 270–90.

Corner, J., *Critical Ideas in Television Studies* (Oxford: Clarendon, 1999).

Dahlgren, P., *Television and the Public Sphere* (London: Sage, 1995).

Dajani, N., 'Television in the Arab East', in J. Wasko (ed.), *A Companion to Television* (Malden, Mass. and Oxford: Blackwell, 2005), pp. 580–601.

Dowmunt, T. (ed.), *Channels of Resistance: Global Television and Local Empowerment* (London: BFI, 1993).

Drummond, P. and R. Patterson (eds), *Television and its Audience: International Research Perspectives* (London: BFI, 1988).

Eden, J., 'Caruso control', *Radio Times*, 5–11 August 2006, pp. 11–12.

Giddens, A. *The Consequences of Modernity* (Cambridge: Polity, 1990).

Gurevitch, M., 'The globalization of electronic journalism', in J. Curran and M. Gurevitch (eds), *Mass Media and Society* (London: Edward Arnold, 1991), pp. 178–93.

Havens, T., *Global Television Marketplace* (London: BFI, 2008).

Herman, E. and R. McChesney, *The Global Media: The New Missionaries of Global Capitalism* (London: Cassell, 1997).

Jameson, F., *Postmodernism, or The Cultural Logic of Late Capitalism* (London: Verso, 1991).

Liebes, T. and E. Katz, *The Export of Meaning: Cross-cultural Readings of 'Dallas'* (New York: Oxford University Press, 1990).

Lull, J. (ed.), *World Families Watch Television* (London: Sage, 1988a).

Mackay, H. and T. O'Sullivan (eds), *The Media Reader: Continuity and Transformation* (London: Sage, 1999).

Rixon, P., *American Television on British Screens: A Story of Cultural Interaction* (Basingstoke: Palgrave Macmillan, 2006).

Sinclair, J., E. Jacka and S. Cunningham, 'New patterns in global television', in P. Marris and S. Thornham (eds), *The Media Reader* (Edinburgh: Edinburgh University Press, 1999), pp. 170–90.

—— (eds), *Peripheral Vision: New Patterns in Global Television* (Oxford: Oxford University Press, 1996).

Sinclair, J., 'Latin American commercial television: "primitive capitalism"', in J. Wasko (ed.), *A Companion to Television* (Malden, Mass. and Oxford: Blackwell, 2005), pp. 503–20.

Thussu, K. D. (ed.), *Electronic Empires: Global Media and Local Resistance* (London: Arnold, 1998).

Whitaker, B., 'Same news, different perspective', *The Guardian*, Media section, 6 February 2006, pp. 1–2.

Zhou, Y. and Z. Guo, 'Television in China: history, political economy, and ideology', in J. Wasko (ed.), *A Companion to Television* (Malden, Mass. and Oxford: Blackwell, 2005), pp. 521–39.

Television Texts
and Narratives

Television Texts and Narratives

Introduction

text an object such as a
television programme,
film or poem, considered
as a network of
meaningful signs that can
be analysed and
interpreted.

narrative an ordered
sequence of images and
sound that tells a fictional
or factual story.

intertextuality how one
text draws on the
meanings of another by
referring to it, by allusion,
quotation or parody, for
example.

flow the ways that
programmes,
advertisements, etc.
follow one another in an
unbroken sequence
across the day or part of
the day, and the
experience of watching
the sequence of
programmes,
advertisements, trailers,
etc.

psychoanalysis the
study of human mental
life, including not only
conscious thoughts,
wishes and fears but also
unconscious ones.
Psychoanalysis is an
analytical and theoretical
set of ideas as well as a
therapeutic treatment.

semiotics the study of
signs and their meanings,
initially developed for the
study of spoken
language, and now used
also to study the visual
and aural 'languages' of
other media such as
television.

This chapter evaluates theoretical frameworks for studying television programmes, advertisements, etc. as 'texts', including methodologies for analysing **narrative**, **intertextual** relations between programmes in a **flow** of different programmes, and **semiotic** approaches to relations between image and sound. These textual approaches are placed in the context of the evolution of Television Studies, where they developed from an assemblage of **psychoanalytic**, semiotic and materialist approaches. Rather than being devised specifically for the study of television, these ideas began in the discipline of Film Studies. Textual approaches to television are powerful ways of discussing the meanings made of television by viewers, but they also have some drawbacks. Textual approaches tend to focus on textual detail at the expense of institutional context and history, and to neglect the ways in which television is understood by audiences. The issues to think about here are:

- ■ how meanings can exist 'in' television texts
- ■ how meanings might depend on relationships between viewers and texts
- ■ how knowledge of production context and history 'outside' the text might affect the meanings which television texts have.

The chapter ranges widely across different television genres and forms, showing how textual approaches to television can explain how meanings are made in them, where these meanings come from and how they might be understood critically. There is a case study at the end of the chapter that shows how semiotic and narrative analysis can be used to study a recent television commercial in some detail.

The language of television

Semiotic approaches to television, as to any other kind of meaning-making activity in society, begin by identifying the different kinds of **sign** that convey meaning in the medium (Bignell 2002a). The principle of semiotic analysis is to begin from the assumption that television has a 'language' that producers and audiences of television have learnt to use. The twentieth-century founder of semiotics, the Swiss linguistics professor Ferdinand de Saussure, regarded spoken language as the most fundamental of human meaning-making practices, and argued that all other media could be understood analogously with spoken language. He sought to explain the functioning of spoken language at a particular point in time, describing the system of language as *langue* and any instance of language use as *parole* (which means 'speech' in French). The 'language' of television would be the whole body of conventions and rules for conveying meaning in the medium, while any example of a particular shot or sequence of television would be an instance of *parole*, an example of this system in use. The language of television consists of visual and aural signs. Television's visual signs include all the images and graphics that are seen on the screen. Aural signs consist of the speech, sound and music which television produces. All of the visual signs on the television screen are two-dimensional, appearing on the flat surface of the screen.

Many of television's visual signs closely resemble the people, things and places that they represent in both fictional and non-fictional programmes. Signs that resemble their object in this way are called **iconic signs**, to distinguish them from signs which themselves have no necessary relationship to what they signify. The word 'cat', for example, is a **symbolic sign**, meaning that the letters on the page or the sound of the spoken word 'cat' is arbitrarily used in English to signify a particular type of furry four-legged animal. A television image of a cat, however, closely resembles the real cat that it represents, and is thus an iconic sign. The conventions of representation in television most often rely on the iconic nature of television images to convey an impression of **realism** whereby viewers accept that the television image **denotes** people, places or cats, for example, which exist in the real world. But this acceptance of the realism of television's denotative signs is reliant on the conventions of composition, perspective and framing which are so embedded in Western culture that the two-dimensional image seems simply to convey three-dimensional reality. The power of these conventions can be seen when television represents objects that do not exist in the real world, such as the spacecraft in science fiction series like *Star Trek* or *Doctor Who*. Often the images of these spacecraft are not images of real objects, or models, but are created entirely by **computer generated imaging** (CGI). Yet because the images of them obey the conventions that audiences recognise from the language of television, viewers can both recognise what they are and accept them as if they were real. These conventions include:

- perspective
- proportion
- light and shade
- shot composition.

Semiotics therefore has a particular interest in the conventions such as these, called **codes**, which govern how signs are used in conventional ways to represent or **denote** believable worlds.

Television signs that denote speech, the ambient noises of a represented environment or the music accompanying a visual sequence are also used according to codes in the language of television. The analysis of television using semiotic methods has tended to focus more on image than sound, but sound is important to the viewer's relationship with what is on the screen. Television screens are relatively small, and watching television often competes with other activities in the same room (such as talking, eating or updating your Facebook page). In order to grab the viewer's attention, sound is used to call the viewer to take notice of the programme. This is very noticeable in television news programmes, which are punctuated with loud brass music to draw the attention of the viewer, as well as to connote the importance of news as a programme genre. Music and sound effects in television programmes are

sign in semiotics, something which communicates meaning, such as a word, an image or a sound.

iconic sign in semiotics, a sign that resembles its referent. Photographs, for example, contain iconic signs resembling the objects they represent.

symbolic sign in semiotics, a sign which is connected arbitrarily to its referent rather than because the sign resembles its referent. For example, a photograph of a cat resembles it, whereas the word 'cat' does not: the word is a symbolic sign.

realism the aim for representations to reproduce reality faithfully, and the ways this is done.

denotation in semiotics, the function of signs to portray or refer to something in the real world.

computer generated imaging (CGI) the creation of images by programming computers with mathematical equations that can generate realistic two-dimensional pictures.

code in semiotics, a system or set of rules that shapes how signs can be used, and therefore how meanings can be made and understood.

signs which direct the viewer how to respond emotionally to the significance of the programme or the action denoted in it. Codes of recording, editing and processing intervene between the sound on **location** or in the studio and the sound that emanates from the loudspeakers in the television set. Sound recordists on location, or sound mixers in the studio, follow conventional codes in setting the levels of sound, and the relative volume of one sound versus another. The distance of a speaker from the camera, for example, might be signified by the loudness or quietness of her speech, while the relative volumes of background music and speech will nearly always be adjusted to allow speech to have priority. Although television images and sounds are often iconic and denotative, seeming simply to convey what the camera and sound recording equipment have captured, these signs have been processed through the various professional norms, industry practices and conventions of meaning-making that have been consciously or unconsciously adopted by both the makers and audiences of television. These ways of working and ways of understanding are among the codes that structure the language of television.

Connotations and codes

The iconic and symbolic signs in the language of television are often presented simply as denoting an object, place or person. But signs rarely simply denote something, since signs are produced and understood in a cultural context that enriches them with much more meaning than this. These cultural associations and connections which signs have are called **connotations**. For example, the head-on shots of newsreaders, wearing business clothes, seated behind a desk in news programmes not only denote the newsreader in a studio, but have connotations of authority, seriousness and formality which derive from the connotations of desks, office clothes and head-on address to the camera. These connotations derive partly from social codes that are in circulation in British society, but also from television codes of news programmes that have been conventionalised over time. Newsreaders speak in a neutral and even tone, which is itself a sign connoting the objectivity and authority of both the newsreader and the news organisation that he or she represents. News presenters are usually shot in medium **close-up**, full face, under neutral lighting. This code conventionally positions the newsreader as a mediator of events, who addresses the audience and connects them with the news organisation's reporters, and with the people who are the subjects of the news. The mediator functions as a bridge between the domestic world of the viewer and the public worlds of news. Even though news programmes now feature newsreaders sitting on desks with their scripts in their hands, or standing up and walking around in the studio, to connote a degree of informality, the desk, the clothes and the head-on address to camera remain because they are so much part of the coding of news programmes.

Television news programmes use music with loud major chords played on brass instruments in their **title sequences**, and these signs carry connotations of importance, dignity and drama. These title sequences also feature computer graphics in fast-moving sequences, **syntagms** in semiotic terminology, connoting technological sophistication. The function of title sequences in television news programmes is to establish the status of news as significant and authoritative, and also to differentiate one channel's news programme from another, providing **brand recognition**.

location any place in which television images are shot, except inside a television studio.

connotations the term used in semiotic analysis for the meanings that are associated with a particular sign or combination of signs.

close-up a camera shot where the frame is filled by the face of a person or a detail of a face. Close-ups may also show details of an object or place.

title sequence the sequence at the opening of a television programme in which the programme title and performers' names may appear along with other information, accompanied by images, sound and music introducing the programme.

syntagm in semiotics, a linked sequence of signs existing at a certain point in time. Written or spoken sentences and television sequences are examples of syntagms.

brand recognition the ability of audiences to recognise the distinctive identity of a product, service or institution and the values and meanings associated with it.

Figure 4.1 Huw Edwards as he prepares to present the *Ten O'Clock News.* © BBC.
Courtesy of BBC Photograph Library.

The title sequences of news programmes, like the title sequences of all television
programmes, share many of the functions of television commercials, in differentiating products that are very similar and endowing them with connotations
supporting a familiar identity. Title sequences are sequences of signs that collectively
signify boundaries between one part of the continual **flow** of television broadcasting
and the rest of it.

It is important to remember that the meanings of television images and sounds
are not naturally attached to signs. The pleasure and understanding which viewers
gain from television often depend on the significance of how signs relate to each
other in a particular context, and it is often misleading to carry over the connotations
of a sign in one context into another. In the long-running police drama series
Inspector Morse, for example, Inspector Morse drove a red Jaguar Mark II saloon.
In combination with the connotations of Morse's affection for real ale, codes of
politeness and love of classical opera, the car had connotations of tradition,
'classicness' and Britishness. By contrast, in the police series of the 1970s (such as
The Sweeney, in which the Morse actor John Thaw played a main character), Jaguar
Mark II saloons were often driven by gangsters and had connotations of the criminal
underworld, the glamour of crime and bravado. In analysing a television programme
semiotically, signs gain their meanings in three main ways:

- by their similarity with other signs in the same programme
- by their difference from these surrounding signs
- by their relationships with uses of the sign in other contexts.

Television relies on its viewers' often unconscious knowledge of codes and their
ability to decode signs and their connotations, and assemble them into meaningful
scenes, sequences and stories.

Television broadcasters' aim is to keep the viewer watching by assembling verbal and visual signs in ways that are entertaining or informative, but different kinds of programme achieve this in different ways. In other words, television **genres** have their own codes and conventions that enable viewers to recognise and expect particular kinds of meaning and pleasure. While many genres of television use very **long shots** (LS) at the beginning of scenes and sequences to establish a physical location, close-up (CU) is very often used in soap opera to denote emotion signified by performers' facial expressions. In general, the greater the genre's emphasis on emotional reaction, the greater the proportion of close-up shots. But while close-up is a signifier of performance in the language of television, and seems highly dramatic, the shot length in soap opera and other emotionally focused dramas is relatively long. Shots are held for quite a long time in order to observe characters' reactions to each other, whereas in action dramas, such as police or hospital programmes, there is less close-up and shorter shot length. Codes of shot composition can also be used differently in different television genres, since static composition (where the camera is still) allows space to contemplate performance in soap opera for example, versus dynamic composition (moving camera) that would produce connotations of disorientation and disorder. Even colour can function as a sign in television programmes: for example, *Strictly Come Dancing* uses bright reds and blues to connote its focus on performance and entertainment, while the hospital drama *Holby City* uses lower levels of lighting and cooler colours to signify a more tense and uncertain environment. In the different versions of *CSI*, the mainly yellow tones of *CSI Miami* signify its sunny resort location, whereas *CSI New York* uses brown colours for the colder and older urban environment of the city. The connotations of signs in the codes of shot type, shot length or colour are meaningful because of their use in particular genres of programme, in relation to other signs in the programme and in contrast to comparable or different programmes.

Narrative structures

Binary oppositions underlie the narrative structures of many television programmes, for example oppositions between **masculine** and **feminine**, or young and old. Thinking of narratives as sets of relations between terms that are opposed or similar to each other is useful in understanding how narrative works in television. The tradition in British sitcom, for example, is to oppose:

- ■ masculinity/femininity
- ■ work/domesticity
- ■ rationality/emotionalism
- ■ intolerance/tolerance.

Humour derives from contrasting these values when they are each embodied in a character, and also from aligning a character who might be expected to represent one side of the binary with the other side. For example, Victor Meldrew in *One Foot in the Grave* was masculine and intolerant, but was made redundant from his job and put in an enforced domestic setting that is conventionally regarded as feminine. This offered numerous occasions to create comedy from his sense of being 'out of place'

genre a kind or type of programme. Programmes of the same genre have shared characteristics.

long shot a camera shot taking in the whole body of a performer, or more generally a shot with a wide field of vision.

binary opposition two contrasting terms, ideas or concepts, such as inside/outside, masculine/feminine or culture/nature.

masculine having characteristics associated with the cultural role of men and not women.

feminine having characteristics associated with the cultural role of women and not men.

BCU
Big close-up

MLS
Medium long shot

CU
Close-up

LS
Long shot

MCU
Medium close-up

VLS
Very long shot

MS
Medium shot or Mid-shot

Figure 4.2 Shot sizes. Photographs courtesy of Jeremy Orlebar.

in a situation. The US sitcom *Frasier* added to this by setting up oppositions between sophistication and crudeness, youth and age, so that Frasier's and his brother Niles's sophistication and relative youth could be contrasted with their father's crudeness and elderliness, for example.

The simplified character positions in sitcoms are too excessive to be '**realistic**' because it is important to the comedy for a character's place in a system of binary oppositions to be clear, in contrast to another character. Sitcom narrative works by setting up oppositions and connections, which by the end of an episode have been laid to rest. The movement of sitcom narrative keeps repeating and developing incompatibilities and compatibilities, playing on the already established position of each character in the system of binaries. But the audience's pleasure partly derives from the anticipation that these conflicts will be resolved satisfactorily. The audience needs to recognise the narrative codes of sitcom and the stakes of the binary oppositions in order to accept the surprising reversals and conflicts that the narrative requires. In sitcoms shot in front of a studio audience, like *Miranda* or *Big Bang Theory*, the interruption of audience laughter and close-ups held on the performers' facial expressions are important generic signs and narrative turning-points. At these points the viewer is invited to recognise the high point of a conflict or reversal among the binary oppositions, and measure its effect on the characters by reading their expressions. The bursts of laughter in the narrative set out the rhythm and pattern in each scene, and punctuate the narrative with stopping-points around which the action turns. This rhythm of stops and starts keeps confirming the position laid out for the viewer to make sense of the narrative and find it funny. The studio audience's laughter confirms the position of the viewer by representing an audience who share the viewer's expected reaction. The collective audience laughing on the soundtrack is a representative of the viewer at home, and occupies a mediating position between the performance of the sitcom and the television audience watching singly or in small groups, where laughing out loud is often embarrassing. The noisy studio audience allows the viewer access to a kind of excessive response which is itself pleasurable, and which can be enjoyed at second hand by the viewer at home.

ACTIVITY 4.1

Write down the binary oppositions and structural patterns that underlie a sitcom you have seen. How many other sitcoms can you list which share some or all of these structures?

Television news consists of narrative reports, and can be analysed as narrative to discover how priorities and assumptions shared by news broadcasters form a code determining which reports have greatest significance within the news bulletin. The reports with the highest **news value** appear near the beginning of the bulletin (in the same way as the front pages of newspapers present some stories as having the highest news value to readers). News bulletins on commercial channels are interspersed with commercials, so that each segment of the programme contains its own hierarchy of news reports. The ranking of reports according to their news value

news value the degree of significance attributed to a news story, where items with high news value are deemed most significant to the audience.

shows how the representation of reality offered by television news is not a **denotation** of events but a narrative mediated by the signs and codes of news television. Binary oppositions – such as those between crime and law, left-wing and right-wing opinions, or home and abroad – are the basis for news narrative. Television news both shapes and reflects the dominant commonsense assumptions about what is significant, since by definition what is deemed significant is what makes the news. News narrative contributes to the process of constructing a commonsense climate of opinion through which audiences perceive their reality. Therefore television news shares with other news media (such as newspapers and radio news) the **ideological** function of naturalising the assumption that the day-to-day occurrences in the public arenas of politics, business and international affairs are what is most important about the daily affairs of a society. Within this field of newsworthy aspects of contemporary life, binary oppositions are again an underlying structure that enables broadcasters and viewers to make sense of the news. News programmes seek to connote **balance** and objectivity by giving approximately equal time to conflicting parties and interested groups who comment on the events narrated in news stories. But balance and objectivity are defined in relation to commonsense assumptions held consensually in society, and these commonsense views are naturalised ideological positions. The definition of the norm is a cultural construct and will therefore shift according to the current balance of power. Some decades ago, for example, the social ownership of major industries and institutions such as railways and telephone networks was part of a norm which interviewers and politicians accepted as the usual state of things. After the **privatisation** of these industries and services this view is no longer the norm, and surfaces rarely in television news, and only as an unlikely possibility. News narrative, despite its commitment to balance and objectivity, measures this balance and objectivity against the currently dominant ideologies in society, which occupy an apparently neutral position.

Television news deals with the potentially infinite meanings of events by narrating them in conventional subject categories, and conventional narrative codes, such as 'foreign news' or 'business news'. These divisions reflect the institutional divisions in news broadcasting organisations, where reporters work in teams of specialist staff. Some news programmes title news stories with captions on the screen next to the news presenter, and these captions connote both the specificity of each news story, which is different from the one before or after it, and also the connection between a particular story and others in the same category. The effect of using this code is to restrict the narrative frameworks that are available for representing the story. Despite the wide-ranging effects and relevance which one news story might have, placing reports in coded categories restricts the viewer's capacity to make connections between one news report and another in a different category, or to bring an alternative narrative structure to bear in understanding the news events.

ideology the set of beliefs, attitudes and assumptions arising from the economic and class divisions in a culture, underlying the ways of life accepted as normal in that culture.

balance the requirement in television news and current affairs to present both sides of an argument or issue.

privatisation the policy of placing industries or institutions in the hands of privately owned businesses, rather than state ownership.

ACTIVITY 4.2

How do the narratives of news programmes use oppositions between 'us' and 'them', 'powerful' and 'less powerful', to reinforce conceptions of social authority and legitimacy?

ACTIVITY 4.3

Analyses of television news have demonstrated the ideological distortions of news. Would it be possible to create television news that would be free of ideology?

The significance of the codes that viewers are invited to bring to bear on programmes can be seen in programmes that use codes deriving from more than one form and genre of television narrative. Television fiction is now rarely seen in the form of single one-off programmes, and is increasingly made in episodic serial forms. **Serials** consist of a developing story divided into several parts, and television soap opera is a special case of the serial form where the end of the story is infinitely deferred. The series form denotes programmes in which the settings and characters do not change or develop, but where new stories involving the continuing characters and setting are presented in each episode. Contemporary television programmes now frequently combine the single setting and new stories in each episode, which are features of the series form, with developing characters and stories episode to episode, as in serials. Robin Nelson (1997) coined the term 'flexi-narrative' to denote fiction like this which adopts the short sequences of action and rapid editing that occur in television advertisements, along with the developing characters and stories found in television soap opera, and the new stories in each episode which are found in television series. The flexi-narrative form is a case of the combination of television forms, but similar mixing and borrowing can be seen within and between television genres, for example in 'dramedy' (comedy-drama) like *Desperate Housewives*.

serial a television form where a developing narrative unfolds across a sequence of separate episodes.

Narrative functions

The theory of narrative has recognised that although the components of narrative are often relatively simple, and organised into binary oppositions and relationships of difference and similarity, there is much in narratives that does not have an obvious functional purpose. Lots of material appears to be redundant. Redundancy consists of the inclusion in the narrative of a number of signs that have a contextual or supporting role. These signs are unremarked, but deepen the consistency and believability of the narrative. They provide texture and tone for the audience. Details of setting, costume, much of the detail of dialogue and some of the narrative action are likely to be redundant from the point of view of getting the story itself across. But in programmes that claim to be **realistic**, redundancy has the crucial effect of embedding the story in a fully realised world. Furthermore, one of the ways that narratives can be most pleasurable and interesting is when the relationship between redundancy and functional narrative components is changed in the course of the story. In detective narratives and whodunits, for example, an apparently redundant detail that seemed simply to lend texture to the fictional world might turn out to be a crucial clue. In science fiction television, redundancy is crucial to establishing a futuristic environment as realistic, in the sense that it has the detail and texture for it to be believable. News programmes are full of apparently redundant information and visual detail. But here, too, semiotics and narrative theory are useful in showing how redundant information actually fulfils important functions in shaping the meanings of news reports.

Television news has to deal with events which are by definition new each day, and to do this it has powerful codes for giving shape and meaning to news reports. Reports make use of four narrative functions (Hartley 1982: 118–19):

- framing
- focusing
- realising
- closing.

Framing is the activity of establishing the news topic, usually done by the mediating figure of the newsreader, who invokes the narrative code in which the report will be presented. For example, political news is usually coded as an adversarial debate. Although mediators such as news presenters speak in a neutral **register** and establish themselves and the news broadcasting organisation as neutral too, the effect of this is to make the setting-up of the narrative code appear invisible to viewers: it seems to arise from the news itself rather than from how it is being presented. Focusing refers to the opening out of the news report into further detail, conveyed by reporters and correspondents who speak for the news broadcasting institution (Hartley [1982: 110–11] calls them 'institutional voices'). The institutional voices develop the narrative by providing background information, explaining what is at stake in the news event, and introducing comment and **actuality footage** that illustrates this. The interviews, reports and comment by people involved in the news event are part of the function known as realising, whereby evidence of the news event and reactions to it from interested individuals and groups are presented. The availability of actuality footage gives important added value to news reports because it is crucial to the narrative function of realising the story. But although actuality footage might seem to be the dominant type of sign in television news programmes, its visual signs never appear without accompanying **voice-over** commentary. While it is possible for visual sequences to narrate on their own, the multiple meanings that images always have can be contained and directed by the reporter's institutional voice on the soundtrack. Realisation therefore tends to confirm the work of the news reporters' framing and focusing activities. Moving out of the news studio to focus and realise news stories allows room for the visual and aural signs in the programme to differ from and affect the news presenter's framing activities. For instance, the connotations of the signs of situation in news programmes have significant empowering or disempower- ing effects in the meanings of news reports. The authority of the newsreaders and commentators in the studio can contrast with the much less empowering presence of a member of the public in the street, or a reporter struggling to speak over the voices of a crowd, for example. Closing refers to the way that a news report moves towards a condensed encapsulation of the report, likely to be repeated in the closing headlines of the news programme, and which presents the **preferred reading** of the report. Closure might involve discounting some of the points of view on the news event that have been represented in the report, or repeating the point of view already connoted by the frame or focus. This movement towards closure is confirmed at the end of reports, but the report as a whole will involve it throughout.

register a term in the study of language for the kinds of speech or writing used to represent a particular kind of idea or to address a certain audience.

actuality footage television pictures representing an event that was filmed live. The term usually refers to pictures of news events.

voice-over speech accompanying visual images but not presumed to derive from the same place or time as the images.

preferred reading an interpretation of a text that seems to be the one most encouraged by the text, the 'correct' interpretation.

Identification

identification a term deriving from psychoanalytic theories of cinema, which describes the viewer's conscious or unconscious wish to take the place of someone or something in a television text.

Television viewers can make sense of television only by taking up a position in relation to it, constituting themselves as an audience. What the audience is watching has to seem to be 'for them', and a relationship can then be constructed with it (whether this relationship to television is marked by pleasure, boredom, anger or frustration). So narrative depends on a shifting pattern of **identification** between the viewer and the programme. Viewers can identify with both fictional and non-fictional performers but also distance themselves from a performer (in order to find him or her funny, for instance, in a sitcom). Viewers can also identify with the studio audience denoted by laughter on the soundtrack (in sitcoms and chat shows for example), taking up a shared position in relation to what the studio audience and home audience have seen. Narrative requires the shifting of the viewer's position into and out of the television programme, and a rhythm of identification and disavowal of identification. But the positioning and repositioning of the viewer as an audience member might succeed or fail for individual viewers in different programmes or parts of the same programme. Narrative lays out positions for its viewers, offering signs and codes that invite the viewers to make sense of and to enjoy what they see and hear, but whether or not viewers actually occupy the position of being-an-audience, and how they inhabit this position, depends on the many variables which compose each viewer's social and psychological identity.

ACTIVITY 4.4

In what ways does audience positioning serve to keep viewers watching programmes? What might happen if audience positioning ceases to work for a viewer?

---

gender the social and cultural division of people into masculine or feminine individuals. This is different from sex, which refers to the biological difference between male and female bodies.

subject in psychoanalysis, the term for the individual self whose identity has both conscious and unconscious components.

The psychoanalytic account of pleasure in watching television argues that there are several identifications which viewers make from moment to moment. The first of these is an identification with the television medium, as something which delivers images of other people, places and times. These images offer to satisfy viewers' desire to experience life differently, as another person or in another place. There are also identifications with all the figures who are presented on the screen, the performers who stand in for the viewer and play out the roles which the viewer might desire to play for himself or herself. There are identifications throughout television narratives with the fictional and non-fictional worlds presented in them, just as in a daydream or fantasy we might imagine worlds where we play all the parts in an imaginary story. Narrative texts are constructed from a network of looks: relationships between the looks of the people on screen, the look of the camera and the viewer's look. The movement of television narrative in this way is analogous to daydream fantasies that allow for identifications with different people and things (imagining being a person, a car, a bird, etc.), including identifications with different **gender** roles. All the possible roles in the narrative are available to the viewing **subject**: he or she can imagine being either the subject or object of a look, and can even occupy a position outside the scene, looking on from a spectator's point of view. The importance of an analogy with fantasy is that the disjuncture of looks and positions in its scenarios appears parallel to the way that television narrative cuts and juxtaposes different shots, different camera looks. Television narrative holds back complete knowledge and total vision to the viewer, thereby maintaining the desire to keep on looking. The desires to look and hear are experienced through the viewer's relations with a set of signs and codes that offer meanings to him or her. Television narratives work by making a pattern out of the many divergent identifications and understandings of the programme, and binding them into coherence. This psychoanalytic model offers a very complex understanding of the processes of watching television, whereby it can be understood in terms of mobile processes of making sense, experiencing pleasure and displeasure, and giving and withholding interest.

The fact that a television screen is a domestic object among the furnishings of a room, and the use of tablet computers and phones for watching television, may diminish the importance of imagined identifications compared to the experience of watching in a cinema, for example. The psychoanalytic approach described here was developed originally for understanding film spectatorship, where film viewers are much more likely to be immersed in narratives. The dark space of the cinema, the large size of the screen and the choice to place oneself in the position of a viewer among an audience of other viewers all militate in favour of much greater involvement in film than viewers often experience watching television. The television theorist John Ellis (1982: 137) pointed out this distinction by describing the viewer's look at television as a 'glance', rather than the concentrated 'gaze' of the film spectator:

> The gaze implies a concentration of the spectator's activity into that of looking, the glance implies that no extraordinary effort is being invested in the activity of looking. The very terms we habitually use to designate the person who watches TV or the cinema screen tend to indicate this difference. The cinema-looker is a spectator: caught by the projection yet separate from its illusion. The TV-looker is a viewer, casting a lazy eye over the proceedings, keeping an eye on events, or, as the slightly archaic designation had it, 'looking in'.

In response to this distinction, television theorists have examined how television narratives offer audience positions for viewers who may be often disengaged glancers rather than immersed spectators. Television has to work hard to get viewers to immerse themselves in programmes and experience intense identifications with its narratives. Television uses a range of narrating figures to address the viewer directly, audiences within programmes with whom the viewer is invited to identify, and representative figures who take the place of the ordinary viewer at home. Each of these strategies of viewer involvement contributes to hooking the viewer into television narratives and encouraging the kinds of immersive identification that psychoanalytic theory has explained.

Television narrators

A very obvious question to ask about the meanings of television programmes is: from where do they originate? Are meanings put there by the person responsible for the

authorship the question of who an author is, the role of the author as creator and the significance of the author's input into the material being studied.

quality in television, kinds of programme that are perceived as more expensively produced and, especially, more culturally worthwhile than other programmes.

director the person responsible for the creative process of turning a script or idea into a finished programme, by working with a technical crew, performers and an editor.

producer the person working for a television institution who is responsible for the budget, planning and making of a television programme or series of programmes.

adaptation transferring a novel, theatre play, poem, etc. from its original medium into another medium such as television.

narration the process of telling a story through image and sound. Narration can also refer to the spoken text accompanying television images.

discourse a particular use of language for a certain purpose in a certain context (such as academic discourse or poetic discourse), and similarly in television, a particular usage of television's audio-visual 'language' (news programme discourse or nature documentary discourse, for instance).

flashback a television sequence marked as representing events that happened in a time previous to the programme's present.

programme's **authorship**, are they the result of how signs, codes and narrative structures work in a text, or are they constructed through the individual interpretations made by viewers, for example? In earlier decades of British television the promotion of television authors enabled television executives to rebuff the accusation that television is without value, and television writers were compared with theatre dramatists, novelists or poets. But the consequence of this has been the mistaken view that the meanings of television programmes are universally shared by all viewers, and are the result of the creator's individual genius and personal vision. The meanings of television are not universal but local (as the differences between, for example, British and American understandings of **quality** and relevance show, see Chapter 7) and are produced within the conventions and moral and cultural values of their time. Authors always negotiate with the other practitioners in the making of television (**directors**, **producers**, designers and script editors, for instance) and are not free to mastermind a unique vision of their own. But within the television industry particular authors have been elevated to high status and publicised for reasons of claiming prestige and attracting audiences. An author can function as a brand, a familiar name that alerts the audience to styles and themes that a writer has explored in the past, and distinguishes the programme from the **flow** of the schedule around it. The marketing of authors as brands occurred in the 1990s and 2000s in relation to dramas by Lynda La Plante, for example (*Prime Suspect, Trial and Retribution*), and classic novel **adaptations** by Andrew Davies (*Pride and Prejudice, Emma, Bleak House*). A few producers have occupied this authorial branding role, such as Paul Abbott (*Shameless, State of Play*) in Britain and Jerry Bruckheimer (*CSI, Without a Trace*) in the US. Popular generic drama, such as the police series or hospital drama, is often authored in a collaborative way, using a pool of writers, and is rarely attached to the name of an author. But if television, even in its most 'literary' form of drama, does not consist of 'messages' put there by an author, there is often the sense in watching television that there is an agency communicating with the viewer. As Sarah Kozloff (1992: 78) explains: 'The "implied author" of a television show . . . is not a flesh-and-blood person but rather a textual construct, the viewer's sense of the organizing force behind the world of the show.' This agency behind narrative appears through the various forms of **narration** used in television.

Analysing narrative requires the distinction between story and **discourse**. Story is the set of events that are represented. They could potentially be told in any order (chronologically, or in **flashback**, for example) and with any emphasis. Discourse is the narrating process that puts story events in an order, with a shape and direction. In any medium, someone or something must be doing the storytelling for the audience, on its behalf, and this agency is the narrator, whether it is a voice, an on-screen performer or simply the agency that viewers reconstruct as the force which controls the arrangement of camera shots, sound and music that deliver the story to them. Some fictional and non-fictional programmes have **voice-over** narrators throughout, or in particular sequences. *Star Trek: The Next Generation* began with a familiar scene-setting narration for the programme as a whole, the 'Captain's log' where a voice-over narrates the setting and situation at the start of each episode's story, and this is followed by the narration at the start of the **title sequence**, beginning 'Space, the final frontier . . . '. Narration can sometimes be found in the title songs of programmes, and episodes of a series may open with voice-over reminding the audience of scenes in a previous programme. A few drama programmes include a voice-over narrator or an on-screen narrator within scenes, as in *Desperate Housewives*. Non-fiction programmes such as wildlife programmes, history programmes such as *Time Team*, commercials, cooking programmes and **reality TV** programmes such as *Big Brother* have narrators. In all of these examples the function of the narrator is to establish a link between the audience and the programme narrative, by inviting the viewer to involve himself or herself in the ongoing progress of the story. Although some programmes make the function of narration explicit in these ways, all television narratives rely on the more complex narration that is made up of camera shots in a narrative progression, often with music helping to link shots together into sequences and to give them an emotional point of view. Sarah Kozloff (1992: 79) notes that 'Music, in film and in television, is a key channel through which the voiceless narrating agency "speaks" to the viewer'. The viewer is aligned with **point of view shots** of characters or performers, alternating with apparently neutral points of view that observe the represented space and the people in it. Programmes shot entirely in point of view shots are extremely rare, but one example is the comedy drama *Peep Show*. Figure 4.3 is a shot from the programme's opening sequence that introduced viewers to this very unusual convention by masking the shot so that it resembles the shape of an eye. The performers in television fiction behave as if the viewer is absent, making it more evident that the camera is the agency conveying their actions to the audience, whereas factual programmes perhaps make narration less obvious because the camera appears more to be a neutral observer. But in each case there is an implied narrator composed from the different camera points of view that have been edited together to form the narrative as a whole.

The significance of narration is partly that the viewer is necessarily positioned by the changing sequence of camera shots, the words of on-screen or off-screen

> **reality TV** programmes where the unscripted behaviour of 'ordinary people' is the focus of interest.

> **point of view shot** a camera shot where the camera is placed in, or close to, the position from where a previously seen character might look.

Figure 4.3 *Peep Show* demonstrates its focus on point of view in its opening sequence.

narrators and the accompanying music in programmes and advertisements. The position of the viewer is the place to which all of them are directed and from where they can make sense as a coherent whole. Television viewers, when they constitute themselves as an audience and answer television's call to join a community of viewers, are making an **identification** with the audience position laid out for them by the signs, codes and narrative structures of the programme or advertisement. In other words the television viewer has occupied the role laid out for him or her by the broadcaster, which is doing the looking on his or her behalf. It is often hard to specify what this institutional narrator is, whether, for instance, it is the production team that has designed and made the programme, or the channel on which it is broadcast. Indeed, both of these vague collective agencies seem to make claims to be the overall narrators of programmes by virtue of the credits and **copyright** ownership information in the end titles of programmes, and by the channel **idents** and logos which appear between programmes and, in the case of some channels, are superimposed in the corner of the screen throughout programmes. In any case the most overarching kind of narrator might be the channel on which programmes are broadcast, since the flow of the period of viewing, no matter how diverse the types of programmes and advertisements that it includes, is held together as a unity by the narrating voice of the off-screen announcers who connect programmes with each other. They are also narrators, saying, for example, 'Join us after the break, when an exotic pudding causes a stir in tonight's episode of *Come Dine with Me*'. This narrating discourse is striking in the fact that it makes explicit the hailing function of television to call on an individual viewer to become part of a collective audience ('join us'), an audience which is conjured up by that address to it.

copyright the legal right of ownership over written, visual or aural material, including the prohibition on copying this material without permission from its owner.

idents the symbols representing production companies, television channels, etc., often comprising graphics or animations.

Signs of the viewer

The television medium brings distant events and uncommon sights, such as the exotic animals of wildlife programmes, or distant events recorded for news programmes, into the private arena of the home. Television has always framed its appeal as a medium on its ability to bring what is different, strange and interesting into the viewer's familiar and domestic world. In this sense television seems to bridge the gap between public and private, and outside and inside. The means of connecting the two, such as by using narrators or representatives of the viewer, are therefore particularly significant to gaining a sense of television's image of itself. But the paradox is that the more television programmes use textual means to include viewers in worlds beyond their own experience, the greater the chance of simultaneously revealing the viewer's own disempowerment and non-involvement. Watching a wildlife programme about the imminent extinction of the tiger might raise viewers' awareness and concern, but might also be a substitute for doing anything about the situation. Broadcasters are concerned to provide a sense of activity and involvement for viewers, whether as part of the **public service** function to show and support initiatives in society or as part of a commercial imperative to encourage consumption of products and services. In either case the ways in which programmes address and position viewers are important subjects of study. Television is a domestic technology, embedded in the home among other technological devices such as radios, computers

public service in television, the provision of a mix of programmes that inform, educate and entertain in ways that encourage the betterment of audiences and society in general.

or stereo systems. These technologies, and the activities that take place with them, compete for attention. Television calls for viewers to take up membership of an audience sharing an experience with millions of unseen others, and thus join in an imaginary community of viewers watching the same thing. This call to belong, and to share the values and experiences of a particular social group or even a whole nation, is parallel to the way in which the French philosopher Louis Althusser (1971) explained the important media theoretical concept of **ideology**. Ideology is a structure in which people are addressed as particular kinds of subject, and take up a position laid out for them by this call, along with the values inherent in the position to which they are called. People become individual **subjects**, subject to ideological values and constituted as subjects by ideology.

The inclusion of viewers in programmes, whether literally or by hollowing out a position for the viewer in the discourse of the programme, is complex in daytime talk shows such as *The Jeremy Kyle Show*. There is a hierarchy of figures, presided over by the host, including professional 'experts' such as doctors and therapists, guest members of the public, the studio audience and the audience of viewers. The role of the host is to mediate between these categories, by representing the viewer's imagined questions and concerns. Television viewers, along with the studio audience, are invited to evaluate the behaviour and opinions of the speakers, so that the position laid out for the viewer is to identify with any or all the speakers, but especially the studio audience, who are the viewer's representatives. Occasionally television viewers are able to participate in the programme by phoning in, and can adopt a confessional discourse and describe their own experiences, or adopt the position of an expert in order to evaluate other participants in the programme. Although phone-ins appear to empower and involve these viewers, the **codes** and connotations of their appearance have disempowering effects. How long they can speak, being heard but not being seen, and being directed by the host, are all means of controlling who can speak, how and in which discursive code. The discourses adopted by speakers from home or among the studio audience tend to match those of the programme as a whole, for example by appealing to personal experiences as proofs of an opinion, or presenting statistical or institutional information in the discursive code of 'objective' professional advice. Talk-show narrative is a series of confrontations between different discourses, each appealing to one of several kinds of authority and legitimacy. The role of the host is to arrange these different discourses into a sequence, acting as a mediating narrator working on behalf of the audience and claiming to represent its concerns.

ACTIVITY 4.5

Can you use an analysis of your own background and experience to explain why you find a particular programme frustrating? What kinds of audience positioning are you resisting?

Television commercials very often contain characters representing the viewer, often someone addressed by an on-screen or off-screen narrator about a difficulty that can be solved by a product (like a household cleaner that will remove stubborn stains). The use of viewers' representatives enables the relationship of the producer and consumer to be dramatised as a person-to-person relationship, and to provide the product with a concrete setting in the household environment. A variant on this structure is the common use of viewer representatives in car commercials, featuring drivers whose representation attempts both to mirror the viewer and also to include an aspirational element (a younger, richer, more attractive version of the target consumer). The narrative function of viewer representatives, therefore, whether they are studio audiences, talk-show hosts or characters in commercials, is to mediate between the viewer and the representation in the programme or commercial. The viewer is invited to identify with his or her representative, and to take up the position laid out by the signs and codes of the programme or advertisement. The viewer is invited to constitute himself or herself as part of an audience, becoming the one to whom the text is addressed.

This becoming-an-audience for the viewer is enhanced by possibilities for **interaction** with programmes and commercials. Comedy programmes invite laughter, television commercials offer puzzles or jokes which the viewer is invited to figure out, and both commercials and programmes provide telephone numbers and websites that offer further information, special offers or competitions. Television shopping channels are of course entirely predicated on this interaction, since the viewer is explicitly addressed as a potential buyer of the products shown on screen. Television sports coverage is constructed in order to invite the viewer's involvement through offering patterns of reaction to the sport directed by the commentator. Studio comment by invited sports experts (former players, managers, sports journalists, etc.) focuses on discourses of evaluation and prediction, and aims to invite the viewer to engage in speculation and judgement in a similar way. This imaginary dialogue between the viewer and the programme therefore lays out codes in which the viewer's response should take place. In sports television, for example, singing football songs and throwing cans of beer at the screen are not expected, whereas knowledgeable debate and respect for the rules and conduct of the game are expected. The use of slow-motion replays in sports programmes is a further means of presenting and encouraging this kind of rational and evaluative critique.

The discussion of signs, codes, functions and narration in this chapter has focused on how television texts are meaningful to viewers, and how viewers are positioned by texts in order to gain pleasure and understanding from them. One of the assumptions behind this kind of analysis is that television does not usually reveal the construction and positioning activities of the text. However, television is an unusual medium in sometimes making its own production, and the failures in its production, a subject for television programmes. But this revealing of behind-the-scenes information and of mistakes in programme production is confined to particular kinds of text. In situation comedy, for instance, it became common in the 1990s for episodes to end with a compilation of **outtakes** and mistakes, or '**bloopers**', from that episode or from several episodes. The animated series *The Simpsons* adopted and made fun of this trend by showing a whole episode supposedly comprised of mistakes, even though animation is made frame by frame and cannot possibly involve these errors. Compilation programmes such as *It'll Be Alright on the Night* are entirely

interactive offering opportunities for viewers to respond to television, by choosing related content ('red button' services) or sending messages by phone or internet.

outtake a shot or sequence which was omitted from a finished programme, because of a mistake during production or an artistic decision.

blooper a mistake by a performer in a programme, or a technical error. The term often refers to humorous mistakes.

composed of outtakes and mistakes from all genres of programme. There is an interesting parallel between these programmes and the compilation programmes of viewers' ridiculous home videos (people falling down, pets doing amusing things, etc.). The widespread use of domestic video equipment, and viewers' increasing familiarity with the means by which programmes are made, has led to a greater sense of equivalence between viewers and programme makers and a less respectful attitude towards television professionals.

ACTIVITY 4.6

Are the best television programmes the ones with the least predictable endings, or the ones that answer all of the questions posed at the beginning? How do standards of value draw on criteria of complexity, plural meaning and innovation?

Television programmes and advertisements invite viewers to gain pleasure and sense by accepting a position laid out by the text, but contemporary viewers are increasingly able to recognise, sidestep and reject these positions. Becoming part of the audience is probably more of a conscious choice than some theories of television text and narrative might admit. In particular, theories of viewer positioning need to be supplemented with studies of audiences' conscious and negotiated relationships with television. Much of what the audience sees on television is performance (in both fictional and factual programmes), and becoming-an-audience is also a performed role which viewers partly unconsciously and partly consciously adopt. For these reasons studies of television texts and narratives are not a self-sufficient set of approaches in Television Studies. They need to be supplemented by studies of real viewers' relationships with television, to explain how some positions for the viewer are taken up and some are not. Chapter 10, which is about television audiences, explores these ideas further.

Case Study: the 'Every Home Needs a Harvey' advertisement

This case study is an analysis of a television advertisement shown first in September 2010. It was made by Thinkbox, a British company that promotes the use of television as an advertising medium. Thinkbox works on behalf of its shareholders, who include the major television channels Channel 4, ITV and Sky. The advertisement, titled 'Every Home Needs a Harvey' and extensive related material can be found at Thinkbox's website, http://www.thinkbox.tv/server/show/nav.1339. It is also available on YouTube and other internet services. The Thinkbox website explains that the advertisement is 'designed to show, in an engaging way, the power of TV advertising to affect people's decisions', and is 'about TV driving instant success in a competitive market'. It is a **metaphor** for the role of television advertising in general. Its audience, therefore, is primarily people who are involved in the television business or the advertising business. But the advertisement gained wide public awareness among a much larger audience, since it was shown on broadcast television not only at

metaphor the carrying-over from something of some of its meanings on to another thing of an apparently different kind. For example, a television narrative about life aboard ship could be a metaphor for British social life (the ship as metaphor for society).

its launch in Autumn 2010, but also over the Christmas period when audience numbers are at their largest, and also in Channel 4's *Ad of the Year* programme on 30 December 2010.

The advertisement begins with a long shot of a corridor (Figure 4.4), establishing the space of the action from a neutral point of view that is not associated with a character. A man and a woman in their early thirties enter the space and begin to move towards the camera. The point of view changes to follow their movement as they look into small cages in which individual dogs can be seen through metal bars, and it is clear that this space is a dogs' home for abandoned or rescued animals. Point of view shots from the couple's position take in the dogs inside two cages, with medium shots from the dogs' positions looking back. The couple move

Figure 4.4 The arrival of the couple.

Figure 4.5 The couple's initial reaction.

on, apparently not excited by the dogs they have seen. A third cage is occupied by Harvey, who is initially static. His space is unusual in that in addition to some expected items like a bowl of water, there is a large flat screen television set mounted on the wall, ideally positioned for the couple to see. Next to Harvey there is a television remote control, and a close-up draws attention to the couple's bemused reaction to the dog and the unusual contents of his cage (Figure 4.5). Harvey picks up his remote control in response to the couple, and the point of view is now increasingly aligned with the couple, since they are about to become Harvey's audience (Figure 4.6). A sequence of moving images appears on the television. Harvey has switched on a television commercial in which he advertises himself, as his image and the text on the screen demonstrate (Figure 4.7).

Figure 4.6 Harvey and his remote control.

Figure 4.7 The start of Harvey's advertisement for himself.

At this point, we can conclude that the commercial uses television's visual and aural signs to tell a story about a dog awaiting a new home. The space of the drama has been represented realistically, according to the codes of point of view, perspective and chronological time that are very familiar in the language of television. There are two human characters who function as viewer representatives; the camera shots are organised around their movement into the space of the dogs' home and their meeting with Harvey, so that the audience is taken on the same journey as theirs.

The visual style of the advertisement changes as, rather than cutting back to show that we are observing the screen in Harvey's cage from the couple's point of view, Harvey's advertisement remains playing without being interrupted by cuts. The framing narrative about Harvey and his situation is replaced by a focus on his advertisement itself. We see Harvey

Figure 4.8 Slippers and warm light indicate a cosy home.

Figure 4.9 Harvey ironing.

undertaking an increasingly unlikely series of tasks in a bright and attractive family home (Figure 4.8). For example, he does the ironing (Figure 4.9), mows the lawn (Figure 4.10), sits in the driver's seat of a family car as he prepares to take the children to school (Figure 4.11), cooks a roast dinner in the kitchen (4.12), plays chess with the family (Figure 4.13), and pulls a duvet over sleeping children (Figure 4.14). Harvey's actions are **metonymies** for domesticity; a sequence of parts representing a whole way of life. The world represented in the commercial has changed from one that denotes a plausible, realistic situation (a couple enter the dogs' home to choose a dog) to an implausible, unrealistic one. But the commercial blurs this distinction between realistic and unrealistic denotation by adopting the same television codes for both parts of the story. Harvey's remarkable exploits doing domestic tasks are shot according to the language of television's conventional use of camera point of view, perspective,

metonymy
the substitution of one thing for another, either because one is part of the other or because one is connected with the other. For example, 'the Crown' can be a metonym for the British state.

Figure 4.10 Harvey mows the lawn.

Figure 4.11 Harvey drives the children to school.

Figure 4.12 Harvey cooks a roast dinner.

Figure 4.13 Harvey plays chess.

composition, colour and lighting. Harvey's actions are embedded in what looks like a realistic world.

The overarching meaning of this sequence of images is that Harvey has made himself indispensable to the daily life of a family. Rather than placing a responsibility on the family that might include the requirement to regularly feed him, take him for walks, clean up after him and control his toilet functions, instead he has taken on family responsibilities himself. He does domestic work and undertakes care responsibilities, thus removing work from the humans who would be expected to look after him. Instead, he looks after them. The advertisement works through a series of reversals, drawing on binary oppositions:

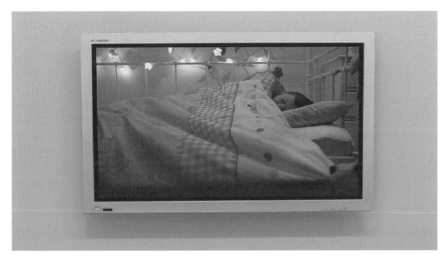

Figure 4.14 Harvey tucks a duvet over a sleeping child.

■ A pet dog is something that needs to be looked after, but instead the dog looks after the people with whom he lives.

■ Dogs do not have the physical coordination, strength or mental capacity to undertake tasks like cleaning windows or playing chess, but Harvey exhibits many impossible capacities.

■ Dogs do not do work, but in Harvey's advertisement humans do not do work themselves or initiate tasks and instead Harvey works for them.

Many of the things that Harvey does are activities that frequently feature in television commercials. The action takes place either in the home, the garden or the family car. Much television advertising is for products that can be used in these places, for cooking, cleaning, furnishing, making domestic labour easier or making the household more attractive. Television advertising presents aspirational images of harmonious family life, convenience and pleasant domestic leisure. In this advertisement, Harvey is the mechanism for making family life run smoothly and pleasantly. He takes the place of the wide variety of products and services, and the efficient ways of using these things, that television advertising most often promotes.

In this way, the things that Harvey does are metonymies for the relationship between advertised products and the comfortable domestic life that they promise to bring about, as Figure 4.15 from the end of his advertisement shows. The camera point of view cuts back to the couple, reminding the viewer that he or she is represented by them (Figure 4.16). The story is left incomplete, however, in that although Harvey has packed a bag in the expectation of leaving with the couple (Figure 4.17) and both he and they appear in the shot, it is never clear whether they take him. The final frames of the advertisement are black screens with the captions 'Discover the power of TV advertising at www.thinkbox.tv' (Figure 4.18) and 'Television: where brands get their breaks' (Figure 4.19). Harvey is the brand in his own advertisement, and it is television that he uses to try to get his 'break' and be adopted by the couple. What we see in Harvey's advertisement is a witty and persuasive demonstration of his usefulness. If the couple in the dogs' home had not seen Harvey's advertisement, they would be unaware of his potential benefits to them. Of course it is also important that Harvey,

Figure 4.15 The closing shot of Harvey's advertisement.

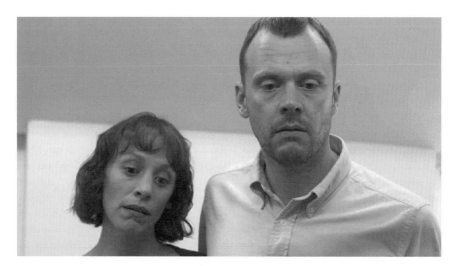

Figure 4.16 The couple react to Harvey's advertisement.

the maker of the commercial, is its star and it is Harvey specifically that the couple should acquire, rather than another dog, or that the couple achieve the benefits that Harvey advertises in some other way. Harvey is selling himself to the couple, and it is television that permits Harvey to do this, in a very short sequence of images that can be delivered to the couple without any need for them to take action themselves. They are an audience.

Thinkbox's commercial has been very successful, as the company's website explains. Not only was the advertisement seen about 260 million times by viewers (some viewers will have seen it multiple times), but associated media such as Harvey's Facebook page (created by the company) and Thinkbox's website also gathered many visitors. Since the advertisement

Figure 4.17 Harvey expects that his advertisement has worked.

Figure 4.18 Thinkbox is linked to Harvey's advertisement.

featured a performing dog, media outlets for dog-lovers also featured it, for example. All of these extensions and spin-offs from the Harvey advertisement increased the likelihood that media professionals but also the wider public would engage with Thinkbox's wider agenda to demonstrate the effectiveness of television as an advertising medium.

But in order to achieve its remarkable impact, the Thinkbox commercial has to control the range of potential meanings that the viewer can take from it. There is a whole range of connotations where the possible meanings of the advertisement would not be beneficial to the Thinkbox campaign, and so these other possibilities need to be overwritten by the preferred meaning of the advertisement. Here are a couple of these alternative interpretations. First, the

Figure 4.19 Television promoted as an advertising medium.

couple in the dogs' home are not accompanied by any children, though the family appearing in Harvey's advertisement for himself comprises at least two children as well as two adults. It is possible that Harvey's advertisement is addressing the wrong people. Indeed, at the end of the advertisement when the camera reverses to see the couple's expression after they have seen Harvey's commercial, they look surprised, uncertain about what they have seen, silent and inactive. Does the couple adopt Harvey? It is not evident that they do. This might remind us that television, as a broadcast medium, cannot target potential consumers very accurately with its advertising. A second interpretation might ask, if the meaning of the advertisement is that Harvey's television advertising is effective, why is Harvey an abandoned dog? He is in a dogs' home, presumably because his previous owners were unable or unwilling to keep him. Perhaps both Harvey and television advertising have been rejected by those who previously experienced them. Indeed, television companies that are dependent on payments from advertisers (companies including Thinkbox's shareholders) have been concerned that their revenue will fall because advertisers choose to buy online advertising rather than pay for television commercials. We can consider this further by thinking about the many connotations that dogs have in British language and culture. Some of the connotations that might apply to Harvey include:

- Harvey adopts a 'hang-dog' expression to gain the couple's sympathy
- Harvey is 'dogged' in his determination to advertise his benefits to the couple
- Harvey is a 'dogsbody' who carries out routine tasks for the family
- Harvey is 'the dog's bollocks', the best companion that the family could wish for.

These connotations are largely positive in the way they are presented in the commercial, though the commercial also has to avoid some negative connotations that are less beneficial to Harvey and Thinkbox. We might think, for example, that Harvey (and thus television advertising) is 'dog-eared'; worn out, overused and out of date. Every sign gains its meaning from the way it is used in a context, alongside other signs, and every text works hard to create a preferred meaning in which positive connotations push aside negative ones. Judging by the overwhelmingly positive comments posted by viewers on YouTube and other internet sites where 'Every Home Needs a Harvey' is available, Thinkbox's campaign succeeded in managing the audience response to the meanings of the commercial in positive ways rather than negative ones.

As yet this analysis has not considered the crucial role of music, and the music in the advertisement goes some way to preventing these potentially negative interpretations from arising in the mind of the viewer. The music in the advertisement is a rock song that was very popular in the mid-1970s, by the Canadian band Bachman-Turner Overdrive. Its title, 'You Ain't Seen Nothing Yet' reflects the chorus of the song and is the most prominent verbal syntagm in it. The pace of the song is relatively fast, and musically it is characterised by a driving beat and powerful chords on electric guitars that convey energy and vitality. Of course the chorus line, 'You Ain't Seen Nothing Yet' refers directly to Harvey's actions in the advertisement for himself, where the narrative structure of the advertisement keeps adding more extraordinary accomplishments, one after another, pushing the narrative of the advertisement forward in a series of short sequences that are cut to match the rhythms of the song. The forward movement, rapid cutting and cumulative impact of the scenes of Harvey's surprising usefulness keeps the viewer from pausing to contemplate any potentially ambiguous and conflicting meanings of the advertisement as a whole.

Of course the makers of television advertisements do not assume that they will be watched in the level of detail presented in this case study. This case study has analysed the advertisement in order to demonstrate how its visual and aural resources are structured in complex ways that build together in a sequence to create meaning and pleasure for the viewer. By analysing the advertisement in this detailed way, the breadth of possibilities for interpreting it can also be considered, to show how narrative in television works not only by connecting related meanings together but also by eliminating or deemphasising meanings that do not serve the apparent intentions of its creators. It is possible to read advertisements 'perversely' as well as 'correctly', and the same is true of any television sequence.

ACTIVITY 4.7

Do all television advertisements address potential buyers of the products they advertise? If not, what function do these other commercials serve?

SUMMARY OF KEY POINTS

■ Methods of close analysis can show how meanings are constructed in television texts.

■ This approach to close analysis relies on analysing the audio-visual 'language' of television.

■ The meanings that can be made from television also depend on relationships between viewers and texts.

- Television programmes use conventions and codes to structure their meanings, and television viewers become expert in recognising conventions and decoding meanings.
- Television guides the viewer by using narrative and offering points of identification where viewers can become involved in programmes.
- A knowledge of the production context and history of a television text can affect the meanings which the television text itself may have.
- The meanings of television have ideological significance that shapes relationships between television texts, audiences and society.

Further reading

Althusser, L., 'Ideology and ideological state apparatuses: notes towards an investigation', in *Lenin and Philosophy* (London: New Left Books, 1971), pp. 121–73.

Bignell, J., *Media Semiotics: An Introduction*, second edition (Manchester: Manchester University Press, 2002a).

Corner, J., *Critical Ideas in Television Studies* (Oxford: Clarendon, 1999).

Creeber, G., *Serial Television: Big Drama on the Small Screen* (London: BFI, 2005).

Ellis, J., *Visible Fictions: Cinema, Television, Video* (London: Routledge and Kegan Paul, 1982).

Fiske, J., *Television Culture* (London: Routledge, 1992a).

—— *Introduction to Communication Studies* (London: Routledge, 1990).

Fiske, J. and J. Hartley, *Reading Television* (London: Methuen, 1978).

Hall, S., 'Encoding/decoding', in S. Hall, D. Hobson, A. Lowe and P. Willis (eds), *Culture, Media, Language* (London: Hutchinson, 1980), pp. 128–38.

Hammond, M. and L. Mazdon (eds), *The Contemporary Television Series* (Edinburgh: Edinburgh University Press, 2005).

Hartley, J., *Understanding News* (London: Routledge, 1982).

Kozloff, S., 'Narrative theory and television', in R. Allen (ed.), *Channels of Discourse, Reassembled: Television and Contemporary Criticism* (London: Routledge, 1992), pp. 67–100.

Lacey, N., *Narrative and Genre: Key Concepts in Media Studies* (Basingstoke: Macmillan, 2000).

Lewis, J., 'Decoding television news', in P. Drummond and R. Paterson (eds), *Television in Transition* (London: BFI, 1985), pp. 205–34.

Masterman, L., *Television Mythologies: Stars, Shows and Signs* (London: Comedia, 1984).

Mullan, B., *Consuming Television* (Oxford: Blackwell, 1997).

Nelson, R., *TV Drama in Transition: Forms, Values and Cultural Change* (Basingstoke: Macmillan, 1997).

Seiter, E., 'Semiotics, structuralism, and television', in R. Allen (ed.), *Channels of Discourse, Reassembled: Television and Contemporary Criticism* (London: Routledge, 1992), pp. 31–66.

Thornham, S. and T. Purvis, *Television Drama: Theories and Identities* (Basingstoke: Palgrave Macmillan, 2005).

Tolson, A., *Mediations: Text and Discourse in Media Studies* (London: Arnold, 1996).

Television Genres and Formats

Television Genres and Formats

Introduction

Genre derives from the French word meaning 'type', and the study of genre has been carried out in relation to television using approaches and terms deriving from the study of genre in film, literature and other cultural forms. This is appropriate since some of the most established television genres derive from types found in other media. For example, the genre of **soap opera** began in radio broadcasting, where continuing **serials** focusing on the emotional relationships of a group of characters were created to address the mainly female audience during the daytime. These radio programmes were called soap operas because they were sponsored by companies producing domestic products such as detergents and soaps. Drama is of course a form deriving from theatre, and in the early years of television broadcasting many fiction programmes were television adaptations of theatre plays. News and current affairs television share conceptions of **news value** and the institutional structures of reporters and editors with newspapers and news radio broadcasting. Entertainment genres such as sketch shows and situation comedy also have theatrical roots in live music hall and variety performance, which were adapted for radio and later became established in television. The study of genre is based on the identification of the conventions and key features that distinguish one kind of text from another, such as the characteristics of westerns, musicals and thrillers in cinema. The study of genre allows theorists to link the conventions and norms found in a group of texts with the expectations and understandings of audiences. In this respect the study of genre aims to explain how theorists and audiences classify what they see and hear on television according to:

- features of the text itself
- generic cues which appear in programme titles
- supporting information in the *Radio Times* or other listings and advertising publications
- the presence of performers associated with a particular genre (in the way that Bruce Forsyth is associated with television entertainment programmes, for example).

As Steve Neale (Neale and Turner 2001: 1) notes: 'Most theorists of genre argue that generic norms and conventions are recognised and shared not only by theorists themselves, but also by audiences, readers and viewers.' Theorists working on genre have disagreed about where genre categories come from:

- Do genre forms arise naturally from the properties of texts?
- Are they categories used by the producers of programmes?
- Are they categories brought by audiences to the programmes they watch?

The answer is that genre is a term used to study each of these things. Furthermore, there is disagreement about whether the task of the theorist is to identify genres so that programmes can be evaluated, or whether the task is to describe how actual audiences make use of genre in their understanding of programmes. From an evaluative point of view, both television theorists and television fans might regard some programmes as transgressing the rules of genre and therefore evaluate these programmes as inferior. For example, some fans of science fiction regard *Star Trek* as lacking the scientific basis of 'true' science fiction and so consider it an adventure series that is simply dressed up with an outer space setting. By contrast, some television theorists might argue that programmes that transgress the boundaries of a genre are more valuable because they potentially draw the audience's attention to the conventional rules of television genre and therefore have a critical dimension. This argument derives from the perception that genre applies most neatly to mass-market **popular culture** texts, so that programmes which are firmly within the boundaries of a genre are regarded as formulaic whereas texts that mix genres are more interesting. For example, *Life on Mars* was a police series set in the 1970s in which the main character seems to have time-travelled there from the present, and confronting him with the outmoded attitudes of the 1970s police is a way of critiquing the conventions of the police series using a science fiction premise. Nevertheless, all texts participate in genre to some extent, and often participate in several genres simultaneously. The study of genre is not only a way of pinning programmes down but also a way of explaining how programmes become interesting and pleasurable by working against genre conventions as well as with them.

Identifying genre and format

The **title sequences** of programmes are sequences of signs that signify the boundaries between one part of the **flow** of television and those parts of the flow that precede and follow them. In this respect, title sequences offer cues to viewers that enable them to identify the genre of a programme. There are many different kinds of **sign** that a title sequence might contain, that will enable a viewer to identify the pleasures offered by a programme, and many of these pleasures are connected to genre. For example, the title sequences of news programmes often contain:

- dramatic orchestral music
- images signifying the global coverage of news events
- the immediacy of news signified by a time of day or a clock
- signifiers of the institutions such as Parliament that are the producers of news-worthy events.

But it is rare for the components of programmes to belong exclusively to a single genre. In news, for example, there are interviews between presenters and experts or officials that are coded in the same ways as interviews in sports programmes. The address to camera found in news programmes can also be seen in sports programmes, weather forecasts or quiz programmes. News programmes contain sequences of **actuality footage** accompanied by a **voice-over**, but similar sequences can be found in **documentary** and current affairs programmes, wildlife programmes and other

popular culture the texts created by ordinary people (as opposed to an elite group) or created for them, and the ways these are used.

title sequence the sequence at the opening of a television programme in which the programme title and performers' names may appear along with other information, accompanied by images, sound and music introducing the programme.

flow the ways that programmes, advertisements, etc. follow one another in an unbroken sequence across the day or part of the day, and the experience of watching the sequence of programmes, advertisements, trailers, etc.

sign in semiotics, something which communicates meaning, such as a word, an image or a sound.

actuality footage television pictures representing an event that was filmed live. The term usually refers to pictures of news events.

voice-over speech accompanying visual images but not presumed to derive from the same place or time as the images.

documentary a form aiming to record actual events, often with an explanatory purpose or to analyse and debate an issue.

format the blueprint for a programme, including its setting, main characters, genre, form and main themes.

factual genres. Although the content of news programmes is necessarily different in each programme because, by definition, the events in the news are new, the **format** of news programmes exhibits a strong degree of continuity. The separation of news programmes into separate items, the importance of the news presenter and reporters as a team which appears regularly in programmes, and the consistent use of settings such as the news studio, logos and graphics make today's news programme look very similar to yesterday's and tomorrow's news. Television commercials also use consistent performers who become associated with a product brand and graphics, logos and music that recur. Television police series personalise law and order in the personas of detectives and policemen, as do other genre programmes such as hospital drama. One of the difficulties in the study of genre in television is identifying which features of programmes are unique to a particular genre, to the extent that these features could form a list enabling the critic to establish the boundaries of a genre.

ACTIVITY 5.1

Examine the brief descriptions of television programmes included in listings magazines and newspapers. How many programmes are described using a genre designation (such as soap opera, teen drama, thriller, sitcom)? Are there other kinds of designation that seem important (such as featured performers, or the mention of writers, directors or producers)? Why are programmes designated in these ways?

---

ideology the set of beliefs, attitudes and assumptions arising from the economic and class divisions in a culture, underlying the ways of life accepted as normal in that culture.

The **ideological** functions of television programmes cross the boundaries between genres. Television police series are structured around the opposition between legality and criminality. Narratives are organised by establishing the central character of the detective or policemen as a personal representative of legality, against whom the otherness of crime and its perpetrators is measured. The television audience is encouraged to identify with the central figure, whereas the criminal is established as an 'other' (an outsider) responsible for disruption. In television news a similar opposition is established between the public, the news presenters and the institution of television news on one hand, and on the other hand the nations, public institutions, perpetrators of crime and the impersonal forces of chance, the weather and natural processes that produce the disruptions and disorder reported in the news. Although audiences recognise television news and television police series as different genres, the ideological oppositions between order and disorder, continuity and disruption animate both genres at the level of structure and narrative. Within television news itself, internal boundaries separate news events into different genres. Separate news items and separate teams of reporters and presenters may be devoted to categories of news event such as party politics, economic affairs and sport. These categories are also arranged in a hierarchy, where party politics and economic affairs are generally considered more newsworthy and significant than sport, for instance. The representation of society in television news depends on the use of a principle of categorisation in order to make sense of events. News could potentially include any event, but depends on a basic categorisation that divides those events considered to be of importance, those events which are newsworthy, from those events that are not. There is an unspoken assumption that society is potentially unified, but further categorisations divide the society into groupings based on relative wealth, age, **gender**, race, institutional power and political outlook.

ACTIVITY 5.2

Nick Lacey (2000: 133) proposes that the elements within texts that need to be examined to identify their genre are: character types, setting, iconography, narrative and style. Try applying this list to two programmes within the same genre. Can you find a programme containing similar elements but which seems to belong to a different genre? If so, what do you need to add to your list of elements to maintain the boundaries of the genre you first looked at? How stable are those boundaries?

Just as categorisation is used in television news to make sense of the potentially infinite events occurring each day, genre categories are used in Television Studies to make sense of the differences between broadcast material and arrange it into hierarchies and groupings. The study of genre in Television Studies has tended to begin from the assumption that what is being studied is complete individual programmes. This is because genre study borrows its methodology from other disciplines such as literary criticism where discrete and complete works (like novels or plays) are the basic units. As discussed earlier in this book, however, television consists of a flow where programmes are interrupted by ads and **trailers**, and where **teasers** may precede the title sequences that declare the beginnings of programmes. For viewers accustomed to **zapping** between channels and fast-forwarding through DVDs, television is experienced in a much more fragmentary manner. On one hand, whole channels are devoted to one genre of programme, on the Syfy Channel, CNN or the Cartoon Network. On the other, as discussed increasingly through this chapter, programmes borrow **intertextually** from a variety of genres and blur the boundaries between them. As Steve Neale (Neale and Turner 2001: 2) argues, 'The degree of hybridity and overlap among and between genres and areas has all too often been underplayed.' But, on the other hand, Neale goes on to note that 'Underplayed, too, has been the degree to which texts of all kinds necessarily "participate" in genre . . . , and the extent to which they are likely to participate in more than one genre at once'. To make sense of the complexity of the contemporary television landscape, viewers become expert in recognising genre, and also derive pleasure from the manipulation of genre and from the ways that television plays with its boundaries.

Because of the instability of genre, it can be useful instead to consider the significance of format, since formats are more stable. Format specifies the ingredients of a programme, to the extent that the programme could be made by another television production company if that company combines the ingredients in the same way. A format is like a recipe, and can be the legal property of its creator so that if another company makes a similar programme, the makers of the new version could be taken to court for 'stealing' the programme idea. For example, the format of *Doctor Who* would include the main character travelling in time and space with a

gender the social and cultural division of people into masculine or feminine individuals. This is different from sex, which refers to the biological difference between male and female bodies.

trailer a short television sequence advertising a forthcoming programme, usually containing selected 'highlights' from the programme.

teaser a very short television sequence advertising a forthcoming programme, often puzzling or teasing to viewers because it contains little information and encourages curiosity and interest.

zapping hopping rapidly from channel to channel while watching television, using a remote control (a 'zapper').

intertextuality how one text draws on the meanings of another by referring to it by allusion, quotation or parody, for example.

Figure 5.1 A dance routine on *Strictly Come Dancing* © BBC. Courtesy of BBC Photograph Library.

companion by means of a futuristic technology, encountering alien societies and dealing with problems of the non-recurring characters that the main characters meet there. The format of *Strictly Come Dancing* (Figure 5.1) would include the ingredients of the host, the judges and contestants who learn to dance and are voted for by the judges and the public.

ACTIVITY 5.3

Examine the schedules of the digital channels in listings magazines or newspapers. Many channels are named after or based around genres. Which genres are these, and which genres do not have channels based on them? What could be the reasons for this?

The generic space of soap opera

It has been customary in Television Studies to define genres by their content and form, but an alternative set of genres could be established by focusing on the representation of fictional space, geographic region or basis in another source text (there could be a genre of literary **adaptation**, for example). It would be possible to divide up television programmes in different ways from the categories customarily used to describe television genres if attention is paid less to the content of programmes and more to their ideology. For example, a genre could be constructed

adaptation transferring a novel, theatre play, poem, etc. from its original medium into another medium such as television.

of television programmes focusing on community. This could include the communities of people inhabiting a shared space in television soap opera, the communities working together in television hospital drama and television police and detective fiction. Within this large generic category, further distinctions could be made to establish sub-genres in which communities are bound together primarily by family and emotional relationships (as in British soap opera), by an institutional hierarchy (as in hospital and police drama) or by the pressure of an external threat (as in *Buffy the Vampire Slayer*).

The significance of space and setting to the definition of a recognised television genre can be seen in the importance of setting in British soap opera. The titles of *Coronation Street*, *Hollyoaks*, *Emmerdale* and *EastEnders* demonstrate how location functions as a force linking characters with each other, not only as a positive basis for community but also as a boundary which characters find it difficult to transgress. Characters in soap opera are in a sense trapped by their location, and their proximity to each other within the space creates not only alliances but also rivalries and friction. The categorisations that link characters together in soap opera such as:

- family relationship
- working relationship
- age group
- race
- gender

function in a similar way as either a positive ground for connection or a source of rivalry and tension. The overlapping of these categories with each other also produces possible stories in soap opera, since one character is likely to belong to several different categories, perhaps working in the local shop, belonging to a family and pursuing solidarity with other characters of the same age group. Soap opera narrative manipulates these connections and distinctions, changing them over time, thus producing different permutations of connection and distinction that form the basis of storylines.

In the genre of soap opera the multiple storylines built around a large group of characters living in the same location produce an impression of rapidly recurring events, since the scenes and sequences in any one episode are likely to involve several different combinations of characters. Short scenes involving different combinations of characters follow each other rapidly, producing forward movement in the storylines. But on the other hand, any one episode of a soap opera usually occurs in a very short space of represented time such as one day or even just a few hours. The exchange of information between characters through gossip and conversation, and the withholding of information which has been revealed to the audience, also encourages the viewer to be aware of developments a long time in the past, to speculate about future events and to experience pleasurable uncertainty about which of the numerous occurrences in any one episode will have effects on the networks of relationships which connect characters with each other. The ways that soap opera works in terms of form have been used as the components to define this genre, but many of the features discussed here are also evident in other programmes which are not in the genre of soap opera but share some of the same elements. For example, hospital drama series such as *Casualty* or *Holby City* share many of the same features in terms of the relationships between characters, the exploitation of the audience's memory of the past and the encouragement of speculation about future events, as well as taking place in a restricted location where a relatively large group of characters enables the tensions in relationships to be explored. The most significant difference between soap opera and television hospital drama is in the degree of narrative closure in individual episodes. Hospital drama and police drama are characterised by narratives in which transitional characters appear and produce a disruption to the social space represented in the programme, and at the end of an episode this storyline is completed.

The police genre: seeing and knowing in *CSI*

The American police drama *CSI: Crime Scene Investigation*, made for the CBS network from 2000, was so popular with viewers in the USA that by 2005 it had spawned the spin-off series *CSI: Miami* and *CSI: New York*. The original *CSI* and its spin-offs have also been sold to overseas broadcasters including Five in the UK. *CSI* is primarily structured through following the work of police forensic scientists, and in common with *Homicide: Life on the Street*, it is much less about physical action than the process of solving crimes. The relationship between visual style and the human body is *CSI*'s greatest innovation (Bignell 2007a). The use of rapid zooms towards and inside body parts or items of evidence (often at extreme magnification) that are often created using computer generated imagery develops the common theme in police series that seeing in a special way is the key investigative activity in the genre (Lury 2005: 44–56). The most important thing that the forensic investigators and the camera do is to look carefully.

CSI is distinctive in its use of long sequences showing the processes of autopsy and the scientific analysis of fragments from bodies or crime scenes. Fluid but very slow camera movements track around the dimly lit spaces of the crime labs while the characters conduct procedures such as examining clothing fibres or skin cells through microscopes, or painstakingly arranging the fragments of an object so they can identify how it was broken. Pace is created in these long sequences by the addition of non-diegetic music, and the camera's elegant dancing motion. The emphasis is on the concentration of the investigators and their systematic absorption in their work, connoting their professionalism and efficiency. Long camera shots produce the impression of continuity through time, and allow the camera to follow characters as they reveal their thoughts and their relationships with each other and their environment. This generosity with time provides the viewer with the opportunity to consider what can be seen, thus providing the audience with relevant clues and encouraging identification with the main characters. Extended shots of the scientists working enforce the viewer's concentration on the detail of how the characters act and react across a sustained period of action. At the same time, these long sequences show the characters moving in space and allow for a physical and emotional distance from them, so that an analytical and critical understanding of the characters can be gained by revealing movements of the body, gesture or costume. This is a distinctly different television code from the rapid alternations of **shot-reverse-shot** and **close-up** which are more common in police drama that focuses on physical action, in which scenes are performed several times with the

shot-reverse-shot the convention of alternating a shot of one character and a shot of another character in a scene, producing a back-and-forth movement which represents their interaction visually.

close-up a camera shot where the frame is filled by the face of a person or a detail of a face. Close-ups may also show details of an object or place.

camera positioned differently each time in order to capture the reactions of one character to another and to provide a coherent sense of fictional space. In *CSI* there is no need for the camera to **pan** quickly between speakers, since scenes move relatively slowly. The effect of this form is to generate a sense of **realism** in following the investigators' work as it occurs. It also has the effect of requiring the audience to observe them and interpret their actions without the camera providing the movements from wider shots to close-ups, and dramatic contrasts that usually offer an interpretative point of view on the action. The segmentation of scenes using rapid cutting and extensive close-up can be analytical, presenting interpretations of character and action, but the long sequences of *CSI* allow the viewer to make sense of space and character in a different way, where he or she must work alongside the forensic investigators to interpret the images.

The camera in *CSI* seems to force objects to reveal their secrets, paralleling the work of the forensic investigators with the looking done by the camera. However, the camera not only matches the investigators' look, but also adds to it, explains it and actively gathers knowledge for the viewer. So one of the functions of close-up, and especially zooms into an object or body in *CSI*, is to link the camera as narrator with the actions of the programme's characters. In fact, the relative lack of conventional physical action in the series is related to this. The stillness and reticence of the characters, especially the chief investigator Gil Grissom, are parallel but opposite to the fluid movement and freedom given to the camera. This also sets up a relationship between present and past. The present is characterised by its stillness, seen especially in the forensic scientists' absorption in their work and the literal stillness of dead bodies or pieces of evidence. But this stillness is made to reveal movement and passion that happened in the past. From the evidence they gather, the team reconstruct a crime that is then either restaged in the manner of a conventional television **flashback**, or an injury to the victim's body is analytically re-enacted by means of CGI, prosthetics and models, so that the processes that gave rise to physical injuries or marks on the body become knowable. In doing justice to the evidence, the forensic reconstruction of the process of the crime gives back a story to a body or an object. The present is therefore known by restoring a past that led to it, and what is seen in the present is explained by another form of seeing that projects a past backwards from that present.

This emphasis on how seeing leads to knowing, and presents are given meaning by the restaging of pasts, has important effects on the significance of the lead actors' performances in *CSI* and again distances the series from the often action-driven drama of the police genre. Referring to critical reaction to the series' beginning, and the principal characters of its Las Vegas, Miami and New York versions, *CSI*'s executive producer, Carol Mendelsohn, explained that

> because CSI was very black and white – the evidence never lies – it was comforting in a grey world. There is comfort when Gil Grissom or Horatio Caine or Mac Taylor are on the case. There aren't many people you can trust in the world today.
>
> (McLean 2005)

However, there is little character development in *CSI*, and only fragments of the characters' domestic lives or past experiences are revealed. This is also something

pan a shot where the camera is turned to the left or turned to the right. The term derives from the word 'panorama', suggesting the wide visual field that a pan can reveal.

realism the aim for representations to reproduce reality faithfully, and the ways this is done.

flashback a television sequence marked as representing events that happened in a time previous to the programme's present.

of an exception to the way in which characters in long-running series are usually explored in greater and greater depth, so that series are drawn increasingly towards the character-based narratives of soap opera. These people who can be trusted are almost unknown except in their roles as professional investigators who see scientifically and know because of how they see. However, the characters' reconstructions of events are hypotheses, and are sometimes wrong. Events in the past are reconstructed fragmentarily, sometimes repeated differently as more facts become clear, and attention is drawn to the processes of investigation. The investigative look is presented as a process of seeing that emphasises its linkage with knowing, and how that link might sometimes be broken. The emphasis on seeing and the process of constructing knowledge about crime in *CSI* are by no means new to the police genre, though they take a distinctively new form in the series. *CSI*'s visual style has given the police genre a new twist, and the series works with audience expectations of the police genre, and also plays with genre because of its emphasis on how evidence of a crime leads to knowledge and a solution to a mystery. *CSI* is exciting television because of its negotiation with genre and its audience's expectations. The conventions of the police genre with and against which *CSI* works are explored further in relation to debates about '**quality**' in US police series and in the case study on *The Wire* in Chapter 7.

quality in television, kinds of programme that are perceived as more expensively produced and, especially, more culturally worthwhile than other programmes.

ACTIVITY 5.4

Series drama on television has tended to develop towards the serial form. Does this potentially mean that all drama tends towards the genre of soap opera? What features of soap opera make it a special form of continuing drama?

Sitcom and the problem of humour

Theorists of television genre have found it very difficult to establish clearly how television comedy programmes, especially sitcoms, work. Obviously the primary characteristic of television sitcom is that it is funny, and this has to do with the relationship between the programme text and the audience. Some components of the programme text can be identified as consistent elements of sitcom, but even these are not exclusive to the genre. Audience laughter, for example, is clearly important to the genre. The moments when laughter breaks into the soundtrack provide cues for the audience about what is expected to be funny. At these points the audience is encouraged to join in with the studio audience laughter and recognise the jokes or comic actions. Within the programme text, jokes and comic actions can be identified to some extent as **signs** of comedy. For example, a surprising contrast can be established between what characters say and what they do. Or in a scene involving two or more characters, surprising contrasts between the **discourse** of one and the discourse of another can provide the misunderstanding or conflict of interpretation that becomes comic. Excessive action such as slapstick or pretend violence can also function in this way. Yet sitcom is not the only television genre where each of these textual elements can be found, since cartoons, shows based on short comic sketches,

sign in semiotics, something which communicates meaning, such as a word, an image or a sound.

discourse a particular use of language for a certain purpose in a certain context (such as academic discourse, or poetic discourse), and similarly in television, a particular usage of television's audio-visual 'language' (news programme discourse, or nature documentary discourse, for instance).

and shows featuring impressionists can also exhibit several of the same characteristics. The genre of sitcom must be composed of a particular combination of elements such as:

- fictional narrative
- self-conscious performance
- jokes and physical comedy
- the presence of a studio audience denoted by laughter on the soundtrack.

Rather than claiming that sitcom has unique characteristics that define the genre, it is necessary to take account of signs and forms that overlap with other television genres. In the comedy series *Campus*, the half-hour duration and small group of characters working together suggest the genre of the sitcom. But the series is shot on location rather than in a studio, and it has moments of extremely unlikely or impossible action that make it surreal rather than (or as well as) funny. In Figure 5.2 the Vice Chancellor of the fictional Kirke University is shot from an angle that emphases his unexplained decision to stand on his desk, and also the colourful dress that contrasts with his masculine beard. *Campus* draws on sitcom conventions, but manipulates them so that the world of the drama feels unstable, unpredictable and unreal.

Television comedy depends more than most kinds of television on the self-consciousness of performance, and the willingness of the audience to engage with the excessive speech and behaviour of characters that are designed to cue the recognition of a social norm and to surpass it in a manner that becomes funny. Frasier and Niles Crane in *Frasier*, for example, are snobbish and self-involved to the extent that their breaking of norms of behaviour becomes funny. The taping of sitcoms in the television studio using three camera set-ups where the set is open at one side to the studio audience underlines the theatricality and performance aspects

Figure 5.2 A university becomes a surreal place in *Campus*.

of sitcom. The fact that actors will allow pauses in their dialogue for audience laughter, even occasionally acknowledging the audience (as happens in the British sitcom *Miranda*), encourages the **identification** of the television audience with the studio audience present at the taping of an episode. Focusing on performance in this way discourages the audience from judging speech and behaviour according to our expectations of normality, and instead suspends these norms in order for them to be reacted against for comic purposes. But these analytical ways of describing how sitcom works are descriptions rather than explanations of how television programmes become funny. What is funny to one viewer may be quite different from what is funny to another, since humour does not only depend on social **codes** and cultural understanding that may be common across a broad age group, nation or region, or **gender**. What is funny also depends on the numerous and largely undiscoverable variables that make up an individual **subject**'s personality. For this reason the only major body of analytical work on comedy derives from **psychoanalytic** criticism, and even this is less a theory of comedy than a descriptive account of how conscious and unconscious factors may predispose individuals to find certain kinds of speech and action amusing.

identification a term deriving from psychoanalytic theories of cinema, which describes the viewer's conscious or unconscious wish to take the place of someone or something in a television text.

code in semiotics, a system or set of rules that shapes how signs can be used, and therefore how meanings can be made and understood.

gender the social and cultural division of people into masculine or feminine individuals. This is different from sex, which refers to the biological difference between male and female bodies.

subject in psychoanalysis, the term for the individual self whose identity has both conscious and unconscious components.

psychoanalysis the study of human mental life, including not only conscious thoughts, wishes and fears but also unconscious ones. Psychoanalysis is an analytical and theoretical set of ideas as well as a therapeutic treatment.

public sphere the world of politics, economic affairs and national and international events, as opposed to the 'private sphere' of domestic life.

niche audiences particular groups of viewers defined by age group, gender or economic status, for example, who may be the target audience for a programme.

ACTIVITY 5.5

Repeated programmes are often those that fall into established genres, and are advertised as 'classics' such as (in sitcom) *Dad's Army*, *The Good Life* and *The Vicar of Dibley*. In what ways might audiences' pleasurable nostalgia for these programmes be the pleasure of their familiar generic form? Are 'classic' programmes always solidly generic?

Talk shows and the performance of morality

The genre of the television talk show has undergone significant changes. Talk shows can be regarded as television representations of a **public sphere**. The public sphere is a conceptual space in which issues of concern to society as a whole can be debated, using the shared discourses and assumptions that are necessary to rational debate. Television provides instances of such debate and constitutes a public sphere, at the same time as contemporary broadcasting atomises individuals within their homes and fragments society into smaller and smaller **niche audiences**. Television's public sphere simulates democratic debate, but at the same time stands in for the lack of collective public debate in ordinary life. American talk shows that rose to prominence in the 1970s, such as the *Oprah Winfrey* show and *Donahue*, focused on individual guests who represented a larger minority constituency that sought a voice. For example, black single mothers, the disabled or people struggling with drug addictions were able to give voice to an underrepresented and stigmatised group, by individualising the problems of that group through the confessional and personal discourse of the guests. This ventilation of personal concerns, connected with the concerns of groups, was itself a mechanism of empowerment and resistance to dominant social values. The contributions of experts on talk shows connected the experiences of the guests to institutional discourses such as medicine, psychoanalysis and civil rights. The translation of personal experience into institutional discourses was also a mechanism of empowerment, though of course it also had the effect of incorporating resistance into society's dominant forms, and converting anger into the more socially acceptable form of televised discussion.

Beginning in the 1980s, however, the genre of the talk show modulated into a much less liberal form of television with much less focus on empowerment and the valuation of resistant and excluded voices. The reason for this change in the genre is that broadcasters' research into audience preferences led to the creation of new programmes, and the reshaping of old ones, to gain new and larger audiences. Graeme Turner (Neale and Turner 2001: 6) notes that 'the cumulative effect of repeated tweaking of the format and content amounts to a change in genre' as 'more finely grained, and more readily available, viewing figures have the effect of influencing content, format and, ultimately, genre'. American television talk shows such as *The Jerry Springer Show* and the *Morton Downey Junior Show* had become by the 1990s as internationally successful as *Oprah Winfrey* had been, but with a very different and much more aggressive attitude to their guests. The hosts of these newer programmes were much more inclined to make accusations against the opinions and behaviour of their guests than to support them in their resistance to a norm. The most commented-upon feature of contemporary talk shows is the prevalence of aggressive physical behaviour when guests confront each other in front of the cameras and the audience. For example, heterosexual couples appear as guests and suddenly it is revealed that the secret lover of one of them is also present without their knowledge. Such confrontations can give rise to fistfights between the guests, throwing furniture across the set and the necessity for burly security guards to intervene from the edges of the television studio to separate the combatants. The role of the host, who has always functioned both as a representative for social norms signified by the collective audience behind him or her and as a mediator between the guest, the audience and experts, has become instead an orchestrator of confrontation and a ringleader encouraging the audience to vent its condemnation of one or more of the studio guests. The prominence of experts has diminished in parallel with this, so that the conversion of social exclusion and violent emotion into the rational terms of institutional discourses is much less the project of the programmes. A remnant of the liberal discourse of empowerment remains at the end of *The Jerry Springer Show*, however, when Jerry delivers his weekly three-minute address direct to camera, containing a more considered homily on the foibles of human nature. Nevertheless the transformation of the talk show genre demonstrates the erosion of these programmes as a public space in which liberal and democratic ideologies of inclusion, empowerment and personal development are enacted in television form. Instead, their ideology has become increasingly focused on the reinforcement of social norms, where audiences (represented by the studio audience) close their ranks against perceived deviance.

A further aspect of this development is the controversial centrality of performance to the talk show genre. There have been celebrated cases (for example in 1999 on the *Vanessa* and *Trisha* shows in Britain) when popular newspapers have revealed that some of the guests have been 'fakes'. Rather than members of the public discovered 'naturally' by programme researchers, these fake guests have been consciously performing their roles in order either simply to appear on television or

spin-off a product, television programme, book, etc. that is created to exploit the reputation, meaning or commercial success of a previous one, often in a different medium from the original.

ratings the number of viewers estimated to have watched certain programmes, as compared to the numbers watching other programmes.

feminine having characteristics associated with the cultural role of women and not men.

to make money from appearance fees and **spin-off** newspaper and magazine features. The appetite for new guests on programmes sometimes broadcast every day during the week has led to the scavenging of guests from one show by the researchers on another, and the creation of an informal pool of guests who can be relied on to give dramatic and emotional performances. In the context of this emphasis on performance and the importance to programme **ratings** of guests' extreme emotional responses or violent outbursts, it is not surprising that the line between a 'genuine' and a 'fake' guest becomes blurred. The importance of the public display of guilt, shame and rage in the contemporary talk show further contributes to the blurring of the boundaries of the genre. These factors link the talk show to the dramatic fiction genre of soap opera, for example, where these emotions and their exaggerated display are the focus of the narrative. Of course, it is no accident in this respect that both talk shows and soap opera are conventionally associated with, and scheduled to appeal to, a feminine sensibility and a female audience. For in Western societies it is a conventional attribute of **femininity** to display emotion openly, and to take an interest in the confessional revelations of others. Indeed the movement of many genres of programme, such as documentary and actuality programmes, as well as soap opera and talk shows towards these conventional attributes of femininity is in itself an interesting development in contemporary television. Programme genres, and their assumed audiences, appear to be moving towards a more generalised social dissemination of femininity.

ACTIVITY 5.6

The preceding section suggested that contemporary television has introduced attributes conventionally associated with femininity (such as emotional display, confession and gossip) into a wide range of programme genres. Are there 'masculine' genres? Which programmes would you include in these genres, and what makes them masculine?

---

documentary a form aiming to record actual events, often with an explanatory purpose or to analyse and debate an issue.

reality TV programmes where the unscripted behaviour of 'ordinary people' is the focus of interest.

schedule the arrangement of programmes, advertisements and other material into a sequential order within a certain period of time, such as an evening, day or week.

Blurred genre boundaries in documentary

It has become increasingly difficult to draw a line in factual television between **documentary** and its related genre of **reality TV**. Television documentary as a genre is associated with documenting the life of society, observing in order to generate revelation and political intervention. Documentary programming has a long history of making social comment and has therefore sometimes been a subject of political controversy. Documentary that claimed this level of significance was evening programming, connected by proximity in the **schedule** and often in terms of the personnel and institutions that made it, with news and current affairs. Reality TV as a genre is a form of documentary in that it is unscripted and features non-actors, but it grew out of the most unremarked and apparently insignificant parts of the daily schedule, namely daytime programming. It was a displacement from one part of the broadcasting day to another, and when reality TV became very popular with audiences (in the late 1990s) it displaced programmes from the genres of conventional documentary, but also popular drama and light entertainment, from their previously dominant positions in evening schedules. With high-profile game-docs and contests like *The X Factor*, documentary sequences have been included that show the contestants being trained, and their reactions to their current standing in the contest, for example. Talent shows took the daytime formats of the game show and the participation programme into the territory of light entertainment. *Big Brother* and *Survivor* welded together the social experiment documentary and the contest, and featured ordinary people in an extraordinary situation. The genre term 'reality TV' has been used differently over time. It was first applied to the combination of surveillance footage, crime reconstruction, voice-over narration and on-screen presentation in programmes such as *Crimewatch UK*. The term was extended to include constructed factual programmes such as *Castaway* where situations were devised for the purpose of shooting them, and **docusoaps** like *Airport* which impose on real events the conventions of soap opera, including character-focused narrative structure, and basis in a single geographical space and community. Looking at reality TV as a genre that increasingly diverges from documentary results in the argument that reality TV loses the authenticity and explanation of documentary, and develops instead towards **spectacle** and performance. What remains from the documentary tradition is the presentation of time as a series of minor incidents unfolding in real time, or the efforts to capture the unexpected and surprising as the programme's subjects go about their business. *Big Brother* is the best-known example of this, where the great majority of screen time denotes very ordinary and undramatic action.

Once Channel 4 had ceased to broadcast *Big Brother* (which was acquired instead by Five), the channel looked for new opportunities in factual television. It returned to documentary in 2008 by means of *The Family* (a format originally created in 1974), with the significant technical innovation of mounting fixed cameras around the subjects' house. Fixed camera documentary was regarded by Hamish Mykura, the channel's head of documentary programming, as a way of delivering 'intimate stories told in a new way' (quoted in Dowell 2011b) and was also adopted for the successful series *One Born Every Minute*, which followed the experiences of staff and patients in a Leeds maternity ward. Mykura contrasted the conventional practice of camera operators shooting on location with the different **aesthetic** that fixed camera shooting offered: 'If people are being followed by a camera all the time they behave in a certain way. With fixed cameras they are more unguarded and more interesting.' In *One Born Every Minute*, remotely controlled miniature cameras are installed in unobtrusive housings on the walls and ceiling of the hospital, with their lenses covered by apertures that conceal where the lens is pointing. The setting of the hospital, in which medical equipment and security systems are also mounted on the walls of corridors and delivery rooms, further serves to make the camera rig relatively unnoticed. Such ambitious fixed camera series require the installation of a large infrastructure of equipment, operator skill in remotely controlling changes from close to long shots in the moment of shooting, careful thought to provide sufficient camera positions to facilitate coherent cutting between points of view at the editing stage, and of course the shooting of very large amounts of footage. But their attraction for producers and audiences is that they create a powerful sense of intimacy, and access to action that seems unmediated and authentic.

Episodes of *One Born Every Minute* are in the genre of documentary in that they denote the working routines of midwives, and provide some insight into the

docusoap a television form combining documentary's depiction of non-actors in ordinary situations with soap opera's continuing narratives about selected characters.

spectacle a fascinating image which draws attention to its immediate surface meanings and offers visual pleasure for its own sake.

aesthetic a specific artistic form. Aesthetics means the study of art and beauty.

process of giving birth. But the majority of screen time is occupied with the interactions of expectant mothers with staff and relatives. The details of human interaction, and how different people respond to the hopes and fears associated with parenthood, are much more prominent than questions of medical policy, institutional politics or public health information. Episodes have a dramatic structure in which sequences alternate between characters, for example the different mothers and relatives in the hours before birth, leading in chronological sequence towards the moment of delivery when the fixed cameras show the birth itself. While births function as the dramatic climax of each episode, the audience is invited to get to know the mothers, staff and relatives in the time preceding the birth, and to sympathise with or criticise the ways that people behave with each other. Referring to a sequence in which a prospective parent considered whether to eat a biscuit, Mykura commented (in Dowell 2011b), 'It is these custard-cream moments that really work' as character drama, rather than the event of birth itself. The association of fixed camera series with reality TV rather than conventional documentary can be seen when established documentary producers criticise this recent trend. The BBC's commissioning editor for documentaries, Charlotte Moore, commented that Channel 4's character-centred factual series lack analysis and public significance:

> When you are trying to purely entertain it is very easy to get something that works and play it again and again through the same prism. It is my job at a public service broadcaster to do more than that. We are not just trying to reflect life, we are trying to peel back the layers.
>
> (quoted in Dowell 2011a)

The issue is one about genre, and whether *One Born Every Minute* should be described as documentary or entertainment.

Similar debates occur around the genre of the series *The Only Way is Essex*, which features young people in south-eastern England. Its participants are young, self-obsessed, and all live in the outer London suburbs of Brentwood, Chigwell and Buckhurst Hill. The independent production company Lime Pictures cast the series from respondents to advertising on Facebook and local media (Raeside 2011). The first to be selected was beautician and model Amy Childs, who had auditioned for *Big Brother*, *The X Factor* and other programmes in the hope of becoming a celebrity. Some of her friends had done the same, and it was from this friendship group that Lime Pictures cast the remainder of the main participants. The series is based around the character relationships among the group, notably the on-off dating between Mark Wright and Lauren Goodger, whose nine-year relationship repeatedly broke up and restarted during the programme's first series. Producers who work on the programme have the task of looking for dramatic storylines that will anchor the everyday interactions between the participants. These storylines are based on the giving and withholding of knowledge, gossip and intrigue that are the staple ingredients of soap opera. The teen soap opera *Hollyoaks* is also made by Lime Pictures. What is at stake, therefore, in *The Only Way is Essex* in the context of reality TV's interest in character, is emotional realism. Rather than documenting and observing, or investigating people in sociological or political terms, the series focuses on expression of emotion.

What distinguishes the performance of reality TV participants from actors in television fiction is the lack of training in creating character that actors will have received, and the consequences for production that result. In constructed reality TV like *The Only Way is Essex*, *The Hills* or *Made in Chelsea*, performances in scenes that have been planned by professional storyline producers are very likely to include moments of inauthenticity from at least some of the characters. Tony Wood, creative director of Lime Pictures, said (in Raeside 2011: 8) in relation to *The Only Way is Essex* that the question of authenticity was intended to be part of the pleasure for viewers in the series: 'At the heart of this was always a desire to put in the audience's mind: "Is it real? Are they acting? Is it scripted? Is it not?" and to leave that as an open question for them.' The devices of fiction in structured reality series include:

■ the use of **point of view** to invite viewer identification with characters
■ music to underscore emotional tone
■ dramatic structuring through editing.

These techniques both invite the audience to engage with reality TV as if it were fiction, but at the same time contrast with the uneven and sometimes inauthentic performance by non-actors that connotes realism. Reality TV is a kind of television that has roots in documentary, and thus it often emphasises immediacy and the role of the screen as a window onto a real world. However, that is rarely a useful way of describing what many contemporary reality TV programmes seem to be interested in. Many examples of reality TV programmes emphasise intimacy, and invite viewers to assess how far the lives of its participants mirror the lives of viewers. Like drama, the intimacy of many reality TV programmes comes from their focus on character, social interaction and emotion. By mixing the ingredients from drama and documentary genres, recent factual television formats have found a prominent place in the television schedule.

point of view shot
a camera shot where the camera is placed in, or close to, the position from where a previously seen character might look.

Case study: animated series

This case study focuses on US animated comedy series, especially *The Simpsons* and *King of the Hill*. *The Simpsons* was created by Matt Groening and screened in the US on the Fox network, and has been widely **syndicated** on other American channels and also overseas, including on BBC and then Channel 4 in the UK. *King of the Hill* was created by Mike Judge, who had previously made *Beavis and Butthead*. These series are highly successful, as measured by their continuing production over many years. *The Simpsons* has run for over twenty series (nearly 500 episodes), while *King of the Hill* has run for thirteen series. The main emphases here are on how the animated series work in dialogue with the convention of the sitcom genre. But although these animated series have much in common with other sitcoms, an investigation of this form needs to take account of the fact that they are created from drawn images and do not feature human performers on the screen. Therefore it is necessary to think about the implications of two-dimensional, 'flat' images in comparison and contrast with the conventional sitcom in terms of visual space and the kinds of narrative that can be told. In animated series, 'impossible' things can happen, because drawn images offer many more possibilities than sitcom drama using real performers. Characters, objects and settings are

syndication the sale of programmes for regional television broadcasters to transmit within their territory.

literally flexible in the animated series. They can be distorted, expanded or contracted, subjected to all kinds of violence, and made to act in ways that are contrary to the laws of physics. The fictional worlds of animated series are much more open than the fictional worlds of conventional sitcom for this reason, but it is also the case that there are genre conventions that place boundaries on what the animated series can do. This case study looks at how the animated series exploits the possibilities of drawn images, and at how these possibilities are given structure and coherence by the conventions of genre.

The individual frames of an animated series are static, drawn images that are made to appear to move because they are placed next to one another in a sequence. A scene in an animated series is composed out of drawings that are similar to each other, but where some elements of the image are changed in one image compared to the previous one. An impression of movement results, and the drawings seem to come to life. They become 'animated', in other words they are given life by their movement, and this is how animation gets its name (Wells 1998). This is the same principle that is used in film-making to create the impression of movement as one film frame is rapidly replaced by the next, and so on. Just as in cinema, it is the difference between one image and the next that creates the narrative movement of the story. The intervals between the images, the gap that separates them, is the precondition for the impression of movement. What is different in the case of animated series is that in filmed sequences the viewer will usually assume that something real was in front of the camera, whereas in animated series there are drawings in front of the camera. Animated series are representations that are constructed out of representations.

One important genre component that animated series take from the sitcom is their setting in a domestic residential environment. The people in the narratives are mainly white, middle-class, heterosexual and live in the suburbs. Most sitcoms are set in houses, usually family homes, away from the centres of important cities. There are exceptions, including the group of young adults who share an apartment in *Friends*, or the group of work colleagues in *The IT Crowd*. But even there, the relationships between the characters come from being put together in the same shared setting (like the shared space of a home), and some of the series' comedy comes from the differences of sex, age and status that make family sitcoms work. The domestic worlds of the sitcom and the animated series match the domestic worlds that television as a medium has been used in, and that many of its programmes represent. Television is a technology designed to be used in the home, by the members of a household, and many of its programmes are set in households and are about the domestic concerns of their audience. This association between television and the domestic world points towards the assumption that television and the programmes that are seen on it are ordinary, indeed the word 'domestic' can mean 'ordinary' in some contexts of everyday speech. Similarly, animations are made out of flat, two-dimensional drawings, and narratives or experiences can be called 'flat' or 'two-dimensional' if they are ordinary and uninteresting.

The most common scenes in *The Simpsons* repeat the same setting, namely the living room where the family watch television (Figure 5.3). They have illegally connected their television set to the local **cable** network, which gives them access to a wide range of channels they have not paid for. Episodes of the series always begin with the family assembling on their sofa to watch television (along with their cat and dog). The series is, among other things, about watching television and about the ways that people interact with what they watch or allow television to wash over them indifferently. The ordinariness of their domestic lives is signified by the repeated return to the sofa and the ordinary room in which it is placed, with a lamp, a plant, one picture on the wall and a rug on the floor.

cable television originally called Community Antenna Television (CATV). Transmission of television signals along cables in the ground.

Figure 5.3 The Simpson family in their living room in *The Simpsons*.

Television animated series adhere to the conventions of visual realism that viewers are familiar with from live-action programmes. Although the images are two-dimensional drawings, they keep to the rules of perspective, where people and objects in the foreground are larger than people or objects in the background. When the separate frames are edited together into a sequence, the space that is represented has continuity from one frame to the next, rather than jumping too quickly from one point of view to the next. Narratives tell stories that have main characters, settings, beginnings and endings. Moments where extraordinary things happen contrast with a fictional world where most of what happens is ordinary and could even be called 'realistic'. In these ways, animated series work hard to draw the viewer's attention away from the fact that they are drawings. But *The Simpsons* and *King of the Hill* use these conventions of realism in animation in order to contrast them with self-consciousness about the fact that they are drawn. Having established an apparently ordinary fictional world, animated series disturb this world.

ACTIVITY 5.7

How are sound effects and music used in examples of animated series you have seen, in comparison to sound effects and music in examples of live action sitcom? What are the main functions of sound effects and music when they accompany drawn images?

Since the characters, objects, settings and narratives of animated series are drawn, extra-ordinary things can happen to them. It is quite possible for characters to explode, be flattened by a steamroller, or be stretched as if they were made out of elastic. Animated series aim for their comic effect by contrasting the ordinary and the extraordinary, in terms of what happens in their narratives and what happens visually to the characters, objects and settings that the drawings represent. Animated series draw attention to the artificiality of the fictional world they represent, where foregrounds and backgrounds are equally distinct and each person, thing or scene might be equally important to the meanings of the episode. Something similar can be seen in the live-action series *Arrested Development*, where a constantly moving camera zooms into and out from the characters and alights in a seemingly arbitrary way on particular objects. It becomes unclear where the significance of a scene lies, and what might be more or less important. In *The Simpsons*, this visual availability of apparently insignificant detail is what allows fans of the series to get interested in the potential meanings of these details and argue about them (see 'The Simpsons Archive' on the World Wide Web: www.snpp.com), for one of the characteristics of these arguments is whether details are mistakes or unfortunate inconsistencies, or whether they might contribute to some deeper meaning of the episodes where they appear.

The settings of *The Simpsons* and *King of the Hill* have this same kind of tension between restriction and freedom. As Alison Crawford (2009) has demonstrated, the use of conventions from the sitcom and from animation are different in this respect, because animation can potentially represent any place and any situation whereas live-action sitcoms are set in a very limited range of locations because of the cost of producing physical sets. The locations of *The Simpsons* include a nuclear plant, the shops, school and meeting places of Springfield, but also neighbouring towns such as Shelbyville, Ogdenville and Cypress Creek, and distant places like London, Paris, Japan or even outer space. However, it is never revealed which state Springfield is in, and in different episodes its physical location appears to change when its closeness or distance from neighbouring towns is shown in quite different ways. The representations of place and space in *The Simpsons* are driven by the requirements of each episode's storyline, rather than each space remaining a part of a fictional world that is consistent between episodes. Sitcoms begin each episode as if the previous ones have never happened, and this allows the series to invoke settings without much consistency from one episode to another (Wood and Todd 2005). A good example of this is the inconsistent location of Moe's Tavern which is usually next to King Toots music shop, but is sometimes seen adjacent to a warehouse and at other times next to Barney's Bowl-A-Rama. The common factor is the sitcom narrative form, where linkages between characters and situations are the motor of the storylines and so the places associated with that storyline can suddenly be as close together or as far apart as the storyline demands.

There is a contrast between *The Simpsons* and *King of the Hill* that is illuminated by the different ways that they use locations. *King of the Hill* takes place mainly in the town of Arlen, in characters' houses and in the local airport, hospital, college, school, restaurants and the office where the main character Hank works. But episodes have also featured other places in Texas and also New Orleans and Mexico. Arlen is in Heimlich County, Texas, and the word 'heimlich' means homely or familiar in German. Its homeliness is signified by the significance of place for its characters, who speak with a Texan accent (especially Jeff Boomhauer who has an almost incomprehensible local dialect) and who match some of the stereotypes of Texan identity. They are conservative in outlook, they are fans of the Dallas Cowboys football team, and they like hunting, barbecues and beer. Arlen is used to explore the culture of Texas in general and the character of Hank and his family and friends in particular. *King of the Hill* is based around character, and character is revealed by environment. That is the reason why *King of the Hill*, unlike the conventional sitcom, has some continuing storylines and the cast of characters changes.

In *The Simpsons* and *King of the Hill*, the facial expressions and movements of the characters' lips when they talk are expressed by simple changes between a few drawn lines that change from being flat to curved. Hank, the main character of *King of the Hill*, for example, has a frowning forehead that is represented by two black lines, and two lines signify his mouth. While the opening title sequence of *King of the Hill* shows the group of main characters moving in front of and behind each other, this is rare in the sequences within the episodes themselves. Similarly, the opening credit sequence of *The Simpsons* moves rapidly from place to place to place and person to person, introducing the location of Springfield and the main characters. The point of view moves from ground level to high up in the sky, swooping around as it follows Bart on his way home from school. But in the main body of each episode, the alternation of points of view is much more stable and conforms to the conventions for live action most of the time, so that visually extraordinary moments are more strongly marked. The bodies of the characters in *The Simpsons* and *King of the Hill* remain static much of the time, and their skin and clothing are not shaded but instead consist of blocks of single colours. Black outlines surround the edges of the characters' bodies and the objects in the frame. The backgrounds in the images are as much in focus as the foreground, and the colours of the backgrounds are as rich as those of the people and objects in the foreground. The movements of the 'camera' (the point of view that shifts to the left or right to change what can been in the frame, for example) are simple **pans** from right to left or tilts up or down. In scenes in the Simpsons' house, for example, the point of view is most often from the edges of the space that is represented (the kitchen, or the living room), as if a camera is positioned in a television studio and looking into the space of a constructed set.

> **pan** a shot where the camera is turned to the left or turned to the right. The term derives from the word 'panorama', suggesting the wide visual field that a pan can reveal.

The implication of these conventions of drawing in animated series is that the viewer is set at a distance from the images on the screen when watching *The Simpsons*, *Family Guy*, *The Goode Family* or *Cleveland*. This distanced visual style allows for a kind of realism that comes about because of the series' relationship with genre conventions. Jason Mittell (2004: 188–94) argues that the realism of *The Simpsons* comes from a tension between animation's possibilities for extraordinary things to happen and the sitcom's conventions of narrative closure at the end of each episode. The conventions of sitcom include the idea that each episode will introduce a new storyline that raises a problem for its characters, and then this problem is resolved. For Mittell, *The Simpsons*' realism comes from the way that it parodies the lack of realism in sitcom. *King of the Hill* or *The Simpsons* have the kind of realism that Ien Ang (1985: 41–50) has described as emotional realism, where viewers understand the lives of soap opera characters as like their own. In *The Simpsons*, the characters are used to explore large-scale social issues like the dangers of nuclear energy, or the idea that television 'dumbs-down' the population and desensitizes people to violence. Mittell (2004: 190) suggests that the series 'uses its cartoon form to pose problems, more akin to those of real life, that simply cannot be solved within a half-hour. The show then regularly solves these unsolvable problems in spite of itself, both parodying the artificiality of the sitcom tradition and demonstrating the power of animation to represent "realities" which cannot be captured in a three-camera studio or before a live audience.' The problems faced by conventional sitcom characters are relatively minor ones, whereas in *The Simpsons*, for example, Homer several times blows up the nuclear plant where he works, and is drawn into an evil mastermind's plans for world domination. Animation can be transgressive in ways that conventional sitcom cannot, because it is distanced from the laws of physics and the consequences of the events that occur. It can take the conventions of domestic sitcom to an extreme by exaggerating the narrative structure of posing problems and solving them, and so at the same time animation can expose the absurdity of those conventions.

postmodernism
the most recent phase of capitalist culture, the aesthetic forms and styles associated with it, and the theoretical approaches developed to understand it.

This play with the conventions of genre is the reason why *The Simpsons* has been described as **postmodern** television. Postmodernism refers to the way that texts in various cultural forms including fine art, film, literature and television use parody, irony and playfulness, both to take part in and to criticise consumer society. Paul Wells (2002: 24) argues that animation has taken on the methods of the artists of the early twentieth century who wanted to explore means of visual expression and perspective by borrowing ideas from advertising images or developing non-representational, abstract ways of painting. This draws attention to the means used to make representations, rather than their content, and in painting this meant drawing the viewer's attention to the flat surface of a work of art rather than thinking of the picture as a window through which the viewer could look into a version of the world. In *King of the Hill* and *The Simpsons* there are still representations of the world (people, houses, trees, etc) and organised storylines. But visually, the programmes keep the flat two-dimensionality of their drawn images in the viewer's awareness, rather than trying to conceal it. Whereas animation has been understood as a medium for children, the self-consciousness that *The Simpsons* and *King of the Hill* are drawn animations works together with their commentaries on significant social issues to shift them away from an address to children and instead positions them as something worthy of adults' attention. As Simone Knox (2006) argues, *The Simpsons* both adopts and comments on its own narratives, allusions and place in popular culture, so that it is both commercially successful as a product and also praised as a critique of commercial media.

SUMMARY OF KEY POINTS

■ Genre study is a way of dividing up and classifying groups of television programmes, and also understanding how viewers make use of genre in order to understand and enjoy programmes.

■ Television theorists have debated whether genre is a property of television texts themselves, or a way for viewers and critics to understand them.

■ All television texts participate in genre to some extent, and often participate in several genres simultaneously.

■ Different genres of television programme address their audiences in different ways, and reveal different assumptions about the interests, pleasures and social meanings of programmes in that genre.

■ Comparing and contrasting programmes from different genres can illuminate the similarities and differences in how television deals with related ideas and themes.

Further reading

Allen, R., *Speaking of Soap Operas* (Chapel Hill, SC: University of South Carolina Press, 1985).

Ang, I., *Watching Dallas: Soap Operas and the Melodramatic Imagination*, trans. D. Couling, revised edition (London: Routledge, 1989).

Bignell, J., 'Seeing and knowing: reflexivity and quality', in J. McCabe and K. Akass (eds), *Quality TV: Contemporary American Television and Beyond* (London: I. B. Tauris, 2007a), pp. 158–70.

—— *Big Brother: Reality TV in the Twenty-first Century* (Basingstoke: Palgrave Macmillan, 2005).

Brunsdon, C., *The Feminist, the Housewife, and the Soap Opera* (Oxford: Oxford University Press, 2000).

—— 'Structure of anxiety: recent British television crime fiction', *Screen*, 39:3 (1998), pp. 223–43.

Buckingham, D., *Public Secrets: EastEnders and its Audience* (London: BFI, 1987).

Clarke, A., '"You're nicked!": television police series and the fictional representation of law and order', in D. Strinati and S. Wagg (eds), *Come on Down?: Popular Media Culture in Post-war Britain* (London: Routledge, 1992), pp. 232–53.

Corner, J., *Critical Ideas in Television Studies* (Oxford: Clarendon, 1999).

—— *Television Form and Public Address* (London: Edward Arnold, 1995).

Crawford, A., '"Oh Yeah!": *Family Guy* as magical realism?', *Journal of Film and Video*, 61:2 (2009), pp. 52–69.

Creeber, G. (ed.), *The Television Genre Book* (London: BFI, 2001).

Dovey, J., *Freakshow: First Person Media and Factual Television* (Cambridge: Polity, 2000).

Dowell, B., 'Moving on from Lagos', *The Guardian*, Media section, 6 June 2011a, p. 3.

—— 'Channel 4 corners market for fixed-camera observational documentaries', *The Guardian*, Media section, 10 January 2011b, p. 2.

Dyer, R., C. Geraghty, M. Jordan, T. Lovell, R. Paterson and J. Stewart, *Coronation Street* (London: BFI, 1981).

Feuer, J., 'Genre study and television', in R. Allen (ed.), *Channels of Discourse, Reassembled* (London: Routledge, 1992), pp. 138–60.

Geraghty, C., *Women and Soap Opera: A Study of Prime Time Soaps* (Cambridge: Polity Press, 1991).

Hammond, M. and L. Mazdon (eds), *The Contemporary Television Series* (Edinburgh: Edinburgh University Press, 2005).

Jacobs, J., *Body Trauma TV: The New Hospital Dramas* (London: BFI, 2003).

Kidd-Hewitt, D. and R. Osborne (eds), *Crime and the Media: The Postmodern Spectacle* (London: Pluto, 1995).

Knox, S., 'Reading the ungraspable double-codedness of *The Simpsons*', *Journal of Popular Film and Television*, 34:2 (2006), pp. 72–81.

Lacey, N., *Narrative and Genre: Key Concepts in Media Studies* (Basingstoke: Macmillan, 2000).

Livingston, S. and P. Lunt, *Talk on Television: Audience Participation and Public Debate* (London: Routledge, 1994).

Lury, K., *Interpreting Television* (London: Hodder Arnold, 2005).

McLean, G., 'CSI: Tarantino', *The Guardian*, New Media section, 11 July 2005, p. 12.

Mittell, J., *Genre and Television: From Cop Shows to Cartoons in American Culture* (London: Routledge, 2004).

Neale, S. and F. Krutnik, *Popular Film and Television Comedy* (London: Routledge, 1990).

Neale, S. and G. Turner, 'Introduction: what is genre?', in G. Creeber (ed.), *The Television Genre Book* (London: BFI, 2001), pp. 1–7.

Raeside, J., 'Virtual reality', *The Guardian*, Media section, 1 June 2011, pp. 6–9.

Shattuc, J., *The Talking Cure: TV Talk Shows and Women* (London: Routledge, 1997).

Wagg, S. (ed.), *Because I Tell a Joke or Two: Comedy, Politics and Social Difference* (London: Routledge, 1998).

Wells, P., *Animation and America* (New Brunswick: Rutgers University Press, 2002).

—— *Understanding Animation* (London: Routledge, 1998).

Wood, A., and A. M. Todd, '"Are we there yet?" Searching for Springfield and *The Simpsons*' rhetoric of Omnitopia', *Critical Studies in Media Communication*, 22:3 (2005), pp. 207–22.

Television Production

Television Production

Introduction

The stages in television programme production discussed in this chapter are:

■ *development*, where programme ideas are being worked out, researched and planned in an audio-visual form appropriate to a certain television **genre**, **slot** and size of budget, and where the **treatment**, budgets and **pitch** are devised.

■ *pre-production*, where after commissioning further research is conducted for **locations** and contributors or performers are selected, the script is written, **storyboards** and production schedules are drawn up, and the design, props, costumes and music are selected.

■ *production*, when the shooting takes place, following the plan outlined in the budget and schedule, using the **director**, performers, presenters, contributors and the technical crew that have been selected and organised at the pre-production stage.

■ *post-production*, when editing takes place, formerly **off-line** at below broadcast quality, then **online** editing is completed, when effects and sound mixing are achieved. At the end of this process final accounts are prepared.

The chapter discusses the many professional roles involved in making television, with emphasis on the creative and managerial roles of producer, director, screenwriter, editor and camera operator. It is not possible in the space available here to provide as much detailed descriptive information about these roles, or the competences needed to carry them out to professional standards, as can be found in the many 'how-to' books on the market about television production. A few such books are listed in the Further Reading section at the end of the chapter. Nevertheless, the chapter considers the different roles in television programme-making and gives an overview of the different stages of the production process, including some of its key terminology. The chapter includes practical exercises that individuals or groups can work on in order to explore these processes for themselves. The aim of this chapter is to develop an analytical understanding of how television production communicates with audiences through the skills and techniques used by professional television-makers. The assumption behind it is that learning about television is not only a critical and theoretical enterprise: television is an industry, a technology and a set of working practices. So the student of television should understand the broad principles of audio-visual composition by learning about the production practices that bring programmes into being, watching a range of television programmes to consider their audio-visual strategies and gaining as much experience as possible of making his or her own short television films in creative and reflective ways.

genre a kind or type of programme. Programmes of the same genre have shared characteristics.

slot the position in a television schedule where a programme is shown.

treatment a short written outline for a programme, usually written for a commissioning producer to read, specifying how the programme will tell its story or address its subject.

pitch a very short written or spoken outline for a programme, perhaps only a few sentences, often used to persuade a commissioning producer to commission the programme.

location any place in which television images are shot, except inside a television studio.

storyboard a sequence of drawn images showing the shots to be used in a programme.

director the person responsible for the creative process of turning a script or idea into a finished programme, by working with a technical crew, performers and an editor.

Television has long been regarded as a producer's medium, meaning that the television producer has the predominant authority over and responsibility for television-making. While there are several other roles that could claim such creative and managerial authority, particularly those of director and scriptwriter, this chapter devotes the greatest space to the key elements of the producer's role. The producer contributes to the process of selecting and working with writers, controls the process of making a programme, and fulfils a responsibility to the television institution that has commissioned the programme by overseeing budgets, personnel, the production schedule and the delivery of the programme. The chapter explains how producers work with a script editor and production assistants in this process, as well as with creative personnel on the production such as the director, performers and designers. As far as possible, the chapter offers a discussion that can apply across the genres of factual and fictional television production, but there are specific discussions of genres that have particular patterns of organisation and production, such as the independent documentary in contrast to the big-budget drama. News is not discussed in this chapter (for news production, see Harrison 2000 and Allen 2010), nor is the making of television commercials, because the emphasis is on the major contemporary modes of drama and documentary and the ways that their production can be explored in simple practical exercises.

off-line editing the first stage of editing a completed programme, where the sequence of shots, sounds and music is established.

online editing the final stage of editing a completed programme, where effects are added and a high-quality version of the programme is produced.

ACTIVITY 6.1

Watch the opening and closing credits of several programmes chosen from different genres (e.g. documentary, news, drama, game show). Compare the total number and different job titles of people listed in the credits. What conclusions can you draw from your analysis about the relative significance of members of the production team (including performers and presenters) in the different genres?

Development

Although the production of television programmes is a linear process from the initial idea to the final broadcast of the programme, making programmes demands anticipation of later stages at every point in the process. An initial idea will need to be shaped so that it will appeal to the audience imagined by the programme-maker. So right from the start the programme-maker will have an audience in mind for the subject, style, genre, aesthetic form and pace of the programme. As the production continues, this sense of the audience may be modified, but it will always be present as a check on the probable effectiveness of each individual decision. At the same time, programmes will have been pitched to producers or commissioning editors, so the idea and the intended process of its realisation will also need to appeal to those people. Although there is potential conflict, then, between the programme-maker's conception of the audience appeal of a programme and the commissioning producer's or editor's conception of the programme's appeal, this degree of difference or similarity may vary considerably. For example, a scriptwriter may be primarily motivated by a sense that his or her documentary or drama production will communicate important messages about gender, ambition, legislation, fear, love, courage or whatever other idea the programme-maker wishes to communicate. The scriptwriter's sense that the audience will be informed, educated or entertained by his or her project may not be shared by the producer or commissioning editor to whom the idea is pitched. In practice there is always a process of negotiation between all of the parties involved in making a television programme, and it is the responsibility of all the parties involved to maintain the integrity of their ideas yet also to be persuaded by the ideas of the others. So tensions, power-struggles and ulterior motives are endemic to television production, as well as the more positive factors of teamwork, creative co-operation and pride in one's expertise.

Whereas cinema has been a medium in which the director has creative control over the film, in television considerably more power is wielded by the producer. Television producers manage all the staff involved in the making of a production, including the director, and have traditionally enjoyed a more secure position in employment. Producers working for large broadcasting institutions will have control over a whole series of programmes, and are likely to employ directors, writers, performers and technical staff on a more ad hoc basis for individual programmes in a series. Even though British broadcasting institutions have contracted out increasing proportions of television production since the 1980s, independent producers as well as producers working for large institutions remain the central figures in the planning, shooting and post-production of television programmes. Producers are primarily managers, but they also work closely with creative staff and require a broad range of knowledge. Their primary role is to lead the team making a programme, to deliver that programme to a deadline imposed by the institution that has commissioned it and to maintain a standard of quality that will ensure approval from industry colleagues and prospects of further work. The skills needed to achieve this include:

- management skills of wielding authority effectively while maintaining the coherence and harmony of the production team
- commitment to the project
- an ability to understand and evaluate the work of others.

copyright the legal right of ownership over written, visual or aural material, including the prohibition on copying this material without permission from its owner.

Since television programmes are subject to a range of legal considerations such as **copyright**, health and safety, and libel and defamation, the producer also needs to know the basics of these legal frameworks as well as the guidelines provided by broadcasting organisations. As producers will be managing technical specialists, such as camera operators, lighting and sound technicians, graphic artists, designers and editors, they need to know enough about these areas of expertise in order to recruit them and manage and evaluate their work.

In many television genres the producer will need writing skills in order to advise scriptwriters and to edit and sometimes rewrite their work, and an understanding of the visual and sound qualities of television that will be used to realise a programme idea or script. In drama programmes producers work closely with writers and may often have experience and skill in writing themselves. Pitching a programme for commissioning will be done on the basis of a storyline created by a writer, and the episodes of a series, serial or a single television film will be planned, shot and post-produced starting from a script bought from a professional writer. The relationships built up between producers and writers are crucial to the success of television programmes. In factual genres such as **documentary**, even though a programme will not be scripted for performance in the same way as a drama, nevertheless producers are required to have some skill in writing. Documentaries also require scripts, often including written sequences of voice-over, and will be pitched and commissioned on the basis of written outlines. As discussed earlier in this book, documentary is a form of storytelling as well as a genre in which realities are represented, and documentary producers need to be aware of **narrative** structure, structures of argument and the production of dramatic effects, all of which are skills inherited from and connected with the written forms of journalism, drama and literature.

> **documentary** a form aiming to record actual events, often with an explanatory purpose or to analyse and debate an issue.

> **narrative** an ordered sequence of images and sound that tells a fictional or factual story.

ACTIVITY 6.2

Use a few short sentences and simple drawings to create a character on which a short drama can be built. Specify as closely as possible the age, gender, race, history and occupation of the person. Think of a simple activity (cleaning shoes, hanging a picture, talking on the phone) that you could shoot using basic video equipment. Draw seven simple pictures in a sequence (a storyboard) to show how the activity could be shot to reveal the character, using only static wide shots, mid-shots and close-ups.

Pre-production

Producers working in **series** or **serial** television depend heavily on the quality of the scripts they can obtain for their programmes. Production planning will typically begin more than a year before any shooting takes place, and at this stage storylines and scripts need to be commissioned and approved. Maintaining connections with writers, and finding new writers to contribute to the series, are therefore important aspects of the producer's job. During the pre-production process producers will often spend considerable amounts of time outside their office in discussions with writers, seeking ideas and negotiating terms for scripts. For a run of thirteen programmes, for example, producers may need to commission several more scripts than will ultimately be used, to allow for late delivery, refusal of a script by the producer or his or her superior owing to cost implications, unsuitability for the agreed format or conflicts with production guidelines or ethical standards. Even when scripts have been delivered, the producer and the script editor will continue to work on them. Revisions may be required in order to make the script shootable within the agreed budget. Extensive rewriting or polishing of the script can be necessary in order to:

> **series** a television form where each programme in the series has a different story or topic, though settings, main characters or performers remain the same.

> **serial** a television form where a developing narrative unfolds across a sequence of separate episodes.

■ maintain continuing characters
■ adapt scripts to the strengths or weaknesses of performers
■ add or remove special design elements or effects.

Because of the numerous other demands on producers, script editors often do much of the detailed work in revising scripts and consulting with writers, and this extensive

Figure 6.1 Example of a storyboard. Courtesy of Jeremy Orlebar.

experience enables script editors to build up expertise and contacts which later enable them to become producers themselves. It is conventionally agreed in the television industry that writers retain credit for the scripts they produce, although in practice the script used during the shooting itself may well have been extensively revised by a script editor and the producer. The authorship of television programmes is therefore difficult to assign to one person: in practice, authorship is a collective activity involving the whole production team.

In television, the rare single television drama and the increasingly common mini-series or low-frequency repeated drama (such as the police drama *Prime Suspect*) are marked by their prominent display of the author's name (Murdoch 1980). The theatrical inheritance in television production leads to the privilege granted within drama to the writer and the notion of creativity. In contrast, all soap operas and high-frequency repeated dramas use a team of writers, either invariant in number or supplemented and exchanged with other writers at intervals. Series are usually commissioned from a single author or an already constituted team of authors, for a contractually agreed number of scripts. Television is regarded by writers as an instrument in which their creative work is distributed to an audience, as well as an occupation that makes them a living. But the script may be altered or drastically changed. It is not simply a transcription of dialogue but also an interrelated set of instructions for all the professional workers involved in production. For the production team and performers, the script directs and restricts their activities. It is the authority to which interpretative and expressive questions are referred, through the figure of the director, who controls the process of realising the written word, such that the script is finally exhausted by being 'translated' into a television programme. In this sense the script is unlike a play text, which not only is performed more than once, but can be transferred between theatre companies and is subject to entirely different interpretations when different directors are in charge of performing it.

Although a producer may have the initial idea for a programme in factual genres such as documentary, he or she relies on researchers to flesh out the details of the topic and find contributors. Researchers in factual television are normally young people with a background or interest in journalism, who are often aiming to move up the professional hierarchy into the role of producer or director. Researchers work for producers, who in turn are employed by executive producers contracted to oversee the making of a series of programmes. The sources of programme research are varied, and include not only resources in the control of television institutions but numerous outside sources, most of which can be accessed free of charge. Researchers will commonly rely on a list of contacts established in earlier projects, such as experts based in academic institutions, government-funded policy units and charities, and a varied collection of people who have contributed to research for previous programmes or appeared in them. These sources do not normally require payment, though researchers can spend a lot of time on the telephone attempting to make contact with them and to shape their contribution into a form that is useful to a programme.

Sources available to researchers within broadcasting institutions are now more accessible with the advent of computer databases, which make access possible to the institution's own archives, previous programmes and libraries of press clippings. However, since programme-making is increasingly contracted out to independent companies who must conduct research at their own expense and using their own facilities, the resources built up by large organisations such as the BBC are not accessible to the researchers working on many contemporary programmes. Research sources such as newspaper archives, libraries and the internet can be important to programme research, but the pressure of time and the requirement to travel make it more likely for today's programme researchers to contact people directly and request instant information. Working in this way demands various skills from researchers, particularly persistence, diplomacy and persuasion, since information sources will normally see their contribution as an additional unpaid responsibility outside their normal work. But organisations that have a vested interest in providing information to publicise or support their cause can be very helpful: for example, charities may be willing to supply packs of information, documents and spokespeople, and may be keen to contribute directly to programmes by providing experts. Clearly, the ulterior motives of research sources and contributors need to be assessed carefully by researchers, and potential problems referred upward to the producer for whom they are working.

New programmes are commissioned on the basis of a **treatment**. This is a short document that organises the ideas on which the programme is based, and provides an indication of its structure, cost and target audience. A treatment normally begins with one or two sentences stating the idea of the programme, followed by an indication of the target audience. Then the style of the production will be outlined, including the creative approach to be taken (for example documentary or drama, location or studio, on-screen narrator or presenter, cinematic or arthouse style,

observational documentary
a documentary form in which the programme-maker aims to observe neutrally what would have happened even if he or she had not been present.

observational or narrated documentary). The structure and content section of the treatment is in effect a condensation of the script, where scenes and sequences are briefly described. A storyboard can be used to give a more precise indication of the key visual sequences in the programme. The treatment will specify the level of equipment used to shoot and edit the programme, and provide background information on the creative team and the skills of the technical staff to be used. The budget completes the treatment. Writing production budgets is a skilled and complex task, but the basic principles are to establish the number of days required to shoot the programme and the editing time required to complete it. These facts will determine the cost of employing the people in front of the camera and behind it, who are employed at daily or hourly rates. Shooting days on location are more difficult to estimate because of such factors as travel to and from locations and between locations, and variables such as weather. Editing time is also difficult to estimate, since sequences cut to music can be very complex to edit, whereas interview contributions to a documentary programme can be edited more easily. On average, a programme-maker could expect to edit about ten minutes of a finished programme in one day. Nevertheless, the basic elements of a budget can be listed on a spreadsheet such as the one shown in Figure 6.2, based on an imaginary two-episode 180-minute medium-to-high-budget drama for the BBC, shot mainly on location. The categories in this budget should be mainly self-explanatory, and are divided into:

■ 'above-the-line' costs relating to the pre-production staff and tasks, and
■ 'below-the-line' costs relating to the period of production itself.

The budget would also be broken down into sub-categories under each of the headings, with each sub-category having an estimated cost attached to it. The 180-minute drama using this budget is quite an expensive production, but usefully illustrates the approximate costs of all commonly used categories of staff and

Budget category	Estimated cost (£)
Story and script	100,000
Producer's and director's fees	150,000
Main cast	75,000
Sub total	**325,000**
Production management	90,000
Assistant director	40,000
Camera crew	50,000
Sound crew	20,000
Editorial staff	55,000
Stills camera staff	1,500
Wardrobe staff	35,000
Make-up staff	15,000
Casting	25,000
Production accountants	50,000
Art department	70,000
Supporting cast	130,000
Stand-ins, doubles and stunts	30,000
Crowd	55,000
Music	50,000
Costumes and wigs	15,000
Productions stores	7,500
Film and laboratory charges	75,000
Studio rental	90,000
Equipment	100,000
Travel and transport	100,000
Studio and other transport	15,000
Hotels and living expenses	60,000
Studio hotels and living expenses	3,000
Sub total	**1,182,000**
Insurances	15,000
Publicity	5,000
Miscellaneous expenses	20,000
Construction labour	10,000
Construction materials	20,000
Set dressing labour	20,000
Operating labour	30,000
Lighting and spotting labour	40,000
Properties	65,000
Special effects	10,000
Location facilities	80,000
Sub total	**315,000**

continued

Finance and legal	75,000
Total above the line	**325,000**
Total below the line	**1,572,000**
Grand total	**1,897,000**

Figure 6.2 Example of a programme budget. Courtesy of Jeremy Orlebar.

service in television production. A low-budget documentary using a small crew, no performers (also known as 'talent') and shooting on less sophisticated cameras would, of course, be much cheaper.

Because of the very high costs of production for prestige drama or wildlife programmes, for instance, co-production deals with broadcasters or production companies in the United States or Europe are a frequent means of support for British programmes. Co-production is increasingly common in all genres of television production. This is not only the case with major broadcasters such as the BBC, which has a long-standing track record of co-production agreements with the United States (Arts and Entertainment Network, the Discovery Channel, the PBS non-commercial channel) and regional broadcasters in Germany and other European countries. Independent production companies in Britain also seek to finance drama by making agreements with programme financiers in a range of countries, such as Canal+ in France, the ABC network in Australia and a range of smaller institutions worldwide. In factual television certain genres, such as the nature documentary, are well-established formats in which co-production contributes significantly to the budget. In the case of nature programmes the key production expense is filming on location, spending large amounts of time and money seeking interesting footage despite difficulties in locating rare animals, coping with difficult weather conditions, working without adequate technical support and recruiting local staff on an ad hoc basis to support the production. But if good-quality footage can be obtained, the resulting programme will be adaptable for translation of its commentary into innumerable languages, and can be sold to a large number of international buyers. Genres in which this kind of translation and suitability to a wide range of markets is more difficult, such as documentaries on British social problems, may be much more difficult to finance by co-production. But even if a co-production deal is forthcoming, producers need considerable expertise in negotiating the legal contractual arrangements. Negotiating with co-production partners for rights to broadcast in particular territories, or for worldwide rights, and making agreements about such potentially lucrative income streams as **merchandising**, and the distribution rights of programmes on DVD for retail sales require specialist legal advice.

merchandising the sale of products associated with a television programme, such as toys, books or clothing.

Television directors are appointed by the producer. This usually occurs on the basis of the producer's previous contact with the director, or the producer's knowledge of the director's strengths and weaknesses as exhibited in earlier work. A director may be known for work in a particular genre, or work that involves the use of particular television forms. For example, some directors specialise in working closely with actors, and may be best suited to television drama where there is the budget and time to develop performances and explore the possibilities of the script prior to shooting. Other directors may be particularly skilled in working quickly on productions with a limited budget and time, where their effectiveness in getting several pages of script shot in a small number of takes would be the primary reason for the producer to employ them. Television drama such as soap opera clearly needs directors with these skills, since performers and characters are already established and the main requirement is to complete the required number of scenes in only a few days' filming. Yet other directors may be schooled in integrating particular technical processes or services into a production. Integrating effects shots, model shots and post-produced digital effects for science fiction television is a particular directorial skill, while directing in inhospitable locations far from base or working with unpredictable animals may be important for the director of a nature documentary programme. Once appointed, the director will be provided with the script and will engage in extensive discussions with the producer about the choices of lesser performers, members of the technical team and the selection of music and costumes, for example. Because the director is responsible for the final look of the programme, and the aesthetic style achieved by the use of vision and sound, he or she has considerable input into the production process, though the responsibility and control of the production will ultimately rest with the producer.

ACTIVITY 6.3

Using the storyboard and brief treatment you created in Activity 6.2, decide how you would cast a performer to play the character, and how you would choose a setting and any costume or props needed without spending any money. How would you use a short voice-over narration in the first person ('I') or third person ('he' or 'she') and some music to give tone and meaning to your seven shots? Write the narration and obtain your music.

Production

It is very unusual to see production equipment and personnel within television programmes. But 'extras' on DVD sets and documentaries about high-profile programmes sometimes give interesting insights into production. For example, the documentary *Lost Revealed* focused mostly on interviews with performers in the American castaway mystery *Lost*, but Figures 6.3 and 6.4 depict brief sequences of the camera operators with their equipment. Both of the images focus as much on the personnel as on the cameras, since the location in a hot seashore setting posed problems for the crew. The most common types of camera and tape or film stock used in television programme-making are:

- *DV*: digital cameras and tape that can be bought from conventional retail outlets, and edited on inexpensive home computer equipment. DV is commonly used in educational institutions and the early stages of vocational training. It is good enough for broadcast.
- *DVCAM*: a version of DV in which the tape used in the camera runs at higher speed, thus recording images that are less prone to momentary drop-out and are more compatible with other equipment. But a shorter recording time results from the faster tape movement.

Figure 6.3 A film camera being used to shoot *Lost*.

Figure 6.4 A film camera being set up to shoot *Lost*.

- *16 mm or 35 mm film*: a format that has become very rare in television production in Britain. The cost of film cameras, film stock and professional editing of footage are rarely justified for television programme-making.
- *HD (High Definition)*: electronic cameras that record images with greater quality than previous digital cameras, producing much more precise detail or 'resolution' that can be seen especially well on new television sets designed for HD programmes.

Human vision is binocular, meaning that having two eyes close to each other but in different positions provides two slightly different images of the world that the brain interprets as a three-dimensional image that has depth and perspective. While cameras are designed to mimic many features of human vision, television pictures are noticeably flatter, so techniques of lighting, sound and shot composition are used to produce the impression of depth and coherence in the space which is shot. Television pictures have also normally been much less visually sharp than cinema pictures. The quest for greater and greater sharpness of image and detail (the resolution of the television picture) has led to the introduction of High Definition (HD) cameras, which the BBC, for example, began using on the prestigious documentary series *Planet Earth* and the drama series *Bleak House* before gradually introducing it for all drama productions. Retail television sets are now being sold that have the screen resolution to display the greater detail visible in programmes shot in HD, and they have already become common. The resolution of television pictures depends on how many lines make up the picture, scanning back and forth horizontally across the screen. Television pictures in Britain are made up of 625 horizontal lines, but HD pictures are made up of at least 720 vertical and 1280 horizontal lines, eliminating much of the fuzziness that can be seen if you look very closely at a conventional television screen. HD also eliminates the flickering effect of conventional 625-line television, and produces a very stable and clear picture, like that seen on a high-quality computer monitor.

Programme-makers have to have in mind the relationships of one shot to another, and when they talk about shots which 'will cut' or shots which 'won't cut' they are describing shots that will connect with the previous and subsequent sequences or not. Shots which will cut are those where the point of view of the camera and the relationships that comprise the shot composition fit the conventions of editing to be used in the programme. Shots which will not cut are those where conventions are not being followed, and for the viewer there will appear to be a leap from one represented space to another, from one camera point of view to another, in a way which does not respect the coherence of the narrative or the coherence of the space which has been shot. In drama, for example, the conventions of a shot-reverse-shot will allow alternations of point of view between speakers so long as the camera does not break the **180-degree rule**. The position of the camera in individual shots and the use of camera movement have to be planned in advance so that one shot will cut with another. In documentary and other factual genres, relationships between shots also have to respect audience expectations of how figures and spaces are represented. **Noddy shots** and **cutaways** are used to provide bridges between shots, and voice-over, music or other sound are also used to produce the impression of coherence and continuity.

180-degree rule the convention that cameras are positioned only on one side of an imaginary line drawn to connect two performers in a scene. This produces a coherent sense of space for the viewer.

noddy shot in television interviews, shots of the interviewer reacting silently (often by nodding) to the interviewee's responses to questions.

cutaway in fictional dialogue or interviews, shots that do not include people speaking. Cutaways often consist of details of the setting or of interviewees (such as their hands).

The Steadicam allows smoother and more complex shots than can be achieved with a hand-held camera, which will be affected by movements of the operator's hands and body whenever the operator takes a step or moves around. Shots where the camera is moving have conventionally been created by placing the camera on a **dolly** equipped with wheels, sometimes running on miniature railway tracks laid on location to facilitate smooth movement, whereas the Steadicam consists of a camera equipped with a complex system of counterweights that stabilise it when attached to an arm linking the camera mounting to a vest worn by the operator. The operator can alter the camera's position on the mounting almost without touching it, and can walk around and turn while the camera remains stable, without shaking or jerking. Although Steadicam operators have to be specially trained to use this cumbersome equipment, it is usually cheaper to employ a Steadicam operator when productions require a number of moving shots, so Steadicam has become common across all genres of television production. Steadicam was developed as a more effective way of creating moving shots in cinema than technology had hitherto allowed, with the aim of keeping the operation of the camera unobtrusive to the viewer and not disrupting the flow of shots within a sequence. Figure 6.5 shows a Steadicam in the production of *Lost*, and the image demonstrates how the camera operator can move while remaining attentive to his position in front of nearby people and the trees and bushes around him. This follows the long-established convention in film and television that the means for creating the visual image should not be apparent to the viewer, and that the technique of shooting should be as 'natural' as possible.

But in some programmes, the sheer versatility and smoothness of Steadicam shots has become a badge of quality and style in itself, drawing attention to the moving camera. The technique is especially evident as a prominent part of a programme's visual style in American drama series such as *ER*, *The West Wing* and *CSI*, where information about complex issues of medical procedure, the workings of American

dolly a wheeled camera platform. A 'dolly shot' is a camera shot where the camera is moved forward or back using this platform.

Figure 6.5 A Steadicam in use during production of *Lost*.

government, or forensic investigation are being conveyed by dialogue. By shooting such sequences with the Steadicam, the characters can continue their conversation while walking together along a corridor or between a series of offices, and the moving camera shots provide an ever-changing background of settings to the conversation, adding visual interest. The Steadicam shot enables the narrative to move between spaces within the setting, and to penetrate different rooms, laboratories or treatment areas in a hospital to give an impression of rapid movement in the narrative of a programme at the same time as information is being conveyed by words. The giving and withholding of knowledge is always important to the unfolding of narrative in television, especially in television fiction. Although much of the time the role of the camera is to deliver significant information to the viewer in order to understand character and plot, the restriction of a point of view and the withholding of knowledge from the viewer can be equally important. Relatively static camera positions, or editing between two or more static camera set-ups in a scene, are conventionally designed to provide the viewer with the best possible view of the activities of the characters in the setting, to deliver the information that the viewer is thought to need in order to understand the narrative. But to place the camera in a position where it can only see partially, or where the view of what is going on in the scene is partially obscured from the camera by objects within the frame, can also have powerful connotations suggesting that there is something more for the viewer to discover, or that the viewer is set at one remove from the action and must wait for further revelations to occur. Moving shots accomplished by Steadicam can contribute to both of these processes.

The moving-camera Steadicam shot can be a way of following characters smoothly from one space to another, maintaining the audience's attachment to the character as he or she accomplishes a series of tasks or engages in several short conversations while walking from place to place. More information can therefore be given to the audience about the character and his or her activities, placing the character against a shifting background of different locations. But on the other hand, using exactly the same technique, the moving Steadicam shot can provide an excess of information because there are too many things to see in the background of the frame, and too many actions or moments of dialogue occur in a sequence for the viewer to be able to trace their meaning satisfactorily. So by delivering such a great deal of information to the viewer as the camera moves and the visible space in the frame changes rapidly, the very excess of information presented to the viewer by the Steadicam shot can paradoxically produce a sense of information overload, or a gap between the understanding of the viewer and the dramatic material being presented in a scene. Furthermore, when it moves with characters who move through the space of the scene, or when it moves independently through the rooms and corridors of a location, giving a sense of the whole space, the camera itself functions as a participant in the scene, like a character itself. These sustained Steadicam shots present an extended experience of time and space that suggests privileged observation of a real world as it is lived, since the real viewer's experience of space and time is that they are seamlessly connected one moment to another and one space to another. But viewers are accustomed to the segmentation produced by editing, and the jumping from one moment to another and one space to another that editing produces. So the Steadicam shot can also be experienced as relatively unusual, and thus not a means of observing a world that is much like the one we experience ourselves, but

Figure 6.6 Shot-reverse-shot. Photographs courtesy of Jeremy Orlebar.

instead a special televisual experience of moving smoothly across an extended time and space that stands out as an exception within the 'language' of television.

The conventional forms of television shooting seem to centre on sets of three. The three most commonly used shot sizes are **long shot**, **close-up** and a range of medium-long and medium close-ups in between. To create a coherent sense of space, sequences often begin with a long shot to establish the environment, followed by alternations between mid-shot and close-up to follow the action. In studio production for both factual and fiction genres, three camera positions are the standard minimum for covering the studio space and offering the director choices of long shot, mid-shot and close-up from each camera. In location shooting for drama, scenes shot with one camera will normally be played three times, with the camera positioned in three different places: a general view for establishing shots and cutaways, with the remaining two positions used for shot-reverse-shot cutting between two points of view on the action. A similar three-position format is used for documentary subjects and interviews, so that mid-shots or close-ups of contributors and presenters can be alternated either with close-ups or with wide shots to be used as cutaways. The reasons for this apparent rule of three are that:

> **long shot** a camera shot taking in the whole body of a performer, or more generally a shot with a wide field of vision.
>
> **close-up** a camera shot where the frame is filled by the face of a person or a detail of a face. Close-ups may also show details of an object or place.

- a single point of view is conventionally regarded as boring
- alternations between two points of view can appear unrelated if there is not a third shot to bridge them
- more than three shot sizes for cameras can appear confusing to audiences.

Published guides to television production focus almost exclusively on the standard conventions for shooting and develop these conventions in much more detail. But as the discussion of Steadicam shows, interesting ways of adapting these rules of three, or even breaking the rules radically, can produce creative and involving programmes.

ACTIVITY 6.4

Going back to your treatment, storyboard and choices of narration and music from the previous exercises, revise your storyboard to make it conform to broadcast conventions of shot size, cutting for narrative coherence, and integration of image, speech and music. Then make changes to some of these aspects of the sequence to try out more radical strategies. You should end up with plans for two different short films.

Shot composition allows the relationships between people, and between people and things, to be expressed in spatial terms. There are basic conventions of shot composition that enable shots to cut together in the editing process. For example, when one character is looking at or speaking to another, the speaker is usually positioned to one side of the frame with a blank space in front of him or her across which he or she can look towards the other person. Similarly, a person walking normally has space left in front of him or her in the shot, into which the person can walk. Static shots of people should always leave a small amount of space above the head so that the person is framed by the environment behind him or her. These conventions are easy to see and understand when watching broadcast television, and have become conventional norms used unthinkingly by television programme-makers. More interesting uses of shot composition contribute to narrative progression and the tone and meaning of television sequences. The distance between speakers in two-shots, for example, and the relative closeness of each of them to the camera, can be manipulated to signify the quality of their relationship and to generate dramatic tension between them. Similarly, positioning characters in frames within the camera frame (such as doorways, windows or mirrors) can create relationships between spatial areas of the frame that **connote** entrapment, or produce a feeling of distance between the audience and the character. Shot composition is inseparable from the issue of point of view, where the camera's closeness to or separation from the action being shot is extremely influential on the audience's relationship with the action and the people carrying it out. For instance, the sense of being involved in the action or kept separate from it, the sense of being given information transparently by the camera or being denied it, are produced by the interactions between shot composition and point of view, and the dynamics of the relationship between one shot and those before and after it.

> **connotations** the term used in semiotic analysis for the meanings that are associated with a particular sign or combination of signs.

The tone and meaning of television sequences can be further enhanced by the use of lighting, sound and music. As a matter of principle, no single element of a shot or sequence carries an intrinsic meaning, but attains its meaning by its interaction with the other elements of the programme in the context of a broader interpretation. Lighting for drama works hand in hand with shot composition to direct the audience's attention to significant aspects of the shot or scene, and light gives texture to the image. Harsh lighting produces strong shadow when cast by a dominant key light, and can evoke fear or mystery. Soft or diffused light has a placid tone and can also connote romance. The addition of gels to light can produce warm colours, or cold and foreboding sensations. In factual and entertainment genres frontal lighting is likely to be used for clarity and coverage of the represented space, supported by **back lighting**. It is worth emphasising that the tone and meaning of a shot or sequence can never be designed by mechanically following a set of rules. Tone and meaning depend on all the elements that contribute to *mise-en-scène*: the lighting, music, sound, shot composition, props and objects in frame, costume, and

> **back lighting** lighting the subject of a shot from behind to provide depth by separating the subject from the background.

mise-en-scène literally meaning 'putting on stage', all the elements of a shot or sequence that contribute to its meanings, such as lighting, camera position and setting.

camera movement. The best book about *mise-en-scène* is actually about cinema (Gibbs 2002), but its discussions apply nearly as well to television. Analysis of key aspects of television *mise-en-scène* is also conducted by Karen Lury (2005). The effective direction of television requires the ability to understand and work creatively with all of the elements of *mise-en-scène*.

ACTIVITY 6.5

Shoot the two different seven-shot films you have planned, using a single static camera. In what ways do the shots 'work' on their own, and in what ways do they require the relationships between shots, and relationships with the speech and music that you have planned in your treatment and storyboard? Why is this?

---

shooting ratio the number of minutes of film used to film a scene or complete programme as compared to the screen time of the finished scene or programme.

During a shoot the details of day-to-day and hour-to-hour activities are the responsibility of a production manager. The production manager is responsible to the producer, and works closely with the director. He or she is responsible for the smooth running of travel, accommodation, catering and the hiring of technicians, equipment and facilities, and may assist the producer by doing reconnaissance (recces) for locations and keeping an eye on the production budget. The production manager will also produce a daily progress report on the shoot. The report lists the starting (call) and finishing (wrap) times of the day's work, the locations used and the time in minutes of screen time shot during the day. Similar calculations will show the number of scenes scheduled to be shot, those actually completed and the number of pages of script completed. From these numbers an average screen time per day can be calculated, and the **shooting ratio** worked out. A shooting ratio of 10:1 is usual for television drama, though an effective and lucky production might manage 7:1. The purpose of all this detail is to record the hours worked, facilities used and supplies of tape etc. consumed during the day, so that progress in keeping to the budget can be monitored. The role of a production assistant (PA) is to log and update changes to the script, to monitor continuity and to ensure that shots match and will cut. The PA logs takes and matches them with the script. The technical crew is headed by the lighting director, who assists the director to achieve his or her desired aesthetic effect by liaising with the camera operator and lighting electricians. The camera operator works the camera and may be the same person as the lighting director. The sound recordist operates sound equipment, sometimes assisted by a sound assistant who will operate microphones and check equipment. Electricians position and adjust lights, and are known as sparks. If there is more than one electrician, the chief is called the gaffer and his or her assistant is the best boy. A grip is a cover-all term for someone who carries cameras and positions them, and lays the track along which cameras can be moved on location. Shoots conducted in television studios will also involve a vision mixer, who selects among the outputs of the different cameras, and a vision controller, who is responsible for the picture quality of cameras. The studio sound supervisor operates a sound mixing desk, the floor manager controls activity on the floor of the studio and is the key link person between the director, performers and contributors, and technical staff. Runners are low-paid staff who support the work of others by running errands, making coffee and generally helping out. Being a runner is often the recent graduate's first job in television.

Post-production

The processes of editing, sound dubbing and adding music are the final and crucial steps of television production and are known by the collective term post-production; they often take place when money is running out and deadlines are approaching. The post-production period is liable to create an overspend on the budget, often due to the interference of the broadcaster or financier attempting to assert control over the programme to improve it or even 'rescue' it. Another reason why post-production can be a long, complex and expensive business is that modern digital editing technology allows for an extraordinary range of interventions that can be made during post-production. The addition of digital effects for cleaning up footage or importing animated elements and complex graphics, for example, is all done after the production shoot at the editing stage. While, on one hand, the availability of inexpensive high-quality desktop computer editing systems can enable students and independent producers with tiny budgets to make effective television programmes, on the other hand the expectations of audiences and commissioning broadcasters have increased as the capability of the post-production technology has expanded. Figure 6.7 is an image from Avid's website advertising its Media Composer equipment, where lighting and the infinite white space around it draw attention to the cool and efficient connotations of its metallic and masculine design.

Editing is crucial to television programme-making. Again, the producer will be heavily involved in the editing process, working alongside a professional editor who

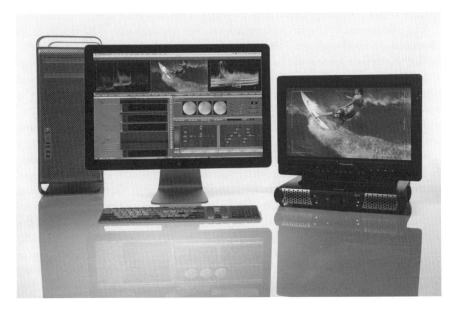

Figure 6.7 The Avid Media Composer Mojo DX Mac CPU. Courtesy of Avid.

final cut the final edited version of a programme that is delivered to the television institution for broadcast.

is expert in the use of contemporary digital editing software and hardware. Although directors have a contractual right to the **final cut** of a programme, in the same way as directors in cinema, the fact that the director is normally employed by the producer for a specific programme, rather than having responsibility for the overall look of any serial or series, means that the director is likely to defer to the producer's authority in the editing suite. Editing used to be done in analogue ('linear') form, but is now digital ('non-linear'). Linear editing involves rerecording selected shots from the original camera tape, choosing them from the camera tape in the order that they are needed in the finished programme. Picture quality is lost in the rerecording process, and it is time-consuming to change the editing decisions made during the process. Digital tape formats became commonly available in the 1990s, and involve the storage of sound and image information as numerical code stored on the tape, in the same way as data is stored on computer drives. Digital editing involves no loss of picture or sound quality when data is moved from the tape to the editing system and downloaded onto an editing master tape. It is also much easier to revise and rework the programme during editing using digital technology. However, the principles of linear editing are useful for thinking through creative decisions, and for this reason students of television production will often be taught its principles. The production team will have ensured their familiarity with all the footage prior to editing, logged it and noted ideas to be used in the edit. The factors in the minds of the director, producer and editor will be:

- possibilities for creating progression through the programme
- the revelation of dramatic or interesting turning-points
- possibilities for intriguing and holding the audience.

The rhythm and flow of the programme will be dependent on the careful structuring of these elements, referring back to the script and storyboard (in drama) to check that the aims of the programme idea are being effectively achieved.

The editing process begins with viewing rushes from the shoot. Particular shots or sequences are chosen for editing, and this process also enables the director to remind himself or herself of the various takes and their possible usefulness. Shots and sequences used to be assembled in an off-line edit, but now the high capacity of computer editing software permits the gradual paring down and simplification of material to be done in a single process. It is likely that chosen shots or sequences will be part of a somewhat longer shot or sequence, so the beginning and ending points desired for the next stage are identified by selecting 'In' and 'Out' points to specify which parts of the chosen shot will be used. The editing software will then be used to produce a rough cut, where the shots are trimmed and ordered more precisely so that the sequences become close to the planned length of the finished programme. The rough cut enables the director to determine the pace and rhythm of the programme, often by cutting on action (where the sequence begins just at the important action rather than including the lead-up to it) and generating interest and suspense by cross-cutting between one scene and another. In documentary, voice-over commentary is written at the rough-cut stage, when the interaction between image and voice can be tried out.

Sound as well as music will contribute to the world evoked on screen, either emphasising what is already present in the image or contradicting it. Sound adds dramatic perspective to images by providing a 'sound point of view' on the action: action in long shot can be accompanied by sound appearing to bring the action much closer to the audience by its volume and clarity; or on the other hand, close-up action can be distanced from the audience by muting or blurring sound. Recorded sound from various locations (seaside, city street, in rooms with different kinds of acoustic tone) or sounds available on CD specifically for use in television productions (sound effects) can be assembled to form a 'library' for use in various projects. In documentary, background sound will be captured by the sound recordist, as well as the speech or other sync sound, for use to cover edits and provide a background soundscape for the programme. In drama, sound can subtly suggest off-screen intrigue, or provide a rhythmical foundation to the programme, as in the ticking of a clock or approaching footsteps. Contrasting sound and image provoke moods and tones that shape the predominant interpretations of action for the audience, while sound montage opens up a whole range of meanings when running parallel with montages of images. These considerations apply not only to sound in general but also to speech. The factors offering connotations in recorded speech include:

- the apparent acoustic source of speech (within the represented world, or from outside it)
- the gender of the voice
- the accent of the voice
- the relative volume of the voice
- the speed of the speech
- the timbre or tone of the voice.

Broadcast television soundtracks are complex layers of sound edited onto the images in the online edit.

ACTIVITY 6.6

Using desktop editing software or whatever non-linear editing you have access to, digitise and log the seven shots you have filmed for each of your two mini-dramas. Record the narration and music, and input them into the editing system. Produce a rough cut of each film, leaving blank spaces and gaps if your image and sound and music tracks do not line up perfectly. How would you fill in these gaps, if any? How would you change your films to make the shots 'cut' better?

Digital editing systems such as Avid are based on the difference between the digital rushes from the shoot that are stored on the hard disk (known as the 'media') and the control information that the computer uses to determine the order of shots (timeline, timecode and editing instructions, known collectively as the 'project'). While the media require large amounts of hard disk storage space, the project is a small document that can be downloaded onto a memory stick and used in another computer. As the edit procedure is carried out, the amount of media stored digitally reduces as selections are made from the whole, based on the instructions contained in the project. Eventually the edit will produce a finished tape or file containing all the right shots and sequences in the right order. The online edit is where this material is fine-tuned, minor repairs can be carried out to unsatisfactory frames, graphics and visual effects are added, and sound and music tracks are attached to images (unless complex sound is being added, where it would be added separately in a dubbing theatre). Online editing effects include transitions between shots such as when one shot is blended seamlessly ('mixed') into another, and three-dimensional effects where moving images can be pasted onto shots and parts of the shot can be shifted around within the frame. All of these online effects can be viewed as soon as they are created, but the computer system needs to render them (process and record them) before the programme can be played back. The resulting programme after online editing is called the fine cut, and at this point the director will review the programme to make minor final changes before the master copy is at last produced.

Making television programmes is extremely gruelling, and it is often hard to tell whether the programme has 'worked' until after it has been completed. The success of a television production is evaluated in several different ways. Newspaper comment on television programmes and the previews of programmes published in listings magazines are available to the public and have important effects in establishing perceptions of the quality of programmes and the attraction of audiences. For the production team, creating good publicity in advance of a programme may be crucial to attracting an audience and establishing a reputation. Gathering a dossier of clippings and reviews can be useful to the scriptwriter, producer or director seeking future employment. But the television industry is a self-enclosed world, with powerful internal hierarchies and codes of shared knowledge, status, competition and gossip. So indicators of success deriving from the industry itself are relatively more significant than indicators deriving from more public sources. The key indicator within the television industry is the response of the audience. This response is determined in terms not only of the total size of the audience but also of the **audience share**. The raw numbers denoting audience size and percentage share are crude, however, and it is therefore also significant to programme-makers to discover more detailed information, such as the distribution of age groups in the audience of their programme, and its social class distribution. It is these numbers which are of most concern to the hierarchy within television institutions such as channel controllers, commissioning editors, heads of network programming, department heads and people occupying the other various roles by which those ultimately in control of the employment of programme-makers are known. Professional reputation among fellow workers within a programme-maker's own specialism, along with recognition from more powerful television executives, are at least as important as recognition by the press and public, since these are the fellow professionals and television executives with whom programme-makers compete and from whom they may gain further prospects of employment.

audience share the percentage of viewers estimated to have watched one channel as opposed to another channel broadcasting at the same time.

ACTIVITY 6.7

How would you evaluate the two simple practical projects you have completed in this chapter using the following different criteria: as training for making conventional genre television programmes; as ways of opening up creative ideas in video production; as mini-dramas that might appeal to viewers (which viewers); as team-building exercises for the people you worked with? How are these criteria connected or opposed to each other?

Case study: the Avid editing system

The basic principles of the Avid and other digital editing systems include:

- the transfer of rushes or 'media' to the computer and logging them so that they can be identified by the software
- the selection of the desired shots and sequences from the media and their ordering into an Edit Decision List (EDL)
- the manipulation of the chosen shots and sequences using the capabilities of the editing software
- the final assembly of the programme from the shots chosen in the EDL.

Cameras automatically record invisible timecode onto the tapes or memory chips used during shooting. But since the same timecode numbers could appear on more than one roll of tape, the editing system will remember each shot for a particular production so that each has a unique number that the system can recognise. It is possible to do an off-line edit on a simpler and cheaper system such as a home computer in order to produce an EDL. The EDL can then be loaded into the Avid or other professional system, and the Avid will automatically select the sequences on the EDL for a high-quality online edit. This enables the programme-maker to save expensive editing time by doing preliminary work using an off-line system that may not be much more complex and expensive than a good domestic computer system such as the Apple iMac.

Editing systems treat camera pictures as objects. The picture is treated as though it were a flat two-dimensional surface, such as a piece of paper. This enables the system to appear to move images by flipping them over so that they look back to front, lifting the corners or edges of the picture as though it were the page of a book, enlarging or reducing the size of the image so it appears to move towards or away from the viewer, and distorting the image as though it were being turned at an angle to the viewer, folded, squeezed or torn. These effects are different from the importation into television editing of techniques that are already possible with celluloid film, such as cutting, fading, tinting and slow motion. They are possible because the image is stored as a sequence of bits of digital information. Because the image has been decomposed into numbers, and these numbers can be manipulated mathematically by the computer and then turned back into an image, the image is 'plastic', meaning that it can be worked on and transformed. Similar processes are used to record and process sound in digital equipment such as the Avid, so that sound can also be manipulated and transformed by the mathematical operations performed by the computer software. It is possible to smooth out jumps between sound sequences, to adjust the pitch and acoustic quality of sound, and layer different soundtracks in relation to each other. However, very complex sound is likely to be completed in a sound studio or dubbing theatre, where specialist audio equipment is available that surpasses the capabilities of online editing equipment designed to work primarily with images.

The first point to note about the Avid system is the different conception of how editing is done, in comparison to the editing of film that preceded both analogue and digital tape editing systems. A piece of film is a material object that can be handled, cut with scissors and chemically processed to bring out different features of the images recorded on it, and bits of film can be pasted together in any order using sticky tape. The experience of editing film is of a closeness to the material and an ability to perceive it through the senses of sight, touch and smell that is akin to the skills of woodworking or oil painting. Editing images and sound captured on tape is quite a different experience. There is nothing to see on the camera tape, and no moving parts inside the memory chips that hold the media used to edit. Instead of physically cutting pieces of tape and sticking them together (although this was done in the early days of magnetic tape for television programme-making), the process is to rerecord selected shots and sequences into another part of the computer memory. Batches of numerical data are being moved around and reassembled inside the computer. But since sequences can be pasted together into any order on the Avid, rather than assembled one after another as used to be the case in non-linear editing, Avid editing is similar to the cutting and pasting done with cinema film.

One consequence of the Avid's capability to treat images as objects that can be manipulated and transformed in digital form is that the possibilities for transforming images and sounds are startling, and it would be rare for any individual television programme to use more than a few of the great variety of processes that the Avid can perform. An Avid Media Composer screen is shown in Figure 6.8, where the complex arrangment of windows and images can be seen. But the camera outputs on the top of the image still appear at the top (as the monitors would do in a cutting room), sitting above the controls that can manipulate the images (just as a vision mixing desk used to be at table-top level, with the monitors above it). The spatial arrangement of the screen in Figure 6.8 harks back to the spatial arrangement of editing suites before computer editing became possible. Whereas in principle the editing of a piece of film could be done with such simple equipment as reel-to-reel Steenbeck editing tables, a sharp knife and some special sticky tape, the Avid cannot be operated without specialist training to understand the architecture of the software that controls it. While the system is logical in its operation, the accompanying technical manual takes about 1,500 pages to explain all of its functions. Editing systems such as Avid are, however, similar to personal computers in that a few training sessions will enable the user to complete basic processes competently, while professional users will be able to accomplish subtle and individual results by adjusting the numerous parameters that are open to modification. The capability of the Avid extends the features of professionalisation and hierarchy in the different employment categories in television production. The technical knowledge required to operate it well consists both of systems thinking and organisation that are common in computer technician work, and of the lateral and creative thinking that characterises direction, lighting camera work and design in television. The editor is highly professional and competent across different kinds of expertise. He or she is also a specialised worker who operates at a particular level in the hierarchy of a

Figure 6.8 The screen of the Avid Media Composer v5 – AMA QuickTime Support. Courtesy of Avid.

trade group. In general, the computerisation and complexity of digital editing produce extended vertical hierarchies of status in the editing profession, and work specialisation that increasingly separates the experience of editors from others in the television industry. This is ironic given that digital technology potentially connects the hardware used to shoot, edit, record sound and display audio-visual media, since it all works on the same principle of translating information into numerical form (digits).

Interestingly, some of the commands on the Avid system refer to one or the other of the cinematic or video editing conventions that preceded digital non-linear systems. The basic command Splice, for example, is called Insert in Avid's main competitor Final Cut Pro, made by Apple. The Splice command inserts material selected from the Source Monitor and marked with an In and an Out point. The term 'Splice' derives from the film editing procedure of physically cutting a strip of frames and splicing or joining one to another. The second most basic and useful command on the Avid interface is Overwrite, which lays a selected sequence on top of another, replacing what was previously there at that point on the timeline. Overwrite derives from the now superseded video editing process by which an audio-visual sequence from a source tape player was recorded onto the edit master at a point where an existing sequence had previously been recorded. The recording head of the video tape player would write the new material over the top of the previous material, leaving no trace of what was there before. The principles of basic editing on the Avid are a combination of the cutting and joining processes involved in film editing, and the transfer and rerecording processes involved in analogue video editing. In a similar way, the timeline displayed at the bottom of the Avid screen represents the project as a linear strip, like a piece of film or videotape. Representing the project in this way provides a useful graphic representation of the programme as it is edited. Jogging and shuttling using the Avid's keyboard or mouse mimic the freeze-frame (jog) and cue and review (shuttle) functions of a videotape recorder, where the play head moves rapidly across the tape and provides a speeded-up version of the pictures. The Avid's Trim mode allows individual shots to be shortened or lengthened by any number of frames, and is particularly useful to refine cuts on action so that the pace of a sequence can be adjusted. As its name suggests, the effect is what would happen if frames of film were snipped from a sequence using scissors, and joined back on to the preceding or following sequence, slightly shortening or lengthening the complete programme. But again, nothing physical happens to the audio-visual information in the Avid, and frames that have been trimmed out using the control remain invisibly present so that they can be restored at any time.

The centre of an Avid system is the software programme loaded onto the computer. Attached to this are the special keyboard which operates the system via a connecting device called a dongle, a storage device in which the digitised rushes or 'media' are stored on a computer hard disk, two television monitors which display media and the cut which is being worked on, sound input devices such as DAT (digital audio tape) players, speakers for sound output and devices for audio-visual input such as videotape players. The Avid is therefore a concrete example of media **convergence**: it can access a wide variety of analogue and digital information sources operating in different formats and standards, and integrate and store these various kinds of input information. By integrating all of these input sources encoded in digital form, it is able to treat them in the same way, manipulate them and produce a new output that can be perceived via the electronic and mechanical devices of the television monitor and loudspeakers. The ways that the Avid separates one project from another in its memory, sets up Bins (like folders on a word processor) containing the digitised rushes or media, and orders the sequences (Clips) manipulated during the edit, all bear no relation to the physical position or arrangement of information in the computer. While the human user requires an interface that separates and categorises these different kinds of information, arranges them in a hierarchy and represents them in understandable ways, the information represented by the interface is virtual. The ability to display representations of media in virtual forms allows the user of the Avid to try out effects, revise and modify the elements of a programme without ever affecting the original form of the media digitised and held in the hard disk drive. It is only at the stage when captions and effects have been added that the Avid editor will declare that he or she has reached the point of Picture Lock. This is where the visual sequences of the programme have been fixed and finalised, and after this is done sound and music will be added until the programme is complete.

convergence the process whereby previously separate media technologies merge together. For example, computers can now send faxes, show DVD films and play music.

SUMMARY OF KEY POINTS

- Studying the professional processes of making television gives a deeper understanding of television institutions, programmes and how meanings are made.
- Development is the stage when programme ideas are being worked out, researched and planned.
- Pre-production is when locations, contributors or performers are selected, scripts are written, storyboards and production schedules are drawn up, and the design, props, costumes and music are selected.
- Production is the shooting stage, when the creative and technical personnel produce the audio-visual raw material for programmes.

■ Post-production includes the editing of the material that has been shot, and the inclusion of effects and a sound mix.

■ The hierarchy of roles in television production, and the ways that technology is designed to be used, reveal assumptions about the relative status of television professional staff, and how images and sound should be put together.

Further reading

Allen, S., *News Culture*, third edition (Buckingham: Open University Press, 2010).

Gibbs, J., *Mise-en-Scène: Film Style and Interpretation* (London: Wallflower, 2002).

Harrison, J., *Terrestrial Television News in Britain: The Culture of Production* (Manchester: Manchester University Press, 2000).

Hood, S. (ed.), *Behind the Screens: The Structure of British Television in the Nineties* (London: Lawrence & Wishart, 1994).

Kauffmann, S. and A. Kennedy, *Avid Editing: A Guide for Beginning and Intermediate Users* (Oxford: Focal Press, 2012).

Lury, K., *Interpreting Television* (London: Hodder Arnold, 2005).

Messenger Davies, M., 'Production studies', *Critical Studies in Television*, 1:1 (2006), pp. 21–30.

Murdoch, G., 'Authorship and organization', *Screen Education*, 35 (1980), pp. 19–34.

Orlebar, J., *The Television Handbook*, fourth edition (London: Routledge, 2011).

—— *Digital Television Production* (London: Arnold, 2002).

Owens, J., and G. Millerson, *Video Production Handbook*, fifth edition (Oxford: Focal Press, 2011).

Staten, G., and S. Bayes, *The Avid Handbook: Advanced Techniques, Strategies, and Survival Information for Avid Editing Systems*, fifth edition (Oxford: Focal Press, 2008).

Tunstall, J. *Media Occupations and Professions: A Reader* (Oxford: Oxford University Press, 2001).

—— (ed.), *Television Producers* (London: Routledge, 1993).

Wayne, M., *Dissident Voices: The Politics of Television and Cultural Change* (London: Pluto, 1998).

Television and Quality

Television and Quality

Introduction

This chapter addresses the question of **quality** in television, and focuses on drama programmes, especially American ones, since this is where academic debates about the meaning of 'quality TV' have been conducted in recent years. Although academic work has largely avoided making distinctions that value one programme or **genre** over another, informal talk about television very often consists of identifying a 'good' programme (or channel or viewing experience). Methodologies deriving from literary and film studies have historically been adapted for the study of television programmes, and their focus on the construction of meaning and the analysis of image and sound produce dominant expectations of what the study of television will prioritise. Studies of television are often concerned to identify features that make a programme **aesthetically** significant, such as visual textures, performers or its legacy as the inspiration for subsequent programmes. The critical evaluation of quality in television depends on attributing value either by claiming that a programme matches the medium's capabilities, or because bringing into television an aesthetic from outside it redresses an inherent predisposition for the medium to be of low quality. The US television theorist Horace Newcomb (1974) argued that the primary attributes of broadcast television are:

- intimacy: television engages viewers with characters and **narratives**
- continuity: television is available whenever we wish to view it
- immediacy: television is closely connected with events occurring around us.

Thus Newcomb suggested that the medium is most suited to working on contemporary social anxieties through narrative forms characterised by verisimilitude and involvement with character and story. He associated visual stylishness, on the other hand, with cinema rather than television.

ACTIVITY 7.1

Think about the ways that you might identify programmes as examples of either 'good' or 'bad' television. Once you have read this chapter, reflect on whether 'good' television is the same as 'quality' television.

In the British context, television has been considered a writer's medium, setting up an opposition between television as an aesthetically conservative medium of dialogue and character, and cinema as more adventurous in style and narrative form. Academic work on television fiction in Britain began by centring on a social **realist** aesthetic, and valued:

- complexity of textual form
- **reflexivity**, in which programmes took account of their own conventions
- the importance of **authorship**
- engagement with contemporary social and political issues.

Canonical status has been attributed to adaptations of 'classic' literature and theatre, or programmes that have assimilated the related value given to authorship in the prestige television play or authored **serial** (Bignell 2007b). The serial *Brideshead Revisited*, based on a novel and made in the early 1980s, is an example of the visually rich and narratively slow-paced form associated with this British prestige drama. In Figure 7.1 the two main characters enter the garden of an Oxford college, where the closing gate of the garden signifies their movement into a privileged world. Since the time of *Brideshead Revisited*, the understanding of quality has become slanted towards programmes that claim political engagement or aesthetic innovation, so that now, a visual look similar to *Brideshead Revisited* does not guarantee that audiences perceive similar visual style as quality TV. The country house period drama *Downton Abbey* is set in a privileged world too, but the shots of stately homes like the shot of Downton Abbey itself in Figure 7.2 have not resulted in the **series** being regarded as quality television. *Downton Abbey* has large audiences on ITV1 and popularity is not strongly associated with quality. As contemporary Hollywood cinema has

realism the aim for representations to reproduce reality faithfully, and the ways this is done.

reflexivity a text's reflection on its own status as a text, for example drawing attention to generic conventions, or revealing the technologies used to make a programme.

authorship the question of who an author is, the role of the author as creator and the significance of the author's input into the material being studied.

serial a television form where a developing narrative unfolds across a sequence of separate episodes.

series a television form where each programme in the series has a different story or topic, though settings, main characters or performers remain the same.

Figure 7.1 British quality drama: *Brideshead Revisited.*

Figure 7.2 *Downton Abbey.*

mise-en-scène literally meaning 'putting on stage', all the elements of a shot or sequence that contribute to its meanings, such as lighting, camera position and setting.

invested in films that base their appeal on spectacle, effects and distinctive directorial intervention in ***mise-en-scène***, the supposed distinction between television and film has gained greater purchase (McLoone 1997). The result has been a relative neglect of television style, especially where style is significant to popular and generic programmes. Furthermore, the interest in British academic work on forms of television realism has focused attention on the cultivation of a style that effaces itself in order to witness character and environment rather than to draw attention to the mediation of narrative by specific audio-visual forms.

Theories of television viewership interact with these conceptions of the specificity of the medium. The viewer has been conceptualised as someone 'casting a lazy eye over the proceedings, keeping an eye on events, or, as the slightly archaic designation had it, "looking in"' (Ellis 1982: 137). Television scholarship has defined the medium as one in which a distracted domestic viewer glances at relatively simple image compositions with low density of visual information, where images are emphasised and anchored by dialogue, sound and music. These assumptions, made initially in the era of live, studio-based, multi-camera television with monochrome pictures, have obstructed detailed work on television's audio-visual style until recently. If audiences watch sporadically, inattentively and continually then complexity, ambiguity and other highly valued aesthetic qualities would be wasted on them. However, contemporary British and US drama series have adopted self-conscious stylishness as a key component of their form and appeal to audiences (McCabe and Akass 2007). Now, studies of television examine generic programmes as examples of how 'good' television opens up the possibilities of apparently conventional forms. Academic work by Robin Nelson (1997), for example, demonstrated how critical emphases on authorship, television plays and a lament for a lost 'golden age' of television drama missed out on the increasing predominance of popular series and also failed to account for audience response or the importance of genre. In recent years, academic publication has increasingly considered the question of quality in new ways.

Identifying quality

Both Simon Frith (2000) and Jane Feuer (2003), discussing quality in UK and US television respectively, argue that quality is defined simultaneously in programmes' aesthetics, technical achievement and the audiences who are targeted. The confusing term 'quality', which has gained increasing prominence in academic work about television, has different meanings in different contexts. Quality television drama means:

- an aesthetically ambitious programme with the literary values of creative imagination, authenticity and relevance, by comparison with what are seen as generic, conventional television productions
- production processes that prioritise strong writing and innovative *mise-en-scène*
- economically valuable television, which valuable viewers (relatively wealthy and educated social groups) enjoy and are willing to pay for.

Programmes that fit these definitions of quality can be found in popular genres such as police and hospital drama or comedy series, as well as in prestigious drama or 'landmark' factual series. Nature programmes produced by Alistair Fothergill and presented by David Attenborough, for example, invest very large amounts of money to capture visually spectacular scenes of animal behaviour. The efforts of a camera operator to capture footage on an ice floe (Figure 7.3) make clear the human and

Figure 7.3 Making the *Blue Planet* natural history series.

technical effort required. The image comes from a documentary, *Making Waves*, which both explained and advertised how the nature series *Blue Planet* was made. However, an important question that arises from this mixing of 'elite' and **'popular'** culture, cinema and television, and one genre with another, is how to ascribe significance and value to television that exhibits these features. For example, it seems quite legitimate to claim that *The Simpsons* is a very important piece of cultural work, at least as important as any contemporary novel, play or painting, because of

- its intertextual complexity
- its self-awareness
- its relevance to today's fragmented media landscapes and audiences.

The values of complexity, self-consciousness, and engagement with cultural issues in *The Simpsons* make it fit the criteria for 'art', yet it is obviously part of popular culture, not least because it is a widely distributed television programme. As the case study in Chapter 5 argued, much of the comedy in *The Simpsons* comes from the reflexive parody of the conventions of, among others:

- other animated series
- television sitcom
- television news
- children's television.

Intertextuality is essential to television. Programmes and advertisements find their place in the schedules and address their audiences by establishing their similarity to and difference from other programmes and advertisements, and from other media texts. At the same time as using these parodic reworkings to criticise the other genres that are referred to, *The Simpsons* celebrates and enjoys mixing up the conventions of the source texts.

Even in the 1970s, Television Studies books addressing television programmes as texts recognised the significance of the mixed formal and informal **registers** in programmes, and the connections these might have to how television addresses its audience and television's relationship with social values. For John Fiske and John Hartley, writing in 1978, the discourse of television was made up of a mixture of what they called 'literate' and 'oral' codes. By this they meant that television programmes have 'literate' components shared with written texts and relatively high-status forms of written communication, since they are 'narrative, sequential, abstract, univocal, "consistent"'. Yet television texts also have features that are more similar to the informal communication of spoken language in anecdotes, folktales or popular songs, in that they are also 'dramatic, episodic, concrete, social, dialectical' (Fiske and Hartley 1978: 125). The literate codes of television underlie the novelistic narrative structures and linear explanatory forms of programmes, and can be regarded as reflecting the unifying and official language of social power, which imposes an ordered view of the world and a system of values and regulations on society. On the other hand, Fiske and Hartley saw the 'oral' features of television as deriving from the organic culture of people's own communities and everyday lives, and in some ways as a representation of people's vigorous popular culture. In the context of Television Studies' critique of the forces of social control, and its valuation of ordinary people and their world-views, the oral mode of television was regarded as a vital and **progressive** element. Television's oral mode seemed to possess radical potential for connecting with a sense of community, validating the ordinary viewer and popular culture. The textual analysis of television programmes still carries a legacy of identifying which programmes have quality because they are 'progressive' and socially challenging, versus identifying programmes which perpetuate formerly dominant social conventions and support the **status quo**.

In all genres, programme-makers try to emulate the success of previous programmes, and also seek new ways of addressing audiences by working on visual style. This has a relationship with genre, since one way of creating innovative programmes is by blending genres together. For example, the hospital drama series *ER* had a mix of generic components that was designed to appeal to American audiences, for whom the interruption of commercials into programmes seems to lead to channel-hopping or **zapping** and loss of involvement in ongoing narrative. Bob Mullan (1997: 60) reports that the novelist and creator of *ER*, Michael Crichton, believed that American viewers

> are incapable of watching television for any length of time unless it is a 'news reality' programme like *The Cops* or a courtroom drama like the O. J. Simpson trial. The only way forward, he believes, is to make drama more dramatic than the news and reality programmes.

The narrative of *ER* was patterned to include periodic bursts of rapid action interspersed with more leisurely character development, and the programme as a whole was segmented into a large number of relatively short scenes. The longer and slower scenes of character interaction drew on the conventions of soap opera, in which reaction by one character to events in the life of another is represented by frequent close-up, emotional cues provided by music and an emphasis on the viewer's memory of past events in the characters' lives to enrich what is happening in the narrative present. By contrast, the shorter scenes of rapid activity, usually scenes in which the doctors respond to the arrival of a seriously injured person, used rapid hand-held camera shots, **whip-pans** and rapid editing. In these scenes the dialogue of characters overlaps, and the noises made by medical equipment accompanied by rapid percussion music add to the sense of urgency and confusion. These action sequences used conventions deriving from **observational documentary** or news footage of action caught on the run by the camera, adding to this the uses of dramatic music and complex sound found in action drama series such as police series. *ER* claimed quality by its innovative mixing of genres and production techniques.

This chapter focuses on quality in television drama, and especially the genre of the police series, to pursue these ideas. Television police series have relatively stable formats, but this also means that interesting stylistic choices can be tried out in them without too much risk. Academic writing about the US police series has focused on common features of the genre (Buxton 1990), the institutions and creators who made programmes (Thompson 1997), or the ideological impact of representations of the police (D'Acci 1994). But there is a need for detailed analysis of television visual style in the police series. Style means the choices that directors and the production team make about:

progressive
encouraging positive change or progress, usually implying progress towards fairer and more equal ways of organising society.

status quo a Latin term meaning the ways that culture and society are currently organised.

zapping hopping rapidly from channel to channel while watching television, using a remote control (a 'zapper').

whip-pan a very rapid panning shot from one point to another.

observational documentary a documentary form in which the programme-maker aims to observe neutrally what would have happened even if he or she had not been present.

- camera movement, framing and composition
- editing and sequence structure
- colour and lighting
- performance and characterisation
- music, sound and the delivery of dialogue
- props and set decoration
- location and the significance of settings.

The conventions of the police series include the introduction of a puzzling crime, a process of investigation and then a resolution. This structure validates ideologies of law and order by demonstrating that police institutions can deal with social disruption. The structure also maps onto the television storytelling convention of dividing the storylines into 'acts', where stages in the narrative progressively move toward resolution. In the US television context, this suits the division of an hour of television into four or five segments separated by commercials. Thus the ideological project of solving crimes is mapped onto a temporal structure and an institutional structure. Style acts as a marker of a programme's distinctive identity and continuity across an evening, a week or a season, establishing a dramatic tone for each episode and the series.

These arguments have been made about the American series *CSI: Crime Scene Investigation* for example, which features a forensic team who examine evidence from Las Vegas homicides and fatal accidents (Rixon 2006, Bignell 2009). The mantle of quality police drama has been inherited by *CSI*, which was for a long time the tent-pole programme in the CBS network's Thursday schedule, the most significant weekday evening. In its second year (2001–2), *CSI* achieved the second-best ratings of any programme and in the following year was top rated. By the fifth series in 2005, the franchise had spawned the spin-off series *CSI: Miami* and *CSI: New York*, and the former was the most watched programme in the world in that year. The original *CSI* continues to be shown in **syndication** in the USA and sold to overseas broadcasters, and contributed significantly to the profile and audiences for Channel Five in the UK, for example. Shown in evening **prime-time** among a group of imported US police series, *CSI* contributed to Five's repositioning in the mid-2000s. The channel had attempted to peel away mass audiences from Britain's main **commercial terrestrial** broadcaster ITV by offering sports coverage, erotica and reruns of US films. But Five subsequently sought a reputation for quality by changing its mix of genres in evening programming, and heavily marketed a small group of imported US programmes. The naming of this strip of programmes as 'America's Finest' referenced not only the slang designation of the police force, but also the claim that these programmes represented the highest quality prime-time imports. Quality and popularity coexisted, and a British television channel sought a reputation for quality by importing US programmes.

syndication the sale of programmes for regional television broadcasters to transmit within their territory.

prime time the part of a day's television schedule when the greatest number of viewers may be watching, normally the mid-evening period.

commercial television television funded by the sale of advertising time or sponsorship of programmes.

terrestrial broadcasting from a ground-based transmission system, as opposed to broadcasting via satellite.

> **ACTIVITY 7.2**
>
> Make a list of five programmes that you think are low in quality: programmes that you might not admit to liking, or even watching at all. Are there common threads linking the programmes on your list (are they daytime television, programmes of a certain format or genre or programmes aimed at a certain audience)? Are the programmes on your list addressed by academic writing about television you have read, and if so how?

Quality and authorship

Early work in Television Studies (e.g. Brandt 1981) engaged with television drama through authorship, because methodologies for discriminating quality could be exemplified in the single television play and the prime-time, high-profile television serial. These were forms that already privileged authorship as both a differentiating **brand** and a guarantor of quality for broadcasters and reviewers. Academic studies legitimated their criteria for selection by drawing on criteria already dominant in the study of literature and theatre drama, such as complexity, social engagement, originality and ambiguity. Unsurprisingly, the resulting selection of programmes consisted of dramas by established male writers of 'serious' television plays or serials. But by our own time, research has questioned the separation of drama into the 'serious' and 'popular' and signalled an interest in reception that came from **sociology** and **anthropology** as much as from literary traditions. An implicit and sometimes explicit discrimination of quality in programmes was replaced by critical **discourses** that used programmes as locations for considering the competing claims of authorship, genre, institution and reception in determining cultural meanings.

In series where visual style is offered as one of the principal attractions of the programme, the director's contribution is significant since the director (working with a cinematographer) is responsible for creating it. Programme producers can exploit auteurism as an indication of quality. When the film director Quentin Tarantino wrote and directed the final episode of *CSI*'s fifth season, the episode garnered an audience of 30 million (McLean 2005), encouraging the identification of a directorial 'signature' by including sequences of body trauma that reference both Tarantino's film work and also the series trademarks of visceral sequences of bodily injury (see the section on *CSI* in Chapter 5). When in 2005 Quentin Tarantino wrote the storyline and directed the two-part episode of *CSI* titled 'Grave Danger', some viewers would already have known that he had worked on the episodes, but when the episodes were screened on Five, the channel made sure that viewers knew about it. The **voice-over** introduction to the programme by Five's continuity announcer informed viewers of Tarantino's involvement, and newspapers, websites and television listings magazines had already mentioned the fact. As with any episode, the director's name appeared in the opening credits of the programme and thus a graphical alert was given to announce Tarantino's role. Having been prompted to regard the involvement of Tarantino as significant, many viewers would have noticed the **intertextual** reference in the episode to Tarantino's preoccupations in the films he directed like *Reservoir Dogs*, *Pulp Fiction* or *Kill Bill*. The films

brand recognition the ability of audiences to recognise the distinctive identity of a product, service or institution and the values and meanings associated with it.

sociology the academic study of society, aiming to describe and explain aspects of life in that society.

anthropology the study of humankind, including the evolution of humans and the different kinds of human society existing in different times and places.

discourse a particular use of language for a certain purpose in a certain context (such as academic discourse, or poetic discourse), and similarly in television, a particular usage of television's audio-visual 'language' (news programme discourse or nature documentary discourse, for instance).

voice-over speech accompanying visual images but not presumed to derive from the same place or time as the images.

intertextuality how one text draws on the meanings of another by referring to it by allusion, quotation or parody, for example.

demonstrate Tarantino's interest in film history, film stars and the extreme violence of 'exploitation movies', for example the sequence in *Reservoir Dogs* in which a captured policeman is tortured by having his ear cut off. The 'Grave Danger' episode of *CSI* included:

- a brief appearance by film star Tony Curtis
- the discovery on a Las Vegas street of a pile of entrails
- the imprisonment of one main character in a transparent coffin, where he is attacked by flesh-eating ants.

It was not essential that viewers recognised the reference to Tarantino's films in order to make sense of the episode, and in fact there was no overt reference to Tarantino in the script; nor were individual camera shots direct imitations of those in Tarantino's films. Instead, the allusions were an enriching aspect of the meaning of the episodes for some viewers, a subtle joke that added a self-conscious **postmodern** playfulness.

postmodernism the most recent phase of capitalist culture, the aesthetic forms and styles associated with it and the theoretical approaches developed to understand it.

The interpretation of texts such as these, and the decision to call them postmodern because of the many intertextual references they contain, depend on the theorist's and the viewer's ability to identify these references. Postmodern play with allusions to other texts needs to be subtle, and to some extent hidden, in order for viewers to enjoy the references and to congratulate themselves on their skill at decoding them. As Robin Nelson (1997: 246) suggests: 'Postmodern texts might be summarily characterized by a formal openness, a strategic refusal to close down meaning. They create space for play between discourses allegedly empowering the reader to negotiate or construct her own meanings.' In this particular episode of *CSI*, Tarantino signalled 'quality' because he is a well-known film director, and the use of a director with a cinema reputation to direct a television programme also implies that a popular television series like *CSI* can borrow some of the cultural status of cinema. The casting of veteran film star Tony Curtis was part of the same strategy to use references to films, film stars and a film director to add a new layer of additional meaning and additional importance to the episode.

Writers and directors are still important creative figures, but so are the producers (who also often write episodes). The ways that US television has been made since about 1980 have given greater creative control over programmes to creator-producer-writers rather than episode directors or screenwriters (Pearson 2005). The same phenomenon has been taking hold in Britain too. These people are known as 'showrunners', and they work in some combination of series creator, writer and producer. They devise programme **formats**, defining the 'look' of programmes in collaboration with the directors. They also outline the main characters, settings and genre components (detective story, family comedy, thriller or more often a combination of these). Once a series format is devised, a robust production system can be established in which numerous freelance writers and directors can contribute to the format, overseen by the showrunner as creator and manager. For example, the subject of this chapter's case study, *The Wire*, was created by David Simon, who made great claims for its innovations in the police genre, but also for its importance more widely in television fiction. Simon argued that *The Wire* took television's possibilities for storytelling more seriously than hitherto, and required the kinds of concentrated attention and commitment from the viewer that might more usually

format the blueprint for a programme, including its setting, main characters, genre, form and main themes.

be expected in the literary novel. While these comments implied that television viewers are usually rather passive and needed to be taught how to view a series like *The Wire*, they also implied that television fiction could aspire to equality with 'serious' art forms.

The valuation of showrunners and screenwriters in discussions and advertising of television fiction has meant that the visual means of realising scripts have received less attention. But the work of actors and directors who create moments of character revelation by means of performance and visual style, rather than the linguistic qualities of the script, characterise the US series that are considered quality television drama. The reason that 'quality television' is often called 'cinematic' is partly because of these emphases on visual style and performance style. Indeed in some programmes (for example, in *The Wire*), dialogue is often spoken too quietly or too quickly to hear. Where programmes investigate the complexities of character and the environments where characters live, they tend to focus not only on dialogue, but also on psychological revelation through facial expression, gesture and movement. These are the main emphases of actor training in Britain and even more so in the USA. US actors are mainly based in Hollywood and cross between work in theatre, cinema and television. This minimises the differences of performance style between the different media and also connects television with film in terms of performance.

ACTIVITY 7.3

Do some research into the 'Method' acting style that is dominant in the USA and also used in the UK for actor training. How might this way of approaching acting work best for some kinds of television drama and less well for others?

Channels and brands in American television drama

Changes in institutional and technological contexts provided the conditions for the changing attitudes in Television Studies to the aesthetics of popular generic programmes. In Britain's 'era of scarcity' (Ellis 2000b: 39–60) or in the USA's period of network dominance, just two or three UK channels and three US networks provided a restricted diet of television that was aimed at mass audiences. Developing a distinctive aesthetic was not very significant when there was a restricted diet of programming for mass audiences, the kinds of programmes that are definitively 'popular'. After this period of what the US network NBC's executive Paul Klein (1975) called 'least objectionable programming', both British and US network television changed significantly during the 1980s and 1990s. From the 1980s onwards the emergence of US cable channels (especially HBO) challenged network dominance, and a culture of programmes for niche audiences came about, supported by programme-related **merchandise** (especially retail videotape and DVD versions) (Curtin 2003). Such series aim to be seen as quality programmes, and:

- encourage sustained viewing by loyal audiences
- create distinctive visual styles and characters

merchandising the sale of products associated with a television programme, such as toys, books or clothing.

■ develop complex storylines across several episodes
■ blend genres together.

In America the phenomenon was mainly dependent on long-running drama series, such as *Hill Street Blues* in the 1980s and *ER* in the 1990s (Thompson 1997). The emergence of 'cult' programmes, repeated viewing, programme-related merchandise and the sale of formats were significantly dependent on the stylishness developed in these serials and series. The US television networks now fund the production of 'must-see' programmes to create strong brands for their programmes and for the network that shows them. The American cable network AMC, for example, gained high public profile for its series *Mad Men*, about advertising executives in the 1960s. Its attention to elaborately recreating the settings and costumes of the era can be seen in Figure 7.4, in which lighting and composition combine to make a dialogue scene visually very satisfying.

This situation questions the continued purchase of the concept of the glance for describing television viewership, since attentiveness is both invited and rewarded by these 'quality' programmes. It also questions the usefulness of the concept of **flow** in describing television's temporality, since flow refers both to the continuous broadcast of programmes one after another (often interrupted by commercials and trailers) and also to the viewing experience as a flowing sequence. Popular programmes that foreground visual style and narrative complexity implicitly attempt to stand outside of flow, and are marketed with such designations as 'appointment television' or 'must-see TV' that draw attention to this claim. The entire cable channel HBO, for example, marketed itself with the slogan 'it's not TV, it's HBO', which among other meanings alludes to visual brands or signature styles in distinction to earlier phases of television. Indeed, the fact that *The Wire* was made by HBO is important to its relationships with other television programmes and audiences. The network screened a range of critically acclaimed television drama series before *The Wire*, including *Oz*, *Sex and the City*, *The Sopranos* and *Deadwood*. HBO markets its services on the basis that it offers 'quality' drama that its

flow the ways in which programmes, advertisements, etc. follow one another in an unbroken sequence across the day or part of the day, and the experience of watching the sequence of programmes, advertisements, trailers, etc.

Figure 7.4 Visual quality in *Mad Men*.

subscribers should be willing to pay to see. It thus deliberately addresses its audience (and people who might be persuaded to join that audience) as a select group, a **niche audience** who demand a superior quality of programme compared to the **free-to-air** television networks (Leverette *et al.* 2008). It took several years for *The Wire* to be acquired for screening in Britain, and the series did not appear on terrestrial television but instead on the **cable channel** FX in 2005. Since FX was not available to any but a small group of British viewers, and in the UK cable channels do not have the same size or status as in the US, relatively few British viewers saw the programme. The FX channel was trying, however, to achieve something like the same significance as HBO as a niche channel, and therefore acquired *The Wire* alongside drama imports from the HBO and Showtime networks. It was noticed by some reviewers in broadsheet newspapers (especially *The Guardian*) but even when the first series was released on DVD in 2005, repeated on FX in 2007, and the British Film Institute in London arranged for David Simon to introduce a screening from series five in 2008, it had taken three years for the series to be noticed by a wider audience. British viewers experienced *The Wire* mainly as a boxed DVD set, therefore, until it was acquired by BBC2 for screening on terrestrial television in 2009.

Television like this is not designed to respond to the traditional notions of the glance and undifferentiated flow that have been adopted for describing television viewing. Quality programmes' creative imagination, authenticity or relevance might instead suggest links with cinema, visual art or theatre, and thus quality comes to mean 'not-like-television'. The distinctive use of style is a reason why generic programmes can become labelled as 'quality' television drama. Stereo sound, CGI and post-production effects technology have offered further opportunities for making visually distinctive narratives. The significance of these different production technologies is to contribute to the audience appeal of programmes when they are launched, and to the appeal of 'landmark' programmes when they are watched again. Style is a way of addressing and retaining viewers who want to see distinctive programmes, and fan audiences and 'cult' or niche programmes are now very significant.

Many of the American series discussed in this chapter were shot on film, rather than videotape or into a digital memory. In the USA, there is a long history of television series production based in Hollywood, using the studios and personnel originally established for cinema. The emphasis on a visual look for each programme can be achieved by drawing on the greater depth of colour, contrasts of lighting and more elaborate camera movement that occur when shooting on film. In contrast, other television forms such as the sitcom or **soap opera** are shot with multi-camera setups and less investment in the look of the finished programme. For film cameras, each shot has to be individually lit and the camera re-positioned. By shooting using single film cameras in both interiors and exteriors, a consistent visual style becomes possible and this look works together with extended narrative arcs, and continuities of settings and characters. We can see how the detective series *CSI* was designed with a signature visual look in mind by considering what its producers and directors put in place in the early episodes of the series.

CSI was created by Anthony Zuicker, and jointly produced by the Hollywood **production company** run by Jerry Bruckheimer (who made *Beverly Hills Cop*, *Top Gun* and *Pirates of the Carribean*, for example). The visual style of strong primary colours and frequent use of extreme close-ups of bodily injury was consciously

subscription payment to a television broadcaster in exchange for the opportunity to view programmes on certain channels that are otherwise blocked.

niche audiences particular groups of viewers defined by age group, gender or economic status, for example, who may be the target audience for a programme.

free-to-air television programming for which viewers make no direct payment.

cable television originally called Community Antenna Television (CATV). Transmission of television signals along cables in the ground.

soap opera a continuing drama serial involving a large number of characters in a specific location, focusing on relationships, emotions and reversals of fortune.

independent production companies businesses making television programmes which can be sold to television networks that transmit and distribute them.

designed to ensure the differentiation of the series from competing programmes. Roy Wagner, *CSI*'s first director of photography, recalled: 'Bruckheimer had demanded a show so stylistically different that a channel-surfing audience would be forced to stop and view the unusual looking images' (Lury 2005: 38). The unusual images included rapid zooms towards and inside body parts created by means of computer generated imagery and props representing body parts. The studio sets use glass, chrome and other reflective surfaces, so that one area can be seen through another. The effect is to layer spaces one in front of another, emphasising the activities of looking, reflecting and observing that the characters carry out. There are often coloured lights in the backgrounds of shots to draw the eye from the foreground to the background. Many sequences in *CSI* are very dark, created by a digital effect that exaggerates colour contrasts and shadows. Slow camera movements around the dimly lit crime labs show the characters conducting scientific investigations of evidence, seeming to indicate a world which is knowable by the characters and the camera. That knowledge is gained by their special kinds of looking such as the technological examination of evidence in the lab, or reconstructions of a crime. But the investigators' hypotheses are sometimes wrong and are very frequently modified. Events in the past are reconstructed fragmentarily, and more evidence often revises them. Thus the camera's ability to convey reliable information is put into question, at the same time as the investigator characters' ability to make sense of the evidence is also challenged.

Visual style is the crucial means for viewers to access a programme's fictional world. By giving and withholding knowledge of that world, visual style shapes what can be known and what the limits of access to it are. For example, the viewer can be made to feel closer or more distant from the character's experience, and the viewer may know more or less than the characters at any given moment. Such a difference of knowledge could produce effects of suspense, comedy or sympathy, for example. The conventions of the police series suggest that just as crimes can be solved, so fictional narrative can understand people, action and society. But the police series as a television form is equally concerned with what can be only incompletely seen, known and resolved (Bignell 2007a). Visual style is concerned with how seeing and knowing works for the characters, how this is presented to the viewer and how the viewer is able to see and know in similar and different ways from them. So **point of view** and the visual realisation of the fictional world are crucial, and by analysing a common fiction genre like the police series, we can see how visual style in some programmes is crucial to quality rather than being secondary to characterisation and story. Those US series considered quality television have shared characteristics, to the extent that they could even comprise a genre:

point of view shot
a camera shot where the camera is placed in, or close to, the position from where a previously seen character might look.

- they conform to audiences' expectations of genre, but also sidestep or extend genre conventions by means of visual pleasure and spectacle.
- they are made as long-running series television but they are 'cinematically' rich in visual terms.
- they have prominent writer-producers and sometimes also prominent directors, who become widely known for their 'brand identity'
- they use US settings and the resources of Hollywood's production system but they are also recognised by British and other international audiences, critics and broadcasters as quality television.

Visual style and the *Doctor Who* brand

The distinctive qualities of the BBC series *Doctor Who* are bound up with its visual style (Bignell 2013), and make connections with the discussion of quality TV in the mainly American context discussed so far. *Doctor Who* was first made in the 1960s era of live, studio-based, multi-camera television with monochrome pictures. However, technical innovations have given *Doctor Who*'s creators new ways of making visually distinctive narratives since the programme was recreated in 2005. These changes since the original 1960s series include:

- shooting in colour
- stereo sound
- CGI and post-production effects
- using High Definition (HD) cameras
- longer 50-minute episodes.

In relation to the reception of programmes, viewers' ability to watch *Doctor Who* on high-specification television sets, and to record and repeat episodes using digital media, also encourage attention to visual style as an indication of quality. For example, visual spectacle using **green-screen** and CGI can function as a set-piece (at the opening or ending of an episode). Shooting on location using HD cameras provides a rich and detailed image texture. *Doctor Who* needs to provide a satisfying experience for this wide range of viewers and viewing contexts. This is because television has become an aspect of media **convergence** culture in the developed world, where production technologies, programme texts and fictional genres cross back and forth from one viewing platform to another. The programme must work on large-screen HD TV sets as well as computer monitors or on the tiny screen of a mobile phone. *Doctor Who* has been leading the BBC's extension of its programmes beyond conventional broadcasting, both to reinforce the programme's powerful brand and to demonstrate the BBC's commitment to convergent technologies. Using *Doctor Who*, BBC has pioneered **spin-offs** such as 'mobisodes', games and SMS feeds. *Doctor Who* needs to be made with these new viewing contexts in mind, and it is a vehicle for bringing the BBC as a brand into the consciousness of the mainly young people who use these new media technologies. These factors affect what *Doctor Who* episodes look like, and how episodes and seasons are structured.

The **production values** of television drama are perpetually increasing (Nelson 2007) and digital technologies have increased the sharpness and complexity of both images and sound. Television is made in very much the same ways as cinema and animation, because of the convergence of television's digital production systems with the technologies used by specialist visual effects companies who work in several media. All original BBC dramas are now shot in HD, and edited and post-produced digitally. The all-digital workflow in production, which can integrate inputs from a range of sources at different stages of production, has been used to drive consumer demand for digital reception technologies like widescreen and HD television sets, projectors and surround-sound. This emphasis on visual quality (and on sound, to a lesser extent) stimulates television makers to exploit its capabilities. Like other contemporary series such as *Spooks* and *Hustle*, *Doctor Who* also accommodates itself to American norms of production and genre expectation. In the commercial context

green-screen
shooting action against a green background so that images from another source can be pasted in to replace the green background.

convergence
the process whereby previously separate media technologies merge together. For example, computers can now send faxes, show DVD films and play music.

spin-off a product, television programme, book, etc. that is created to exploit the reputation, meaning or commercial success of a previous one, often in a different medium from the original.

production values
the level of investment in a television production, such as the amount spent on costumes, props, effects and sets.

of overseas sales, where *Doctor Who* will be seen on overseas commercial channels, its form needs to accommodate four 'acts' per episode that will be separated by commercial breaks, so each segment will have a development that leads to a moment of tension or suspense.

ACTIVITY 7.4

Visit the website of BBC America. How does the channel promote itself in terms of 'quality' and how is this connected with the channel's British origins?

Quality drama in the UK and USA can be defined in part by how it recruits involved and active viewers by offering aesthetically challenging programmes that combine visual spectacle with dramatic complexity. *Doctor Who* is screened in the USA on the subscription cable channel BBC America. BBC America positions itself alongside HBO and other cable networks that address the 'quality' audience of wealthier and more educated viewers. When Steven Moffat took over the show-runner role for *Doctor Who* in 2009, the tone and visual style of the series was deliberately altered to emphasise a fantasy or fairytale quality, not only in the writing but also in the visual look of the episodes. The HD cameras, lenses and the directors of photography that were used to shoot the episodes, are a way of making television that has a lot in common with cinema. Moffat's new series declared an interest in the visual set-piece from the very start of the first episode he was showrunner for, 'The Eleventh Hour'. The TARDIS hurtles over London at the height of several hundred feet, with its doors hanging open and the Doctor dangling out, and then crashes into Amy Pond's garden. The pace and changing point of view in the sequence seem calculated to encourage an appreciation of visual excitement. The sequence contributes little to the plot or to the exploration of character, but it encourages a sense of awe and admiration for its expertise, and in this respect it is comparable to the opening 'hook' sequences of blockbuster action movies, where the cinema viewer is quickly rewarded with an exciting opening. In the opening TARDIS flight of 'The Eleventh Hour', the rapid movement is a visual tour-de-force in itself. It is a helicopter shot that has been digitally overlaid with studio-shot green-screen sequences of the Doctor dangling from the TARDIS, and it is the roller-coaster pace of the editing of the sequence that is responsible for its impact as much as the visual content of any particular shot.

Doctor Who's first showrunner from 2005 was Russell T. Davies, who reshaped the format by planning lengthy story arcs that comprise both set-piece action sequences and moments of high-budget spectacle. Davies's work can be seen as an attempt to transcend the perceived limitations of visual style in the *Doctor Who* format. In an interview (Sleight 2011: 15), Davies said that 'the thing that enticed me to do *Doctor Who* [was] – big pictures. Television doesn't do that enough; most television is people sitting there talking.' Davies' and Moffat's approaches are linked by their commitment to story arcs that link stories together and lead to extended, two-part finales. But CGI is also used in 'invisible' ways to enhance the drama rather than to draw attention to itself. For example, in the shooting of the eleventh season finales 'The Pandorica Opens' and 'The Big Bang', the director Toby Haynes reported (Spilsbury 2010: 30) that the effects team from The Mill had specially sent a camera crew to Kew Gardens in London to shoot the leaves of tropical plants so that these detailed shots could be merged into the digitally created jungle of an alien planet environment for close-ups. Here, CGI and especially shot frames were knitted together so that the CGI sequences appeared equally as realistic as the shots made in the studio using 'practical' (physically constructed) props and sets. CGI in *Doctor Who* is used to create monsters and other entities that are intended to appear as though they are physically present in the fictional world, or else CGI is used in ways that conceal post-production work and should be unnoticed by the viewer.

ACTIVITY 7.5

What can you find out about the careers of Russell T. Davies and Steven Moffat before they became showrunners for *Doctor Who*? Do you think their previous work would have given them a reputation for making 'quality TV'?

As well as overseeing the making of a specified number of hours of drama, Moffat is the manager of a very valuable commercial asset. Part of his job is to protect and enhance the *Doctor Who* brand. The *Doctor Who* franchise is a significant contributor to BBC Worldwide's income from overseas sales and merchandising. It is not just the look of the screened episodes that counts, but also how they function as products in themselves and exist in a relationship with further non-televisual products that express that visual look in another medium. The possibility of recording time-shifted episodes and rewatching them has an impact on the attention given by viewers to spectacular sequences and special effects, as well as on the dramatic moments of character revelation and the unfolding of extended story arcs (Kompare 2005, 2006). In the UK context, *Doctor Who* has maintained a large audience for its first broadcast showing, but has also gathered large audiences in repeats on the BBC3 digital channel, on the iPlayer internet-based delivery system and in time-shifted recordings where viewers watch the episodes at a time subsequent to their first broadcast. While the 2008 series in which the Doctor was played by David Tennant averaged 7.2 million viewers compared to Moffat and Matt Smith's 2010 season at six million viewers, these figures look very different when time-shifted recordings are included. Viewing of recordings from Sky+ and other systems raise the audience of the 2010 series finale to 6.7 million viewers and a near 37 per cent **audience share**. The BBC claimed an average audience for Matt Smith's Doctor of seven million viewers. The scheduling of the finale was also significant, since *Doctor Who* had to compete with the Wimbledon tennis championships and World Cup football.

Texts in the wider *Doctor Who* franchise include behind-the-scenes commentary on how special effects work is achieved, for example in the *Confidentials* series; box set DVD extras and **interactive** media outlets that expand the narrative. When 'The Eleventh Hour' was advertised in late March 2010 before its first screening, Moffat's opening sequence of the TARDIS over London was made available on the BBC

audience share the percentage of viewers estimated to have watched one channel as opposed to another channel broadcasting at the same time.

interactive offering the opportunity for viewers to respond to what is broadcast, by sending signals back to the broadcaster (along a cable or phone line, for example).

teaser a very short television sequence advertising a forthcoming programme, often puzzling or teasing to viewers because it contains little information and encourages curiosity and interest.

storyboard a sequence of drawn images showing the shots to be used in a programme.

website and the interactive 'red button' digital television service. It is significant that it was this high-speed effects sequence that was chosen as the **teaser** for the series, to showcase its visual appeal. Moreover, a series of short videos about the making of the effects sequence was added to the website and red button feed. The pre-visualisation artist Dan May explained how he constructed the CGI animation from a **storyboard**, and James Swanson, director of photography for the helicopter sequence, described the experience of making it. The forces that impact on *Doctor Who* are dynamic and often contradictory. Emergent technologies of production and reception, like shooting in HD or watching on Blu-ray, have made it possible for a long-running series programme like *Doctor Who* to emulate what Moffat and other members of the production team perceive as 'cinematic' visual quality. What they mean by this encompasses several aspects of the production:

- the greater level of visual detail that can be captured by the camera, which leads to greater attention to the details of make-up, costume, set dressing and lighting
- the integration of special effects into episodes. Although many effects are still created by models, prosthetics or props, the notion of visual quality predominantly means post-production effects created by CGI
- visual scale that is most clearly seen in set-piece action sequences, often at the beginnings or ends of episodes.

Moffat's aim of an expansive, large-scale, visually sumptuous look for *Doctor Who* has had to be realised inventively with restricted budgets, and this has often brought benefits in adapting storylines to available resources and strengthening the attention to character that has always been central to the format.

ACTIVITY 7.6

Choose a recent episode of *Doctor Who*, and analyse it to identify specific examples that could demonstrate that the programme is 'quality TV' according to definitions discussed in this chapter.

Quality US police drama before *The Wire*

Much of the commentary from the producers, viewers and writers about *The Wire* made it appear distinct from the television surrounding it, and even depicted it as a programme that is not television at all as it is conventionally understood. In reality, *The Wire* could be more accurately thought of as a programme that draws on a tradition of quality police dramas and borrows from traditions in other genres too, as this chapter's case study argues in more detail. Indeed, one of the things that defines what genre means is the idea that genres shift over time, mix with each other and change their relationships to each other. This can even include self-conscious allusions by programmes in one genre to programmes in other genres, and the American television theorist John Caldwell (2008) has argued that in the past couple of decades and more, television professionals have deliberately moved towards this hybridity between genres and this self-consciousness about their conventions. The ongoing storylines but different focal points in the separate seasons, combined with episodes that develop characters and storylines in a combination of free-standing incidents and sections of longer narratives arcs, make the series hard to classify. It is in a tradition of innovative genre dramas that mix the series and serial forms. The narrative of *The Wire* is certainly complex, with several storylines running at the same time and a large cast of main characters (Mittell 2006, Nanicelli 2009). Although this makes the programme distinctive compared especially to older, mainstream police and detective dramas, some of its components are routinely found in other television genres. Multiple narrative strands and a large group of characters are found in all television soap operas, for example, though soaps do not move towards a conclusion; and like soap opera the programme's narrative is carried by its dialogue rather than set-piece moments of remarkable visual style.

Around the beginning of the 1980s, it became increasingly common for television drama to combine the one-off storylines that are components of the series form with the serial form's ongoing development of characters and storylines across episodes. At the same time, television directors used more cuts within and between storylines, getting straight to moments of action or psychological revelation. The reason for these changes was the attempt by US television networks to peel audiences in high-income and well-educated **demographic** groups away from the emergent cable networks. To begin this section's account of a few of the quality police dramas that laid the foundations for *The Wire*, it is useful to begin with *Hill Street Blues*, a series that started at the beginning of the 1980s just as US television underwent the changes discussed. *Hill Street Blues* was not a ratings success and finished its first season as the 87th most popular programme that year (Feuer 1984: 25–8). However, the series was renewed for another year by NBC because it gained significant numbers of affluent urban viewers in the18 to 49 age group, for whom advertisers would pay premium rates. The series was also critically praised and eventually won the Emmy award for Outstanding Drama Series five times. We can see from this contextual information how the popularity of *Hill Street Blues* with mass audiences was less important than its popularity with a 'quality audience', and its recognition as high quality by informed commentators in the television industry.

> **demography** the study of population, and the groupings of people (demographic groups) within the whole population.

Hill Street Blues followed a group of uniformed police and detectives based in an urban police station. It ran from 1981 to 87 on the NBC network in the USA, and was created and executive produced by Steven Bochco and Michael Kozoll for the MTM company. It was the first in a long run of critical successes that established Bochco's reputation as a television 'auteur'. Bochco and Kozoll had co-written the police drama *Delvecchio* in 1976–7, while Bochco himself had written scripts for the detective dramas *Ironside* and *McMillan and Wife* in the 1970s, for example. He was the story editor and chief writer for *Columbo* in 1971. So *Hill Street Blues* was created by a team who had long experience of the genre conventions of police drama. *Hill Street Blues*' complex serial and series storylines were woven around about a dozen recurring characters (Stempel 1996: 227–36), and the actors in the programme overwhelmingly consisted of performers who had already worked either in Bochco's previous series, with the MTM company in other workplace series, or in the *Police Story* series of 1973–77 (Kerr 1984: 150). *Hill Street Blues* had a level of 'realism' that was ground-breaking at the time, and this was conveyed by a visual style that was borrowed from US **documentary**. In particular, the series imitated *The Police Tapes*, a documentary series made on portable video cameras for the PBS network in 1976.

> **documentary** a form aiming to record actual events, often with an explanatory purpose or to analyse and debate an issue.

Reviews of *Hill Street Blues* on its US debut in January 1981 and its British premiere in early 1982 focused on its realism (Jenkins 1984: 184–6) and the US television critic Todd Gitlin (1983: 274) opened his chapter on the series with the bald statement that '*Hill Street Blues*'s achievement was first of all a matter of style', in other words its documentary style.

ACTIVITY 7.7

The MTM company that produced *Hill Street Blues* was a pioneer in making 'quality' television fiction in the USA. What can you discover about how its other programmes conformed to genres you are familiar with (like sitcom or hospital drama) but also used genre in innovative ways?

The director of the pilot for *Hill Street Blues* and the first four episodes, Robert Butler, had a long career in television drama going back to live studio plays and had also worked with Bochco on *Columbo* (Gitlin 1983: 290). Making the episodes subsequent to the pilot in blocks of four enabled Butler (and later directors) to save time and money by shooting locations for more than one episode at the same time, thus providing opportunities for more elaborate lighting and rehearsal. The overall effect was to prioritise the visual look of the series, and to allow the performers to develop an ensemble style of acting, where they each contributed to making the fictional world seem authentic and coherent. This made it possible to develop a hybrid of comedy and realism that worked by choreographing multi-character scenes in a crowded studio set, with relatively few exterior scenes. Nevertheless, the large cast and complex filming process made production very expensive, and Bochco was asked to quit his job as producer in 1985 (Marc and Thompson 1995: 225).

Hill Street Blues is a hybrid of many different genres. It is a workplace drama like some sitcoms of the 1970s, such as *M*A*S*H* in which US doctors serve in the Korean War. *Hill Street Blues*' documentary style portrays the city as a 'war zone' while infusing it with comedy. According to Paul Kerr (1984: 148–9), NBC network head Fred Silverman prompted the creation of the series by asking for a hybrid of *M*A*S*H*, the police sitcom *Barney Miller*, the gritty police film *Fort Apache, The Bronx* and the television drama series *Police Story*. As in a documentary, some shots are unsteady so that they look as if they were filmed with a hand-held camera, and the action may be obscured by objects or by people in the frame. These observational techniques are combined with editing techniques that illuminate the fictional characters and their storylines. An improvisational acting ensemble was hired to create ambient sounds of conversation that was added to the episodes in post-production (Gitlin 1983: 294). Thus the style of *Hill Street Blues* was carefully designed to convey a messy realism that placed the viewer in the midst of the police's experience. Scenes outside the police station followed the police, rather than establishing the place before their arrival. The consequent giving and withholding of information in *Hill Street Blues* contrasts with detective series that give the viewer privileged access to the fictional world in advance of the main character's encounter with it.

By the 1990s Steven Bochco had become a highly respected creator of television series that were renowned for their innovation and their ability to attract the knowledgeable, wealthy viewers that American television channels wanted because such viewers were attractive to advertisers. Bochco went on to create the police drama *NYPD Blue* with David Milch, and the series ran on the US ABC network from 1993 to 2006. Like *Hill Street Blues*, there was extensive use of mobile camera, but unlike the earlier series, it used prominent music to underscore emotion. The lead actor Dennis Franz played Lt. Andy Sipowicz, and had appeared in other Bochco productions (*Hill Street Blues*, *Bay City Blues* and Milch's *Hill Street* spin-off *Beverly Hills Buntz*, for example). While Bochco was seen as the author of the series, he was working with a relatively constant team of collaborators behind and in front of the camera. In terms of visual style, *NYPD Blue* was distinguished by its moving camera, fluid shot composition, percussive music track and use of slow motion. A shocking decision (later used in many other series) was to apparently fatally wound Sipowicz in the opening episode, seeming to break the convention of the police series that the main characters will always survive unscathed. The first and second episodes were written by Milch, and shot over twenty days in Los Angeles at 20th Century Fox studios and on location in New York's Lower East Side (Milch and Clark 1996: 27). New York location sequences featuring the city's skyline or subway stations were shot to establish place, and studio shots in Los Angeles used back-lighting in contrast with natural light to signify the strong shadows created by New York's tall buildings and neon lights (Fisher 1996). The visual style uses a wandering camera with off-centre composition and constant reframing, apparently uncertain about where the centre of action is. The series producer Greg Hoblit labelled this the 'fishing pass' technique, and it was used alongside fast **pans** from one speaker to another as if the camera were reacting to unexpected events. Hoblit called this fast panning style the 'flicking eye' technique or 'dektoring' (after the US director Leslie Dektor), and in the early seasons it was *NYPD Blue*'s distinctive trademark.

pan a shot where the camera is turned to the left or turned to the right. The term derives from the word 'panorama', suggesting the wide visual field that a pan can reveal.

This brief look at US television police series can most usefully end with the series that established the reputation of the creator of *The Wire*, David Simon. *Homicide Life on the Street* was screened on the NBC network from 1993 to 99, then syndicated on the Lifetime cable network in the USA, and has also been imported by Channel 4 in Britain. The series was based on the book, *Homicide: A Year on the Killing Streets* by the *Baltimore Sun* newspaper reporter David Simon, who spent a year with the Baltimore police's homicide unit. The producer and screenwriter Barry Levinson initially planned to adapt the book into a cinema film (Troy 1997), having been attracted by the book's distinct sense of place. Levinson's conception of the television series emphasises its locations, which are distinct from the more usual police series locations of Los Angeles and New York. Levinson even required *Homicide*'s writers to work on-site in Baltimore (Troy 1997), so they could understand the place and how Baltimore residents speak. The co-executive producer Tom Fontana commented that: 'What attracted Barry [Levinson] and me to the material is that these are thinking cops . . . they can be articulate. They can have a way with language that the audience will enjoy watching' (Troy 1997). The series allows characters to speak at length, and the viewer sees Baltimore through the characters' interactions with each other in dialogue. The directors use **long takes** to extend the viewer's experience of time. Generically, *Homicide* shifts between comedy and crime drama and is not so much focused on solving crimes as gaining insight into the experiences of the detectives themselves.

long take an imprecise term denoting a longer than usual uninterrupted camera shot.

Case study: *The Wire*

The Wire is an American police series created by David Simon, a journalist and television writer, together with Ed Burns, a teacher and former police officer. It was made by the US cable television network Home Box Office (HBO) and ran for five series between 2002 and 2008 (Rose 2008). *The Wire* has an evolving storyline arc (Kinder 2008) that runs across four seasons of thirteen episodes and a final season of ten episodes, and each season is based around an institutional organisation (MacMillan 2009). The first season was based around a police investigation into organised drug-dealing, and was set in the American city of Baltimore. While the police themselves were central characters, there was equal attention to the lives of the mainly black young men who ran the drug supply organisation in the city's public housing estates ('the projects'). The first series included some of the political complexities of the police department and the politicians seeking to control and influence its work. This interest in the powers behind the scenes was extended in the second and subsequent series. In the second season, the impact of post-industrial recession on manual workers is explored using the port of Baltimore as the main location. The third season considers whether political institutions in the city can offer hope for improvement. The fourth season deals with the school system and the ways it provides or frustrates opportunities for children. The last season is set among newspaper and television workers and asks how they might encourage reflection on the problems of the city. David Simon is seen (and sees himself) as the creator and controller of the world of *The Wire*, as an auteur, and outside of the series he shares in the mastery of the fictional world as much as the main characters who also attempt to understand the reality they inhabit within the programme.

The Wire may be attractive to viewers not only for its qualities as fiction, but also because it matches television's ability as a medium to address the concerns of its viewers about contemporary anxieties. The programme is explicitly about how crime, corruption and social disorder should be managed, and how those people with responsibility for dealing with social problems might contribute to those problems at the same time as they try to solve them. All police drama is about the topic of law and order, but *The Wire* specifically features storylines about contemporary issues including:

- the role of surveillance
- how America's 'war on drugs' is fought
- how terrorism and 'the war on terror' have affected attitudes to policing.

The Wire addresses these narrative themes in a highly 'realistic' way by means of its visual style and uses of sound. Just as the literary novel is regarded as the most 'realistic' of literary genres, so *The Wire* aims for a kind of television realism that matches the characteristics that the literary theorist Raymond Williams (1977) outlined. Its creators claim that it authentically represents the city of Baltimore and uses Baltimore to accurately represent the social, economic and political problems of an urban America where traditional industries and communities have broken down. Baltimore is, in a sense, a character in *The Wire* as much as any of its human characters. The narrative pace of *The Wire* is very slow and there are very few climaxes. For example, most of the first season is devoted to the plans to set up a wire tap in order to gather evidence on a drug-dealing organisation. In genre terms, *The Wire* works against the viewer's expectations because of the lack of fast-paced action (Mittell 2009). Its organisation into seasons also means that many of the main protagonists from season one do not even appear in subsequent seasons. However, the similarity that they share is the location and narrative world of Baltimore itself. Settings create a kind of symbolic geography of the city, where some characters (like the teenage drug dealers) can be at home in a place (such as the wasteland around the public housing projects) where others (the police) are alien outsiders. In Figure 7.5, taken from the first episode, the camera position is at a distance from the drug dealers on the sofa in the projects. That distance, and the presence of a clothes line obscuring the top of the shot, draws attention to the problem that outsiders have in accessing the drug dealers' space. The police, and to some extent the politicians and media workers of *The Wire*, are able to move between places to make sense of them and their interrelationships, while the less powerful local population are stuck in their neighbourhoods.

These distinctions of belonging or exclusion are also evident in the kinds of speech that characters use. Slang and nicknames are used extensively by the characters, and this makes it evident that they belong to overlapping or occasionally separate social worlds that are expressed in their language. For the police and other institutional professionals, there is also technical language that is specific to their jobs. Season one was based around setting up a wire tap to record conversations that could be presented as evidence in court. Battles to control the urban environment of Baltimore are fought in part by imposing one kind of language on another, for example when witnesses to crime are required to give their evidence in 'normal' English rather than in local slang. The police try to intervene in, and travel among, the different linguistic communities of Baltimore and sort out the hierarchy of power among them by speaking and listening. The police employ a 'translator' who transposes the overheard conversations of the wire tap into 'normal' English. The character Bubbles is a drug addict and informer who crosses the boundaries in the city and also eventually crosses over from addiction and the criminal underworld to 'normality' and 'normal' speech.

Despite being a very speech-oriented series, much of the dialogue breaks the television convention that sound will convey information clearly (Altman 1986). Viewers were prepared

Figure 7.5 Drug dealers in *The Wire*.

for this by the first season's opening caption 'Listen carefully', and DVD versions of *The Wire* are available with subtitles. With a screening on terrestrial television, a considerable number of viewers were also able to record it and re-watch it. At the same time in the late 2000s, academic studies of *The Wire* began to appear (Potter and Marshall 2009, Vest 2011). Newspaper articles on *The Wire*, as well as other sources such as internet discussion boards, offer frameworks for how to approach a viewing of the series. The predominant tone of these surrounding texts is admiration for the achievement of the production team and especially the writer–creator, David Simon. *The Wire* has been increasingly understood as a high-quality text that rewards repeated viewing and further study, so that an enriched and more complex response to the programme can be gained. Academic Television Studies have not only argued recently that television programmes can and should be approached in this way (Akass and McCabe 2004, 2005; McCabe and Akass 2006), but that *The Wire* in particular is suited to this kind of approach. Once a programme is available as a DVD, the possibility of giving it sustained attention over a period of concentrated viewing is much more likely than if a programme is watched in weekly episodes. Viewing on DVD permits re-watching that is suited to *The Wire*'s complex storylines and fragmentary, slang dialogue that is hard to hear on first watching.

In common with most police and detective series, the law enforcement officers of *The Wire* need to understand the urban environment in which they and the people they encounter operate. This can be seen in the police series that preceded *The Wire*, including *Homicide: Life on the Street*, *NYPD Blue* and *The Shield*. These series of the 1990s and 2000s themselves draw on narrative structures and visual styles that have been important to police series of decades before. The police series has a range of sub-genres, and the one that *The Wire* fits best is the sub-genre of the police procedural. This form tracks the police in their everyday work, and places them in the culture of the police institution. This culture is distinct from one where individuals operate on their own (often against the system, as maverick cops) or where work colleagues have family-like relationships. In the first series, the police detective McNulty is the focus for this investigation of the city and the struggle to understand and control it. McNulty is accompanied by protagonists on the other side of the law, such as the drug gang leader Omar and the itinerant addict and informer Bubbles. But none of them are able to comprehend the complexity of the fictional world, and instead the alternation between their stories and their experiences of the city are held together by the ability of the camera to follow them and see from their points of view.

This case study shows how *The Wire* fits the criteria explored in this chapter for identifying quality television. It is innovative, complex, engaged in significant debates about the politics of the contemporary city and its problems and offers the pleasures of an extended and rich fictional world. But thinking in terms of the emphases of Television Studies, a focus on *The Wire* also raises some questions about what quality means. *The Wire* rewards attention to its literary qualities, as an ambiguous, complex and relevant work and as an example of authorial creativity. These ways of evaluating television tend to envisage value as being determined by how much a programme is not like other television but is instead like a novel, or an art film. It has been ascribed a similar value to a literary novel, and this is also partly because of its extended narrative with evolving storylines. Extended serial forms permit television programmes to create a fictional world in great detail and to represent the points of view of many characters. This scale is also a means to portray a fictional world that *The Wire*'s creators want to critique, and it allows them to show how the dynamics of personal and social relationships are affected by the workings of power and politics in that world. So the programme is also specifically televisual, especially in its exploitation of serial form.

SUMMARY OF KEY POINTS

- Quality in television has been assessed by comparing programmes with texts in other media, such as cinema, theatre and literature.
- Quality in television has also been assessed by analysing how programmes make creative use of television's distinctive features as an audio-visual medium.
- The contributions of key authorial figures, and the social status of a programme's audiences, are aspects of quality as much as the characteristics of a programme itself.
- Producing quality programmes is important to promoting the brand identities of the production companies and channels that make and show the programmes.
- The concept of quality television has changed its meaning over time, and changed its relationships with genre.

Further reading

Akass, K. and J. McCabe (eds), *Reading Six Feet Under: TV to Die For* (London and New York: I. B. Tauris, 2005).
—— *Reading Sex and the City* (London and New York: I. B. Tauris, 2004).
Altman, R., 'Television sound', in T. Modleski (ed.), *Studies in Entertainment: Critical Approaches to Mass Culture* (Bloomington: Indiana University Press, 1986), pp. 39–54.
Bignell, J., 'The look: style, technology and televisuality in the new *Who*', in A. O'Day (ed.), *Doctor Who: The Eleventh Hour* (London: I. B. Tauris, 2013).
—— 'The police series', in J. Gibbs and D. Pye (eds), *Close Up 03* (London: Wallflower, 2009), pp. 1–66.
—— 'Seeing and knowing: reflexivity and quality', in J. McCabe and K. Akass (eds), *Quality TV: Contemporary American Television and Beyond* (London: I. B. Tauris, 2007a), pp. 158–70.
—— 'Citing the classics: constructing British television drama history in publishing and pedagogy', in H. Wheatley (ed.), *Re-viewing Television History: Critical Issues in Television Historiography* (London: I. B. Tauris, 2007b), pp. 27–39.
Brandt, G. (ed), *British Television Drama* (Cambridge: Cambridge University Press, 1981).
Buxton, D., *The Police Series: From The Avengers to Miami Vice* (Manchester: Manchester University Press, 1990).
Caldwell, J. T., *Production Culture: Industrial Reflexivity and Critical Practice in Film and Television* (Durham, NC and London: Duke University Press, 2008).
Curtin, M., 'From network to neo-network audiences', in M. Hilmes (ed.), *The Television History Book* (London: British Film Institute, 2003), pp. 122–5.
D'Acci, J., *Defining Women: The Case of Cagney and Lacey* (Chapel Hill: University of South Carolina Press, 1994).
Ellis, J., *Seeing Things: Television in the Age of Uncertainty* (London: I. B. Tauris, 2000b).
—— *Visible Fictions: Cinema, Television, Video* (London: Routledge and Kegan Paul, 1982).

Feuer, J., 'Quality drama in the US: the new "Golden Age"?', in: M. Hilmes (ed.), *The Television History Book* (London: British Film Institute, 2003), pp. 98–102.

—— 'MTM enterprises: an overview', in J. Feuer, P. Kerr and T. Vahimagi (eds), *MTM: 'Quality Television'* (London: British Film Institute, 1984), pp. 1–31.

Fisher, B., 'Behind the scenes at NYPD Blue with Brian J. Reynolds', International Cinematographers Guild, 1996, available at: http://www.cameraguild.com/interviews/chat_reynolds/reynolds_NYPD.htm.

Fiske, J. and J. Hartley, *Reading Television* (London: Methuen, 1978).

Frith, S., 'The black box: The value of television and the future of television research', *Screen*, 41:1 (2000), pp. 33–50.

Gitlin, T., *Inside Prime Time* (New York: Pantheon, 1983).

Jenkins, S., 'Hill Street Blues', in J. Feuer, P. Kerr and T. Vahimagi (eds), *MTM: 'Quality Television'* (London: British Film Institute, 1984), pp. 183–99.

Kerr, P., 'Drama at MTM: Lou Grant and Hill Street Blues', in J. Feuer, P. Kerr and T. Vahimagi (eds), *MTM: 'Quality Television'* (London: British Film Institute, 1984), pp. 132–65.

Kinder, M., 'Re-wiring Baltimore: the emotive power of systemics, seriality, and the city', *Film Quarterly*, 62:2 (2008), pp. 50–7.

Klein, P., 'The television audience and program mediocrity', in A. Wells (ed.), *Mass Media and Society* (Palo Alto, CA: Mayfield, 1975), pp. 74–7.

Kompare, D., 'Publishing flow: DVD box sets and the reconception of television', *Television & New Media*, 7:4 (2006), pp. 335–360.

—— *Rerun Nation: How Repeats Invented American Television* (New York: Routledge, 2005).

Leverette, M., B. L. Ott and C. L. Buckley (eds), *It's Not TV: Watching HBO in the Post-Television Era* (London and New York: Routledge 2008).

Lury, K., *Interpreting Television* (London: Hodder Arnold, 2005).

MacMillan, A. 'Heroism, institutions, and the police procedural', in T. Potter and C. Marshall (eds), *The Wire: Urban Decay and American Television* (New York: Continuum, 2009), pp. 40–63.

Marc, D. and R. Thompson, *Prime Time, Prime Movers: From I Love Lucy to L.A. Law – America's Greatest TV Shows and the People Who Created Them* (NY: Syracuse University Press, 1995).

McCabe J. and K. Akass (eds), *Quality TV: Contemporary American Television and Beyond* (London: I. B. Tauris, 2007).

—— *Reading Desperate Housewives: Beyond the White Picket Fence* (London: I. B. Tauris, 2006).

McLean, G., 'CSI: Tarantino', *The Guardian*, New Media section, 11 July 2005, p. 12.

McLoone, M., 'Boxed in?: the aesthetics of film and television', in J. Hill and M. McLoone (eds), *Big Picture, Small Screen: The Relations between Film and Television* (Luton 1997), pp. 76–106.

Milch, D. and B. Clark, *True Blue: The Real Stories Behind NYPD Blue* (London: Boxtree, 1996).

Mittell, J., 'All in the game: *The Wire*, serial storytelling and procedural logic', in P. Harrigan and N. Wardip-Fruin (eds), *Third Person: Authoring and Exploring Vast Narratives* (Baltimore: MIT Press, 2009), pp. 429–38.

—— 'Narrative complexity in contemporary American television', *The Velvet Light Trap*, 58:1 (2006), pp. 29–40.

Mullan, B., *Consuming Television* (Oxford: Blackwell, 1997).

Nannicelli, T., 'It's all connected: televisual narrative complexity', in T. Potter and C. Marshall (eds), *The Wire: Urban Decay and American Television* (New York: Continuum, 2009), pp. 190–202.

Nelson, R., *State of Play: Contemporary 'High-End' TV Drama* (Manchester: Manchester University Press, 2007).

Nelson, R., *TV Drama in Transition: Forms, Values and Cultural Change* (Basingstoke: Palgrave Macmillan, 1997).

Newcomb, H., *Television: The Most Popular Art* (New York: Anchor, 1974).

Pearson, R., 'The writer/producer in American television', in M. Hammond and L. Mazdon (eds), *The Contemporary Television Series* (Edinburgh: Edinburgh University Press, 2005), pp. 11–26.

Potter, T. and C. W. Marshall (eds), *The Wire: Urban Decay and American Television* (New York: Continuum, 2009).

Rixon, P., *American Television on British Screens: A Story of Cultural Interaction*, (Basingstoke: Palgrave Macmillan, 2006).

Rose, B. G., 'The Wire', in G. R. Edgerton and J. P. Jones (eds), *The Essential HBO Reader* (Lexington: Kentucky University Press, 2008), pp. 82–91.

Silverstone, R., *Television and Everyday Life* (London: Routledge, 1994).

Sleight, G., 'The big picture show: Russell T. Davies' writing for *Doctor Who*', in S. Bradshaw, A. Keen and G. Sleight (eds), *The Unsilent Library: Essays on the Russell T. Davies Era of the New Doctor Who* (London: Science Fiction Foundation, 2011), pp. 15–28.

Spilsbury, T., 'Shooting stars', *Doctor Who Magazine*, 426 (20 October 2010), pp. 26–30.

Stempel, T., *Storytellers to the Nation: A History of American Television Writing* (New York: Syracuse University Press, 1996).

Thompson, R., *Television's Second Golden Age: From Hill Street Blues to ER* (New York: Syracuse University Press, 1997).

Troy, P., 'Sixty-minute men and women: writing the hour drama', *Written By*, September, 1997.

Vest, J. P., *The Wire, Deadwood, Homicide and NYPD Blue: Violence is Power* (Oxford: Praeger, 2011).

Williams, R., 'A lecture on realism', *Screen*, 18:1 (1977), pp. 61–74.

Television Realities

Television Realities

Introduction

Realism is a particularly ambiguous term in the analysis of television. One meaning focuses on what is represented: that actual scenes, places and people are represented rather than imagined or fictional ones. A second meaning refers to television's representation of recognisable and often contemporary experience, such as in the representation of characters in whom the audience can believe, or apparently likely chains of events. This meaning of realism relies on the familiarity of the forms and conventions, the **codes** that represent a reality. But, finally, another meaning of realism would reject the conventions of established realistic forms, and look for new and different forms to give access to the real. In each of these meanings, however, realism assumes the separation of the text from a reality which pre-exists it. This chapter discusses the different ways that television represents the real, in a range of different **genres**. This involves considering the different methodologies that can be used in Television Studies to approach these issues, and the strengths and weaknesses of different means of answering related questions. The chapter also discusses television representations of particular groups, especially those defined by gender or race, with attention to their differences in different television forms and genres. The chapter includes a case study on a hybrid of fictional and factual television, the **drama-documentary** or docudrama, and explores the critical arguments advanced about this form of programme.

There are three central questions that have informed work in Television Studies on the issue of representation. Each of the questions stems from an initial assumption that television has connections with the real world of culture and society in which it exists. Earlier chapters have noted that the television medium has a continuing interest in the present moment, in documenting what is happening now, and engaging with the lives lived by its viewers. This is connected with the fact that television began as a medium of live broadcasting, and still broadcasts both live programmes and programmes that are not live, but masquerade as being live. So the question of representation in television is connected to the issue of realism. The three concerns that Television Studies has addressed about representation are:

- who is doing the representing? – a question about production.
- what is represented and how is this done? – a question about codes and conventions.
- how are representations understood by audiences? – a question about reception.

Each of these questions draws attention not only to content, but also to the forms and processes of representation. In Television Studies, television is approached as something that is actively made by someone, using particular textual forms to communicate some meanings and not others, with meanings that are not simply delivered to the audience but that are appropriated and used by them in complex ways.

Quantitative research: content analysis

In contrast to many of the theoretical methodologies discussed in this book, there is a long tradition in the social sciences, including the study of television, that seeks to find empirical data to answer research questions. As John Fiske (1990: 135) explains, the aims of empiricism are to:

- collect and categorise objective facts
- form hypotheses and explain them
- eliminate human bias from the process of investigation
- devise experimental methods to prove or disprove the validity of the data.

Content analysis works by gathering a sample of material to be studied – such as a group of television programmes broadcast on the same day, or programmes that feature representations of a particular gender, economic or ethnic group – and devising a method for subdividing the sample into relevant units that can be counted. While content analysis is sometimes used as a method of television analysis on its own, it is more common for it to be deployed as one of several different methodologies, including, for example, **textual analysis** or audience research. Content analysis is quantitative in that, rather than making an interpretation of the meanings of selected components of television programmes, it attempts to offer precise information on the relative quantities of one kind of representation or another, so that these can be compared with each other. The method is effective when there is a sufficient quantity of recorded material available to be analysed. Since it is now quite easy to record television and amass a considerable volume of potential research data, content analysis is not difficult to carry out on the medium, though the design of a study and the specific methodology used to answer any particular research question can be difficult to establish.

textual analysis a critical approach which seeks to understand a television text's meanings by undertaking detailed analysis of its image and sound components, and the relationships between those components.

There are five steps to take in conducting a content analysis:

- selecting the sample
- defining the categories to analyse
- reviewing and coding the data
- analysing the data
- drawing conclusions based on the results.

Using a term from statistical analysis, the sample of material to be analysed is called a 'population'. The population might be, for example, all of the programmes, advertisements, trailers and other linking material broadcast on Five between 6.00 a.m. and midnight on a particular day. Or it might be all of the situation comedies broadcast on **terrestrial** channels in the month of October 2012. The sample will be chosen to answer a research question. A research question might be, for example, how many acts of violence involving the use of firearms appeared in programmes,

terrestrial broadcasting from a ground-based transmission system, as opposed to broadcasting via satellite.

advertisements and other kinds of broadcast during the hours of Five's programming that have been recorded. Clearly, the most productive answers to a research question will depend on having a suitably large sample population to study. The aim of content analysis is often to provide a snapshot that gives a reliable sense of the frequency of representation of a particular chosen type of content. When television analysts have sought to conduct studies of the representation of particular groups of people on television, they have often adopted content analysis in order to produce representative quantitative figures that may be interesting in themselves, or useful to compare and contrast with other samples that have been analysed in the same way.

Once the research question has been decided, and the sample population recorded, the analysis of data usually requires the definition of categories of content. For example, in a content analysis of the representation of disability in television programmes, it might be useful to separate the categories of physical and mental disability, perhaps introducing further sub-categories representing a range of types of disability. It can be a long and frustrating activity to apply all of the categories and sub-categories to the sample population and to record the data. The application of categories to the sample is called coding, since each instance of relevant content will be represented in a numerical form. As the analysis goes on, it may also be necessary to refine the categories or even to reassess the usefulness of the research question. Categories of content may be too vague and too difficult for the researcher to assign to cases that seem to belong to more than one category. Nevertheless, the end result of the coding and recording process will be a numerical count of the instances in each category, so that these can be displayed in a useful way, in a graph, table or pie chart, for example. The next step will be to analyse the data; computer packages for analysing statistics are now often used for this purpose. Some knowledge of the significance of statistical analysis is necessary at this stage, in order to understand how to use procedures involving standard deviation, means, medians and modal distributions, for instance. Once the data have been analysed by these methods, it will then be possible to draw inferences and make interpretations about the results, and also to relate them to other kinds of research methods (such as textual analysis or audience research) that may have been used to address the research question.

ACTIVITY 8.1

If you were conducting a content analysis to find out how often black characters have leading roles in television detective fiction series, what kind of sample 'population' of programmes would be representative of television programming? What decisions would you take about how much material to study, and what 'leading role' means?

Figure 8.1 Images of the 9/11 attacks in New York, in *102 Minutes that Changed America*.

Factual television

For workers in the television industry, the non-fiction programmes discussed in this chapter fit into the category of 'factual' television. This category includes programmes which feature non-actors on screen, in the modes of:

- documentary
- drama-documentary (also called docudrama)
- docusoap
- reality TV

Programmes such as these aim to represent reality, to dramatise events which occurred in the past, or **denote** real people in a continuing serial. A clear example is the documentary *102 Minutes that Changed America* (Figure 8.1) in which sequences shot on 11 September 2001 were assembled to document the attacks on the World Trade Center in New York. In this image, amateur footage captures a moment when pedestrians in Times Square in New York stood watching live pictures of one of the Twin Towers burning. The shot conveys the immediacy of a real event, and the responses of those who were in Manhattan on that day. It might seem that television technology and the conventions of television programme-making are used in these examples as neutral media for representing personalities and situations that already existed, or would have existed even if the programme were not being made. But many programmes that appear to be factual cross into the

documentary a form aiming to record actual events, often with an explanatory purpose or to analyse and debate an issue.

drama-documentary a television form combining dramatised storytelling with the 'objective' informational techniques of documentary. Abbreviated as 'dramadoc' or 'docudrama'.

docusoap a television form combining documentary's depiction of non-actors in ordinary situations with soap opera's continuing narratives about selected characters.

denotation in semiotics, the function of signs to portray or refer to something in the real world.

reality TV programmes where the unscripted behaviour of 'ordinary people' is the focus of interest.

territory of fictional entertainment because they are based in situations designed for television. *Big Brother* is the best-known example of this type of television, a '**reality TV**' programme where members of the public are chosen to appear, in a house specifically built for the programme, and are aware that they are being recorded twenty-four hours a day. Similarly, some programmes aim to reconstruct events which actually happened, such as the crimes reconstructed in *Crimewatch UK*, but use actors performing scripted dialogue and action to do this. Some apparently real events in television programmes become performances, and some performances are designed to be equivalent to real events. Television realism is a flexible category, containing at one end of the spectrum news footage which claims to document events occurring independently of the fact that they are being recorded, and at the other end drama entertainment programmes which claim to be realistic but are constructed for television. Television realism is a matter both of content and of the conventions or codes which structure the representation seen on the screen. It is the interaction between what is on television and the ways in which an audience understands a programme that is at the heart of television realism. Television has a 'language of realism' which programme-makers and audiences share.

In relation to forms of realism, television factual programmes aim to present information about the diverse ways in which people live and to broaden the horizons of understanding for the audience. In the documentary *Welcome to Romford*, for example, split-screen is used so that viewers can see both the face of a taxi-driver and the faces of the passengers he is carrying (Figure 8.2). Television audiences are invited to experience the lives of others through the mediation of television documentary forms, for example, so that television realism carries an assumption of social responsibility.

- Television realism aims both to mirror society to itself and to show the diversity that exists within a society which is assumed to have an overall unity.
- Television realism constructs a sense of an organic and unified culture, partly by exhibiting the complexity and diversity of culture.
- Television realism consists of a negotiation between ideas of unity and difference, familiar and unfamiliar, and thus performs an **ideological** role in shaping the norms of society.

ideology the set of beliefs, attitudes and assumptions arising from the economic and class divisions in a culture, underlying the ways of life accepted as normal in that culture.

Figure 8.2 A taxi driver and his passengers, seen in split-screen in *Welcome to Romford*.

Conventional documentary techniques such as interview and observation were used in *Dispatches: Britain's Secret Slaves*, to offer evidence by means of personal testimony from women who worked illegally, without pay, as domestic servants in Britain (Figure 8.3). Frontal shots of their testimony and subtitles were used to present evidence of this disturbing and largely unknown problem. A companion programme to this documentary, *I Am Slave*, shown on the same day, used dramatisation to explore how a young girl in Africa was drawn into the slave trade and came to Britain as an unpaid servant. In Figure 8.4, it is clear that conventions of costume, lighting and composition from drama (rather than documentary) were adopted in this dramatisation, to present factual information in a storyline featuring actors who could draw out the emotional responses of a victim of this situation.

Because of the assumption that television can and should reflect society to itself, there have been many controversies about whether specific groups are represented fairly. For example, in July 2009, the female choreographer Arlene Phillips was replaced as a judge on BBC1's *Strictly Come Dancing* by Alesha Dixon. Dixon has a Jamaican father and is thus from a mixed-race background, so it can be argued that her presence on the panel of judges made a contribution to a broader racial representation on the programme since her fellow judges were all white men. But on the other hand, there was an outcry in British newspapers at the time because Dixon was aged thirty-one and Phillips was sixty-six. It is much more difficult for women to continue their television career when they reach middle-age than it is for men. There are many high-profile male presenters in factual programmes who continue well into their later years, like the entertainer Bruce Forsyth and the wildlife presenter David Attenborough.

Figure 8.3 Personal testimony in the documentary *Dispatches: Britain's Secret Slaves*.

Figure 8.4 Dramatisation explores contemporary slavery in *I Am Slave*.

One of the ways that channels try to improve their record in catering for minority audiences is to employ more people from minority groups in programme-making, on the assumption that this will change the programmes that appear on the screen. In June 2006, the BBC secured Mary Fitzgerald, formerly head of diversity at Channel 4, to work for the BBC as editorial manager of cultural diversity. The role involved working with the controllers of BBC channels, programme commissioners and programme-makers inside the BBC to encourage them to employ a wider range of people behind the camera and in front of it. Although the BBC has targets for employing minority staff, they are not easily enforceable and changes have recently been notable mainly in the use of women newsreaders from non-white backgrounds. The BBC makes programmes itself, but also commissions programmes from **independent production companies**, and it can be a challenge to influence these independent companies to improve their diversity. This is especially the case since many of BBC's **prime time** programmes (like soap opera and drama series) are made by BBC itself and the aim of introducing non-white characters can be enforced. In programmes made by independent producers this is more difficult. However, non-white characters in prime time drama programmes have tended to be marginal and appear only for a handful of episodes. In making news programmes, too, the production staff at all the larger channels remain overwhelmingly white (and often male). Given the recent political focus on Muslim people in Britain and abroad, because of war in Iraq and Islamist terrorism, television executives are particularly keen on diluting the dominant presence of white journalists, reporters, news editors and other programme production staff, in the hope that this will lead to news programmes that connect more effectively with Muslim and non-white people in Britain.

The major problems that television faces in increasing diversity are:

■ Policy initiatives in large television institutions are laid down by senior management but may have little impact on the day-to-day work of busy programme-makers.

independent production companies businesses making television programmes which can be sold to television networks that transmit and distribute them.

prime time the part of a day's television schedule when the greatest number of viewers may be watching, normally the mid-evening period.

- Diversity can seem like an add-on extra in programmes and in the way television institutions work, and potentially threatens existing staff and ways of working.
- High-profile individuals from minority groups conceal under-representation of minorities in the broad mass of producers and performers in television.
- There is little impetus from the majority of the audience for greater diversity in television, and it is audiences that matter to television programme-makers.
- Minorities (black, disabled, gay or Chinese people, for example) do not have the same concerns or the same kinds of cultural identity, but are treated as if they did.
- People from minorities are perceived as having 'problems' that define them as victims, threats to society and outsiders through stereotyped portrayals.
- Thinking about minorities assumes the presence of a unified majority, though the majority white British population is very diverse.

ACTIVITY 8.2

Who are the black or Asian characters in soap operas you have seen? Are there ways in which their ethnicity is important to continuing stories? Why is this?

Audiences and race

The reasons why the representation of different races and cultures on television matters are that:

- Social cohesion is enhanced by seeing and knowing about people different from you.
- Broadcasting in Britain should address all of the audience, not just some of it.
- Viewers pay for programmes (though the licence fee or by buying products advertised on television), so they are all entitled to be represented.
- People from minority groups are keen to see representations of people like them.

These reasons all assume the principles of **public service broadcasting**, which involves the idea that television will contribute positively to British society, offer something to all viewers and represent the nation to itself.

In 2006, the audience data collection agency BARB released figures for the ten programmes most popular with black viewers in the year from May 2005 to 2006. They averaged out the audience size when dealing with series, where audiences can fluctuate from week to week, and included imported programmes shown on British channels. The results were:

public service
in television, the provision of a mix of programmes that inform, educate and entertain in ways that encourage the betterment of audiences and society in general.

1 *EastEnders* (BBC1, soap opera): 250,000 black viewers
2 *Everybody Hates Chris* (Five, imported US sitcom): 186,000
3 *Champions League*, Barcelona v Chelsea (ITV1, sport): 174,000
4 *Champions League*, Real Madrid v Arsenal (ITV1, sport): 170,000
5 *Charlie's Angels: Full Throttle* (Five, film): 156,000

6   *Con Air* (BBC1, film): 154,000
7   *Waterloo Road* (BBC1, drama): 151,000
8   *Bodyshock: Half Ton Man* (Channel 4, factual): 147,000
9   *Holby City* (BBC1, drama): 147,000
10   *My Family* (BBC1, sitcom): 144,000

Although *EastEnders* tops the list, the list contains surprisingly few of the drama and factual programmes for which British television producers and academic critics make claims for quality or importance. There are two Hollywood films, two programmes consisting almost entirely of sporting coverage and one imported US sitcom. This seems to support the argument that the main channels and the evening schedules do not cater appropriately for black viewers (Newton 2011). The question remains as to whether some programmes might appeal to black viewers more than to non-black viewers, or in other words, which programmes' audiences contain the greatest share of black viewers.

The list changes when considering which programmes included the largest proportion of black viewers in their audience, in comparison to the number of non-black viewers watching that programme. The programmes in 2005 to 2006 attracting the most black viewers as a proportion of their audience were:

1   *Everybody Hates Chris* (Five, imported US sitcom)
2   *Animal Attraction: Cheaters* (Five, factual)
3   *Cold Turkey* (Channel 4, factual)
4   *Charmed* (Five, imported drama)
5   *The Real Flying Saucers: Stranger than Fiction* (Five, factual)
6   *Two and a Half Men* (Five, imported US sitcom)
7   *The Child Who's Older than her Grandmother* (Five, factual)
8   *Gay Vicars* (Channel 4, factual)
9   *Capturing the Friedmans* (Channel 4, film)
10   *The Seven Year Old Surgeon* (Five, factual)

There has been an assumption that black viewers will prefer to watch programmes featuring black characters, and the popularity of *Everybody Hates Chris*, featuring a mainly black cast including the stand-up comedian Chris Rock, supports this. Following the same logic, in recent years BBC1 screened the black sitcom *The Crouches* (written by two white male authors) and BBC2 screened the series *Babyfather*, but both had short runs, were not well received by critics and did not gain significant audiences. According to the director of programmes at Five, Dan Chambers, who was interviewed when these figures were published in the press (Armstrong 2006), it is the broadly appealing genre of the sitcom that has most potential to offer black audiences representations of themselves, and it is sitcom where British television is failing black audiences most: 'Where do ethnic minority audiences go to find their role models on TV when it comes to sitcoms?' Even *Everybody Hates Chris*, though clearly important to black audiences, did not draw a very large audience overall, with one million viewers on average. But the terrestrial channel whose programmes routinely gain the smallest audience sizes, Five, seems surprisingly popular with black viewers in comparison to its majority white audience.

Channel 4, by contrast, whose remit has included the provision of programmes for minority audiences, has fewer programmes than Five in the top ten by share of black viewers. Mary Fitzgerald, editorial manager for cultural diversity at Channel 4 (quoted in Armstrong 2006), summed up the black audience as 'a very selective audience looking for strong content and a strong storyline and very keen on good factual shows. I don't think there's a huge difference between the demands of black viewers and white viewers.' Nevertheless, the BBC responded to a perception that British television does not serve black and Asian viewers by commissioning comedy sketch shows featuring black and Asian performers, such as *The Kumars at No. 42*, *3 Non-Blondes* and *Little Miss Jocelyn*. The comedian and actor Sanjeev Bhaskar starred in the drama *The Indian Doctor*, as a GP arriving to work in the Welsh valleys in the 1960s (Figure 8.5). This image from the first episode is composed to emphasise the contrast between the all-white population of the Welsh village and the doctor and his wife, positioned in the centre of the frame and costumed very differently from the other characters.

Figure 8.5 Arriving in a Welsh village in *The Indian Doctor*.

ACTIVITY 8.3

Which racial and ethnic group do you belong to? Do you consider that your group is represented correctly on British television, and what might 'correctly' mean? How might television representations of your group affect your sense of who you are?

Realism and television technologies

Television programmes are coded as transcriptions of the real world, but they are assembled from the different discourses of image and sound that are available in the 'language' of television. Television cameras admit rays of light through a lens on to an electronic grid which registers them as quantities of red, green and blue. These signals are encoded for transmission, and the television set converts them into the pixels that make up the television picture. In sound recording, the recording mechanism isolates and intensifies some sounds and not others. It produces an implied perspective on the sound source, representing sound through the hidden electronic processes of recording, transmission and reproduction. Television realism is reinforced by the combination of sound and image, each providing references to and 'evidence' of the smooth unity of the television text as a transcription of reality. There is a separation between the objects or people which are recorded and the recording itself. Since television uses technologies of recording images that seem to transcribe realities 'objectively', or in **semiotic** terminology 'denotatively', television images acquire the status of evidence. But because of this separation, because they are representations of realities rather than realities themselves, television representations are ideological: they encode social points of view that condense, displace or forget social relationships.

semiotics the study of signs and their meanings, initially developed for the study of spoken language, and now used also to study the visual and aural 'languages' of other media such as television

Programmes often conceal the work of their production, just as other kinds of product made for our mass society (such as tins of soup, cars, newspapers or clothes) are abstracted from the work processes and institutional arrangements which created them. Products like these are called **commodities**, and in the early twentieth century the German theorist Walter Benjamin (1969: 212) argued that mechanical reproduction processes which give rise to the media of photography, cinema and now television substitute 'a plurality of copies for a unique existence'. Television images are 'copies' of reality not in the sense that they are fakes, but in that they are the result of a mechanical process and circulate remotely from the physical body of their producer. Television's 'copies' of reality can be distributed widely, and are seen at the same time by mass audiences either on their own or in groups. Media images produced by mechanical reproduction free what has been recorded from its social and historical environment, and (to some extent) from control by the state or elite groups. The interpretation of television images is not controlled by these contexts and social relationships, either. Three of the effects of this are that:

- television images seem to float free of the frameworks which determine them
- television images circulate in culture as commodities
- television images are separated from the people, places and events which were recorded.

iconic sign in semiotics, a sign which resembles its referent. Photographs, for example, contain iconic signs resembling the objects they represent.

These effects occur despite the **iconic** relationship between those people, places and events and the images themselves.

ACTIVITY 8.4

Consider the limits on the ways the term 'realistic' can be used about television: are there ways in which science fiction or fantasy programmes – such as *Doctor Who* – can be realistic? What criteria for realism are you using to formulate your answers to this question?

Contemporary **digital** technologies for recording and editing television, and for transmitting it over networks, pose a potential challenge to the iconic realism of the medium. These digital processes extend the process of unfixing the image from its referent, its maker and its social and historical determinants. Digitisation:

- increases the ease of manipulating images
- allows the transmission of images as electronic units of data along phone cables in the global communications system at high speed and across national boundaries
- permits the digitisation of existing footage into electronic data which can be stored and accessed remotely
- allows the **convergence** of television with interactive systems.

New technologies have modified the realist claims of television, so that digital images, or the grain of video (which is recorded digitally onto the analogue medium of magnetic tape) can connote immediacy, in surveillance video footage, for example, in the same way as the visibility of photographic grain produced by chemical recording in film, and apparently proving the simultaneity in time and space of the person who made the recording and the event which has been recorded. The photographic grain of film, which is inseparable from the celluloid on which it is carried, is an iconic sign and physical trace of the object photographed. This separation of the production of the registering material from the activity of making the image by exposing the chemical surface to light underlies film's claim to show reality as it occurred. But we know that post-production effects are used in film to alter images. In digital recording, images and sound are converted into numerical values which can be easily manipulated in the computer. Although they seem like different media, with film seeming to show what was really before the camera more reliably, both technologies' claims to realism are mythical.

There is a correspondence between thinking of realism as a set of codes that document recognisable realities and thinking of society as constituted by the exchanges of speech and expression between individuals. Realist television forms assume the transparency of the television medium, just as society assumes transparent communication between individuals. In the same way that different kinds of people use different **discourses** deriving from their social class, gender, religion or political outlook, so television realisms represent realities in ways that are recognisable to some viewers and not others. If television realism can never match its codes and conventions to the different versions of reality which actual viewers experience, we need to ask how the notion of realism has become such a widely understood and

digital television television pictures and sound encoded into the ones and zeros of electronic data. Digital signals can also be sent back down cables by viewers, making possible interaction with television programmes.

convergence the process whereby previously separate media technologies merge together. For example, computers can now send faxes, show DVD films and play music.

discourse a particular use of language for a certain purpose in a certain context (such as academic discourse, or poetic discourse), and similarly in television, a particular usage of television's audiovisual 'language' (news programme discourse or nature documentary discourse, for instance).

widely used criterion for discussing and evaluating television. The answer to this problem is to understand how some forms of realism have become dominant codes, and why.

The dominant form of realism in television, labelled by theorists 'classic realism', roughly coincides with the epoch of modern industrial society. It can be seen in the majority of television fiction programmes, and also affects the representation of people in factual television programmes and documentary. Individuals' character determines their choices and actions, and human nature is seen as a pattern of character differences. These differences permit the viewer to share the hopes and fears of a wide range of characters. The comparisons and judgements about identifiable human figures represented on television are reliant on a common code of judgement, a notion of 'normality', which is the terrain on which the viewer's relationships with characters can occur. Classic realism represents a world of psychologically consistent individual **subjects**, and addresses its viewers as the same kind of rational and psychologically consistent individual. The action of the television text is to establish communication and offer involving **identification** with the images it shows. Individual television texts need to be constructed as wholes that promise intelligibility and significance. The realist assumption of the match between the television text and a pre-existing reality underlies this process, by posing the image as equivalent to a real perception of recognisable social space. This depends on the equivalence between what and how the viewing subject might see and be seen, and what and how the television point of view might see and be seen. So the category of the rational perceiving subject is the connecting assumption shared by the viewer and television, and by his or her world and the world represented on television. The viewer's varied and ordered pattern of identifications makes **narrative** crucial to classic realism, for the different kinds of look, point of view, sound and speech in narrative are the forms through which this communication between text and audience is produced.

subject in psychoanalysis, the term for the individual self whose identity has both conscious and unconscious components.

identification a term deriving from psychoanalytic theories of cinema, which describes the viewer's conscious or unconscious wish to take the place of someone or something in a television text.

narrative an ordered sequence of images and sound that tells a fictional or factual story.

British soap opera and realism

The television form of British soap opera exhibits several kinds of realism, for it is a continuing form, flowing onward like our conventional experience of time in reality. British soap opera's social realism derives from the historical circumstances in 1960 when the first regular British soap, *Coronation Street*, was created. The portrayal of Northern working-class life contains the same nostalgia for community which was being dramatised in the cinema films and television and theatre plays of the late 1950s, at a time when this culture was no longer representative of how most British people lived. Community is always already lost, and persists as the impossible dream of binding separated families and groups together.

Soaps are multi-character dramas, and their stories, settings and concerns are embedded in the mythologies of community in national popular culture. They appear to 'reflect' the real experience of being part of a community, with their fictional worlds functioning as a microcosm of 'ordinary life'. But the condensation and narrative progress that are necessary to television fiction mean that soaps do more than 'reflect'. There are very frequent breaking-points in soap opera families and communities (such as divorce, birth, death, gossip and antagonism between characters), which enable new stories to begin. So while the foundations of soap opera reflect ideological norms in being centred on the family, community and regional identity, it is the lack and disturbance of these structures that drives the narrative. Plots are often based on 'common-sense' wisdom about human nature, like 'pride comes before a fall' and 'a little knowledge is a dangerous thing'. These common-sense axioms are the ideological assumptions that underlie dramatic dilemmas. Charlotte Brunsdon (1981: 35) has explained that

> The coherence of the serial does not come from the subordination of space and time to linear narrativity, as it does in classical narrative cinema, but from the continuities of moral and ideological frameworks which inform the dialogue . . . although soap opera narrative may seem to ask 'What will happen next?' as its dominant question, the terrain on which this question is posed is determined by a prior question – 'What kind of person is this?' And in the ineluctable posing of this question, of all characters, whatever their social position, soap opera poses a potential moral equality of all individuals.

The action in soaps takes place within a set of values that provide the norms for characters' lives, and, even though characters continually violate these norms, they remain bound by them and have to learn to adjust to them or suffer the consequences. While the narrative of the serial poses these moral questions of its characters, the leakage of these questions out of and back into the realities of the viewer's life, and out of and into other media discourses, such as newspaper stories, spreads them across society as a whole. It is soap opera realism that allows this transfer between fiction and reality, and enables soaps to claim social responsibility and public service functions. Soaps are an arena for debates about morality and social behaviour in modern societies, and pose television institutions as socially responsible. The proof of this concern is measured by the responses of viewers (in phone-ins, viewers' letters and audience **ratings**) to programmes. But there are no issues without the media to represent them and direct them back to their source in society, so the important question for Television Studies becomes how particular forms of address and representational form are used to 'reflect' and respond 'responsibly' to social life.

The realism of soaps depends not only on their construction and form within their television **genre** but on the discourse generated around them. The stories about soap operas in newspapers and television listings magazines offer information and advertise soaps in ways that support the kinds of realism established by the forms of the programmes themselves. The soaps are represented as entirely familiar: the articles profiling the actors presuppose familiarity with the names, identities and major events in the lives of the characters; and the fascination with what will happen, and with the continuing production of the series, particularly in relation to the changes in personnel among the actors, helps to support the creation of a continuous present in the soaps. The television industry is able to publicise its soaps extensively, while maintaining secrecy about forthcoming events in the narrative. But the popular press is also involved in the comparison and testing of the soap narratives against reality, running articles on the 'real' people of the East End of London, and on the lives of the actors in *EastEnders*. The exaggerated **melodramatic** forms of soap opera narrative (its use of comic, grotesque or stereotypical characters, for instance) play

ratings the number of viewers estimated to have watched certain programmes, as compared to the numbers watching other programmes.

genre a kind or type of programme. Programmes of the same genre have shared characteristics.

melodrama a form of drama characterised by exaggerated performance, a focus on reversals of fortune and extreme emotional reactions to events.

against its realism, and the viewer's pleasure must therefore partly depend on his or her recognition of the mediation of realism by television forms and institutions. The back-and-forth movement between fiction and fact in these discourses both maintains their separation from each other and shows how interdependent they are, testifying to the unstable border between what is considered 'real' and what is a performance or representation of reality. The television theorist Robert Allen (1985: 85) has argued that 'soap opera trades narrative closure for paradigmatic complexity', meaning that although soaps, like life, never end, the result of this is that very large numbers of narrative strands can be kept going in parallel. For any one character, change and unpredictability are the norm, but in the long run this has no effect on the community as a whole. Yet, at any one moment, a change in any character will affect all the other characters with whom he or she comes into contact. The realism of soap opera refers not only to this apparent unpredictability and change but to the programme's consistently represented world and fidelity to its own fictional identity.

The shifting relations of characters in soap opera are paralleled by the shifting of the camera's points of view, that give access to the widely differing people and locations that appear in each episode. *EastEnders*, like all soaps, represents a community with a regional identity. It has a residential setting in an urban area, as does *Coronation Street*. In *EastEnders*, flows of characters and interaction between them occur in Albert Square, around and through which characters walk, and the various shops, pubs, houses and the market where characters meet. There is a sense that there is no escape from Albert Square, but the roads into it also lead outwards, to Walford and the rest of London, allowing the diffusion of the action towards the edge of the represented space and the invasion of that space from the outside. Sandy Flitterman-Lewis (1992: 224) has argued that within the rooms and other smaller spaces where scenes are set, the camera does not create a consistent space by alternating establishing shots and **shot-reverse-shots** in order to situate the drama securely for the viewer, 'for what the reverse shot accomplishes in the soap opera is something altogether different. The quality of viewer involvement, instead, is one of continual, momentary, and constant visual repositioning, in keeping with television's characteristic "glance".' The movement of the narrative point of view allows the sense of incompletion and future necessary to soap opera form. This maintenance of 'the now' is supported by the emphasis in journalistic discourses on each soap's identity and unity as it unfolds in this week or this year.

shot-reverse-shot
the convention of alternating a shot of one character and a shot of another character in a scene, producing a back-and-forth movement which represents their interaction visually.

ACTIVITY 8.5

In what ways do the realisms of British soap operas depend on the mythologies and stereotypes that represent the regions of Britain in which the soaps are set? Does this make them more or less realistic?

Realism and ideology

Television realism places the viewer in the position of a unified subject 'interpellated' with, or folded into, the discourses of a dominant ideology (Althusser 1971), subjected (made into a **subject**, and subject to the ideology) to a version of reality in which he or she misrecognises that reality and misrecognises himself or herself. This theory of how ideology in television separates the subject from his or her 'real' self shares its structure with the French psychoanalyst Jacques Lacan's theory of subjectivity. For Lacan (1977) the subject is the result of a division between his or her 'real' self and the means (such as words, photographs or other representations) through which the subject comes to know himself or herself. Theorists of television have therefore turned to **psychoanalytic** theory in order to explain how individuals are hailed into ideology and subjectivity by the experience of watching television. One of the consequences of the ideologies of television realism is a contradiction between the viewer's working activity, where he or she is producer, and his or her leisure activity, in which he or she is positioned as a consumer. Althusser makes the point in his essay that ideology is not just a question of ideas circulating in people's heads but is inscribed in certain material practices. The reactionary practice of television realism involves the entrapment of the viewer in a position of apparent dominance and control over the represented reality offered by television's discourses about reality. Realist television discourse resolves contradictions by representing a unified and rational world of causes and effects, actions and consequences, moral choices and rewards or punishments. It distances the viewer from the contradictory and ambiguous dynamics of reality and suggests that political action to intervene in the ways that reality is produced from day to day is unnecessary.

If television, particularly realist television, is performing ideological work in concealing a more correct vision of social and political realities, the makers of television might be under an obligation to draw the attention of the viewer to the non-equivalence of television and reality. According to this view, television cannot be a 'true' representation, but it may be a medium in which the beginnings of a recognition of the true state of affairs could occur. In this context realism is no longer a reflection of an exterior reality but one of the forms in which representations and audiences connect with each other. The makers of television must draw the viewer's attention to his or her relationship with the medium in order to make him or her recognise the social relations that this relationship involves. So perhaps the strangeness or unrealistic nature of television versions of reality might draw the viewer's attention to the fact that he or she is watching a representation and not a reality. When familiar recognitions and identifications break down, viewers might grasp what it is that the relations between television and audience, and between real and representation, involve. This strategy is known as 'critical realism', and involves recognising a relationship between the television text and material social realities, yet resisting the television text's transcription of reality as if television were a neutral medium, so that the work of the forms through which representation takes place is recognised as not natural but cultural and constructed.

News and liveness

One of the uses of photography has been for military surveillance, first by placing cameras in balloons to observe enemy troops and positions, and now modern uses of satellite surveillance and computer enhancement of images continue this aim to provide a superior and powerful vision of space and detail beyond the capacity of

subject in psychoanalysis, the term for the individual self whose identity has both conscious and unconscious components.

psychoanalysis the study of human mental life, including not only conscious thoughts, wishes and fears but also unconscious ones. Psychoanalysis is an analytical and theoretical set of ideas as well as a therapeutic treatment.

the human eye. The broadcasting of such images, however, is controlled by military institutions:

- by allowing or withholding access to the action
- by exercising powers to censor information, or
- by encouraging television crews to self-censor the images they acquire.

War and conflict are the occasions when television's power to show reality is most evident, but also when it is most subject to attempts to control it. Viewers have become increasingly accustomed to seeing television images of events almost at the same time as they occur, and the attraction of television as a medium relies in part on its ability to broadcast events live. The excitement of live television derives not only from the sense of participation and presence at an event which live broadcasting provides, but also from the assumption that what we see and hear in live broadcasting is unmediated, uncontaminated and accurate. When sports events such as the Olympics or the FA Cup Final are broadcast live, or when a national event such as a royal wedding or the occurrence and aftermath of disasters are broadcast, it is the accidental detail and unpredictable unfolding of events which are fascinating. And now, because live broadcasting is relatively rare, those things that are broadcast live gain a particular importance. Live events are those that are assumed to have a universal importance for society. Live television gives the audience access to an 'other' space and also to an alternative time: the viewer's present and the present experience of others in a distant place are equivalent but different. The caption 'live' is significant in itself, for it means 'alive', connoting that a living reality for other people is being shown, and is open to the audience's involvement.

Contemporary networks of electronic mediation allow digital images denoting realities to be circulated around the world from television news crews back to their producers at home, and also to the news agencies which sell packages of news pictures to broadcasters. Television technologies are not neutral, and the capacity to circulate images denoting realities has political effects. One example of this is the perception of the Third World by Western television audiences, where some categories of event are the most frequent versions of reality denoted in news and current affairs television. Large-scale political violence and natural disasters are the predominant form of news image broadcast of Third World countries and developing countries such as India. Media theorists have studied the patterns of regional and global news coverage, and discovered that, although the greater part of news imagery relates to the country in which news is made or to the neighbouring countries, it is the United States and other Western nations which appear in news coverage as the active makers of news, while countries in the developing world are portrayed as the passive suffering objects of news events. These divisions between active makers of the news and passive sufferers of news events are parallel to the division between the rich Western nations which intervene in world affairs and control world institutions such as the World Bank or United Nations, and the relatively impoverished and politically disempowered nations in the rest of the world.

ACTIVITY 8.6

Collect samples of television news stories relating to nations in Africa. What patterns do you find in the kinds of stories about Africa, and the ways in which they are represented in image and sound? What conclusions can you draw from this exercise?

The documentary mode

Factual programmes denote society, and inform and educate the audience both about aspects of life with which they are familiar, and aspects signified as unfamiliar. Factual programmes make the 'other' into the familiar, and make the familiar seem 'other' by denoting it in unfamiliar ways, and are a key part of the contemporary television landscape. This is in part because the denotation of different aspects of society in factual programmes is part of television's public service function.

John Corner (2006: 90) draws attention to what he calls an 'economy of intensity' in documentary:

> The regularity of such material is often a key requirement and it may vary in its nature from scenes of violence through angry interaction and verbal abuse to scenes of celebration and joy (for example, the moment of arrival of good news; the reunion). It may close down entirely around personal testimony, the intensity of a "speech event", perhaps a personal revelation or other form of disclosure or difficult recollection, signalled not only in its content but by changed forms of speech and facial demeanour.

Clearly these kinds of moments in documentaries are dramatic, but Corner notes that this mixes together two meanings of the word 'drama'; first, something that is sensational or surprising, and second, something that is scripted or fabricated by the programme-maker. Surprising or intense moments can be introduced in documentary by, for example, the use of surveillance footage that shows something shocking happening, like a crime being committed, an accident taking place, or police action. Surprising moments can take place when people do surprising things in a situation that has been set up in advance, but where the actions or speech of the participants (in *Big Brother*, for example), could not be pre-planned.

In order to produce the impression of realism in television documentary, several very unnatural procedures have to be carried out. The documentary subject will almost always be aware that he or she is being recorded, witnessed or even pursued by the camera operator, and often also by a sound recordist. Once the footage has been gathered, the documentary-maker will edit the footage together in order to produce a coherent argument or a narrative. While the finished programme may acknowledge the presence of the documentary-maker, it is often the case that documentaries imply that the subject is behaving 'naturally' or at least representatively. So there is a tension between producing a documentary that is representative and 'accurate', and providing the audience with a programme that conforms to the conventions of argument or storytelling. It is this tension that gives rise to the complaints and occasionally legal cases brought by documentary subjects against documentary-makers, where the subject claims that he or she has been misrepresented or made to look foolish. The assumption of accuracy that always accompanies the documentary mode brings with it the danger of claims of misrepresentation. Techniques such as covert filming, or showing the documentary-maker on screen developing a relationship with the documentary subject, are two different ways of coping with these problems.

To attract viewers and guide their understanding, story has always been important to documentary. It can be created in a range of ways (Corner 2006: 92–4). Re-enactment can show the unfolding of events that occurred in reality in the past and were not observed by the camera. A voice-over commentary can describe, explain or make an argument that has a sequence and a story-like flow. The presenter can seem to find things out, leading the viewer through a story of discovery and understanding. It is not only the observation of the documentary subject that provides an impression of reality in documentary television but also the inclusion of supporting **narration**, testimony or expert commentary. These devices make links with other factual genres, where:

narration the process of telling a story through image and sound. Narration can also refer to the spoken text accompanying television images.

- ▪ the authority of a narrator provides coherence and continuity
- ▪ testimony of members of the public supports the authenticity of the programme
- ▪ expert commentary provides backing for the assertions and arguments of the programme-maker or the figures appearing in the programme.

Devices such as these are found in, for example, sports programmes, science programmes, nature programmes and current affairs. It is always the case that television programmes gain their meanings by their similarity to and difference from each other, and the overlap of codes and conventions among them. Some documentary conventions connote unmediated reality, such as hand-held camera, 'natural' rather than expressive lighting and imperfect sound, while other conventions connote drama, argument and interpretation, such as voice-over, narrative structure and contrastive editing.

metonymy the substitution of one thing for another, either because one is part of the other or because one is connected with the other. For example, 'the Crown' can be a metonym for the British state.

The device of **metonymy** in documentary enables part of reality to stand for the larger real world that it represents. One day in the life of a hotel metonymically stands for any other day. The work of an inner-city social worker stands metonymically for that of all inner-city social workers. Specific images or sequences, or specific documentary subjects, have metonymic relationships with the reality of which they are a part. This device is one of the unstated assumptions that enables television programmes to claim implicitly that they represent society to itself, and connect the specific subjects of programmes to larger social contexts. But the impression of realism in television depends on the relationship between the codes of the programme and the codes available to the audience for interpreting it. Kilborn and Izod (1997: 39) use the term 'accommodation' to describe the shaping of documentary programmes to accord with the assumed knowledge of the audience. Documentaries about hotels or social work accommodate themselves to some extent with ideological assumptions about hotels and social workers that circulate in society. Television's claim to present the real rests on the ideologies shaping that reality for the audience.

Case study: docudrama

Television drama-documentary retells events, often recent events, in order to review or celebrate them. It is one among many ways for television to 'work through' reality, processing it in order to explain, tell stories about, investigate or speculate about reality (Ellis 1999). The key figures and turning-points of the story are often familiar to the audience, though opening statements and captions make clear the factual basis of docudramas, while disclaimers may state that some events and characters have been changed, amalgamated or invented. Derek Paget's (1998: 82) definition of drama-documentary is that it

> uses the sequence of events from a real historical occurrence or situation and the identities of the protagonists to underpin a film script intended to provoke debate . . . The resultant film usually follows a cinematic narrative structure and employs the standard naturalist/realist performance techniques of screen drama.

Drama-documentary offers a single and personalised view of a dramatic situation, in which identification with central figures allows access for the audience, but where the documentation of an historical situation 'objectively' sets these identifications into a social and political context. Narrative provides the linkage between the forms of documentary and of drama, as John Caughie (1980: 30) describes: 'If the rhetoric of the drama inscribes the document within narrative and experience, the rhetoric of the documentary establishes the experience as an experience of the real, and places it within a system of guarantees and confirmations.' British docudrama is based in carefully researched journalistic investigation, and follows the conventions of journalistic discourse such as the sequential unfolding of events and the use of captions to identify key figures. It has become more common then ever in recent years as a way of speculating in a fictional drama about how real threats to society might impact on Britain, for example in *Gas Attack* and *Smallpox 2002*, each of which explored the consequences of terror attacks by small groups of extremists.

The hijacking of four airliners on 11 September 2001, each of which crashed in the United States with no survivors, gave rise to a substantial group of docudramas that could address the causes and significance of the attacks with greater scope than conventional documentary. Because none of the hijackers or passengers could bear witness to the events in person, reconstruction and dramatic speculation on the events as they affected those directly involved could be developed with the assistance of expert opinion, journalistic investigation and the exploration of the institutional response to the crisis. Channel 4's *The Hamburg Cell* dramatised the lead-up to the destruction of the World Trade Center towers, and the destruction of the World Trade Center and the experience of those inside the building and their rescuers was dramatised in the BBC's co-production with the Discovery Channel, *9/11: The Twin Towers*. These programmes bore witness to public and political events with international recognition, but recent histories where no cameras had been present were also explored in British docudramas about political controversy. These included Peter Kosminsky's docudrama for Channel 4, *The Government Inspector*, which dramatised the events preceding the apparent suicide of a government scientist searching for Iraq's supposed 'weapons of mass destruction', and Michael Winterbottom's Channel 4 docudrama *The Road to Guantanamo*, which concerned the capture of three British Muslims and their deportation to an illegal US prison camp. Docudrama moved into the territory of investigative documentary, especially to address high-profile events that had a bearing on controversial issues of racism, terrorism and preparations for war that were supposedly justified by acts of terrorism.

The growth in television docudrama in Britain since 1990 was caused by several factors. The Broadcasting Act of 1990 affected existing television institutions by increasing competition and budgetary pressure. The Act reduced budgets for television programmes originated by the BBC and the commercial broadcasters, because it required them to commission 25 per cent of programme time from independent producers. The effect was to place greater emphasis on 'value for money', and to increase internal competition between the departments within the major broadcasters, now competing against outsiders as well as each other (Born 2004: 172–3). Even in larger institutions, support for conventional documentary waned. Referring to Granada Television's docudrama output around 1990, the company's head of current affairs from 1987 to 93, Ray Fitzwalter (2008: 85–6) lamented the reduction in resources for investigative programmes and the pressure on ITV to maximise revenue by courting mass audiences. This was also the period when docusoap rose to prominence in prime-time, moving out of daytime programming to gain high ratings in part because of its focus on performance (Corner 2002). Programmes like *Driving School*, *Airport* and *The Cruise* competed with long-running drama series like *London's Burning* or *The Bill* and key participants became media celebrities. In drama, the major broadcasters invested significant budgets in high-profile projects, but the escalation of cost above inflation led to aversion to risk and strategies to secure continuing audiences by perpetuating strong formats or building drama projects around star actors who had been placed under contract. Series and serial formats such as *Casualty* or *Inspector Morse* reduced risk, maintained audience loyalty and reduced production cost. In this environment, docudrama was able to attract co-production finance and distribution deals with overseas television channels, since fact-based narratives seemed to offer audience appeal and reduce risk, and they could be cast with strong performers.

The production of docudrama can therefore be seen as part of a larger-scale strategy to draw on both the perceived success of factual entertainment like docusoap, and the building of scripted drama around star actors. In some cases, the subjects of docudrama and the casting of star performers could facilitate external production funding or overseas distribution. For instance, Georgina Born (2004: 167) reports that at the end of the 1990s, BBC single dramas co-produced with the American cable channel HBO could attract US investment of as much as £1.5 million, more than three times as much as the average hourly cost of a BBC drama series at that time. British producers sell themselves on high production values and quality when marketing dramas at international trading fairs such as MIPTV in Cannes. With a high profile in factual **formats** and drama, Britain is second to the US in global programme sales, and UK television exports rose 21 per cent in 2005 to £632 million. Exports to the US are by far the largest sector of the UK programme trade, generating £228 million in 2005. BBC Worldwide was the largest exporter, earning £171 million, although smaller producers improved their performance following new regulations introduced in 2004 that gave them more control over their programme rights (Holmwood 2006). US factual filmmakers have become increasingly occupied in making fact-based drama and a transnational English-speaking market has developed for the form (Rosenthal 1999, Lipkin 2002). Since the 1990s and across the television landscape, narrative dramatisation in docudrama, in more conventional documentary and in docusoap has been attractive to programme-makers for a range of practical, institutional and aesthetic reasons.

Docudrama is scripted and acted, so it makes performance into its primary and acknowledged focus of interest, within a narrative that aims to inform its audience and to make events accessible (Bignell 2010). The criteria that viewers bring with them centre on questions of authenticity, but authenticity depends on the match or mismatch between the expressive

format the blueprint for a programme, including its setting, main characters, genre, form and main themes.

performance techniques used by witnesses or actors and the factual base that legitimates them. Docudramas draw on performance modes from fictional television forms and invite audiences to deploy their knowledge of fiction codes, while the factual base invites the viewer to evaluate narrative in relation to the real events, settings and people represented, and also in relation to other media representations. But as Tobias Ebbrecht has commented in making a similar argument around docudramas based on witness testimony about the Second World War, actors validate docudrama narrative by inhabiting the identity of a person from the past, while the people whose lives they are re-enacting validate the docudrama's promise of authenticity. Actors 'become part of contemporary memory culture' and the programme 'takes part in the construction of a national culture of public memory' (Ebbrecht 2007: 37). Viewers' existing knowledge about past events and people works together with television docudrama narrative.

ACTIVITY 8.7

Research docudramas featuring actors who play well-known real people (like Winston Churchill or Queen Elizabeth II). To what extent do you think they were cast because they look like the person they portray?

Key events or elite figures function as hooks around which the marketing of docudrama programmes can be organised. For example, Figure 8.6 is the title caption from *When Boris Met Dave*, dramatising the relationship between David Cameron (who became Prime Minister) and Boris Johnson (who became Mayor of London) when they were at university together. The actors playing the two characters face the camera, to aid the viewer's identification of who they are playing, while costume and make-up (especially the blond hair for which Johnson is known) also work with the character names in the caption to make clear that the drama is about people whom the viewer will recognise. Such dramas are promoted as factual

Figure 8.6 The opening title of *When Boris Met Dave*.

public sphere
the world of politics, economic affairs and national and international events, as opposed to the 'private sphere' of domestic life.

documents of the main character's personal struggles, revealing their private lives and their private reactions to public events, often events in the **public sphere**. Figure 8.7 is from the docudrama *The Queen*, at a moment when the then Prime Minister Margaret Thatcher has a private meeting with the Queen. Moments like this are never recorded in real life, but the docudrama provided a fictionalised reconstruction of what the meeting may have been like. The pairing of the characters in the frame in Figure 8.7, with lighting emphasising their faces and expressions, demonstrates that this is a docudrama about what their relationship reveals about each of their characters. The documentary base in docudramas is signalled by opening statements about the accuracy of the content, and action representing their public appearances is counterposed and given significance through psychological and emotional turmoil. Patterns of speech and gesture that are familiar from television news footage are recreated. Performance motifs work alongside melodramatic narrative form to aid viewer recognition of the lead characters, and an accretion of previous representations makes promoting these docudramas easy.

The Channel 4 docudrama *The Deal* (2003), for example, was a recreation of a meeting between the Labour Party politicians Tony Blair and Gordon Brown at London's Granita restaurant after the death of Labour Party leader John Smith in 1994. The drama was written by Peter Morgan and directed by Stephen Frears. In *The Deal*, Brown agrees to allow Blair to stand unopposed for the Labour leadership thus enabling Blair to become Prime Minister at the 1997 election, in exchange for a promise that Brown would direct domestic policy and would be Blair's successor as Prime Minister. Blair was played by Michael Sheen and Gordon Brown by David Morrissey. Sheen has become associated with playing not only Tony Blair, but also other real people, in docudramas for both television and cinema. He played the football manager Brian Clough in the cinema film *The Damned United*, also scripted by Peter Morgan, and Sheen played Blair again in the film *The Queen*, directed by Frears and written by Morgan. *The Deal*'s producer Andy Harries has a long track record of making fact-based dramas anchored around a major performer, such as *The Last Hangman* (starring Tim Spall), *See No*

Figure 8.7 Margaret Thatcher meets the Queen in *The Queen*.

Evil: The Moors Murders (starring Maxine Peake), *Longford* (starring Jim Broadbent), and *The Special Relationship* in which Michael Sheen again played Tony Blair and the American actor Dennis Quaid played the US President, Bill Clinton.

Records of the private conversations that *The Deal* and these other docudramas dramatise were not available to the programmes' writers directly; although the events depicted in the docudramas were known to have happened, the details had to be reconstructed dramatically. *The Deal* begins with an opening caption that declares 'much of what follows is true'. This is a quotation from the opening of the cinema buddy-movie *Butch Cassidy and the Sundance Kid* starring Paul Newman and Robert Redford, so the allusion to the film signals a buddy relationship between Blair and Brown. The name of the writer, Peter Morgan, followed the first caption, announcing the programme's connection with scripted forms as much as with fact. The use of actors in *The Deal*, then, facilitates a factual narrative that could not meet documentary standards of accuracy, offering the lure of behind-the-scenes access to key political decisions that are presented as a face-to-face conversation.

The Deal draws on a way of representing history that explains decisive moments by exploring the role of key individuals in them. *The Deal* draws attention to performance, presenting Tony Blair as a politician whose public persona was a brilliantly crafted performance. The docudrama contains flashbacks to Blair's television appearances and also his preparations for them, sitting in the make-up artist's chair and putting up with the lengthy process because, he says, 'I always wanted to be an actor'. The repeated use of television interviews presents Blair as someone suited to a style of leadership that promotes his personality and is designed to appeal to the media. Peter Morgan's script both legitimates its version of the facts by integrating news footage into fictional acted sequences, and minimises the distinction between them. It is sometimes hard to tell which sequences in *The Deal* are **actuality footage** and which are acted reconstructions. Scheduling affected this blurring of fact and fiction, since *The Deal* was broadcast as part of a Channel 4 'Tony Blair season' in September 2003 and was preceded by the documentary, *Inside the Mind of Tony Blair*. In *The Deal*, acted sequences of Sheen's performance are edited into actuality footage that was also used in the *Inside the Mind* documentary. Docudramas about public figures always set up a tension between reconstruction and actuality. But *The Deal* takes this a step further by making performance part of its theme. If Blair can be thought of as an actor playing a politician, Sheen's realistic performance as Blair presents the paradox that this reality was already a performance.

> **actuality footage** television pictures representing an event that was filmed live. The term usually refers to pictures of news events.

Docudramas that represent public figures negotiate between several narrative modes. They bear witness to public events at the same time as they promise an insight into personality and private psychology. They reference media representations of the central figures and sometimes incorporate actuality footage alongside reconstruction. In docudrama, interviews with real or fictional subjects – alongside dramatised reconstructions – emphasise moments of crisis or transformation. The aim is to allow the audience to reflect on the forces impacting on individuals, and on how individuals respond to those forces. The question audiences are invited to ask is 'What was it like to be there?' As a subset of the documentary mode, docudrama can emphasise immediacy, where television offers a window onto the world around its viewers and represents public affairs. However, many docudramas are interested in intimacy and character. They aim to set up a mirroring relationship between the viewer and the people featured in the programme, where the viewer can imagine what he or she might do in the same situation that the characters face. Docudrama has worked with the interdependent documentary and dramatic resources offered by the cultural forms in television.

SUMMARY OF KEY POINTS

■ Realism in television can refer to the conventions used in particular forms of programme to convey the impression that something real is being represented adequately.

■ Television audiences are accustomed to realist conventions and expect realism from some kinds of programme, such as news and documentary, more than others.

■ The study of television representation includes the question of which television institutions, for example, are representing certain groups, in what ways and for what reasons.

■ The methodology of content analysis is a statistically based method for finding out about representation in samples of television, whereas textual analysis interprets and evaluates television representations.

■ Studying representations involves considering how audiences understand and respond to the representations of people they see.

■ The factual genres of television have a special relationship to realism because they seem to represent something that would have happened anyway. But fictional programmes also make use of realist conventions, in their representations of place, character and narrative. Docudrama mixes the two modes together.

Further reading

Allen, R., *Speaking of Soap Operas* (Chapel Hill, SC: University of South Carolina Press, 1985).

Armstrong, S., 'Go figure: Black viewing', *The Guardian*, Media section, 22 May 2006, p. 9.

Benjamin, W., 'The work of art in the age of mechanical reproduction', in *Illuminations*, ed. H. Arendt, trans. H. Zohn (New York: Schocken Books, 1969), pp. 219–54.

Bignell, J., 'Docudrama performance: realism, recognition and representation', in C. Cornea (ed.), *Genre and Performance: Film and Television* (Manchester: Manchester University Press, 2010), pp. 59–75.

—— *Big Brother: Reality TV in the Twenty-first Century* (Basingstoke: Palgrave Macmillan, 2005).

Born, G., *Uncertain Vision: Birt, Dyke and the Reinvention of the BBC* (London: Secker & Warburg, 2004).

Brunsdon, C., 'Crossroads – notes on soap opera', *Screen*, 22:4 (1981), pp. 32–7.

Bruzzi, S., *The New Documentary: A Critical Introduction* (London: Routledge, 2000).

Buckingham, D., *Public Secrets: EastEnders and its Audience* (London: BFI, 1987).

Campion, M. J., *Look Who's Talking: Cultural Diversity, Public Service Broadcasting and the National Conversation* (Oxford: Nuffield, 2005).

Caughie, J., 'Progressive television and documentary drama', *Screen*, 21:3 (1980), pp. 9–35.

Corner, J., '"A fiction (un)like any other"?', *Critical Studies in Television*, 1:1 (2006), pp. 89–96.

—— 'Performing the real: documentary diversions', *Television and New Media* 3:3 (2002), 255–69.

—— *The Art of Record: A Critical Introduction to Documentary* (Manchester: Manchester University Press, 1996).

—— 'Presumption as theory: "realism" in Television Studies', *Screen*, 33:1 (1992), pp. 97–102.

Cottle, S. (ed.), *Ethnic Minorities and the Media* (Oxford: Oxford University Press, 2000).

Cumberbatch, G., S. Gauntlett and V. Lyne, *Minority Group Representation on British Terrestrial Television: Key Findings, 1993–2003* (London: BBC/Ofcom, 2004).

Dahlgren, P., *Television and the Public Sphere* (London: Sage, 1995).

Dovey, J., *Freakshow: First Person Media and Factual Television* (Cambridge: Polity, 2000).

Ebbrecht, T., 'Docudramatizing history on TV: German and British docudrama and historical event television in the memorial year 2005', *European Journal of Cultural Studies*, 10:1 (2007), pp. 35–55.

Ellis, J., 'Television as working through', in J. Gripsrud (ed.), *Television and Common Knowledge* (London: Routledge, 1999), pp. 55–7.

Fiske, J., *Introduction to Communication Studies* (London: Routledge, 1990).

Fitzwalter, R., *The Dream that Died: The Rise and Fall of ITV* (Leicester: Matador, 2008).

Flitterman-Lewis, S., 'Psychoanalysis, film, and television', in R. Allen (ed.), *Channels of Discourse, Reassembled* (London: Routledge, 1992), pp. 203–46.

Geraghty, C., *Women and Soap Opera: A Study of Prime Time Soaps* (Cambridge: Polity Press, 1991).

Gray, H., *Watching Race: Television and the Struggle for 'Blackness'* (Minneapolis, Minn.: University of Minnesota Press, 1995).

Gripsrud, J., *The Dynasty Years: Hollywood Television and Critical Media Studies* (London, Routledge, 1995).

Hall, S. (ed.), *Representation: Cultural Representations and Signifying Practices* (London: Sage, 1997).

—— 'Black and white television', in D. Morley and K. Chen (eds), *Remote Control: Dilemmas of Black Intervention in British Film and TV* (London: BFI, 1996), pp. 13–28.

Havens, T., '"The biggest show in the world": race and the global popularity of *The Cosby Show*', *Media Culture & Society*, 22:4 (2000), pp. 371–91.

Hobson, D., 'From *Crossroads* to *Wife Swap*: learning from audiences', *Critical Studies in Television*, 1:1 (2006), pp. 121–8.

Holmes, S. and D. Jermyn (eds), *Understanding Reality Television* (London: Routledge, 2004).

Holmwood, L., 'Mipcom showcases the best of British', *The Guardian*, Media section, 9 October 2006, p. 2.

Jhally, S. and J. Lewis, *Enlightened Racism: The Cosby Show, Audiences, and the Myth of the American Dream* (San Francisco, Calif.: Westview, 1992).

Kilborn, R. and J. Izod, *An Introduction to Television Documentary: Confronting Reality* (Manchester: Manchester University Press, 1997).

Lacan, J., 'The mirror stage', in *Ecrits: A Selection*, trans. A. Sheridan (London: Tavistock, 1977), pp. 1–7.

Lipkin, S., *Real Emotional Logic: Film and Television Docudrama as Persuasive Practice* (Carbondale, IL: Southern Illinois University Press, 2002).

Livingston, S. and P. Lunt, *Talk on Television: Audience Participation and Public Debate* (London: Routledge, 1994).

Lusted, D., 'The popular culture debate and light entertainment on television', in C. Geraghty and D. Lusted (eds), *The Television Studies Book* (London: Arnold, 1998), pp. 175–90.

Mills, B., 'Comedy verité: contemporary sitcom form', *Screen*, 45:1 (2004), pp. 63–78.

Nelson, R., *TV Drama in Transition: Forms, Values and Cultural Change* (Basingstoke: Macmillan, 1997).

Newton, D., *Paving the Empire Road: BBC Television and Black Britons* (Manchester: Manchester University Press, 2011).

Nichols, B., *Introduction to Documentary* (Bloomington: Indiana University Press, 2001).

—— *Blurred Boundaries: Questions of Meaning in Contemporary Culture* (Bloomington: Indiana University Press, 1994).

—— *Representing Reality: Issues and Concepts in Documentary* (Bloomington: Indiana University Press, 1991).

Paget, D., *No Other Way to Tell It: Docudrama on Film and Television* (Manchester: Manchester University Press, 2011).

—— 'Acting a part: performing docudrama', *Media International Australia*, 104 (2002), pp. 30–41.

—— *No Other Way to Tell It: Dramadoc/Docudrama on Television* (Manchester: Manchester University Press, 1998).

Piper, H., 'Reality TV, *Wife Swap* and the drama of banality', *Screen*, 54:4 (2004), pp. 273–86.

Roscoe, J. and C. Hight, *Faking It: Mock-documentary and the Subversion of Factuality*, Manchester: Manchester University Press, 2001.

Rosenthal, A. (ed.), *Why Docudrama?: Fact-Fiction on Film and TV* (Carbondale, IL: Southern Illinois University Press, 1999).

Thornham, S. and T. Purvis, *Television Drama: Theories and Identities* (Basingstoke: Palgrave Macmillan, 2005).

Winston, B., *Claiming the Real: The Documentary Film Revisited* (London: BFI, 1995).

Television You Can't See

Television You Can't See

Introduction

An analysis of the kinds of image not allowed to appear in television programmes can tell us a lot about the television medium. Cutting images involves assumptions about how audiences watch television, and how television images can be meaningful to us. The decision to cut an image must be based on the ability to identify and determine what that image represents. So the act of seeing and making sense of the television image is the first precondition for censorship. Furthermore, the significance of what the image might mean for a viewer (for the person cutting it himself or herself, and for another hypothetical television viewer) draws on assumptions about the image's **effects**. Cutting out an image is motivated by a concern about how the image might provoke a response in the viewer who sees it. Television censorship, then, is a topic where questions of **ideology**, the **semiotics** of the television image, and pleasure and repulsion (what we enjoy seeing and what we would prefer not to see) are fundamental. Paradoxically, looking at what we cannot see can tell us much about what seeing and understanding mean.

effects measurable outcomes produced by watching television, such as becoming more violent or adopting a certain opinion.

ideology the set of beliefs, attitudes and assumptions arising from the economic and class divisions in a culture, underlying the ways of life accepted as normal in that culture.

semiotics the study of signs and their meanings, initially developed for the study of spoken language, and now used also to study the visual and aural 'languages' of other media such as television.

Free speech and regulation

The American Constitution, largely because of the global power and influence of the United States, has been an influential statement on the right to free speech. The First Amendment (added in 1787) to the Constitution of the United States declares that 'Congress shall make no law . . . abridging the freedom of speech or of the press'. A similar statement was included in 1948 in the United Nations Universal Declaration of Human Rights, in Article 19: 'Everyone has the right to freedom of opinions without interference and to seek, receive and impart information and ideas through any media regardless of frontiers.' The European Convention on Human Rights seeks to protect freedom of speech in Article 10: 'Everyone has the right to freedom of expression. This right shall include freedom to hold opinions and to receive and impart information without interference by public authority and regardless of frontiers.' But this grand statement is soon subject to qualifications:

> The exercise of these freedoms, since it carries with it duties and responsibilities, may be subject to such formalities, conditions, restrictions or penalties as are prescribed by law and are necessary in a democratic society, in the interests of national security, territorial integrity or public safety, for the prevention of disorder or crime, for the protection of health and morals, for the protection of the reputation or rights of others, for preventing the disclosure of information

received in confidence, or for maintaining the authority and impartiality of the judiciary.

But the claim that restrictions will be those that are necessary in a democratic society is misleading. The obstacles to free speech are normally determined not by a democratic process but instead by the interests of the elite groups, especially governments, that have the power to determine standards of conduct. These are the people who determine what 'the public interest' may be, for example. In media theory, members of the elite group that have the power to determine what information can be circulated are referred to as '**gatekeepers**'. These include, among others, the executives of television companies, the editors of television news programmes and the producers of television programmes in all genres. The gatekeepers make use of both published **regulations** and guidelines about programme content, and their own internalised sense of what it is right and wrong to broadcast. Broadcasting organisations are ultimately dependent on government, since it controls the level of the BBC **licence fee** and the renewal of the commercial channels' licences to broadcast. So while direct censorship is uncommon in Britain, television companies are reluctant to bring themselves into confrontation with government.

gatekeepers the critical term used for the people and institutions (such as television commissioning producers or regulatory bodies) who control access to television broadcasting.

regulation the control of television institutions by laws, codes of practice or guidelines.

licence fee an annual payment by all owners of television sets, which is the main source of income for the BBC.

ACTIVITY 9.1

Look up the current BBC Producers' Guidelines or the guidelines for a commercial channel on the channel's website. What do these say about the reasons for not broadcasting some kinds of programme content, and in what ways might these restrictions be necessary 'in a democratic society'?

Broadcasting in Britain is largely self-regulated on the basis of codes and guidelines drawn up and interpreted by **Ofcom**, a body appointed by the government to supersede the previous regulators the Independent Television Commission (ITC) and the Broadcasting Standards Commission (BSC). Ofcom oversees the activities of all broadcasters to 'further the interests of citizens in communication matters', and was set up by the Communications Act of 2003. The purpose of creating Ofcom was to reduce the confusion that broadcasters and the public have felt in dealing with different television regulators – Ofcom regulates television programmes, radio and telecommunications including mobile phone wavelengths and landlines. It establishes rules on the mergers of media companies and investigates complaints. Ofcom is required to 'further the interests of consumers', so it monitors bad language, violence and sexual scenes on television channels, including BBC programmes that have previously been regulated by the BBC itself. Its guidelines require broadcasters to treat controversial subjects accurately and impartially both in news and in other kinds of programme, and to refrain from expressing an editorial view of their own. Broadcasters must also not make programmes that include anything that could offend against good **taste** or **decency**, or that could encourage crime or lead to disorder. There are severe penalties such as fines, or, in the case of

Ofcom the Office of Communications, a government body responsible for regulating television and other communications media in Britain.

taste and decency conformity to the standards of good taste and acceptable language and behaviour represented on television, as required by regulations.

commercial companies, the withdrawal of their licence to broadcast that can be applied if broadcasters commit serious offences against regulation. The effect of this is to introduce a culture of self-censorship among programme-makers, who know that regulators will review potentially controversial programmes and are required to investigate serious complaints made by viewers. Ofcom's standards are expressed in its Broadcasting Code, which addresses the issues of harm and offence, impartiality and accuracy in programmes, fairness and privacy, and ways that programmes can be sponsored by commercial organisations. Probably the best-known of its rules is the way that children are protected from harm that may be caused by screening violent or sexual content at times when they might be viewing. Broadcasters have for a long time agreed on a 9.00 p.m. '**watershed**', before which time programmes that could be offensive or disturbing to children will not be broadcast.

watershed the time in the day (conventionally 9.00 p.m.) after which programmes with content that may disturb children can be shown.

But 'harm and offence' can refer to many different things. Among the demands made of Ofcom was the requirement in 2006 to investigate whether advertising 'junk food' during children's television programming might have health implications. The reason was that the health effects of obesity among children had become a matter of major concern, and government believed that advertising foods high in fat, salt or sugar encouraged children to consume these foods. The restrictions, supported by organisations like the National Heart Forum, were that the advertising of junk food during children's programmes was banned in programmes aimed at young children. Ofcom commissioned research on the likely impact of this advertising ban on children's health, and calculated that it would reduce child obesity and therefore save about £1 billion currently spent on medical treatment for overweight children. The producers of television programmes for children were concerned that these proposals would make children's television a loss-making programme type, since the revenues deriving from advertisements would not be enough to cover the cost of making the programmes. The independent producers and makers of animated programmes who create the great majority of children's television, represented by their trade organisation Pact, estimated that the financial turnover in their sector of the industry could fall between 12 and 50 per cent. Since the profit margins on children's programmes are already relatively small, this impact has meant that the only major producer of children's programmes left is the BBC, which was already the biggest producer of this genre of television. The organisations representing independent producers, and organisations lobbying for the important role of children's television in child development and creating young people's sense of cultural identity have argued unsuccessfully that a government subsidy is necessary to guarantee the survival of television for children.

The decision about banning junk food advertising to children was closely related to other considerations affecting ITV's future planning and how it is regulated by Ofcom. Before 2006, ITV spent about £30 million per year on new children's programmes, commissioned from independent producers and amounting to half of the total money spent on children's programmes by the biggest commercial broadcasters ITV, Channel 4 and Five put together. But since children's programmes are not as profitable as programmes aimed at a family or adult audience, ITV sought to reduce its commitment to providing children's programmes, a commitment that is part of its responsibility as a public service broadcaster. The public service commitment also requires ITV to provide religious programmes and regional programmes, which, together with children's programmes, are three genres that make it very little money in return. ITV claimed in 2006 that it spent 30 per cent of its £850 million budget for the ITV1 channel on these genres. Factual entertainment and comedy are much more lucrative for ITV and its competing channels. Children's ITV (CITV), beginning at 3 o'clock on weekday afternoons, was regularly beaten in the ratings by *Countdown* and *Deal or No Deal* on Channel 4, thus reducing the amount that ITV could charge advertisers to place ads in its afternoon schedule, because ITV's programmes had smaller audiences. ITV wanted to reduce the number of hours of children's programming on ITV1 from eight hours per week to two hours. The body representing independent television producers, Pact, reported in 2006 that the number of hours of new children's programming on the main public service channels had already fallen from nearly 25 hours each week in 2000 to less than 20 hours in 2004. Although programmes for children have been part of the British television landscape since the beginning of the medium, commercial pressures, competition between the large numbers of channels now available, and wider political concerns about public health have come together to threaten this genre. The regulator, Ofcom, had to find a compromise between the widely supported idea that children's programmes are a good thing, beneficial to society, and the realities of the new age of multi-channel television. The outcome was that ITV moved children's programmes to its digital channel CITV, leaving the BBC as the main provider of children's programmes via its CBBC and CBeebies channels.

ACTIVITY 9.2

What are the arguments for including children's programmes on the main channels BBC1, ITV1 or Channel 4 or Five, rather than on separate children's channels?

While Ofcom has a largely negative role in that it determines what may not be shown, it also positively requires broadcasters to include in their schedules diverse programmes, programmes of 'quality', regional and educational programmes, and to maintain standards of political neutrality. Programme-makers retain close links with the regulator, and will often approach Ofcom at an early stage in the planning of a potentially sensitive programme to gain an opinion on whether it is likely to give rise to concerns over content or tone. It is not only written guidelines that are used by television companies to represent and disseminate standards of taste and decency. The internal culture of television production is involved too, since programme-makers use their experience and knowledge of industry histories, controversies and legal challenges to find rules-of-thumb that guide them as they plan and produce programmes. It can seem that high-profile cases of intervention by regulators are lamentable examples of programme-makers' creative freedom being attacked by distant, often ill-informed outsiders to the television production process. While this might occasionally be the case, it is more usual that problems with programmes could have been foreseen, either by the programme production team specifically or by the institutional culture within production organisations, which always provides a sense of the limits and sphere of freedom of action that programme-makers can expect. The contacts maintained between broadcasters and regulators are of course not just cosy ones, but they do form part of the day-to-day business of television executives and producers, who are aware that a good relationship between programme-makers and regulators smoothes the way for problems and challenges to be anticipated and avoided.

An issue which regularly gets a lot of coverage in the media itself, and which appears to be of concern to a substantial minority of television viewers, is the representation of sex and sexuality on British television. The representation of sexuality on television in Britain has been problematic because of the location of viewing. The fact that the television is physically located in the domestic environment leads to the fear that unsuitable material may be watched by children and cause embarrassment to adults watching with them. The informal codes of behaviour governing family life that are imagined by the producers and regulators of television mean that bad language, sexual scenes and violence are considered to be outside the norms of behaviour expected in the family, and outside the norms of behaviour deemed good for the family audience. However, it is notable the degree to which attitudes to sex on television have liberalised over the decades of television's existence. The next section gives a brief overview of this history.

A brief history of sex on British television

1931: The statue of Ariel, a spirit representing broadcasting, situated on the front of the BBC Broadcasting House headquarters, had its penis shortened on the orders of Lord Reith, the first Director General.

BBC programme guidelines on radio broadcasting were very strict, and extended not only to programmes but also to their presenters. Newsreaders could be sacked if they were involved in a divorce. The BBC *Policy Guide* on **variety programmes** for 1948 contained strict rules on the subject of jokes that could be broadcast in BBC radio comedy. Prohibited subjects included:

variety programmes
entertainment programmes containing a mix of material such as songs and comedy sketches.

- lavatories
- effeminacy in men, and
- honeymoon couples.

These subjects are understandable to us today as possibly offensive because of their connections with bodily functions, homosexuality and heterosexual sex. But we can see how what is offensive changes over time by noting the other subjects that were of concern to the BBC in the 1940s. Two other groups who were not allowed to be mentioned were chambermaids (stereotyped characters who were portrayed as sexually available in lewd jokes about hotels and aristocratic country houses) and travelling salesmen (who were supposedly free to engage in temporary sexual relationships while they moved around the country on business). Evidently, what is offensive to standards of taste and decency depends on the norms of a culture at a particular time, and in a particular location. Taste and decency are cultural concepts, not standards that arise by nature. They are the products of **ideology**, the system of beliefs and assumptions that shapes people's beliefs and attitudes, and which changes according to the social and political character of a given group or national population.

As we have seen in earlier chapters in this book, ideologies are always in conflict with each other, and in a state of change. Even though in the early days of television the BBC decreed that nothing could be broadcast that was in bad taste or offensive to public feeling, television performers looking for ways of attracting large audiences challenged this. Successful comedians used innuendo to replace some of the more explicit material that they used in their music hall and theatre performances. The competition with ITV was important for the BBC, and audiences were significantly attracted not only by big-name performers, but also by downmarket material. Different forces were and are still involved in an often unconscious negotiation and conflict over what the standards of taste and decency should be, forces such as:

- television executives
- television performers
- audiences
- regulators
- the press.

1958: Sexuality was significant to teenage viewers and was evident, for example, in the pop music programmes on which openly sexualised performers appeared.

As the category of the teenager became significant in Britain in the 1950s, television fulfilled its obligation to show society to itself partly by producing programmes for this audience. For television the key issue is that it is a mass medium, increasingly available to all **classes**, and in this period a majority of British households began to own or rent television sets. It was in this context that the BBC satire programme *That Was the Week That Was* began in 1962. The programme was regarded as a primary offender in the loosening of national morals, and the Clean Up TV Campaign was initiated to combat it. Mary Whitehouse (author of the book *Cleaning Up TV*, 1967) was the leading figure in this movement. She objected, for example, to the BBC sketch comedy show *Between the Lines*, produced by BBC Scotland in 1964. It was broadcast at 6.35 p.m. on Thursday evenings, a time regarded as family viewing, and starred the actor Tom Conti in a sketch where his voice-over reveals his sexual curiosity in a young woman he meets at a dance. Mary Whitehouse's chief opponent was the Director General of the BBC in the early 1960s, Hugh Carleton Greene, portrayed by Whitehouse as a purveyor of pornography and a corrupter of society.

In television, programmes claiming highbrow qualities were able to deal with sexual matters. Productions were able to depict sexuality, although no nudity or explicit sexual behaviour was shown on screen, as in the BBC adaptation of the play *In Camera* (*Huit Clos*) by Jean-Paul Sartre in 1964, and the BBC adaptation *Bloomsday*, a version of James Joyce's 1922 novel *Ulysses*, in 1965. This drama featured the sexual arousal of the character Gerty McDowell on the beach, depicted by cutting between the character's orgasmic expressions and shots of exploding fireworks. Documentary series such as *Man Alive* were also able to undertake serious investigations of contemporary sexual behaviour, recognising the effect of liberalisation of the laws on homosexuality, contraception, abortion and divorce.

class a section of society defined by their relationship to economic activity, whether as workers (the working class) or possessors of economic power (the bourgeoisie), for example.

1965: The BBC Wednesday Play Up the Junction *attempted to represent realistically the lives of young working-class women in London, including sexuality and a shocking scene depicting a back-street illegal abortion.*

realism the aim for representations to reproduce reality faithfully, and the ways this is done.

The aim for **realism**, coupled with a desire to compete with ITV for high ratings, led to unheard-of frankness about sex and its consequences. Perhaps the most significant aspect of this move was its focus on young women. Female desire seemed to have been newly discovered by television. It was particularly significant that working-class women were depicted in active sexual relationships, rather than a particular liberated sector of the middle class in programmes aimed at the middle class themselves. The BBC's high-profile drama slot *The Wednesday Play* attracted audiences of fifteen or eighteen million, so its depictions of sexuality were necessarily socially significant since they triggered public discussion and press coverage.

Similarly, the immensely successful drama serial *The Forsyte Saga* on BBC in 1967 depicted rape within marriage for a mass audience, and brought this issue into public consciousness in a new way. After the episode which dealt with the rape of Irene Forsyte by her husband Soames, as an assertion of his power over her when she appeared to be unfaithful to him, the television review and commentary programme *Late Night Line-Up* conducted a poll of viewers asking whether the husband or the wife was in the right:

■ Fifty-four per cent of viewers supported Soames.
■ Thirty-nine per cent supported Irene.
■ Seven per cent were indifferent.

The issue was not whether the BBC should have screened the scene of marital rape, but was about the morality which might enable Soames to feel justified in punishing his wife in this way for her waywardness. The 1968 play by Nigel Kneale, *The Year of the Sex Olympics*, depicted a society in which television was used to pacify its mass audiences by broadcasting a diet of explicit sex. By combining the **format** of the game show with the expert evaluation and competitive qualities of television sports programmes, the play debated the future of television as a mass entertainment medium and the possibility of its manipulation as a form of social control.

format the blueprint for a programme, including its setting, main characters, genre, form and main themes.

The representation of sexual behaviour involving scantily clad young people has certainly been a feature of television history over the past forty years. Pan's People, the dancers on the BBC chart show *Top of the Pops* in the 1970s, were renowned at the time for their sexualised mode of dancing, and invited the viewer both to gaze **voyeuristically** and also to share an ethic of liberation and promiscuity that their dancing appeared to represent. Under the banner of art, Ken Russell's film for the BBC arts programme *Omnibus*, *The Dance of the Seven Veils*, was a **drama-documentary** on the life of the composer Richard Strauss and included numerous scenes of simulated sex. The 1973 BBC drama *The Operation* was the first programme to depict oral sex performed on a man, and the ITV drama *A Point in Time* depicted group sex using naked actors in an exterior location in the same year. The play also featured the first penis to be shown on television. Although the representation of homosexuality was most often in the camp humour of such television comedy personalities as Dick Emery and Larry Grayson, occasionally drama and documentary programmes represented it.

voyeurism gaining sexual pleasure from looking at someone or something that cannot look back.

drama-documentary a television form combining dramatised storytelling with the 'objective' informational techniques of documentary. Abbreviated as 'drama-doc' or 'docudrama'.

1974: The BBC drama Girl *depicted the first lesbian kiss on British television, some twenty-five years before the soap opera* Brookside *claimed to be breaking this boundary.*

Alastair Milne, later BBC Director General, objected personally to Dennis Potter's drama *Brimstone and Treacle*, due to be transmitted in the *Play for Today* slot in 1976. It not only suggested that good consequences could derive from evil actions, and thus challenged conventional morality, but also dealt with the rape of a severely disabled young woman in a suburban living room by a man who was clearly an incarnation of the devil. The play was never banned under broadcasting regulatory law, but was instead withdrawn from transmission by the internal self-censorship of BBC programme executives. Also in 1976, the BBC depicted numerous scenes of nudity and sexual activity in *I, Claudius*, a costume adaptation in which such scenes could be plausibly justified, and in the same year Andrea Newman's serial *Bouquet of Barbed Wire* was broadcast on ITV. This drama featured a suburban family and the numerous sexual relationships within and beyond it, including the husband and his secretary, the wife and her son-in-law, the daughter and her many lovers, and the father's unrealised incestuous desire for his daughter. Clive James, a television critic of the time, described the drama as 'The House of Atreus transferred to Peyton Place', in a reference to the extraordinary violence and sexual complication in the Greek tragedies of Oedipus and his family, and the popular contemporary American television **melodrama** serial *Peyton Place*.

The election of Margaret Thatcher as Prime Minister and the beginning of Conservative government in 1979 appeared to provide a political platform for conservative morality and censorship in broadcasting. Mrs Thatcher's espousal of 'Victorian values' seemed likely to lead to much tougher regulations on what could be depicted, and a return to repressive and infantile representations of sexuality such as the comedy programmes fronted by Dick Emery and Benny Hill. Both of these comedians had programmes in the top twenty highest-rated shows of 1980, drawing on the working-class vulgarity of music hall and seaside postcards. In costume drama two major BBC productions, *The Borgias* of 1981 and *Cleopatra* of 1983, failed to gain audiences despite their combination of apparent historical seriousness with nudity. The arrival of Channel 4 into the British television landscape in 1982 changed the representation of sexuality, however. Since its remit was in part to cater for minority audiences, some of these audiences would necessarily be those with interests in alternative depictions of sexuality.

> **melodrama** a form of drama characterised by exaggerated performance, a focus on reversals of fortune and extreme emotional reactions to events.

1982: The youth audience was one of the first audiences targeted by Channel 4, both in programmes conventionally displaying erotic imagery such as the pop videos on The Tube, *and also in programmes specifically targeting audiences defined by their sexuality such as the gay community in* One in Five *(1983).*

Paradoxically, Thatcher's free market policies and the value given to social groups with economic power led to the increased public visibility and visibility on television of groups such as gay people and British Asians, who were economically significant and whose interests and identity could in part depend on the representation of their sexual identities. Indeed the 1990 BBC drama *Oranges Are Not the Only Fruit* dealt explicitly with the linkage between ideological repression expressed through religion and the liberation of its apparent opposite, lesbian sexuality. Channel 4's policy of screening 'art films' also increased the level of physical sexual activity on television under the rubric of culture. The screening in 1984 of Derek Jarman's film *Sebastiane*,

pan-and-scan
capturing a section of an
image and enlarging it to
fill the television frame, a
technique used to fit
wide film images into the
square television screen.

for example, was problematic because Channel 4 was prohibited from including a scene depicting an erect penis. **Pan-and-scan** technology was used to shift the penis below the level of the frame. In 1986 Channel 4's film season included the use of red triangles at the top corner of the screen in order to alert viewers to potentially offensive content.

The realisation in the mid-1980s that AIDS was likely to be a significant threat to the UK population led to a dramatic reversal in policy on the discussion and representation of sexual activity on television. In 1987 especially, the year in which a massive government information campaign was launched, television discussion of the varieties of sexual behaviour and the mechanics of sex was unprecedented. Ironically, the severity of British broadcasting regulations in earlier decades led to a worry that the television audience was severely under-informed and at risk from sexually transmitted diseases. Channel 4's programme *Sex with Paula* in 1987, which involved Paula Yates chatting to pop stars about their attitudes to sex, was withdrawn by Channel 4 and never broadcast because it appeared to promote promiscuity. Writers, producers and programme controllers in all British broadcasting organisations were very careful always to depict 'safe sex' in any television programme.

ratings the number of
viewers estimated to
have watched certain
programmes, as
compared to the
numbers watching other
programmes.

The BBC transmitted Dennis Potter's serial drama *The Singing Detective* in 1986, at a time when the government had begun to give significant attention to AIDS. The play's most controversial scene involved cross-cutting between the central character's mother having sex in the woods with her lover while her son observed them unseen from the undergrowth, and an elderly man dying of a heart attack in a hospital ward while a large hypodermic was pushed into his heart in an attempt to save him. Penetration, life and death were forcefully linked. Controversy followed in the tabloid newspapers, but the furore was deliberately provoked by the production team in order to boost the **ratings** of the third episode, in which the scene occurred, after the ratings of the first two episodes were lower than expected. When Potter's drama *Blackeyes* (BBC 1989) represented female nudity, but in addition used deliberately voyeuristic camerawork combined with agonised discussion of its eroticism in the voice-over spoken by Potter himself, Potter as a writer, director and voice-over artist far exceeded the norms of representation of sexuality on British television in the 1980s. For although it had become common to discuss sexual activity in current affairs, documentary and other **public service** discussion genres, the dramatic representation of sexual activity had become increasingly self-censored by broadcasters as a result of the AIDS crisis.

public service
in television, the provision
of a mix of programmes
that inform, educate and
entertain in ways that
encourage the
betterment of audiences
and society in general.

audience share the
percentage of viewers
estimated to have
watched one channel as
opposed to another
channel broadcasting at
the same time.

Changes to broadcasting regulations opened the way to satellite broadcasting and cable television in Britain during the 1980s, and during the 1990s the **audience shares** acquired by broadcasters such as Sky became a significant concern for terrestrial channels. Satellite and cable broadcasters had already been able to offer greater sexual content in programmes than their terrestrial competitors, by offering dedicated channels such as the Playboy Channel, and terrestrial broadcasters began to compete on the same terrain by increasing the degree of sexual content in their own programmes. Since the Conservative government of the 1980s had relaxed broadcasting regulations, the primary concern for broadcasters was market share, in other words the acquisition of valuable audience segments. This was significant not only in terms of total audiences, in which mainstream terrestrial channels succeeded in maintaining their dominance, but more importantly in terms of the acquisition of audience groups of high value to advertisers. The most valuable group was the young, whose high disposable income and willingness to spend on inessential and impulse purchases were especially attractive. Furthermore, while audiences in their thirties and over could be expected to watch the most television, audiences in the eighteen to twenty-five range watched relatively little television. The youth audience was, and remains, simultaneously economically attractive yet also elusive.

1990: Channel 4's The Word, *in which hedonistic sexuality and the eroticisation of the talk-show and chart-show genres became highly controversial, was part of efforts on the part of television broadcasters to capture the youth audience.*

Yet in 1994, a television commercial for Neutralia shower gel in which a model briefly revealed a nipple was hastily shifted to after the 9.00 p.m. watershed. The depiction of sex was still controlled by powerful regulation and self-censorship, although discussion of sex, especially in a documentary or in ironic comedies on youth television, had become common. In 1997 the youth audience was offered, for example, *Ibiza Uncovered* by Sky, in which the relatively uninhibited desire of a group of young British holidaymakers to have as much sex as possible in their fortnight away was documented in some detail. The eroticised youthful body had become a commodity for the attraction of youth audiences, and also a source of titillation for the older viewer. The launch of Channel 5 depended on the depiction of sexuality since the channel had very small amounts of working capital, not all of the UK population could receive its signal and it had a very small budget to spend on programmes. In order to gain the 5 per cent audience share required for the channel to satisfy its backers, it concentrated on what its first chief executive, Dawn Airey, called 'films, fucking and football'.

ACTIVITY 9.3

Channel Five no longer schedules many films and programmes that could be described as 'erotic'. Does this show that the channel has achieved its own distinctive place among its competitors, or that other digital channels have taken over the provision of sexual content instead?

Taste and decency today

The force dominating the representation of sexuality on contemporary television is no longer the issue of what can or cannot be shown, or what can or cannot be discussed. Instead, it is the context in which sexuality is represented. When in 2011 the comedian Miranda Hart included a scene in her popular BBC sitcom *Miranda* where she sucked a penis-shaped lollipop, a range of taste and decency issues were considered by BBC executives (Plunkett 2011). The programme was shown on BBC2, and Janice Hadlow, Controller of the channel, discussed the sequence with Jana Bennett, director of BBC Vision. The sitcom was originally commissioned for showing after the 9.00 pm watershed, but was moved to an earlier time when sexual content is more thoroughly policed. Because of the family audience expected during the early evening, the scene was re-shot so that the lollipop was less easily visible.

Figure 9.1 Christina Aguilera performing a song that featured in *The X Factor*. Photo © Lester Cohen/WireImage/Getty.

There was also a debate over whether Hart was licking the lollipop or sucking it, since sucking seemed to have a more erotic connotation. While the incident is in itself somewhat ridiculous, it shows that several factors come into play at present in relation to taste and decency:

- What can be seen on the screen, and how clearly can it be seen?
- What channel is the programme on?
- What time of day is the programme scheduled for?

These factors were important when in 2010 viewers complained to Ofcom about simulated sex in the breakfast television programme *This Morning* on ITV1. There were no naked bodies, and the item on *This Morning* was intended to offer advice to couples experiencing sexual problems. But some viewers found the content disturbing because it was screened on one of the main channels, at a time of day when children could be watching. Similarly, there was controversy when the pop stars Rihanna and Christina Aguilera performed sexualised dance routines during the final programme of *The X Factor* talent show in 2010 (Hewlett 2011). The issue revolved around the fact that *The X Factor* is on the main channel ITV1, is shown in the early evening, and is watched by both adults and children (often viewing together in the same room). But for Ofcom to tighten its rules about what can be shown before 9.00 pm would not address some of the changes that now affect British television and British society:

- Ofcom has less control over minority digital channels where sexual content is much stronger, than it has over the dominant mass audience channels like ITV1.

■ Viewers can download programmes at a different time of day from their original broadcast, record them and view them later, or find them on the internet.

Smaller channels are much more likely to be sanctioned and fined than the major channels like ITV or BBC, because of their lesser expertise in applying regulations in advance of broadcasting programmes and because they assume much greater tolerance among their viewers for sexual content. For example, Ofcom found that the companies Bang Channels and Bang Media had breached the Broadcasting Code with their programmes *Early Bird* and *The Pad* in November 2010. In these programmes, broadcast in the early morning on a channel called Tease Me available on Sky and Freeview, young scantily-clad women stroked themselves, adopted sexual body-positions, and jiggled their breasts, among other things. The aim was to invite viewers to phone premium-rate chat lines, whose numbers were advertised via on-screen captions, and the programmes were considered by Ofcom to be a form of 'participation TV', and thus both a kind of advertisement and also an interactive television programme. Ofcom decided that the Tease Me programmes had caused offence against generally accepted cultural standards, and that the programmes could be seen by children because of the time of day when they were broadcast. But the 2010 decision was not the first time these channels had been found in breach of regulations, having been warned in 2009 and found in breach several times earlier in 2010. Ofcom has found it challenging to get the producers of adult erotic programming to understand the regulations and to comply with them.

Much of the regulation of television is based on the perceived need to protect children from programme content that may be disturbing to them. Although this may seem to be a straightforward notion, it is worth considering how the idea of childhood is constituted. From a **semiotic** point of view, 'childhood' makes sense only in distinction to 'adulthood'. Of course it is adults who are responsible for broadcasting regulations, and who make decisions about what children should or should not see on television. For adults, childhood is a time in their own lives and in the lives of other adults that is inaccessible to them except in memory or by imagining what it must be like to be a child. In the developed nations of the Western world childhood is seen in two contrasting ways. Our current conceptions of childhood began to be developed around the beginning of the nineteenth century. On one hand, children have been regarded as:

■ irrational
■ immoral
■ in need of adult guidance.

There have been high-profile incidents (such as the abduction and murder of the toddler James Bulger by two teenage boys) that seem to show that children can be dangerously violent, uncivilised and threatening. But on the other hand, children are also regarded as:

■ innocent
■ naturally predisposed to be good
■ uncontaminated by adults' problems.

It is very common to see representations, including many representations on television, of children as cute, endearing and able to teach adults lessons about how to see the world more clearly. There is a continuing conflict between these two quite different meanings of childhood, and, when considering how television regulations protect children, it is important to remember that the meanings of childhood are both contradictory and the product of adult thinking.

ACTIVITY 9.4

List the ways in which children are represented on television as cute and innocent, and as uncivilised and threatening (don't forget to include advertisements). How are representations of childhood tied into the bigger issue of humankind as 'naturally' predisposed to goodness or to evil?

---

effects measurable outcomes produced by watching television, such as becoming more violent or adopting a certain opinion.

Children watching television have been a focus of study for several decades. In the 1950s and 1960s, for example, researchers in the United States attempted to devise experiments in which the **effects** of television on children could be discovered (see Bandura 1977 and Himmelwhite *et al.* 1958, for example). This kind of research has been heavily criticised, since the settings in which it took place, the kinds of television shown to children and the methods used by the researchers were very artificial and distant from the ways in which children normally watch television. Despite the flaws in the research, there were in any case very few increases in aggressive or anti-social behaviour that could be observed in the children the researchers studied. Nevertheless, work such as this provided sufficient material to support campaigns for the regulation of children's television in order to protect what were seen as vulnerable audiences from programmes that might turn children into anti-social adults. Another result of this research was to campaign for the teaching

media literacy the skills and competence that viewers learn in order to understand easily the audio-visual 'languages' of media texts.

of '**media literacy**' in schools, with the aim that if children understood how television representations were constructed, and were equipped with study skills to analyse narrative and character, for example, they would be better able to negotiate the meanings of television for themselves. More recently, the developing strands of work described in this chapter, in which more sophisticated methods of studying audiences were devised using interviews conducted at home or in more real-world settings, have been used to attempt to find out how children make meanings from their television viewing, and how their television experience fits into their broader social lives.

Several books have been published by the media academic David Buckingham (1993a, 1993b, 1996), who draws on the range of audience research techniques discussed in this chapter to explore both parents' and children's reactions to television. Some of this work focuses on cognitive issues, in other words, what adults and children understand from television consciously; other strands of the research focus on children's emotional and unconscious responses to television. The results show that both watching television and talking about television programmes play a significant role in the process by which children learn to understand themselves, other people and society. Some of children's interaction with television involves learning and using knowledge of television codes and conventions (media literacy), such as the differences between television genres, narrative forms and placing programmes in context by deploying knowledge about the production processes involved in the making of programmes. It appears that the more children know about television codes and conventions and production processes, the more they are able to control the emotional reactions that are provoked by programmes. This seems to support the arguments made by academics and educators that the teaching of television and media in schools performs a useful social function. But, interestingly, some of the more controversial aspects of children's viewing of television seemed also to be both useful and important to them.

It is known that children sometimes consciously seek out disturbing programmes containing violence or sex, and programmes in the genres of horror or action adventure which broadcasting regulations seek to protect them from. Buckingham (1996) found that the function of watching these programmes for children was to test their own maturity in coping with troubling emotions. In other words, watching programmes that could be disturbing was part of children's effort to grow up, to understand the adult world and to anticipate being part of it. A key concept in understanding this process is **modality**. Adults use the recognition of modality in order to judge whether representations are realistic, or whether they are fantastic or comic, for example. Children watch violent, sexual or otherwise potentially disturbing programmes in order to learn how to deploy an understanding of modality, and thus to share the viewing practices of adults. Indeed, children's television programmes commonly feature central characters who are childlike even though they may be adults, thus representing the negotiations that real children in the audience make about their difference or similarity to adults and their place in the adult world. Characters in children's television programmes who are actually children are also commonly active in the narrative because adults fail to deal with a problem, or are incompetent. Academic research on child viewers seems to confirm that for children the most important aspect of watching television is that it provides a resource for working through conscious and unconscious understandings of their identity, and their social position in relation to adults. Watching television is pleasurable for children, but it is also an essential part of their gradual integration into society as a whole.

modality the fit between a fictional representation and the conventional understanding of reality. High modality describes a close fit, and weak modality a distant one.

ACTIVITY 9.5

To what extent do adults (like children) watch television not only in order to enjoy it, but also to test their reactions to disturbing issues such as violence or sex? How might modality be useful in explaining adults' use of the concept of realism as a standard against which to judge and evaluate programmes?

Protecting children from television content that could be disturbing or in some way bad for them is connected to assumptions about how other vulnerable groups in society can be adversely affected by television. Since television programmes and television regulations have been largely made by well-educated and socially powerful elite groups in society, the underlying ideology of television regulation has considered the less socially powerful and less well-educated mass audiences of television as vulnerable and prone to bad influences in the same way that children might be. Theodor Adorno and the **Frankfurt School** considered that the mass media perpetrated what we now call 'dumbing down' and encouraged the mass audience's fascination with trivia, immorality and indiscriminate consumption. There is a long tradition among commentators on television to consider mass audiences as 'them' in contrast to the more sophisticated 'us' represented by those commentators themselves. The mass audiences of television have been regarded as childlike and in need of protection. One of the ideological assumptions behind television regulation is that viewers (or at least some of them, who are not as sophisticated as the people who make programmes or frame television regulations) are not able to discriminate for themselves between programmes that have socially positive meanings and programmes that could encourage anti-social or dangerous behaviour. The way that broadcasting regulations refer to children or to vulnerable adults can be regarded as a way of justifying the ability of a small group in society to legislate for what the majority are able to understand.

Attitudes perceiving the television viewer as a vulnerable person who needs to be protected tend to regard the viewer as an object, as a person separate and different from that small group of people who frame broadcasting regulations. The gradual liberalisation during the twentieth century of regulations on television programme content is partly the result of a recognition of this problem, and the granting to television viewers of greater agency and discrimination. Rather than thinking of the television viewer as a passive object that television programmes can directly affect, perhaps causing the viewer to imitate anti-social behaviour seen on the screen such as violent, sexually excessive or illegal behaviour, more recently television viewers have been thought of as people whose relationships with television are more complex. Rather than simply imitating what they see on the screen, viewers are now understood as being aware of how television operates as a medium, and how the images and sounds on television are not the same as real life but are representations of it. This issue of how the audience is considered increasingly as a subject rather than an object, and how television viewers understand what they see in diverse and complex ways, is the subject of the next chapter in this book, which considers television audiences and how they can be studied and understood.

Theories of regulation

Television programmes are **commodities**, offering pleasure to their viewers through the payment of money, whether via advertisements, subscription or a licence fee. When considered from a perspective informed by Karl **Marx**'s studies of economics, the real meaning of nudity, violence or sexual activity in television programmes can be found in how programmes work within the exchange system of the **capitalist** economy. Viewers will pay money to see images of nudity or violence, for example, by subscribing to 'adult' television satellite or cable channels. Television regulators largely support the position of television within the capitalist system, and are prepared to accept the exploitation of images of sexuality or violence as long as this is cloaked by an acceptable justification. This justification is the result of the

Frankfurt School
a group of theorists in the mid-twentieth century who worked on theories of contemporary culture from a Marxist perspective. Key members, notably Theodor Adorno and Max Horkheimer, left Nazi Germany in the 1930s to work abroad.

commodity
a raw material or product whose economic value is established by market price rather than the intrinsic qualities or usefulness of the material or product itself.

Marxism the political and economic theories associated with the German nineteenth-century theorist Karl Marx, who described and critiqued capitalist societies and proposed Communism as a revolutionary alternative.

capitalism
the organisation of an economy around the private ownership of accumulated wealth, involving the exploitation of labour to produce profit that creates such wealth.

discourses of **narration**, **genre** and form that contain images of sexual behaviour, violence or some other challenging content. Television representations mobilise the viewer's desire to see and hear these exciting or arousing images, and fix them in narratives. The question for regulators is how excessive the meanings and effects (such as sexual arousal or disposition to commit violent acts, for example) of programmes might be. But, as earlier chapters of this book have argued, the audio-visual representations on television never have only one meaning, but many. Since television texts are '**polysemic**', it is hard for television regulators or campaigners (and for academics and students) to find a secure set of rules to describe the images and sounds that should be cut out. The meaning of television representations can appear to be immediately readable because many of them are 'realistic' (in semiotic terminology, television signs are **iconic** and **indexical**). Television regulators, just like academics writing analyses of television programmes or students writing essays, try to decode the meanings of television programmes. Regulating television involves processes of 'translation' that aim to determine the meanings of programmes, and so this always leaves room for debate about whether a programme really means what a regulator thinks it does.

Meaning in a television programme, the way that different images are linked systematically together, depends on how each moment is contained and limited by the moments around it. In most television programmes all the various components of the programme are ordered by narrative (whether a fictional story, a non-fictional documentary treatment or a news story, for instance), with the aim that the programme will make sense for the viewer. Meanings are coded and systematised. Programme-makers aim for each moment to fit well with the next, and they avoid excessive stillness, too much movement, undecideable, meaningless images or images that are shocking and seem to leap right out of the programme's narrative flow. By setting up the regime in which programme-makers self-censor their programmes, regulators are taking further what programme-makers already do. They aim to cut what is excessive, while preserving the coherence, smoothness and comprehensibility which television culture already takes as the norm. The operation of television self-censorship at the programme-planning stage or later in the editing suite depends on isolating particular images or sequences from the flow of the programme's narrative, identifying them as problematic and then removing them in a way which does not challenge the coherence of the programme as a whole. What is at stake in this is therefore the **denotation** of something that might be worthy of being cut out, and its relationship with the meanings of the programme.

Some of the laws that govern television regulation, in Britain as elsewhere, require that a television image must be cut out if it denotes something that is prohibited. Regulators make use of a list of acts and words that television programmes are not allowed to represent, and programme-makers know these rules and make changes during post-production, only occasionally requiring regulators to intervene. For example, obscene words were 'bleeped out' from *Big Brother* when it was shown in mid-evening, and in one programme from the salacious talk-show *So Graham Norton* a webcam image of a woman playing the penny-whistle with her vagina was technically processed to blur the details of the whistle's relationship to her body. In these two examples, programme-makers were following guidelines on taste and decency that do not in themselves have legal status. But some of the laws of the land in Britain can apply to television programmes. For example, the Protection of

narration the process of telling a story through image and sound. Narration can also refer to the spoken text accompanying television images.

genre a kind or type of programme. Programmes of the same genre have shared characteristics.

polysemia the quality of having multiple meanings at the same time. Texts such as this are called 'polysemic'.

iconic sign in semiotics, a sign which resembles its referent. Photographs, for example, contain iconic signs resembling the objects they represent.

indexical sign in semiotics, a sign which is the result of what it signifies, in the way that smoke is the result of fire.

denotation in semiotics, the function of signs to portray or refer to something in the real world.

Children Act states that no image of a child in a sexual situation can be shown (on television, as well as in other media such as magazines or newspapers). So in programmes in the documentary series *The Hunt for Britain's Paedophiles*, videotapes and photographs that the police had seized as evidence had to be obscured by black bars or blurred patches so that television viewers could not see them in detail. It is important to recognise that the regulation of television depends on the ideological assumptions about what is acceptable and what is unacceptable in a given culture. In other words, television regulation and censorship are a political matter that is potentially open to debate, and not self-evident or natural. At present television images of naked women's bodies have become more acceptable than images of naked men: television programmes cannot denote an erect penis, although they can denote female genitals in some non-sexual programme contexts (such as medical documentaries). Television regulation is also affected by the **genre** that a programme occupies.

Some laws, such as the Obscene Publications Act (1959), can be contested by arguing for the good intention of a programme, for example that it is in 'the public interest', or that it is artistically excellent. In other words, questions of **authorship** and **aesthetic** value are also significant. The Obscene Publications Act defines obscenity as something whose effect as a whole is to 'tend to deprave and corrupt persons who are likely, having regard to all relevant circumstances, to read, see or hear the matter contained or embodied therein'. For the Act, a programme might be considered obscene because of what is represented, but it can be legal because the intention and effect of the whole work is artistically excellent or morally improving. It is for this reason that programmes claiming to be '**quality** television' can contain more graphic violence, more explicit sexual behaviour or more obscene language than programmes that cannot easily make a claim to be 'quality'. The Channel 4 drama serial *Queer as Folk* did not show explicit images of homosexual sex (it was after all performed by actors and therefore sex was simulated rather than real), but there were numerous scenes in which penetrative sex and other kinds of homosexual activity were represented. Because *Queer as Folk* was an authored drama, with high production values and a recognised 'artistic intention', its representation of homosexual sex was able to be much more graphic than in any previous British television drama.

Television regulation of taste and decency tells us a lot about how television is organised in society, and how our assumptions about the meanings of programmes and the interpretative activity of audiences work. Television regulation attempts to control the meanings the viewer can consume, and thus it is about the regulation of the viewer as much as the regulation of what the television set shows. Since television is a business and an industry, regulation predominantly follows the pattern of how society controls the channels of consumer culture more generally (in film, book publishing or advertising, for example). Regulation intervenes by naming, describing and prescribing ways of seeing and hearing. This rests on presumptions about how viewers perceive what they see and hear on television, how they identify with or are repulsed by the meanings of television programmes and how they might imitate what they see and hear or be prompted to adopt modes of behaviour that are represented. Inasmuch as television viewers' understandings and desires are not straightforwardly the product of television images and sounds, but are instead negotiated by viewers in complex ways involving images, sounds and the ideologies

authorship the question of who an author is, the role of the author as creator, and the significance of the author's input into the material being studied.

aesthetic a specific artistic form. Aesthetics means the study of art and beauty.

quality in television, kinds of programme that are perceived as more expensively produced and, especially, more culturally worthwhile than other programmes.

of culture in and around them, television regulation needs to be understood in this wider framework of social and political life.

ACTIVITY 9.6

Is it acceptable for adults subscribing to cable or satellite channels to see greater violence or sexual content in programmes than is currently seen in free-to-air broadcasting? Could you draw up a list of images, actions or words that would be acceptable in subscription television but not in free-to-air television, and how would issues such as programme genre and format affect this?

Case study: reporting conflict

The coverage of war and conflict in recent years has been dramatically affected by the ability of television news to convey very recently recorded, moving images and sound both from battlefield sites and also from locations behind the lines, from where journalists can relay information. This case study focuses on the control of television reporting on television, and also how the recent role of social media (like YouTube and Facebook) has supplemented television coverage and influenced it. Television coverage had a dramatic effect on the perception of conflict not only in Britain but also internationally, shaping its representation. Television has overtaken newspapers as the dominant source of news in Britain and other developed nations. This is partly because broadcasting regulations demanding '**balance**' and 'objectivity' govern television news, but not newspaper publishing. Another key consideration, which is the focus of this section, is the value of immediacy in television news deriving from its incorporation of **actuality** pictures and live reporting. Television news programmes can, on rare occasions, incorporate live footage during programmes, although the technological complexity of doing this can make news producers wary of links with news crews in distant locations. News programmes are planned to the second, so the immediacy of live **ENG** footage potentially conflicts with the desire to connote orderliness and authority in news broadcasting. A more common use of ENG footage is therefore to create packages where sequences of actuality pictures have been edited together with a voice-over by the news reporter. The package will be of a known length and can be combined with live studio discussion and other commentary. But since television news attracts its audience with the promise of seeing and hearing news events happen, especially when they are happening live, there is both a professional pride for broadcasters and a hook for potential audiences in using actuality footage. Therefore on-screen captions denoting a live report and the frequent mention of the word 'live' in the pieces to camera by news presenters are a notable feature of television news programmes.

There is a hierarchy of **news value**, in which live actuality pictures are the most attractive to the producers of television news programmes, followed by actuality pictures which have been pre-recorded, and finally those stories which cannot be illustrated by actuality footage or other visual forms, such as an interview, and which are the stories least likely to appear in the producer's running order for a programme. News programmes depend on a mythology in

balance the requirement in television news and current affairs to present both sides of an argument or issue.

actuality footage television pictures representing an event that was filmed live. The term usually refers to pictures of news events.

electronic newsgathering (ENG) the use of lightweight cameras and digital technology such as portable satellite transmission dishes to record and transmit news pictures and sound.

news value the degree of significance attributed to a news story, where items with high news value are deemed most significant to the audience.

Figure 9.2 A US soldier plays soccer with an Iraqi boy in Mosul, Iraq, Wednesday 26 October 2005. Photo by Mohammed Ibrahim. © EMPICS

which the television audience can apparently directly witness any significant events occurring anywhere in the world. Television news claims to denote events objectively and immediately, offering a neutral and transparent channel of communication. The iconic quality of television images, which appear simply to record what is unfolding in front of the camera, are key signifiers of this mythology of transparency in television news and in other television factual genres. The word 'television' means seeing at a distance, and television news is a central example of the mythology underlying the medium. For almost everyone in the television audience, the public world of politics, war, business and natural catastrophe is distant, but television news advertises its ability to connect the relatively isolated and disengaged viewer with this more dramatic and apparently important reality. Television news bridges the gap between public space and private space, which has ambivalent ideological effects:

- On one hand, the audience is linked by the medium of television with the wider public world.
- On the other hand, this wider world is shaped according to the codes and conventions of television news, and necessarily remains at a distance from the audience.

The institutional and representational structures of television news simultaneously involve the audience and disempower it.

The chance to circumvent the institutions and professional practices of television news is offered by the newer media of web-based video services and social media. Recently there has been much interest in the newer media as a way of representing conflict and war, especially where national governments restrict access to the traditional media for their citizens. In October 2011, the Arabic Al Jazeera channel broadcast a film by Ibrahim Hamdan about the people who shot videos of popular uprisings in Tunisia, Egypt and Libya, called *Images of Revolution* (available on the web at www.aljazeera.com/programmes/aljazeeraworld/2011/10/2011101 974451215541.html). This documentary feature programme aimed to tell the story behind video footage of the uprisings that had been shot by people in those countries on their mobile phones. Many of the phone videos were uploaded onto the internet and subsequently used by news television broadcasters to illustrate news stories about the events. The filming of the uprisings was a news story in itself, since television news channels also debated whether the mobile phone footage had stimulated the uprisings in the Middle East to become more widespread and larger in scale, since people in the countries concerned could view the phone footage on the internet. The filmmaker Ibrahim Hamdan located the people who had shot footage of protesters and the often violent responses of the government military forces to the protests. In many cases he was able to interview the video-makers at the locations where they had shot their films. In *Images of Revolution*, it becomes clear that the mobile phone film-makers were middle-class, well-educated people who had access to the internet – people who were students or professional workers. Commentary by experts in the film explains how the rapid growth in the use of mobile phones and social media sites (like Facebook) in the few years preceding the uprisings of 2011 led to the presence of a significant number of interconnected individuals with interests in changing the political make-up of their countries in the Middle East.

ACTIVITY 9.7

Visit the website for Al Jazeera's English service (www.aljazeera.com). Although the channel is a global news service, how do its current programmes demonstrate its interests in Middle East news or news affecting that region?

The governments of the region exercised tight control over the conventional broadcast media of radio and television, and also over newspaper reporting. But social media networks enabled individuals to communicate with each other, and to post still images and moving video publicly, thus cementing the politically active people together and providing access for themselves and the outside world to disturbing video footage of the uprisings and the military responses to them. Images showed people gathering in large numbers in public places to express their discontent with their governments' regimes and violent acts of repression by military and police forces, like the use of water cannons or tear gas directed at the protesting crowds. These images and video were used by Al Jazeera and other television companies to realise news stories. Television news could give their stories a basis in fact by showing actuality footage of events, despite the news journalists' inability to get to the uprisings themselves because of restrictions imposed by the governments. As discussed in Chapter 4 in relation to news narratives, actuality images like these ground news stories in visual evidence. But in the case of video shot by individuals witnessing the protests, an added layer of authenticity was created because of the opportunity for non-professional video makers to generate the images themselves.

In some of the videos, the sound of the video-makers crying out in shock when protesters were beaten or even shot by police can be heard. Sound as well as image signified the emotional intensity of events and invited viewers of the videos to be similarly appalled. Ordinary people became news gatherers and news reporters, 'citizen journalists' bearing witness to events and bringing them to the attention of the wider world. The video-makers were not impartial, however, since their decision to film and publicise the rebellions they witnessed was motivated by a desire to take part in the political battles over the future government of their countries. Content provided by non-professional video makers is a powerful addition to the conventional television news function of bearing witness to events. This is especially the case when the reports by users come from places where professional journalists are unable to get access, whether because they are prevented by official regulations or because an event happens in an inaccessible place. In a study of how audience-generated material was used by the professionals at BBC News, Wardlaw and Williams (2010) found that this material conformed to some of the conventional news values shared by news programme-makers. The material was new, had a strong sense of giving the audience access to events, and was used to bear witness to developing new stories. But it also posed challenges for the ways of working that news professionals are accustomed to, and the strategies of the television institutions for which journalists work. When Neil Thurman (2008) interviewed the editors of British online news websites, he found that journalists were quite defensive when offered the option to incorporate audience-generated material. They were concerned about the legal issues of who had ownership of the footage, how it might be used in conjunction with their own work, and about the challenge to the professional practices and reputation of journalists and news organisations that could be posed by incorporating material made by amateurs.

The availability of a mass of information about the world around us via television, and now by internet media, led to arguments by John Ellis (2000b: 9) and Roger Silverstone (2007) that audiences gain a new sense of social and political responsibility. When we can see things that we were not able to see before, it is not plausible to deny responsibility or involvement in the actions of others. Of course there is a difference between being present at an event and witnessing the event on television, for example by watching the news. But even though a television viewer in Britain might not have been present during the popular uprisings in the Middle East in 2011, that viewer can still gain a strong sense of being informed and involved by watching actuality pictures on the television news or by accessing news websites that show video footage of them. The dramatic footage included in news bulletins, shot by professional camera operators or by amateurs on their mobile phones, can provide an intense impression of truthfulness and implicate the television viewer in a sense of responsibility. Indeed, viewers can respond by conventional means such as writing letters to their member of Parliament, or talking to people they know, but they can now also leave comments on the webpages associated with television news broadcasts, and comments on the blog webpages of internet news channels. The opportunities for participation in public affairs, and the building of a community of active citizens, were already increased by the mass media culture of the twentieth century and are now intensified in the interactive media landscape of the present time. In the case of the uprisings in the Middle East in 2011, social media and citizen journalism are reactions to the perception by the video-makers that television in their own countries did not represent protest and government action accurately, or even at all. The images and video footage shot in Libya, Tunisia and Egypt were, in part, a desire for television that the viewers in those countries could not see. The availability of social networks and internet video compensated for a lack in the television of the region. But once the images and video had appeared on the internet, they could be re-broadcast and re-used by television, in news coverage on television around the world.

SUMMARY OF KEY POINTS

■ Preventing audiences from seeing something on television relies on an often unacknowledged theory of how audiences might be affected by what they see.

■ It has been impossible for researchers to prove that what television viewers see has a definite effect on their behaviour.

■ The ways in which the censorship and regulation of television happen in any society depend on the ideologies of that society, and change as the norms of society change over time.

■ Conflicting ideas about freedom of speech, versus the protection of vulnerable viewers, have marked the ways that censorship and regulation happen in Western societies.

■ Institutions such as Ofcom lay down guidelines and rules about what can be shown on television.

■ In times of war and other political crises, television regulation and self-regulation is much more evident than at other times in Western societies, and reveals the significance that television is thought to have on its audiences' understanding of events.

■ The possibility for ordinary people to create videos that can then be shown on television or via the internet offers new opportunities for national media regulation to be evaded.

Further reading

Badsey, S., 'The influence of the media on recent British military operations', in I. Stewart and S. Carruthers (eds), *War, Culture and the Media: Representations of the Military in Twentieth-century Britain* (Trowbridge: Flicks Books 1993), pp. 5–21.

Bandura, A., *Social Learning Theory* (London: Prentice Hall, 1977).

Baudrillard, J., 'The reality gulf', *The Guardian*, 11 January 1991, reprinted in P. Brooker and W. Brooker (eds), *Postmodern After-images: A Reader in Film, Television and Video* (London: Arnold, 1997), pp. 165–7.

Bignell, J., 'Writing the child in media theory', *Yearbook of English Studies*, 32 (2002b), pp. 127–39.

Buckingham, D., *Moving Images: Understanding Children's Emotional Responses to Television* (Manchester: Manchester University Press, 1996).

—— *Reading Audiences: Young People and the Media* (Manchester: Manchester University Press, 1993b).

—— *Children Talking Television: The Making of Television Literacy* (London: Falmer, 1993a).

Ellis, J., *Seeing Things: Television in the Age of Uncertainty* (London: I. B. Tauris, 2000b).

Freedman, L. and E. Karsh, *The Gulf Conflict 1990–1991: Diplomacy and War in the New World Order* (London: Faber, 1993).

Gillespie, M., 'Ambivalent positionings: the Gulf War', in P. Brooker and W. Brooker (eds), *Postmodern After-images: A Reader in Film, Television and Video* (London: Arnold, 1997), pp. 172–81.

Hewlett, S., 'Why the Daily Mail has it in for Ofcom', *The Guardian*, Media section, 13 June 2011, p. 3.

Himmelwhite, H. T. *et al.*, *Television and the Child: An Experimental Study of the Effect of Television on the Young* (London: Nuffield Foundation and Oxford University Press, 1958).

Kellner, D., *Media Culture: Cultural Studies, Identity and Politics Between the Modern and the Postmodern* (London: Routledge, 1995).

Livingstone, S. and R. Das, *Public Attitudes, Tastes and Standards: A Review of the Available Empirical Research* (London School of Economics, 2009). Available at http://eprints.lse.ac.uk/25117/1/Public_attitudes_tastes_and_standards.pdf.

Lury, K., *British Youth Television: Cynicism and Enchantment* (Oxford: Oxford University Press, 2001).

Norris, C., '"Postscript": Baudrillard's second Gulf War article', in P. Brooker and W. Brooker (eds), *Postmodern After-images: A Reader in Film, Television and Video* (London: Arnold, 1997), pp. 168–71.

Plunkett, J., 'Miranda's dilemma', *The Guardian*, Media section, 29 August 2011, p. 2.

Poster, M., *The Second Media Age* (Cambridge: Polity, 1995).

Silverstone, R., *Media and Morality: On the rise of the Mediapolis* (Cambridge: Polity, 2007).

Thurman, N., 'Forums for citizen journalists? Adoption of user generated content initiatives by news media', *New Media and Society*, 10:1 (2008), pp. 139–57.

Walker, I., 'Desert stories or faith in facts?', in M. Lister (ed.), *The Photographic Image in Digital Culture* (London: Routledge, 1995), pp. 236–52.

Wardlaw, C. and A. Williams, 'Beyond user-generated content: a production study examining the ways in which UGC is used at the BBC', *Media Culture and Society*, 32:5 (2010), pp. 781–99.

Whitehouse, M., *Cleaning Up TV: From Protest to Participation* (London: Blandford, 1967).

Television Audiences

Television Audiences

Introduction

This chapter discusses how broadcasters gain information about audience sizes, and why this information is significant to them. An important matter to bear in mind when reading this chapter is that numerical, quantitative information does not reveal answers to the questions about why and how people watch television. But since the measurement of audiences in terms of numbers of viewers is crucial to the economics and organisation of television, this chapter discusses ways of studying this. The Dutch television theorist Ien Ang (1991, 1996) has analysed the practices of audience measurement, and shown that broadcasters have an insistent desire to find ways of measuring audiences. But audience measurement techniques set limits to the kind of conclusions that can be drawn from them. Audience measurement:

- is statistical
- is based on samples of viewers, and
- results in generalisations about what viewers find pleasurable.

Another very significant issue is why audiences watch television programmes, whether they enjoy them and what role television programmes play in their lives. These are qualitative questions, questions that require information about the value people attribute to television, rather than statistical information.

Television Studies theorists regard the television audience not as a relatively uniform mass but instead as a complex set of overlapping groups with different allegiances, backgrounds and interests. The effect of this is to shift the object of study from the television programme, as a text, to the television audience responding to this text. The key concept in the discourse of Television Studies – the plurality of meanings – is still in use, but is now applied not only to the many meanings of programme texts, but to the many different ways in which audiences might interpret programmes. It could be argued that earlier critical methodologies focusing on the text privileged the role of the critic himself or herself in determining the correct meaning of television programmes, assuming that the meanings discovered through analysis were those that the audience was taking from programmes. By focusing on the audience, often by setting up situations in which the researcher listens in person to the talk of actual viewers, Television Studies has granted more power and authority to ordinary viewers and undercut, to some extent, the mastery of academic discourse over the subject that it aimed to discuss. In undertaking these newer methods of research, Television Studies has also paid much more attention than it had done previously to groups of people excluded from study. In particular, television viewers belonging to ethnic subcultures, women viewers, children and the elderly began to be the subject of research, and their responses to television were taken seriously. Because the researchers working in Television Studies are generally critical of the power relationships operating in contemporary society, audience studies also provided an opportunity to find new sources of potential **resistance** to the ways that the television business is organised, and to the conventional and **ideological** meanings that are discovered in the majority of programmes by close **textual analysis**. Rather than looking for instances of television programmes that could be held up as examples of resistant texts, researchers looked for groups among the television audience that could be characterised as resistant viewers.

The competition between television channels and methods of delivering television by **terrestrial** and **interactive** means, have made competition for audiences more and more significant. The total television audience has become increasingly fragmented, although the number of hours per week that the average viewer watches has remained at about four hours per day. Broadcasters aim to capture a significant share of the available audience for their own programmes, especially if their source of funding is advertising. Clearly, broadcasters can charge advertisers substantial amounts of money to put advertisements on their channel only if a large or valuable audience group is watching that channel when the advertisement is shown. The same concerns are also important to broadcasters that are not funded by advertising. The BBC gains its income not through advertising but through the payment of the **licence fee**. But the government is unlikely to keep increasing the cost of a licence fee, and might even abolish the licence fee altogether, if the BBC is not gaining audiences comparable to those of the commercial channels. Broadcasters compete against each other to achieve large audience sizes for their programmes (**ratings**) and to encourage viewing of their own programmes rather than the competing programmes on other channels that are shown at the same time (**audience share**).

ACTIVITY 10.1

Which activities might compete for the time of the valuable eighteen to thirty-five age group and persuade them to watch less television? What connections might there be between time spent watching television and economic prosperity, rates of employment and ways of using leisure time apart from watching television?

The economics of watching television

Television programme-making has to be paid for. While cinema audiences pay for films by buying tickets to see them (and buying products associated with films), television viewers pay indirectly either by buying the television licence, paying for subscriptions to providers like Sky or by buying products that are advertised in television advertisements. Commercial broadcasters sell audiences to advertisers by estimating the size of audience expected to view a particular programme and estimating the composition of the audience (in terms of its age, gender and economic power). According to the size and composition of the audience, the broadcaster charges advertisers a particular sum of money per thousand viewers that it expects to view a certain programme. The assumption behind this is that viewers are

---

resistance the ways in which audiences make meaning from television programmes that is counter to the meanings that are thought to be intended, or that are discovered by close analysis.

ideology the set of beliefs, attitudes and assumptions arising from the economic and class divisions in a culture, underlying the ways of life accepted as normal in that culture.

textual analysis a critical approach which seeks to understand a television text's meanings by undertaking detailed analysis of its image and sound components, and the relationships between those components.

terrestrial broadcasting from a ground-based transmission system, as opposed to broadcasting via satellite.

interactive offering the opportunity for viewers to respond to what is broadcast, by sending signals back to the broadcaster (along a cable or phone-line, for example).

licence fee an annual payment by all owners of television sets, which is the main source of income for the BBC.

ratings the number of viewers estimated to have watched certain programmes, as compared to the numbers watching other programmes.

audience share the percentage of viewers estimated to have watched one channel as opposed to another channel broadcasting at the same time.

economically active in making purchases during the time that they are not watching television. So although it may seem that watching television is a respite from the activities of earning money and spending it, the viewer's economic activity is the precondition that enables television programmes on commercial channels to be made.

Jhally and Livant (1986) establish parallels between the nineteenth-century economist and political theorist Karl **Marx**'s theory of labour and watching television. For part of the time that people are at work, they are engaged in socially necessary labour. This is the time spent doing the work that generates the money to pay people's wages. For the remaining hours spent at work, people are engaged in surplus labour, which makes the money that generates profit for the **capitalist** (the owner of the business). In the hours people are not at work, they are engaged in the reproduction of labour: sleeping, eating, recuperating in order to be ready to go to work the next day and do the same things all over again. The same model can be applied to commercial television broadcasting. Television networks make their money by selling advertising time. The commodity that is sold by the network is audience time. In a parallel with Marx's concept of labour power, 'watching power' is the cost of reproduction, in other words the cost of the programme. During socially necessary viewing time, audiences watch the advertisements equivalent to the amount of money the programmes have cost the network to produce. In surplus viewing time, audiences are watching advertisements solely for the profit of the networks, since the production of programmes has already been covered during socially necessary viewing time.

For example, a programme might cost £800,000, which is the amount paid by the network to the television producers who made it. This programme might last twenty-four minutes, with another six minutes filled with advertisements. One thirty-second advertisement might bring in £100,000 in payments to the network by advertisers. Six minutes would allow twelve of these thirty-second advertisements, bringing £1,200,000 into the network. So, for this thirty-minute slot:

- the network income is £1,200,000
- the costs of broadcasting are £800,000
- making a surplus for the network of £400,000.

Once the operating costs of the network have been deducted from this figure, the rest is profit, for which Marx used the term surplus value. From the audience point of view, four of the advertisements during the six-minute break are socially necessary labour time, generating the £800,000 needed to cover the cost of the programme. The other eight advertisements watched by the audience in the six-minute commercial break are required to generate profit for the network. The price of advertising varies according to whether the programme in which they are placed is a free-to-air broadcast programme or an on-demand programme that a viewer has chosen to watch by selecting it from an online menu. In 2011 an advertiser would expect to pay about £20 per thousand viewers watching a **scheduled free-to-air** programme, whereas the same number of viewers would cost the advertiser about £25 for an on-demand programme. The reason for the difference is that younger viewers in the 16–34-year-old age group are more likely to watch on-demand programmes, and it is these viewers who comprise the most attractive market

Marxism the political and economic theories associated with the German nineteenth-century theorist Karl Marx, who described and critiqued capitalist societies and proposed Communism as a revolutionary alternative.

capitalism the organisation of an economy around the private ownership of accumulated wealth, involving the exploitation of labour to produce profit that creates such wealth.

schedule the arrangement of programmes, advertisements and other material into a sequential order within a certain period of time, such as an evening, day or week.

free-to-air television programming for which viewers make no direct payment.

for advertisers because they spend most freely on the products and services advertised on television. In 2010, ITV's *The X Factor* brought an income of more than £100 million from television advertising, with one thirty-second commercial costing advertisers £150,000 (Sweeney 2011).

The maximisation of profit by television networks depends on decreasing socially necessary viewing time and increasing surplus viewing time. This can be done by:

- selling shorter commercials which have proportionately higher cost per second
- reducing the cost of programmes
- reducing the amount of non-income-generating time by making programmes shorter and including more commercials.

Since advertisers pay for audiences' viewing time, they need to know that audiences are watching the commercials. The '**people meter**' is a mechanism for monitoring this, in which people in a household punch in their personal identification number when they begin to watch television and punch out the number when they leave. This is very similar to punching in to work in a factory, and punching out at the end of the day. While it might seem strange to equate watching television with doing paid work, the analogy is actually very close. It is just that we are accustomed to thinking of television viewing as leisure (the opposite of work), and separating it from the harsh calculations of profit and loss that govern life in highly developed societies such as Britain. But television is a business and an industry in which television viewers are increasingly regarded as a market, and could also be understood as participants.

people meter a device resembling a television remote control, used in sample households to monitor what viewers watch. Viewers record which channels they watch and for how long.

ACTIVITY 10.2

If people watching television are generating income for television broadcasters by allowing them to charge advertisers to place commercials, why are viewers not paid by broadcasters to watch (viewers are, in a sense, 'working' for the broadcaster)? How does your answer illuminate the role of television as a 'leisure activity'?

Ratings: measuring audiences

BARB, the television audience research body, introduced a new audience panel on 1 January 2010, covering 5,100 households (www.barb.co.uk). The results are crucially important to programme **schedulers** and channel controllers, who make decisions each week based on the overnight viewing figures provided by BARB. About £3 billion a year in advertising revenue is traded on the basis of BARB figures, and, as Bob Mullan (1997: 16) notes, 'Counting the numbers of viewers allegedly watching television at certain times of day or night is essential to the requirements of advertisers as they attempt to target "audiences" and maximise their promotional messages.' BARB's new household panel is the first entirely new panel to be recruited since 2002. BARB selects its group of households so that it is as representative as

BARB (Broadcasters Audience Research Bureau) the independent body that gathers and reports viewing statistics on behalf of UK television institutions.

possible of the whole British television audience. It chooses households from various regions of the country, comprising different combinations of household types, some with children, some without, across a range of ages and economic backgrounds. Complex statistical methods are used to ensure that the whole sample is representative, and that the results of the audience research information can be reliably multiplied to give national figures. Viewing on computers or on catch-up services like the BBC iPlayer are also included in the measurement of viewing. Opportunities to commission, continue or cancel a television programme are significantly determined by BARB research, because the BARB figures tell television companies what 'works'. Fiction programmes have always attracted the largest audiences, and programmes in the long-established **genres** of soap opera and the police drama, for example, as well as talent shows like *The X Factor* and sports coverage, are still the most popular according to BARB ratings.

genre a kind or type of programme. Programmes of the same genre have shared characteristics.

John Ellis (2000a: 28), considering the changing significance of audience ratings and targeted niche audiences, explains:

> Numbers still matter in that they provide the bench-mark for the performance of the channel as a whole. But overall audience numbers can only be increased by a subtle strategy of targeting particular sections of the audience on competing channels and providing something that will appeal to or satisfy them more . . . audiences can be specified according to age, class, gender, region, pattern of viewing and even by their degree of appreciation of the programme.

niche audiences particular groups of viewers defined by age group, gender or economic status, for example, who may be the target audience for a programme.

The BBC has built on its well-known brand, with its values of 'quality' and trustworthiness, to introduce channels that address **niche audiences** and particular **demographic** groups and rival the companies dominating the current multi-channel landscape. BBC3 is targeted at young adult audiences, while BBC4 addresses an older audience and viewers in more wealthy social groups, for example.

demography the study of population, and the groupings of people (demographic groups) within the whole population.

The audience for ITV's terrestrial programmes has been getting older for many years, and has a typically lower average income than the BBC's audience. ITV1 has made various attempts to attract younger viewers and viewers with the higher disposable incomes that are attractive to advertisers. BARB and the broadcasters themselves use a standard breakdown of the population into groups according to their economic and social position. Highly paid professionals make up the 'A' group, lower-management and clerical workers form the 'B' group, while the 'C1' group consists of skilled manual workers. Less attractive groups to advertisers, such as people in temporary employment, people living on pensions and the unemployed, are the least attractive groups in the population, represented by the codes 'C2', 'D' and 'E'. It is evidently very important for broadcasters that their audience contains a high proportion of the most economically and socially powerful people in the national audience.

preferred reading an interpretation of a text that seems to be the one most encouraged by the text, the 'correct' interpretation.

Audiences can be regarded as distant and unknowable, as objects rather than subjects or agents who act on their own initiative. The alternative view to this is that television audiences have an active agency and are not simply passive objects positioned by television texts so that they lap up a single '**preferred reading**'. By considering audiences as active, it is possible to take account of the complex social and cultural contexts in which television viewing takes place, and in which television programmes are made. As Bob Mullan (1997: 18) has argued,

Figure 10.1 Rehearsing a performance in *Glee*.

Viewers often, but not always, engage in meaning-making: they do not always sit there empty-minded awaiting edification. When a viewer watches television they do not leave their histories at the living-room door: neither do they abandon their cultural, class, racial, economic or sexual identities, nor do they forget either their media knowledge of comparable programmes, information in newspapers, and other aspects of the infrastructure of television viewing.

From this '**active audience**' perspective, audiences are not regarded as masses, crowds or mobs whose behaviour appears from the outside to be irrational and uncontrollable.

Targeting audiences

Television programme-makers devise new programmes not simply on the basis of ideas that they are interested in, but in order to target and attract particular audiences. The information provided to them by BARB about existing programmes gives them some basis for understanding that particular kinds of **format** are attractive to certain audiences (for example, that significant numbers of young adult viewers enjoy **observational documentary** programmes with strong continuing characters, leading to a wave of **docusoap** programmes). The popular American series *Glee*, about singers rehearsing and performing at college, drew on the success of youth drama about teenagers, combining this with the narratives of auditioning, putting on a show and popular music performance in talent shows (Figure 10.1). As we can see from this image, the programme adopted a visual style in which the camera was positioned in the place of a live audience to see a performance. But in other sequences, the drama adopted the conventions of the drama serial to follow the interactions of the characters. Information deriving from past ratings is not always reliable, so single pilot programmes of new formats are routinely made and shown

active audience television audiences regarded not as passive consumers of meanings, but as negotiating meanings for themselves that are often resistant to those meanings that are intended or that are discovered by close analysis.

format the blueprint for a programme, including its setting, main characters, genre, form and main themes.

observational documentary a documentary form in which the programme-maker aims to observe neutrally what would have happened even if he or she had not been present.

docusoap a television form combining documentary's depiction of non-actors in ordinary situations with soap opera's continuing narratives about selected characters.

focus groups small groups of selected people, representing larger social groupings such as people of a certain age group, gender or economic status, who take part in discussions about a topic chosen for investigation.

to **focus groups** comprising carefully selected individuals of a certain age, gender and social background. Moderators are employed to lead the discussions in the focus group, in a similar way to how teachers ask questions and lead the discussion in a class. Drama programmes are an exception to this practice, since making a single programme from an intended series is expensive and may not provide a representative sample for the focus group to discuss. But even drama programmes are shown to focus groups once they have been completed. The results of the focus group discussions give the broadcasters a sense of the elements of a programme that can be emphasised in trailers and in advertising, and suggest how and when a new programme might be scheduled.

The aim of a focus group discussion conducted for a broadcaster is not only to find out whether audiences might enjoy a planned programme. It is important for the broadcaster to fit the programme into the existing habits and routines of audiences' television viewing. For example, participants might be asked whether they would prefer to watch the new programme at 7.00 p.m. or 8.00 p.m., and whether it would be best placed on a weekday or at the weekend. Finding out whether viewers might prefer the new programme to a competitor on another channel can enable schedulers to make decisions about whether the new programme should aim to inherit the same audience as a similar competing programme, and whether to place the new programme directly against its competitor. Since the majority of viewers watch television accompanied by other members of their household, participants in the focus group might also be asked whether they would be embarrassed to watch the new programme with their children, with their parents or with their spouse. Or, by contrast, participants might be asked whether this would be a programme that would attract the whole family to watch at the same time, perhaps around a mealtime. Clearly, focus groups represent very small samples of the total viewing audience, and the results derived from such studies can be unreliable. A further difficulty with using this methodology is that viewers tend to make judgements based on what they already know. It is very difficult for people to give an opinion on something that is really new, without comparing and contrasting it unfavourably with programmes they already like. It is for this reason that television broadcasters are criticised for producing a diet of television that always seems the same. Once a particular genre or format has been successful (such as talent shows, police or hospital drama) there is a tendency for programme-makers to keep delivering more of the same, since they know it works.

ACTIVITY 10.3

Think about the trailers you have seen for new programmes recently, and, if you can, record two or three so you can analyse them in detail. You can also find programme trailers on YouTube or other video websites. What aspects of the trailers (their visual and aural signifiers, signs of genre and their placing between particular current programmes) seem calculated to address a certain audience, and a certain mode of viewing?

Active audiences

In the 1980s, new ways of understanding how audiences understand the **codes** of television programmes were explored, and the most prominent of these is called the 'encoding–decoding' model. This work by the media academic Stuart Hall (1980) argued that programmes contain dominant ideological **discourses**. These are encoded in programmes through the production practices of programme-makers that result in conventional forms of narrative structure, invitations to the audience to identify with particular characters and the telling of stories that reflect taken-for-granted social meanings. Hall was interested in the factors that might affect the encoding of these meanings and also how audiences might decode them. Since the images and sounds of television are **polysemic**, it can never be guaranteed that audiences will make sense of the programme in a way that is consistent with the meanings encoded in it. Hall argued that television programmes contain a 'dominant' or '**preferred**' **reading**, and thus limit the range of ways in which audiences can interpret the programme. However, the encoding–decoding model is subject to three important criticisms. First, it is easier to determine preferred meanings in programmes that are primarily intended to convey information, such as news programmes. Drama and other kinds of fiction tend to offer more alternative understandings of the action represented in them, and therefore a greater range of possible interpretations. Secondly, the encoding–decoding model does not make it clear whether preferred meanings are part of the television programme itself, whether they are something that can be identified after analysis by a media theorist, or whether they are actually in the minds of audiences. The third criticism is that the ideological values encoded in television programmes seem to be so powerful according to this model that they cannot be challenged. It is clear that some programme-makers produce radical and alternative programmes, so it remains to be explained how the conventions of communicating meaning in television leave a space for change.

In a study of how different audience groups made sense of *Nationwide*, a current affairs magazine programme shown in the 1970s, David Morley (1980) selected groups according to their social and economic background. He asked the different groups to watch selections from *Nationwide*, and tested Stuart Hall's encoding–decoding model against their responses. He found that many of their comments did not seem to justify the model. These actual viewers did not understand *Nationwide* primarily in the categories of 'dominant', '**negotiated**' and 'resistant' readings. There were two main reasons for this:

■ Characteristics of the groups that were not directly related to their social and economic position were affecting his results. The gender and ethnic background of people seemed to be just as important as their economic status.
■ Many of the viewers in Morley's groups found *Nationwide* irrelevant to them, or were not able to make much sense of the programmes they had seen.

The conclusion that Morley drew from this was that audience research should pay much more attention to the knowledge and experience that viewers brought with them to watching television. This knowledge and experience are termed the viewer's 'cultural competence' or 'cultural capital'. On the basis of what viewers already know

code in semiotics, a system or set of rules that shapes how signs can be used, and therefore how meanings can be made and understood.

discourse in television, a particular usage of television's audiovisual 'language' (news programme discourse, or nature documentary discourse, for instance).

polysemia the quality of having multiple meanings at the same time. Texts like this are called 'polysemic'.

negotiated reading a viewer interpretation of a television text where the viewer understands meaning in relation to his or her own knowledge and experience, rather than simply accepting the meaning proposed by the text.

and understand, they have reactions to television that are as much to do with pleasure and frustration as they are to do with the issues of social and political position that Morley had focused on. Much of the audience research that is discussed in this chapter takes off from the two problems that Morley identified in these earlier studies.

Attention and involvement

Aiming to provide a way of distinguishing between the different levels of attention that television viewers give to the programmes they watch, Jeremy Tunstall (1983) distinguished between primary, secondary and tertiary involvement with media. The most concentrated kind of attention he refers to as 'primary involvement'. This is where the viewer concentrates closely on what he or she sees and hears on television, to the exclusion of any other activity. Of course many television viewers are also doing something else while they are watching television. The kind of attention where viewers are sometimes distracted is categorised as 'secondary involvement'. In a situation like this, the viewer is paying attention to the television screen some of the time, and listening to most of the sound, but might also be doing something else like flicking through a magazine, using a laptop to browse the internet or keeping an eye on the children. The lowest level of attention is called 'tertiary involvement'. Here the television viewer is paying only momentary attention to television while being engaged in another activity that demands concentration. For instance, the viewer might be cooking a meal while a television set in the kitchen is switched on, so that he or she scarcely sees any of the images on the screen and is only occasionally listening to the sound. Some people use media technology in ways that had not been envisaged by its creators, such as leaving a television set on all day as a deterrent to burglars when all the occupants of the house are out. Clearly the level of involvement in television makes a lot of difference to the meanings that viewers can make of what they see and hear. Television in contemporary culture is so deeply embedded in the routines of everyday life that the viewer's involvement with it can vary enormously. When studying television it is important to remember that there will be a whole spectrum of ways in which actual viewers engage with programmes.

ACTIVITY 10.4

Think about your own television viewing in relation to concepts of primary, secondary and tertiary involvement. How is the range of ways that you watch television affected by your daily routines? What kinds of programmes succeed in gaining primary involvement from you, and why?

Some television programmes are constructed in order to attract viewers to engage with them at the level of primary involvement. This is the case, for example, with news programmes. Main evening news bulletins are scheduled at fixed points such as 6.00 p.m. or 10.00 p.m. Their scheduling already carries the connotation that news programmes are important, and that viewers could and should make an appointment to view them. News programmes begin with loud and dramatic opening music, calling the viewer's attention to the television set and announcing that something important is about to be broadcast. The implication is that viewers should stop what they are doing and pay attention, granting primary involvement to the programme. Once the programme begins, the opening shot is normally a head-on address to the viewer by the presenter, who welcomes the viewer by saying 'good evening'. A situation of dialogue is constructed by this address to the viewer, and the viewer is invited to take up the position of someone being spoken to directly, someone who is paying attention to what is being said. News programmes are complex television texts, in which a large number of segments are linked together. There are likely to be:

- sequences in which the news presenter is speaking directly to the viewer
- sequences of news reportage
- dialogue between the presenter and experts in the studio or reporters live in a location where a news story is occurring
- displays on the screen of graphics, maps, statistics and diagrams.

News is a very rich **semiotic** text that is constructed to demand attention from the viewer. That attention is rewarded by allowing the viewer to gain information from a variety of viewpoints and by means of a variety of semiotic codes that convey meanings in different ways.

semiotics the study of signs and their meanings, initially developed for the study of spoken language, and now used also to study the visual and aural 'languages' of other media such as television.

Some of the time, it is likely that the complex television texts of news programmes succeed in attracting and rewarding primary involvement from their viewers. But it is also likely that the density of news programmes often passes the viewer by. A few hours after watching the news, or even a few minutes after watching it, many viewers will find it very difficult to remember each of the news stories presented, let alone the nuances of the different points of view and fragments of information that the programme has offered. Instead viewers will construct for themselves a sense of what is important in the news, often based as much on their pre-existing knowledge of ongoing news stories, and on other information sources such as newspapers and gossip, as on a particular news programme itself. Some of this cultural knowledge of news must be shared among large numbers of people, since it is this shared but specific news knowledge which enables news quizzes such as *Have I Got News for You* (a **satirical** television programme based on current news stories), or phone-in radio programmes to be both comprehensible and entertaining. The embedding of programmes in a **flow** of television over a period of time, and the distractions present during viewing, as well as the whole complex of factors that predispose viewers to be interested in some news items and not others, are all factors that tend to dissolve the detail of what is seen on television into the diffuse fabric of everyday life. This could be seen as a failing, in that television has to struggle so hard against the other aspects of people's lives that it has in many ways a relatively weak power to shape and inform. Yet, on the other hand, this criticism is based on the assumption that television should indeed shape and affect its audiences in this dramatic way. Audience researchers have been more sceptical about the role of television in society. They have argued instead that television should be regarded as only one of the very many ways in which people make sense of their reality. Although television is important, it needs to be understood as part of everyday life.

satire a mode of critical commentary about society or an aspect of it, using humour to attack people or ideas.

flow the ways that programmes, advertisements, etc. follow one another in an unbroken sequence across the day or part of the day, and the experience of watching the sequence of programmes, advertisements, trailers, etc.

Qualitative audience research

ethnography
the detailed study of how people live, conducted by observing behaviour and talking to selected individuals about their attitudes and activities.

anthropology
the study of humankind, including the evolution of humans and the different kinds of human society existing in different times and places.

Ethnographic studies of television audiences take their methodology from the academic discipline of **anthropology**. Anthropology began in the nineteenth century, and means the study of humankind. It was part of the expansion of the methods of the experimental physical sciences (such as biology or chemistry) into the arena of human activity and initially focused on the study of 'primitive' peoples living in the underdeveloped territories controlled by the empires of Western European nations. The ideology underlying these early anthropological studies was a belief in the possibility of human progress, from tribal cultures to the industrial and technologically developed societies from which the anthropological researchers themselves came. It was assumed by anthropologists that over time all human societies would evolve in more or less the same way, into industrial, democratic and bureaucratic cultures. However, anthropology has questioned some of these assumptions, and argued that there is no necessary forward movement of human societies towards a particular form. The underdeveloped non-technological societies that still exist in some parts of the world are no longer regarded as in some way 'behind the times' or as throwbacks to an earlier phase in the development of the human race. But anthropologists still seek to understand how different cultures function, and whether there are consistent structures that underlie human culture, family relationships and ways of organising work, leisure and identity. Research on television audiences asks some of the same questions, by seeking to understand how television

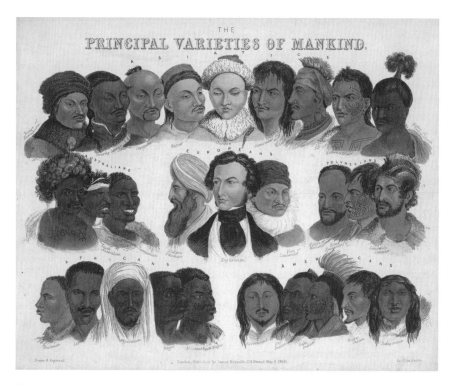

Figure 10.2 Engraving showing the 'Principal Varieties of Mankind' by John Emslie, 1850. Courtesy of the Science Museum, Science & Society Picture Library.

functions in relationships between people, and affects the ways in which people's daily lives and understandings of themselves are formed. Yet one of the legacies that remains from the history of the discipline of anthropology is that the researcher is normally in a much more socially powerful position than the respondents that he or she interviews and studies. Ordinary television viewers are interesting to researchers because they are different, even exotic, rather like the 'primitive' tribal people who were the subjects for early anthropological projects.

Television audience researchers aim for what the anthropologist Clifford Geertz (1967) called a 'thick description' of audience behaviour. This involves discovering 'a stratified hierarchy of meaningful structures in terms of which [social behaviours] are produced, perceived and interpreted, and without which they would not . . . in fact exist' (Geertz 1967: 7). The observation must be interpreted in relation to the cultural frameworks that make it meaningful, so that the ethnographer can interpret what he or she observes. The television ethnographer's results are therefore interpretations of the subjects' interpretations of his or her own actions and thoughts, and often those of other people too. Ethnography is a form of textual analysis, and interpreting audiences reveals the intricate, singular and different ways in which people make interpretations of their world and think about their own cultural behaviours. Layer on layer of interpretation is produced, and the best kinds of audience research explore not only the results obtained from the research, but also the constructed quality of the ethnographer's text. Ethnographic researchers are writers, and the observing, transcribing and interpreting functions involved in their work are not as separate as the 'scientific' history of the discipline might imply; in fact the different functions that researchers perform affect each other. Doing audience research requires the ethnographer to adopt several identities at different times, or at once:

- participant
- observer
- recorder
- author
- interpreter
- theorist.

Commonly, researchers reflect on their agendas but try to present viewers as sharing either the same enthusiasms or the same political views as themselves. But television audience researchers, who often say that they themselves belong to the subcultures they study, have to remember that what they do is a cultural practice that will itself inevitably alter and affect the behaviour they observe.

Academic studies of television audiences using ethnographic methods are difficult to evaluate. They are most often carried out by talking to respondents who have voluntarily put themselves forward as research subjects, and who are therefore likely to have something they want to say about television. The methods used to find respondents can give rise to a number of problems in the design of audience research studies. Some researchers have used the method called 'snowballing', in which one person takes on the responsibility to find another who will participate in the study, then that person finds another volunteer, and so on. While this methodology is less artificial than trying to select a panel of respondents who are representative in some way, it inevitably produces a self-selected group. Other researchers have placed advertisements in magazines or on websites, for example, and reviewed the responses they receive. Here, of course, those people who respond have something that they wish to communicate, and they also communicate in writing. The formalities of writing letters or emails include the need to organise material, to be polite and to choose a language that may distort information by formalising it; they are all problems that this methodology has to address. When writing down their reactions, viewers may consciously or unconsciously modify their responses by putting them into the disciplined forms that are conventional when writing to people whom we do not know personally. Talking can present some of the same problems, when respondents can tailor what they say in order to give the answers that they think may be most interesting to the researcher, or that present them in the most interesting light, for example. Ethnographic research on television viewers is still relatively recent in the discipline of Television Studies, and few of the academics who have carried it out have been trained in the methodologies of anthropology or sociology from which ethnography derives. But researchers have become increasingly conscious of these problems, and books and articles presenting their findings now almost always contain explanations of their methodology and draw attention to the limitations of their results.

ACTIVITY 10.5

If you wanted to design an ethnographic study of how elderly viewers respond to daytime drama programmes, how would you go about selecting a sample of viewers, deciding on the questions you wanted to ask and analysing your results? What problems might you encounter in conducting your study, and how could you minimise or solve these problems?

Interviews are commonly used by television makers (production companies, channels or advertising agencies, for example) to understand what viewers think of programme ideas or completed programmes. Interviewing has also become more common in academic Television Studies, where researchers have interviewed producers, writers, actors and executives. Viewers are interviewed in order to understand why they watch television, what they watch and what appeals to them or turns them away from some kinds of programme, such as violent or sexual content (Hill 1997). In each of these contexts, qualitative interviews are used; in other words, the interviewer gathers information and then interprets its significance, rather than asking straightforward yes or no questions. Qualitative interviews provide primary data, the raw material for drawing conclusions based on evidence. But they can also be used to explore an area of research to see whether there are more questions that need to be asked.

The different ways of conducting interviews have been a topic of research for decades, as experts in the social sciences have refined their techniques in order to do effective commercial research on consumers (to improve products and services, or to create new ones) and also to study social phenomena such as television viewing habits or opinions about violence on television. There are four types of interviews: structured, semi-structured, unstructured and focus group interviews (Arksey and Knight 1999, Lunt and Livingstone 1996, May 2001). They vary across a spectrum from using a preordained set of questions, asked in a particular order (structured interviews) to a group discussion where the interviewer and the participants have a conversation that can veer off in unexpected directions (focus group discussion). The less structure there is in the choice of questions to ask, the more an interview is likely to yield useful qualitative information, but the more the interviewer will need to interpret the results and consider what the significance of the answers may be. In focus group interviews, the aim is to make the interview as much like a conversation as possible, so that questions and answers lead on from each other. When a range of different interviewees are involved, their responses can be compared with each other, and individual responses can reveal the ways in which one person's views are different from another person's.

When planning how to gather information from interviews, the researcher needs to make a series of decisions that will affect what kind of interviews to use and who to invite to be the interviewees. Clearly, the main research question will guide these initial decisions, such as who the best interviewees would be and what the best interview method would be to gather the kind of information required. But further issues that might seem less obvious include where the interview ought to be conducted. The consensus among social scientists is that qualitative research should be carried out in a 'natural' setting, rather than in an artificial setting such as a laboratory, because research into how people experience the social world should aim to make interviewees behave as much as possible as they would in everyday situations (Seale 1999). For this reason, interviewers usually do not say very much in advance to their interviewees about what the questions are going to be. On one hand, having a sense of what the interview is about can be helpful to the interviewee because it allows them to prepare some thoughts before the interview, so that they are not anxious about being caught off-guard. On the other hand, researchers find pre-prepared answers less useful than answers given on the day, because pre-prepared answers might be influenced by all kinds of constraining factors like an interviewee's fear of looking stupid, or trying to give an answer that the interviewer seems to want. Once an interview has been completed, the researcher will need to interpret it and extract information that helps to answer the initial research question, or modifies it in new directions. Interviews provide many kinds of evidence, and not all of it concerns the actual content of the answers to questions. Hesitations, misunderstandings of a question and apparently irrelevant digressions can be revealing about the interviewees' attitudes to the topic they are being asked about.

Fan audiences

Viewers who regard themselves as fans of particular programmes are a special subgroup of television audiences who reveal some of the strengths and weaknesses of ethnographic audience research. As with the other research discussed in this chapter, the main emphasis has been on how fans gain pleasure from their close relationship with television programmes, and how their relationships with television provide fans with kinds of social identity that are desirable to them. The way that fans actively appropriate television culture can be regarded as an unusually extreme but revealing instance of how all television viewers take possession of the programmes they watch, and assimilate the meanings of programmes into their own lives. Fan communities are self-selected groups of people who have decided to identify themselves closely with programmes, and with fellow television viewers who also devote special attention to the same programme. Prominent programmes whose **fan cultures** have been investigated by television researchers include *Doctor Who*, *The X-Files*, *Buffy the Vampire Slayer* and the original *Star Trek* and its many subsequent spin-offs. It is notable that these programmes fall into the category of science fiction or fantasy television, since one of the arguments of audience research on their fan communities is that being a fan is itself crucially tied up with constructing fantasies that provide the scenario for fans to re-imagine themselves differently and to experiment with the possibilities and limits of their interests and desires. When a new actor takes over the role of Doctor Who, for example, or when a popular enemy of the Doctor reappears in a new episode, the programme's fan community extensively debates the good and bad points of storylines and performances. Figure 10.3 shows Matt Smith as the Doctor, confronted by his old enemy the Daleks. In this shot, a familiar confrontation that has happened in *Doctor Who* since 1963 is staged by placing both of them in the frame at opposite sides, emphasising their implacable enmity.

The range of ways in which fans take possession of a television programme for themselves, and redirect its components and meanings for themselves, has been described by the media theorist Henry Jenkins (1992) as 'textual poaching'. Drawing the analogy with poachers who illegally capture animals or fish to eat from land or rivers that are owned by someone else, Jenkins argues that fans invade the territory of television programmes that are created, controlled and owned by the 'official' television culture of professional programme-makers. Rather than viewing

fan culture the activities of groups of fans, as distinct from 'ordinary' viewers.

Figure 10.3 The Doctor confronts a Dalek in *Doctor Who.*

programmes according to the preferred readings encoded by their creators, fans pick out the elements that are of interest to them and make them function in new ways. For some audience researchers there is a heroic aspect to this, whereby fans are considered as a resistant audience that refuses to adopt the conventional position laid out for it by a television programme, and instead re-appropriates programmes in ways that contradict the aims of their creators and owners. Indeed, fans operate in similar ways to the creators of television programmes, producing alternative products that supplement or take the place of industrially produced television programmes. For example, fans:

- create websites about their favourite programme
- set up and distribute magazines and newsletters
- organise collective cultural events such as conventions.

These activities can be regarded as resistant, in that they promote ways of viewing, talking about and restaging programmes that take possession of the original and change it in interesting ways. But on the other hand, fan culture reproduces many of the ways in which 'official' television production culture works. Fans discriminate between insiders (who belong to the world of fan culture) and outsiders (who do not belong), just as television professionals seek to preserve their elite position within the industry and normally deny access to members of the audience. Fans produce and circulate texts and products, in parallel with the ways that programme-makers produce and circulate texts and products. The cultural competence that fans seek to possess (such as detailed knowledge about their favourite programme) is a form of capital that gives them status within their community. In a similar way, television programme-makers accumulate insider knowledge about their business and also accumulate financial capital and profit for themselves and the broadcasting organisations for which they work.

While some media audience cultures can claim a degree of cultural unity, this unity is sustained in distinction to national and global media cultures that they cannot change. The theorist of fan cultures Henry Jenkins (Tulloch and Jenkins 1995) conducted studies of the attitudes to *Star Trek* of a range of different groups, including science students at the Massachusetts Institute of Technology (MIT) and members of the gay *Star Trek* fan group the Gaylaxians. Jenkins points out that the MIT students largely share the ideological values of the programme, such as faith in human progress, the ability of science to solve social problems and value attributed to the technology represented in *Star Trek* and the technology used to represent it in special effects. Members of this group are hardly a resistant audience because they are highly educated middle-class males who are destined to be among the professionals who wield social power. In his study of the Gaylaxians, Jenkins (Tulloch and Jenkins 1995: 264) notes that

> Resistant reading can sustain the Gaylaxians' own activism, can become a source of collective identity and mutual support, but precisely because it is a subcultural activity which is denied public visibility, resistant reading cannot change the political agenda, cannot challenge other constructions of gay identity, and cannot have an impact on the ways people outside the group think about the issues which matter to the Gaylaxians.

The more that an audience is identified by researchers as an emblem of resistance to the dominant norms of television and contemporary society, the less likely it is that this audience group will be able to exert any actual power to create change in either television or society.

But some of the television audiences studied by ethnographic researchers do not have a constituted identity at all, except when an identity is attributed to them by the researcher doing the ethnographic work. In a discussion of some of the many studies of women viewers of soap opera, for example, Ien Ang and Joke Hermes (1996) have pointed out that researchers have a tendency to assume that the responses of particular research respondents are representative of the larger group made up of women viewers in general. The results of talking to one small sample of women can be made to stand for all women (often restricted to those of a certain social class or race) in order to make an argument about how this entire group is likely to understand and enjoy television. The impetus behind much audience research is to value the voices of viewers in a dominant television broadcasting culture which largely excludes them, and thus to claim the agency of the audience, and also to claim that audience research itself can have political agency as a way of intervening in the discussion of the politics of contemporary culture. The British television academics Julia Hallam and Margaret Marshment (1995) made a study of women viewers of the British three-part BBC television serial *Oranges Are Not the Only Fruit* (1989, based on a novel of the same name by Jeanette Winterson). After completing interviews with their sample of viewers, Hallam and Marshment (1995: 14) concluded that the diversity of viewers' responses 'remained within a recognizable "we" of common experiences and pleasures which seemed to owe much to our common positions as women'. The researchers claimed (1995: 3) that

> we were not 'looking for' negotiated or resistant readings among the respondents . . . but our feminist standpoint does need to be taken into account. We hoped to find that they did like [the serial] and did interpret it in line with the preferred reading because . . . it would . . . thus constitute a significant feminist anti-homophobic intervention in popular culture.

Since research is always carried out with an explicit or implicit research agenda or set of research questions, there is a tendency for academic publication of audience research to find the answers that it has already aimed to find. After all, it is much more interesting to read about research findings where positive results have been obtained, than studies where the research subjects had little coherent to say, or where the design and methodology of the research were found to be flawed.

The growth of the internet has provided television fans with extensive possibilities for communicating with each other. To take the example of *Doctor Who*, this British science fiction adventure series began in 1963 and ran until 1996, and there was a long gap until it was revived in 2005. Nevertheless, in 2002, despite the lack of new programmes for the fans to discuss, there were more than forty *Doctor Who* newsgroups and chat forums running on the internet. These web resources consisted of fictional stories written by fans, websites devoted to actors appearing in the programme, fan magazines and sites offering non-professional films of *Doctor Who* made by fans. John Tulloch (Tulloch and Jenkins 1995: 145) describes the central fan activity as 'the power to gloss', meaning the power of television fans to interpret and reinterpret programmes for themselves and to engage in dialogue and debate with each other around questions of interpretation. Henry Jenkins (1992: 86) argues that

> Organised fandom is, perhaps first and foremost, an institution of theory and criticism, a semi-structured space where competing interpretations and evaluations of common texts are proposed, debated and negotiated and where readers speculate about the nature of the mass media and their own relationship to it.

By engaging in such debates, fans are able to display their cultural capital of knowledge about the programme, and the debates and discussions themselves constitute a fan community. The possibility of potentially endless debate about interpretation enables the fan community and its activities to continue indefinitely, even when (as in the case of the science fiction series *Blake's 7*, for instance) there are no new programmes to discuss. Series television, such as the long-running programmes that have tended to be the focus of fan interest, is normally written by a wide range of writers, may feature different actors who join and leave the series over the period of its run, and the narrative structure, thematic concerns and settings (the components of the programme format) may change. These discontinuities allow broad scope for fan interpretation, and for making value judgements about the success or failure of particular episodes or groups of episodes.

The overwhelming majority of comments posted to newsgroups on television programmes consist of comments on the broadcast episodes. The majority of fans are interested in the official productions associated with television programmes, and the **merchandising** products produced under licence that are connected to them. So although the internet provides a virtual community for television fans, only a very small proportion of fan activity has to do with media production itself, and instead it is concerned with consumption. As John Fiske (1992b: 44) notes, 'the emphasis is not so much on acquiring a few good (and thus expensive) objects as accumulating as many as possible'. Being a fan means acquiring the cultural capital of knowledge about television programmes, and also amassing the commercial objects such as videos and DVDs that make it possible to 'possess' the programmes. Being a fan is a means not only of resisting the dominant interpretations shaped by programme-makers and taking possession of the meanings of television programmes for oneself, but also of positioning oneself as a consumer of the commodities that programme producers now increasingly use as valuable streams of income to fund further programme-making. Knowing that fans are likely already to have amassed videotape copies of programmes, it then became common for the owners of franchises such as *Star Trek* and *Doctor Who* to re-release programmes on DVD with tempting extras such as interviews with cast members or producers, so that fans would buy the original programmes all over again. The desire for a complete collection of programmes with the best possible image and sound quality stimulates the desire to amass commercial objects among the fan community. So although television fans are in a sense the heroes of audience research in Television Studies, since they are the viewers who most actively respond to television programmes and engage most consciously in alternative and resistant practices prompted by television programmes, fans are also complicit with the television industry and the structures

merchandising the sale of products associated with a television programme, such as toys, books or clothing.

and assumptions that underlie it. Indeed, fan culture is a response to a cultural disempowerment that derives from being a member of the audience rather than a producer of programmes. No matter how active, resistant, knowledgeable or interested a television fan may be, his or her activities and those of the fan community have little effect on the ways that the television industry works or on the television programmes that are produced.

ACTIVITY 10.6

Search on the web for the 'official' BBC site for *Doctor Who*, and also for the 'unofficial' sites created by and for fans of the programme. How similar and how different are the 'official' and 'unofficial' sites in terms of how they address their users? What might the reasons be for these similarities and differences?

Case study: television scheduling

John Ellis (2000a: 25) has argued that the composition of a television schedule is parallel to the operations involved in editing during the programme-making process:

> Instead of combining shots and sounds into a sequence and sequences into a programme, as an editor does, the scheduler combines whole programme units into an evening's flow, whole evenings into a week, whole weeks into a season, and whole seasons into a year.

Scheduling is therefore an activity of selection and combination, just as editing is, and schedulers aim to offer audiences a variety of programmes that have relationships between them of a similar kind to the relationships between the moments and sequences of an individual programme. Some programmes will have connections between them (in the same way that a current affairs programme may be scheduled after the news), while others will be placed next to programmes that have a quite different genre and format (a Hollywood film might follow Premiership football). Although in the early years of television production the lengths of programmes and their interrelationships with each other were subject to little overall planning, by the 1980s standard programme lengths such as thirty minutes and one hour had produced grids of time slots such as were already common in broadcasting in the United States.

Schedules are planned on the basis of assumptions about the nature of the television audience and the ways in which audiences watch. Television schedules on the main terrestrial channels (BBC1, BBC2, ITV1, Channel 4 and Five) have for a long time been planned around the ways that hypothetical family audiences organise their time. For example:

- children come home from school at the end of the afternoon
- main meals are usually eaten in the early or mid-evening
- young children are expected to go to bed at around 9.00 p.m.

In general, the early evening contains shorter and more diverse programmes, while the later evening offers adult viewers longer and more complex forms and formats. At the level of the year as a whole, new programmes are traditionally introduced around September, when the holiday season has finished and family routines get back to normal as school time begins. In the summer people watch less television because they are more likely to be outside in the warmer weather, so the summer period contains more repeated programmes and fewer programmes that broadcasters have invested significant money in or attach greater importance to. At a particular point during the year, expected events such as the football Cup Final, the Eurovision Song Contest or Christmas celebrations will require the schedule to be rearranged and specially planned.

Of course the schedulers for one channel will need to take account of what its competitors have planned. There are several possible responses to competition. The purpose of scheduling is to gain audience share and audience ratings. Schedulers are working in the interests of the broadcasting channel for which they work, and not for the producers of individual programmes. Therefore, an individual programme which might seem to be worthy of a prominent place in the schedule might be moved to a much less attractive spot because of a strategic decision about the programming which a competing channel is offering at the same time. The schedulers for one channel might go 'head to head' with the competition and place a programme likely to attract large audiences against a high-rating programme on a competing channel. Or alternatively, the scheduler might accept that the ratings battle is lost in that time slot, and schedule a programme that was never likely to be a ratings winner, thus conceding the ratings battle to a strong competitor. Occasionally, an unusual scheduling decision can work to make a programme stand out from its competitors. The mini-series *Torchwood: Children of Earth* was shown on consecutive evenings in 2009. This scheduling pattern is unusual, and the programme was screened in the summer, when audiences are smaller than in the autumn or spring. But it achieved higher than expected ratings, probably in part because of this exceptional scheduling that was trailed extensively in advance. This science fiction drama also posed a mystery in its first episode, about why all the children of Britain seemed suddenly to become immobile (Figure 10.4). These images of children frozen like statues were

Figure 10.4 Children suddenly freeze into immobility in *Torchwood: Children of Earth.*

visually arresting, and to find out the solution to this enigma, viewers had to watch subsequent episodes. But they only had to wait until the following day to see one.

British schedulers keep in contact with their competitors at other channels, under regulations which require them to exchange information about each other's programming one week beforehand. The power to commission new programmes is in the hands of the executives at broadcasting channels, but schedulers have an important role to play in identifying programmes which are likely to gain audiences, based on information schedulers have about what audiences have watched in the past. So schedulers provide recommendations to commissioning executives and thus have an important influence on which programmes are made. John Ellis (2000a: 26) goes as far as to say that the schedule is

> the locus of power in television, the mechanism whereby demographic speculations are turned into a viewing experience. And it is more than that as well, for any schedule contains the distillation of the past history of a channel, of national broadcasting as a whole, and of the particular habits of national life.

However, schedulers are subject to a vicious circle that depends on their use of audience data to identify a good or bad scheduling decision:

> The success or failure of a particular scheduling strategy is measured by the same methodology that suggested it in the first place. A problem with audience size or composition produced by a particular programming policy is identified through using the BARB figures. This leads to changes in that policy, whose success is measured by using the same BARB data.

> (Ellis 2000a: 35)

public service in television, the provision of a mix of programmes that inform, educate and entertain in ways that encourage the betterment of audiences and society in general.

stripping in television scheduling, placing a programme or genre of programme at the same time on several days of each week.

prime time the part of a day's television schedule when the greatest number of viewers may be watching, normally the mid-evening period.

The BBC needs to attract audiences large enough to justify the levying of the licence fee, and at the same time to provide **public service** programmes. The factors affecting scheduling on commercial channels like ITV are somewhat different: decisions have commercial implications in terms of ITV's income from advertisers, which is based on the size and composition of audiences available to watch advertisements during programmes. Programmes about home improvement are likely to be shown at times when people are considering doing work on their houses, for example on Fridays and Saturdays, when major DIY superstores will be open for people to purchase materials. ITV is unlikely to show DIY programmes on Sundays, when viewers will already have completed their shopping for such items. This British situation is becoming much like that in the USA, where programmes are generally scheduled in **strips**, for example soap operas in the afternoon, sitcoms in **prime time**, drama in the late evening. Each American network channel's schedule is similar to those of its competitors, but the variety and unexpectedness that we find in Britain has been threatened for some time. David Liddiment, then head of ITV, spoke at the 2001 Edinburgh Television Festival (his speech was reprinted in Brown and Wells 2001), and said:

> Numbers now seem to be the only universal measure for excellence we have: how many, how much, how often. We are losing sight of the innate value of programmes in our fixation on the successes that can be measured by profit, profile or performance. The relentless quest to find out what viewers want and then give it to them has made for sameness as we all seek to engineer the same schedule.

> (Brown and Wells 2001: 3)

By evaluating audience figures, channel controllers and schedulers identify patterns of audience movement. For example, a 'pre-echo' is an audience group intending to watch a programme starting shortly, thus increasing the audience for the programme scheduled just before the one they are interested in. 'Echoes' are audiences inherited from a programme that has just been broadcast. Now that British programmes tend to fit into the grid of half-hour and hour-long slots, there are more 'junction points' at which large numbers of viewers may switch from one channel to another. For example, at 10.00 p.m. news has been broadcast on both BBC1 and ITV1, and the 9.00 p.m. watershed is a point at which programmes aimed at a more adult audience can begin, resulting in a tendency for all channels to change the kinds of programme available at 9.00 p.m. or 10.00 p.m. This produces a junction where audiences may choose to move to one channel or another. 'Tent-pole' programmes are those that can be relied on to gain a large audience, thus lifting up the trend line showing audience size, like the ridge pole of a tent. Schedulers might also position a programme with a relatively low audience between two popular ones, hoping to inherit audiences from the preceding programme and to pick up audiences expecting to see the following one, producing 'hammocking', whereby a less popular programme is held up by those on either side.

ACTIVITY 10.7

Look for examples of relationships between programmes on the same channel in the current television schedules that seem to represent 'tent-poling' and 'hammocking'. How much 'head to head' competition can you see between popular programmes scheduled at the same time on two different channels?

News programmes fulfil the regulatory requirement for broadcasters on the main channels to inform their audience about contemporary events, but can also be used to control the audience's patterns of viewing because they occur at junction points. An early-evening news programme may encourage viewers to remain watching that channel for subsequent entertainment programmes in mid-evening prime time, while late-evening news occurs when adult-oriented programmes are shown. After the 9.00 p.m. 'watershed', when children are presumed not to be watching, the long late-evening news can hold viewers to remain on the same channel for the programmes that follow. However, since viewers now watch programmes at times other than when they are broadcast, the placing of programmes around junction points is going to change. According to BARB figures, in 2011 as many as 20 per cent of viewers watched programmes on catch-up services like the BBC's iPlayer, or by recording them and watching them later ('timeshifting'). For example, it has become normal for an episode of *EastEnders* to have over 8 million viewers at the time of first broadcast, but a further 1.5 million viewers watching at a subsequent time. *Top Gear* might achieve an audience of 8 million when first screened on BBC2, and another 2.5 million viewers watching later on iPlayer.

Scheduling is still hugely significant in British television, though some of the changes occurring in broadcasting in the present and near future may well change the ways in which it is done. Timeshifted viewing at a time following the first broadcast of a programme, the proliferation of channels and the threats to conventional terrestrial television from falling advertising revenues are some of the significant factors that schedulers worry about now. The introduction of personal video recorders – such as the SkyPlus box – also have an effect on scheduling, since viewers become schedulers themselves. The personal video recorder offers a searchable programme guide from which the viewer can choose programmes that are stored digitally in the hard drive. Since all the programmes stored on the machine are there to be watched whenever the viewer wishes, and in any order, now that this technology has been widely adopted it renders much of the scheduling effort that currently takes place potentially redundant. Nevertheless, for the moment it seems likely that viewers will still want to see the free programmes that are available simply by switching on the television when the daily routines of life in British households allow them the opportunity to do so. Scheduling remains a crucial activity in shaping audiences.

SUMMARY OF KEY POINTS

■ The measurement of audiences and prediction of how they respond to television are important to television institutions' economic success and the planning of programmes. Television schedules are designed to attract and hold audiences, and studying schedules reveals how television channels conceive of their audiences.

■ The increasing number of television channels, broadcasting hours and systems of delivery (such as Freeview, cable and satellite) has fractured television audiences into smaller niche groups, and some audience groups are more sought-after than others, usually because of their economic or social status.

■ To address and hold particular audiences, television producers change programmes, create new programmes, mix the genre conventions used in programmes and look for opportunities to increase viewers' involvement in programmes.

■ Television Studies has developed ways of understanding how audiences make meanings from television, and debated the significance of television in everyday life. Television Studies researchers have sought to reduce the distance between them and the ordinary viewers they study, in order to understand and value everyday television viewing.

■ The television audience is considered not as a uniform mass, but instead as a collection of diverse groups whose personal and social experiences shape their responses to television.

■ Television Studies has taken a particular interest in audiences from groups with relatively little social power (such as children, fans of cult programmes and women at home), and their use of television to express their identities and form social networks.

Further reading

Allen, R., 'Audience-oriented criticism and television', in R. Allen (ed.), *Channels of Discourse, Reassembled: Television and Contemporary Criticism* (London: Routledge, 1992), pp. 101–37.

Ang, I., *Living Room Wars: Rethinking Audiences for a Postmodern World* (London: Routledge, 1996).

—— *Desperately Seeking the Audience* (London: Routledge, 1991).

—— *Watching Dallas: Soap Operas and the Melodramatic Imagination*, trans. D. Couling, revised edition (London: Routledge, 1989).

Ang, I. and J. Hermes, 'Gender and/in media consumption', in I. Ang, *Living Room Wars: Rethinking Audiences for a Postmodern World* (London: Routledge, 1996), pp. 108–29.

Arksey, H. and P. Knight, *Interviewing for Social Scientists* (London: Sage, 1999).

Brown, M. and M. Wells, 'How did it rate?', *The Guardian*, Media section, 27 August 2001, pp. 2–3.

Bruhn Jensen, K. (ed.), *News of the World: World Cultures Look at Television News* (London: Routledge, 1998).

Dickinson, R., R. Harindranath and O. Linné (eds), *Approaches to Audiences: A Reader* (London: Arnold, 1998).

Dovey, J., *Freakshow: First Person Media and Factual Television* (Cambridge: Polity, 2000).

Dowmunt, T. (ed.), *Channels of Resistance: Global Television and Local Empowerment* (London: BFI, 1993).

Drummond, P. and R. Patterson (eds), *Television and its Audience: International Research Perspectives* (London: BFI, 1988).

Ellis, J., 'Scheduling: the last creative act in television', *Media, Culture & Society*, 22:1 (2000a), pp. 25–38.

Fiske, J., 'The cultural economy of fandom', in L. Lewis (ed.), *The Adoring Audience: Fan Culture and Popular Media* (London: Routledge, 1992b), pp. 30–49.

Geertz, C., *The Interpretation of Cultures: Selected Essays* (London: Fontana, 1967).

Geraghty, C., 'Audiences and "ethnography": questions of practice', in C. Geraghty and D. Lusted (eds), *The Television Studies Book* (London: Arnold, 1998), pp. 141–57.

Hall, S., 'Encoding/decoding', in S. Hall, D. Hobson, A. Lowe and P. Willis (eds), *Culture, Media, Language* (London: Hutchinson, 1980), pp. 128–38.

Hallam, J. and M. Marshment, 'Framing experience: case studies in the reception of *Oranges Are Not the Only Fruit*', *Screen*, 36:1 (1995), pp. 1–15.

Hill, A., *Shocking Entertainment: Viewer Response to Violent Movies* (Luton: University of Luton Press, 1997).

Hobson, D., *Crossroads: The Drama of a Soap Opera* (London: Methuen, 1982).

Holmes, S. and S. Redmond, *Framing Celebrity: New Directions in Celebrity Culture* (London: Routledge, 2006).

Jancovich, M. and J. Lyons (eds), *Quality Popular Television: Cult TV, the Industry and the Fans* (London: BFI, 2005).

Jenkins, H., *Textual Poachers: Television Fans and Participatory Culture* (London: Routledge, 1992).

Jhally, S. and B. Livant, 'Watching as working: the valorization of audience consciousness', *Journal of Communication*, 36:2 (1986), pp. 124–43.

Lewis, L. (ed.), *The Adoring Audience: Fan Culture and Popular Media* (London: Routledge, 1991).

Lunt, P. and Livingstone, S., 'Rethinking the focus group in media and communication research', *Journal of Communication*, 46:2 (1996), pp. 76–98.

May, T., *Social Research: Issues, Methods and Process*. 3rd Edition (Buckingham: Open University Press, 2001).

Morley, D., *Television, Audiences and Cultural Studies* (London: Routledge, 1992).

—— *The 'Nationwide' Audience* (London: BFI, 1980).

Mullan, B., *Consuming Television* (Oxford: Blackwell, 1997).

Ruddock, A., *Understanding Audiences: Theory and Method* (London: Sage, 2001).

Seale, C., *The Quality of Qualitative Research* (London: Sage, 1999).

Storey, J. *Cultural Consumption and Everyday Life* (London: Arnold, 1999).

Sweeney, M., 'TV advertising still needs an Xtra factor', *The Guardian*, Media section, 30 August 2011, p. 6.

Tulloch, J., *Watching Television Audiences: Cultural Theories and Methods* (London: Arnold, 2000).

Tulloch, J. and H. Jenkins, *Science Fiction Audiences: Watching Doctor Who and Star Trek* (London: Routledge, 1995).

Tunstall, J., *The Media in Britain* (London: Constable, 1983).

Beyond Television

Beyond Television

Introduction

In this final chapter, the book concludes with a study of how television is responding to its **convergence** with the newer media of personal computers, mobile communications and social networks. It is always risky to speculate about the future, but this chapter considers the extent to which television has recently changed as a medium and how it might change in the coming few years. The next stage in the development of television is to integrate the delivery of programmes with the ability for viewers to access the World Wide Web at the same time as they are viewing. In 2010, about half (12 million) of the households in Britain **subscribed** to pay television, and the other half were viewing the **free-to-air** broadcasting on the traditional broadcast channels, via a Freeview set-top box or a free satellite dish system. Many viewers supplement their watching of television as broadcast by using the catch-up services like iPlayer, or by using computers to access video on YouTube. So viewers are already accustomed to watching television in non-traditional ways. For the established broadcasters whose core activity has been to broadcast **analogue** television, namely the BBC, ITV, Channel 4 and Five, the culture of convergence – in which television and **interactive** internet services come together – challenges their dominance of the television landscape. For these traditional broadcasters, their dominance would be challenged if increasing numbers of viewers subscribe to pay television services in order to experience the new interrelated television and web services. At present, this is a moment of change where it is not clear whether audiences are going to demand viewing that combines television programmes, broadcast at a specific time and watched at the time of their broadcast, with access to the web and computer applications. But it looks as if viewers will want to use such services, and there are many technology and communications companies who are keen to sell the equipment that makes it possible to do this.

From the perspective of academic Television Studies, it is important to ask whether the questions posed in the past about television are still relevant, and whether the methods of study used in the discipline are still appropriate to analyse what is happening now (Brunsdon 2008). This chapter reflects on the recent ways that the delivery of television to viewers, and the ways that viewers interact with what they watch, suggest trends that might be significant. The overall argument of the chapter is that there are strong continuities between the recent place that television has had in British society and the ways that it is developing. While significant changes are taking place, they seem to be evolutionary rather than revolutionary. The chapter considers some of the evidence for the argument that television as we know it is about to cease to exist, but the chapter argues that the supposed 'death of TV' is actually a myth rather than a reality.

---

convergence the process whereby previously separate media technologies merge together. For example, computers can now send faxes, show DVD films and play music.

subscription payment to a television broadcaster in exchange for the opportunity to view programmes on certain channels that are otherwise blocked.

free-to-air television programming for which viewers make no direct payment.

analogue broadcasting signals in waves of varying frequency. Analogue signals require greater space or 'bandwidth' than digital signals, and do not allow interactive response from viewers.

interactive offering the opportunity for viewers to respond to what is broadcast, by sending signals back to the broadcaster (along a cable or phone line, for example).

ACTIVITY 11.1

Do you watch television programmes on a computer or mobile phone? If so, are there also times when you watch on a television set? What are the reasons why you watch using these different technologies?

Figure 11.1 Watching television on an iPad. © Yunus Arakon/ istockphoto.

Television as an interactive medium

Television programmes and up-to-the-minute rolling news still have a preeminent place in how people engage with and make sense of their world. In 2010, a dramatic general election in Britain led to a coalition government comprising the Conservative and Liberal Democrat parties. Television debates between the leaders of the main political parties were a high-profile live television experience, and the debates themselves together with associated coverage set the terms for how the political issues determining the election were presented. Television has always been associated with liveness, and an engagement with events that are happening in the present. Because of the time it takes to gather information and go to print, newspapers are always likely to deal with immediate events less quickly than radio or television. There is a long tradition in which major events of public interest encourage people to switch on their televisions to see the key players in the unfolding events and benefit from the differing opinions of commentators and experts. Although social media like Facebook and Twitter also offer an experience of immediacy, television remains a key means for people to experience and understand the present.

ACTIVITY 11.2

Which genres of programme rely most on being broadcast live? Why is this?

Although interactive television, where viewers can respond directly to programme content, is a decisive and important development in contemporary television, viewers have always interacted with television. There are many **genres** of programme that invite the viewer to become involved and to participate remotely. For example, television coverage of sport routinely addresses the viewer as a witness watching the sport along with television commentators and spectators at the event. The spoken **discourse** of sports commentators also routinely invites viewers to make judgements about the performance of the sportspeople and to evaluate their success. The positioning of cameras in television coverage of sport provides a much closer view of the action than is normally available to spectators at the event itself, and cutting between camera shots allows the television viewer to identify with the efforts and emotions of the competitors. The production and editing of television sport are designed to promote viewer involvement and to stimulate viewers' interaction with the event as it is taking place.

In a similar way, television talk shows address the viewer as someone taking part in the discussion. Expert commentators, often professionals such as psychologists, therapists or lawyers, appear in television talk shows and provide specialist opinion, while studio audiences engage either by individual audience members making comments of their own to the host or the guests, or simply by cheering, booing or laughing, for example. Television viewers are invited to **identify** with the experts, their guests or the studio audience at various points in the programme. Occasionally, talk shows also include opportunities for viewers to phone in and speak directly to the host and to ask questions or make comments. Although most of the time viewers of talk shows are involved only virtually, by responding to the programme only within their own viewing space in the home, nevertheless, as with sport's progress on television, the **format** and staging of the programme address the viewer as someone interested and involved in an ongoing discussion. A space is 'hollowed out' for the viewer to occupy, in which an active response and involvement is required.

Strategies such as these are intended to stimulate active viewing of television programmes, where viewers give their full attention to what they are seeing and hearing, and where there may be opportunities for action by the viewer. It is generally supposed by advertisers that the greater the attention given by television viewers to programmes, the more chance there is that viewers will also give their attention to advertisements screened before, after and during them. From an advertiser's point of view, of course, it is very important that viewers watch and remember the advertisements they have seen on television. Advertisements often include opportunities for viewer activity. These may simply be invitations for the

genre a kind or type of programme. Programmes of the same genre have shared characteristics.

discourse a particular use of language for a certain purpose in a certain context (such as academic discourse or poetic discourse), and similarly in television, a particular usage of television's audio-visual 'language' (news programme discourse or nature documentary discourse, for instance).

identification a term deriving from psychoanalytic theories of cinema, which describes the viewer's conscious or unconscious wish to take the place of someone or something in a television text.

format the blueprint for a programme, including its setting, main characters, genre, form and main themes.

viewer to get a joke, to solve a puzzle or simply to figure out what product an advertisement is selling. Being intrigued by a visually interesting advertisement, and enjoying its wit, are in themselves the kinds of activity that make the advertisement and its product more memorable. But there are further strategies that advertisers can use, such as providing telephone numbers and internet addresses that invite viewers to seek further information immediately about a product or service. A particular case in which the strategies of advertisements and programmes merge together, is in television shopping channels. These of course address the viewer as a potential buyer of the products that are displayed, and the presenters of shopping programmes address the viewer directly in describing and recommending products. Displays of prices, availability and special offers appear in windows on the screen, along with the telephone number that the viewer can use to purchase a particular product. Shopping channels also sometimes use short segments in which viewers who have rung in to buy a product are interviewed briefly by the presenter about why they found a product attractive, and whether they would recommend a product having used it before.

But true interactive television goes much further than this. **Digital television** systems can allow television viewers to choose programmes from a menu available on an on-screen programme guide. Viewers can also call up additional information about programmes, and access brief television segments that support the programme they are watching. Wildlife programmes, for example, may have supporting material giving further information about the animals seen in the programme, or providing further footage that was not included in the eventual edited version. The technology of 'picture-in-picture' allows this material to appear in smaller windows within the television screen, or for the viewer to see what is being broadcast on another channel. It has been suggested for a long time that it will also be possible for viewers to see alternative endings of drama programmes, or to change the relationship between **narrative** sequences in a way that is already possible with DVDs. The technological development that allows all of these opportunities to exist is digital television. The viewer becomes much more active, and more like the 'user' of a computer, so that contemporary television viewers are sometimes referred to as 'viewsers'.

With a range of around a hundred or more available digital channels, conventional television listings publications are difficult to use for viewers of digital television. Instead, electronic programme guides are available on the television screen. These look similar to the grids that are already common in listings publications such as *TV Guide* in the United States. They are in effect lists of time slots where, for a particular time period, all of the programmes available on all channels are shown. Viewers can scroll up and down through these lists and view information about particular programmes. Electronic programme guides are easiest to use when programmes are of standard lengths, such as thirty minutes, one hour or two hours for programmes such as films or football matches. In the multi-channel environment of the United States, even in terrestrial broadcasting, the use of standard programme lengths makes it easier for viewers to **zap** between channels, and the introduction of interactive television more widely in Britain produced greater standardisation of programme lengths for this reason. It also seems that the broadcast of digital interactive programmes has disrupted the conventional pattern of television **schedules**. Because digital television makes it easy to choose to view a programme at a variety of different starting times (because the same programme is shown by perhaps three or four

digital television television pictures and sound encoded into the ones and zeros of electronic data. Digital signals can also be sent back down cables by viewers, enabling interaction with television programmes.

narrative an ordered sequence of images and sound that tells a fictional or factual story.

zapping hopping rapidly from channel to channel while watching television, using a remote control (a 'zapper').

schedule the arrangement of programmes, advertisements and other material into a sequential order within a certain period of time, such as an evening, day or week.

different channels, on different days and at different times, on Channel 4, E4 and E4+1, for example) the viewer's chance to catch a programme is greatly increased. The power of television schedulers to control when audiences watch programmes diminishes, and television viewers become schedulers themselves.

In the digital television environment there are more broadcasting channels, and therefore smaller amounts of money per channel and per programme to spend, because the audience sizes for particular programmes are correspondingly smaller. The costs of making programmes are therefore more difficult to recoup from advertisers, and need to be generated from the subscriptions paid by the viewers of interactive digital television channels, or from one-off payments made by viewers to see a particular programme. Subscription and **pay-per-view** are becoming economically significant in Britain, and it seems likely that these modes of viewing will increase in importance. Interactivity has changed the forms and formats of television programmes. When interactive betting or phone voting are the primary ways of generating revenue, increasingly programmes are structured to include opportunities for competition among the people appearing in them, and the possibility of a range of different outcomes within programmes and at their conclusion, so that viewers are able to vote for the results. The ways that audiences view programmes, identify with and relate to people appearing on television, and follow storylines, also change. But new developments in technology of any kind are more likely to be adopted when they enhance a service that already exists, or offer services that are linked to an established **brand** (Johnson 2007). As John Storey (1999: 125) has argued, people's media use is strongly influenced by their habits and routines, since

> cultural consumption is a practice of everyday life. Cultural commodities are not appropriated or used in a social vacuum; such usage and appropriation takes place in the context of other forms of appropriation and use, themselves connected to the other routines, which together form the fabric of everyday life.

pay-per-view specific television programmes (such as sports events or films) offered to subscribers on payment of a fixed, one-off fee.

brand recognition the ability of audiences to recognise the distinctive identity of a product, service or institution and the values and meanings associated with it.

ACTIVITY 11.3

If you were trying to 'pitch' an interactive programme to a broadcaster, which programme format and genre might you choose in order to include plenty of opportunities for viewer interaction? How would you respond to the broadcaster's concerns about the profitability of your programme (the balance between programme cost and potential income)?

The growth of interactive television

From the perspective of the television broadcaster, interactive television began as an enhancement to existing programmes, and was a 'premium service' that viewers could be charged additional money to use. For some years it was difficult, however, to find ways of making money from digital television in Britain. Shopping, voting and online betting can be provided through interactive television services, and convergence with email and phone services means that viewers can enter phone competitions (on premium rate phone-lines) and post comments on programmes. Digital television also allows games to be played over the line. Interactive shopping through the television set has attracted relatively small numbers of users compared to shopping on the World Wide Web on computers, and it currently seems that it is mainly voting for competitors in game shows that could be profitable uses of the interactive technology.

The programme that had the greatest early success with interactive television was *Big Brother*, at the beginning of the 2000s. In the case of *Big Brother*, the relationships between the programme and its website was no longer one of an 'original' text and an add-on that enhanced the programme or perpetuated audience interest in it beyond transmission. The two were integrated, planned at the same time, and interdependent. This makes *Big Brother* an important pioneer of convergence in media culture. The interactive services associated with *Big Brother* were created by the Victoria Real agency. Endemol, the company that created *Big Brother*, owned a 50 per cent stake in the agency and bought it outright in 2003. *Big Brother* was sponsored by, among others, the telephone company O2, which offered text updates and sought to associate itself with the programme and enhance the value of its own brand. The convergence between media means not only that programmes are being made for broadcasting on the web, and web-based services are being connected to programmes, but also that convergence provides ways for consumers to flow between media such as the internet, mobile telephones and television. Programmes have become able to perpetuate their life beyond the run of an individual series, by encouraging their audiences to interact with programmes after they have finished, and also by drawing audiences to programmes when they begin, since those programmes already have a presence in other media. When Channel 4 planned its second series of *Big Brother* in 2001, it introduced interactive services accessible through its digital television channel E4, as well as on the World Wide Web. Since the programme had already established brand recognition, and viewers of the first series had already been able to interact with the programme on the internet, Channel 4 was able to enhance the second series in ways that audiences already understood. *Big Brother* had a large audience among the eighteen to thirty-four audience, and this group is more likely than others in the British population to have access to interactive television technology (and also to the internet). Viewers of *Big Brother* were able to take part in interactive games using their remote-control handsets, and could also vote for the exclusion of contestants, take part in quizzes and gain access to additional information and video coverage. So *Big Brother 2* and *3* had numerous benefits for Channel 4 in attracting and maintaining a valuable youth audience, stimulating the use of and demand for digital interactive services, and promoting the brand identity of a programme closely identified with the channel.

For the 2004 series of *Big Brother*, Channel 4 changed its offerings on the internet to give greater priority to interactive services. In 2003, interest from internet users dropped by half after the first week of screening, but in 2004 hits on the *Big Brother* site placed the programme second only to the BBC's weather information pages. The managers in charge of interactivity at the production company Endemol speculated that the revival in the use of interaction was a result of the casting of

Big Brother where more conflict and more titillation were on offer. For the first time, the 2004 version of the website carried content that could only be seen there and had to be paid for by users. The content included behind-the-scenes documentaries and extended footage. The free streaming of coverage that marked the first series of *Big Brother* was no longer available. With its access to the families and friends of the contestants, the official website was able to present webchats and brief written reports that could extend the information available to users. The material on the programme site aimed also to divert its users to other services offered by Channel 4, such as its pages on cars and property. In a newspaper article about Channel 4's financial prospects, Maggie Brown (2004b) reported that the channel expected to lose 20 per cent of its audience by 2012, as multi-channel increases and grabs some of its audience and advertising revenue; ways to hook the audience and keep it by using interactive web-based services therefore became more significant. Text messaging and interactive services brought in the relatively small amount of £2 million in 2004, including *Big Brother*. In 2004 Channel 4's share of the audience was divided up into:

- 13 per cent share of viewing in homes with only analogue television
- 11 per cent share in homes with the Freeview multi-channel set-top box
- 6 per cent share in homes subscribing to Sky Television.

The channel expected its overall share to fall to 8 per cent when terrestrial television was switched off. In this context, maximising the revenue from interactive services associated with programmes, and especially strong brands like *Big Brother*, was going to be crucial to any channel's continuing health. But *Big Brother* was acquired for Five and began a new series on that channel in 2011, thus leaving Channel 4 with the question of how it would compensate for this with programmes that would be equally significant.

Having gained much experience with interactive programmes on *Big Brother*, Channel 4 commissioned a batch of new documentaries in 2010 that drew on content from the web and offered audience interaction. They developed the focus on ordinary people in **documentaries** that has been evident in British television since the high-profile **docusoaps** of the 1990s. *Seven Days* aimed to promote audience involvement by offering real-time chat online with the people featured in the programme, and was shot and edited all in the same week to convey immediacy. Two other documentaries, *Life in a Day* and *One Day on Earth 10.10.10* gathered programme material from people who had posted short films about themselves on the web. It is an indication of the extent to which television-makers now perceive the web as parallel and complementary to their work, rather than a competitor with it, that the director of *Life in a Day*, Kevin Macdonald, secured funding for the programme by approaching YouTube, which provided his programme budget via sponsorship from the technology company LG (Bulkley 2010). Since *Life in a Day* drew material from YouTube, there was expectation that it would promote YouTube to potential users. Television producers and television channels now look for ways to exploit the convergence of television with other media, and ways to stimulate interactivity.

documentary a form aiming to record actual events, often with an explanatory purpose or to analyse and debate an issue.

docusoap a television form combining documentary's depiction of non-actors in ordinary situations with soap opera's continuing narratives about selected characters.

ACTIVITY 11.4

In what ways are television programme-makers competing with video sharing sites like YouTube, and in what ways are their interests complementary?

Research by James Bennett that drew on his earlier work (2006, 2008) used interviews with a wide range of programme commissioners and programme producers to understand the role that multi-platform media play in recent BBC television policy. The BBC initially aimed to undertake 360° commissioning, which meant creating not simply television programmes, but interconnected material for television and a range of other media platforms, such as websites and social networks. Programmes with strong brand identities like *Doctor Who* have benefitted from this idea, and Figure 11.2 is an image from the downloadable game that BBC launched to accompany the television series. Very recognisable elements of the *Doctor Who* brand can be seen here, notably the image of Matt Smith as the Doctor, and his space–time vehicle the TARDIS. But primarily what the BBC did was deliver conventional television programmes for broadcast and for catch-up viewing on the iPlayer, with some supporting webpages and social media. The broadcast television programmes took the lead. This was because of the legacy in the television industry of thinking about broadcasting (rather than interactive delivery of content), so that staff working for television companies continued to do their work in much the same ways as they did before. A high degree of inertia constrains the creative experimentation that could go on in a multi-platform media world. Similarly, the makers of digital content, like web designers and interactive software producers, are happy to stay in their own field rather than engage with television broadcasters.

Government imposed significant cuts to BBC budgets in 2010, and the BBC responded with a strategy called 'Delivering Quality First'. Its aims were to do fewer things, but to do them better. Just as before, James Bennett found that the BBC actually placed its emphasis on making programmes for conventional broadcast and

Figure 11.2 The *Doctor Who* 'Victory of the Daleks' downloadable video game.

on making computer applications that would deliver broadcast programmes to audiences. While programmes and the services associated with them could be delivered to the audience in many ways via conventional television and by new media outlets, broadcast television was placed at the centre of BBC activity. Making television programmes costs much more than making digital multi-platform content, so within the television company more attention is likely to be lavished on making programmes. The size of the television audience for programmes is also much larger than the number of users of interactive services, and the combined effect of these circumstances is to give greater value to broadcast output than to multi-platform content, and to encourage the perception of non-broadcast content as an added extra.

The success of iPlayer reinforced the central role of making television programmes, since iPlayer's role is to deliver programmes through the internet. Creative ways of using interactive media require time, staff effort and money. For the production team of a programme, there is rarely the available staff or the time to develop custom-made interactive services. And since the production team for a programme is likely to be assembled from people employed on short-term contracts to service the programme project up to its completion, rather than permanent staff who are always available, the maintenance of complex multi-platform interactive services would in any case be difficult to resource once the programme itself has been broadcast.

Some programme-makers have been innovative, however. At the BBC and at Channel 4, for example, particular high-profile programmes have been chosen to exploit the potential of interactivity. For commercial broadcasters especially, for example Channel 4, it is possible for programme webpages to offer users links to commercial sites or products; the owners of programmes and formats have a financial incentive to do this since they can make additional money from the commercial companies to whom they direct users from the programme website. For example, the Channel 4 series *Embarrassing Bodies* had very complex web resources, including interactive tests that users could take to check the status of their health, and links to many external organisations connected with health and well-being (www.channel4 embarrassingillnesses.com/). Younger and technologically sophisticated viewers are not only a valuable **niche audience** for programme-makers, but are also the group that are most likely to be conversant with how to use internet services. At the BBC, younger viewers are the future payers of the licence fee, and thus significant to the BBC even though it is not a commercial organisation. The BBC's drama series *Being Human*, for example, addressed to young adult viewers, had a complex web-based service called 'Becoming Human'. On the programme webpage in preparation for its launch in 2011, Sarah Clay, BBC Multi-platform Drama Commissioner, wrote:

niche audiences particular groups of viewers defined by age group, gender or economic status, for example, who may be the target audience for a programme.

> The fans of Being Human are incredibly active online, so we wanted to give them something they could really get their teeth into. The Becoming Human online extension doesn't just consist of nine episodes, the narrative extends beyond that with daily clues in the form of press cuttings, anonymous tips, CCTV footage, mobile phone clips . . . giving the online audience the chance to follow the mystery on the blog as it unfolds.
>
> (www.bbc.co.uk/blogs/beinghuman/2010/10/new_
> series_becoming_human.html)

ACTIVITY 11.5

How can television broadcasters use websites and social media to extend the public service aspects of programmes? Are factual programmes the only ones that do this?

Viewers' interaction with programmes

The appearance of new media formats seems to proclaim a realignment between the audience and the text, and *Big Brother* was at the forefront of the exploitation of young audiences' familiarity with technology, such as the internet and interactive technologies where the users are able to choose and change what they watch. When interactive users are able to influence and reconfigure texts, this can have the effect of producing a greater sense of authenticity and belief in the liveness of the material. Research by Janet Jones (2004) suggested that these interactive formats reduce viewers' suspicion of how what they see is being mediated by programme-makers, building on the convergence of new media with television in order to produce a sense of immediacy by drawing on the apparent authenticity of live and interactive material. Authenticity is often produced by the relationship between the live and the mediated, which exist in tension with each other. Jones's research on how people remember experiences in the different levels of mediation offered by different media platforms, shows that the first encounter creates a frame for subsequent memories of that moment. In *Big Brother*, the media platforms were the broadcast television signal, either live or edited, broadcasting over the web, broadcasting over interactive television channels, and automatic messaging systems that sent notification of significant events to the user's mobile phone. Where there is less mediation because of a live broadcasting context, such as the E4 channel or a web broadcast, this produces a more detailed memory of a moment than in a more highly mediated form like recorded highlights. Audiences for less mediated material show a greater diversity of remembered moments, and a more personalised recollection of those moments, suggesting that live broadcasts are good ways of involving viewers in television watching and making television viewing significant to them.

There are significant differences between the technological platforms in which viewers encounter programmes that may be broadcast live, broadcast in the form of recorded highlights, streamed over the web or disseminated by short messages to mobile phones. The live broadcast of *Big Brother* on E4 had low mediation in that although there was some editing for **taste and decency** and legality, it was marked as live with a caption 'live' on the screen, and the material itself was both visual, auditory and graphical. Relatively unmediated live broadcasts offer the opportunity for the viewer to actively interpret the material and create meanings for him or herself. The messages broadcast to mobile phones had comparatively high mediation, since they consisted only of short text similar to newspaper headlines, and very brief descriptions of events. The messages were sent within twenty minutes of the occurrence of an event, so despite their high mediation, they were close to the temporality of live broadcasting. These messages provided viewers with only a limited set of interpretive possibilities, since the input was restricted to the written

taste and decency conformity to the standards of good taste and acceptable language and behaviour represented on television, as required by regulations.

form of verbal messages. The broadcasts of recorded highlights in the evening Channel 4 schedule exhibited a high degree of mediation, since any event was enfolded within **voice-over**, editing of visual material, graphics on the screen and also music. The recorded programmes had much less temporal closeness to the events, since programmes usually referred to events that occurred in the *Big Brother* house on the previous day. Viewers were provided with primarily visual information, which framed events using a very varied range of points of view mixed with information presented in graphical or caption form. These evening broadcasts restricted the opportunities for viewer interpretation, though less so than for mobile phone messages. The work by Jones suggests that the viewers' emotional engagement is restricted by a high degree of mediation. Overall, watching live television appears to present opportunities for interaction that are not present in recorded programmes.

So far it has not been profitable for television programme-makers to invest in interactivity within the content of fiction programmes. The telecommunications and cable television company NTL announced in March 2000 that it had allocated a fund of £5 million that would be spent over five years to develop interactive television drama programmes. This was planned to be a joint venture with Channel 5, whereby Channel 5 would screen this interactive drama and thereby persuade more viewers to purchase the hardware such as digital television receivers and set-top boxes manufactured by NTL that are necessary to view such programmes. The pilot programme that Channel 5 commissioned from the **independent production company** Leisure Time was to be a crime drama. But knowing that the only profitable use of interactive television at that time was in betting, Channel 5 adjusted the specifications for the programme to include an element of competition. It would therefore be possible for viewers to make bets about the fates of the characters and increase the element of suspense in the narrative. However, in 2001 the project was abandoned as being too complex and expensive. Making a drama programme that has multiple simultaneous plot lines, each of them accessible to viewers making choices through their remote-control handsets and thus composing different programmes according to the choices they have made, is an extremely expensive and complicated business. The programme-makers are asked in effect to write and produce the equivalent of several different conventional programmes, and find ways of linking up narrative segments, plot events and character development so that the choices made by the viewer would continue to result in a meaningful and enjoyable programme.

But there are ways of introducing interactivity by more simple means, and at Christmas 2006, ITV tried an interesting experiment with its popular **soap opera** *Emmerdale*. The regular character Tom King was killed in mysterious circumstances and many of the programme's villagers were suspects in the murder. ITV set up a website in which viewers could take part in solving the crime, by providing a virtual tour of the village in which users could pick up items and look for clues in the pub and the farms where the serial is set. Written diaries or 'blogs' appeared on the website in which regular characters gave their opinions on the crime and who might have committed it, and users could put questions to the character Shadrach who was stationed in the Woolpack pub. Users who signed up on the website could receive emails each week, supposedly written by characters in the serial, where new clues and hints gave new information that might lead to the finding of Tom King's killer.

voice-over speech accompanying visual images but not presumed to derive from the same place or time as the images.

independent production companies businesses making television programmes which can be sold to television networks that transmit and distribute them.

soap opera a continuing drama serial involving a large number of characters in a specific location, focusing on relationships, emotions and reversals of fortune.

The first clue posted on the website was an anonymous letter, saying: 'You've lied. You've cheated. You've stolen. You've murdered. The law can't get you. So I will.' This kind of exercise does not require the writing of several different strands of storyline in *Emmerdale*, since the solution to the puzzle of who killed Tom was not in the hands of the viewers and could be decided in advance by the production team. The only difficulty was keeping the identity of the killer secret until the producers were ready to reveal it.

The prominence of voting as a means of gathering revenue for interactive television has important consequences for audiences' relationships with television, and more generally as an index of shifts in the **ideology** of television culture. As this section has argued, voting is used to stimulate the involvement of the viewer in programmes, since supporting a game show contestant produces a tangible reason for the viewer to focus exclusively on what he or she is watching. There are significant differences between this kind of involvement with television and the conventional ways in which Television Studies has discussed the viewer's relationship with programmes. Conventionally, the viewer's relationship to programmes has been thought of in terms of identification with the patterns and rhythms of narrative and identifications with characters and people represented, and in terms of an ebb and flow of attention across the flow of a period of watching time. But casting a vote forms a link between the space of viewing and the represented space in the television programme, increasing viewer involvement and interest. It is now common for viewers to vote for contestants on *Strictly Come Dancing* and other programmes with interactive elements, taking part to reject or promote their favourite performers. If interactive voting becomes widespread and socially significant, there is likely to be a change in the ways that people conceive of their reality. Society could be considered primarily in terms of success and failure, winners and losers, and the ability of individuals to take risks in order to succeed. The forces of chance and fate, rather than planning, effort and consistency of action, may acquire increasing importance. The sense that society is a collective community may reduce in importance compared to individualism and competition. Ideological assumptions such as these give support to the increased short-term thinking, acceptance of risk and unpredictability and diminished social cohesion that are currently found in more capitalist societies such as the United States, as compared to Western European nations.

> **ideology** the set of beliefs, attitudes and assumptions arising from the economic and class divisions in a culture, underlying the ways of life accepted as normal in that culture.

ACTIVITY 11.6

In what ways does viewer voting in talent shows and reality TV give viewers power over programme content? How important is this viewer power?

Interactivity and sociability

The viewing context, such as watching television with other members of your family or with your best friends, for instance, affects viewing experience. People watching with their families will often be persuaded to watch something they do not enjoy, whereas watching a favourite programme with a group of friends might help to confirm a person's shared relationships with members of that group. John Storey (1999: 114) summarises this social role of television viewing by arguing that:

> Watching television is always so much more than a series of acts of interpretation; it is above all else a social practice. That is, it can be a means to isolate oneself . . . or to make contact with other family members . . . In these ways, the cultural consumption of television is as much about social relationships as it is about interpretations of individual programmes.

While employed adults watching television might use television as a reward after a hard day at work, their reasons for watching and the pleasures they gain might be quite different from, for instance, those of teenage girls watching MTV with their friends. Audience researchers have also studied people's talk about television. Information about who talks about television, to whom, where and how (for example in the school playground, at work, in pubs or when meeting other people for the first time) reveals the different roles television can play in making, breaking and maintaining social relationships. Researchers have looked at how 'television viewing is generally a somewhat busy activity, interrupted by many other activities and routinely accompanied by talk, much of it having nothing to do with the programme being watched' (Storey 1999: 16). For the discipline of Television Studies in general, the shift of interest on to viewers and audiences rather than on television programmes as texts has focused on 'active' rather than 'passive' viewing, and provided good reasons to value the kinds of viewing and kinds of television programme on the basis of how people use them in their daily lives. Rather than being passively positioned by the semiotic **codes** of a television programme, viewers can now be understood as makers of meaning. Watching television requires viewers to draw on their personal histories and their cultural, class, racial, economic or sexual identities, and to use their cultural competence, gained from media knowledge of comparable programmes and the various information sources available to them, to construct a relationship with the television programme in the context of their cultural lives.

code in semiotics, a system or set of rules that shapes how signs can be used, and therefore how meanings can be made and understood.

There are already some viewers who regularly watch television programmes with their laptops in front of them or their internet-enabled phones switched on, so that they can instantaneously send messages to their friends about what they are watching, contribute to Twitter conversations or post comments on fan websites. A survey in late 2010 by the research company Thinkbox showed that 60 per cent of people say that they simultaneously watch television and go online two or three times a week, while a third of those participating in the survey claimed to watch television and simultaneously use the internet every day (Armstrong 2010). About half of these people were using internet shopping sites while watching programmes, and thus not using interactivity to do things that were directly related to the programme, but 44 per cent of the people surveyed were using social networks to post messages while they watch television. Television writers and producers monitor online activity relating to at least some of their programmes, and this feedback from viewers can influence decisions about future programme-making. The producer Daisy Goodwin, from the independent production company Silver River that made the factual entertainment series *Giles and Sue Live the Good Life*, commented: 'The Twitter feed has convinced the BBC to commission another series, on the basis of how enthusiastic and how young the audience is' (quoted in Armstrong 2010).

Gathering information from social networks about what viewers like or do not like about programmes is a significant enhancement to the information about the size and composition of audiences that broadcasters already receive from **BARB**. It is also significant in another way, since it has the effect of raising the profile for programmes that attract a high volume of social networking response. Within social networks themselves, a high volume of comment has the effect of spreading the word about a programme to a widening community of users, and thus potentially increasing the audience for the programme. Media outlets like newspapers, breakfast television and talk shows also take an interest in what is popular on social networks in order to find ideas for items in television programmes or feature articles in newspapers. So a high volume of viewer comment on social networks also leads to a snowball effect where programmes are referred to or discussed in other programmes and in non-televisual media. Programmes become 'watercooler TV', the subject of informal conversation at work or at school, but now also in conversations on interactive media platforms rather than face-to-face. Some of this social network profile can be encouraged by writers and producers placing surprising or controversial moments in programmes, in the hope that high volumes of Twitter comments or posts to websites will be generated. Moments like this are referred to as a 'Twitter bomb', dropped deliberately into a programme. On the other hand, it could be argued that social networking while watching television is clearly an indication of viewer distraction, in which a programme has failed to generate attentive viewing of the programme itself.

BARB (Broadcasters Audience Research Bureau) the independent body that gathers and reports viewing statistics on behalf of UK television institutions.

ACTIVITY 11.7

How would you weigh up the claim that social networking about television programmes is evidence of viewer involvement with them, versus the claim that it is evidence of distracted viewing?

How new is new?

The BBC's iPlayer service for viewing television programmes on computer has been very successful, and other companies have been trying various ways to link television with other domestic digital technologies. The Apple computer company offers its own set-top box, for example, BT Vision was a project by the telephone and internet service provider to corner the interactive television market, the internet search company Google linked programmes with web services, and the Sony PlayStation 3 can stream video over broadband connections to connect with the BBC iPlayer. In this context, it might seem that watching television has decisively changed, but evidence does not bear out this claim.

For the 2011 Edinburgh Television Festival, a survey of media use was commissioned from the company Deloitte (2011). The aim of the survey was to see whether predictions of the death of television were borne out by the ways that British viewers access media content. It has been argued for several years that the conventional delivery of television programmes by broadcast to domestic television sets was about to be replaced by new ways of viewing. Viewers were expected to abandon conventional television and watch programmes on demand by selecting them from a menu of content offered either by the traditional television channels or by aggregators: companies that run portals giving access to programmes from many different channels and providers. The internet was expected to be the main technology for delivering audio-visual material. If this were true, there would also be consequences for what television programmes are like. The idea of liveness would be replaced by selecting ready-made programmes from a menu, and rather than watching programmes from start to finish in the BBC domestic living room, people would watch more individually on computers, telephones and portable pads around the home, on trains, in airports and all kinds of other locations.

But the results of the 2011 survey showed that the average British person has been watching increasing amounts of television, 90 per cent of it on conventional television sets at the time when programmes are first broadcast. The average British person watched more than four hours per day of television from the middle of 2010 to the middle of 2011. However, it is also clear that repeating programmes, making them available to download on personal video recorders, and making them available on catch-up services like iPlayer has also had an effect. The ITV1 **period drama** *Downton Abbey*, set in a stately home in the early years of the twentieth century, was a Sunday night programme in a very established genre and was ITV1's most popular programme in 2010. The first three episodes of its first seven-part series were watched by an average of 7.7 million viewers, but a further 1.5 million viewers watched it after its first broadcast. It has become important for television companies to understand the significance of timeshifted viewing. George Entwistle (2011), the director of BBC Vision, explained in a newspaper article that the BBC had introduced new ways of measuring audiences in response to the ways that programmes become available in a range of forms at a range of times. The new audience measurement indicator called Live Plus 7 was introduced to measure how many people, using any technology, watched a particular programme in the seven days from first transmission. Although the sports quiz *A Question of Sport* on BBC1 had 2.8 million viewers when first transmitted at the end of July 2011, after seven days the audience had risen to 5.4 million. The BBC's science fiction drama *Torchwood* had 4.2 million viewers when first shown, rising to 6.3 million during the subsequent week. Clearly, significant numbers of viewers do not watch programmes when first broadcast but choose to watch at a range of times that suits them. But overall, for all channels, on-demand viewing on the BBC iPlayer, SkyPlus, YouTube and other services accounted for only about 7 per cent of television viewing in 2010. While new ways of viewing may herald a change in what television is in Britain, the change is happening slowly.

Some programmes seem more attractive to online viewers than others. Entwistle (2011) reported that iPlayer was an especially attractive way to view the BBC3 programme *Russell Howard's Good News*, for which 16 per cent of the audience were iPlayer viewers. Timeshifting, where viewers watch programmes at a later time than first broadcast, was used to watch about 10 per cent of the BBC output across all genres, but 26 per cent of the viewing of BBC drama was by timeshifting in May 2011. Drama has always been a key attraction for audiences, and viewers use timeshifting so that they do not miss programmes that they perceive to be important and attractive. It seems that the impact of new ways of delivering television, and

period drama
television fiction set in the past, most often the nineteenth or early twentieth centuries.

audience interaction with programmes on the internet and social networks, is much greater for some programmes than others and is also an indication of the value that viewers give to the programmes they most enjoy. Entwistle reported that the 2011 season of BBC's business competition *The Apprentice* attracted half a million hits on the programme website in the first week of the series. Across the series as a whole, online viewing of episodes amounted to 15 million views. When, at the end of the series, the winner of *The Apprentice* was announced, there were 150,000 mentions of the programme on Twitter. Television programmes are both the subject of social media interaction and a driver for people to use interactive technologies. In 2011 the BBC soap opera *EastEnders* had about 2.3 million followers on Facebook, and the fantasy drama *Being Human* had a third of a million. The live nature programme *Springwatch* had 220,000 Facebook followers. These examples are further evidence that social networking activity functions as an enhancement to programmes that already have large established audiences, and may encourage further viewing and deeper engagement with programmes.

The traditional broadcasters came together to launch a new set-top box in 2011 called YouView. BBC, ITV, Channel 4 and Five worked jointly with the telecommunications companies BT and TalkTalk to develop the YouView service, combining three kinds of watching experiences:

- delivery of programmes as broadcast, like conventional television
- ability to select and view programmes on demand, available from a large menu of choices.
- applications like those found on an iPhone, enabling users to access social networks and internet sites.

Existing digital television services like Freeview and Sky already provide an on-screen electronic programme guide (EPG) that shows the television schedule in graphic form. The new YouView service will have an EPG of a similar kind, where viewers can select which current broadcast programme they wish to watch from a range of channels. But the programme guide can move forwards and backwards in time, so that viewers can scroll back to the previous day's or the previous week's programmes and select one to download and watch. Rather than having to use a computer to visit the catch-up websites from BBC, ITV or any other broadcaster, the YouView television screen will give access to each of these broadcasters' catch-up services, all available from the same screen. YouView was scheduled to launch in 2012, when users would be able to post messages and chat online while watching a programme, or they could go to shopping sites like Amazon to order products. The idea is that this will enhance viewing in new ways, so that, for example, viewers watching a football match could post comments about the game while it is going on. Or viewers who are watching a cookery programme could order a cookbook online. While these kinds of social networking and purchasing can already be done using different pieces of technology such as a television, a laptop computer and a phone, for example, YouView makes it possible to do all of these things from the same screen at the same time.

New ways of delivering and using television certainly add to the opportunities for audiences, and impact on the ways that programme-makers and schedulers think about their work. But the evidence of recent surveys of actual viewers is that they are likely to continue to watch most of their television at home, on television sets, at the time when programmes are first broadcast. Watching programmes at times other than their first broadcast, by timeshift recording, happens mainly in the few days following first broadcast, and viewing online via a computer remains a minority way of watching television. For Television Studies, there are sufficient continuities in television of the past, present and future for the approaches explored in this book to maintain their usefulness (Turner and Tay 2009). For instance, television still comprises programmes that are understood in the frameworks of genre, and some programmes have the status of cultural events (Ellis 2012). Television is by no means dead, and the ways it is changing make it even more interesting and important as a subject for study.

SUMMARY OF KEY POINTS

■ New ways of delivering programmes to viewers, and for viewers to experience and interact with programmes, are changing television's role as a medium.

■ But television has always had a developing and changing relationship to the other media that it complements or competes against.

■ Interactivity with television is enhanced by the convergence of television with computers, internet communications, mobile phones and recording devices.

■ New ways of using television build on the medium's capacity to generate and shape social interactions between people.

■ For television-makers, building up strong brands while exploiting media convergence helps them to shape and adjust to the changes in how television is used.

■ Viewers are going to enjoy opportunities to use television in both 'old' and 'new' ways, so understanding the past, present and future prospects for the medium is increasingly important.

Further reading

Armstrong, S., 'Are two screens better than one?', *The Guardian*, Media section, 22 November 2010, p. 3.

Bennett, J., '"Your window on the world": The emergence of red-button interactive television in the UK', *Convergence*, 14:2 (2008), pp. 161–82.

—— 'The public service value of interactive TV', *New Review of Film and Television Studies*, 4:3 (2006), pp. 263–85.

Bennett, J., and N. Strange (eds), *Television as Digital Media* (Durham, NC: Duke University Press, 2011).

—— 'The BBC's second-shift aesthetics: Interactive television, multi-platform projects and public service content for a digital era', *Media International Australia*, 126 (2008), pp. 106–19.

Brown, M., 'The £100m crisis at Channel 4', *The Guardian*, Media section, 11 November 2004b, pp. 8–9.

Brunsdon, C., 'Is Television Studies history?', *Cinema Journal*, 47:3 (2008), pp. 127–37.

Bulkley, K., 'A focus on the future', *The Guardian*, Digital Vision supplement, 25 October 2010, p. 1.

Deloitte, 'Perspectives on television in words and numbers', 2011, available at http://www.deloitte.com/view/en_GB/uk/industries/tmt/5d44f5fe4e0f1310Vgn VCM2000001b56f00aRCRD.htm.

Ellis, J., 'The end of TV? I don't think so', *Critical Studies in Television* blog, 9 January 2012, http://cstonline.tv/end-of-tv-not.

Entwistle, G., 'Net gains are mutual benefits', *The Guardian*, Media section, 22 August 2011, p. 4.

Jenkins, H., *Convergence Culture: Where Old and New Media Collide* (Cambridge, Mass.: MIT Press, 2006).

Jermyn, D. and S. Holmes, 'The audience is dead; long live the audience!: Interactivity, "telephilia", and the contemporary television audience', *Critical Studies in Television*, 1:1 (2006), pp. 49–57.

Johnson, C., 'Tele-branding in TV III: the network as brand and programme as brand', *New Review of Television Studies*, 5:1 (2007), pp. 5–24.

Jones, J., 'Emerging platform identities: *Big Brother* UK and interactive multi-platform usage', in E. Mathijs and J. Jones (eds), *Big Brother International: Formats, Critics and Publics* (London: Wallflower, 2004), pp. 210–31.

Storey, J. *Cultural Consumption and Everyday Life* (London: Arnold, 1999).

Turner, G., and J. Tay (eds), *Television Studies after TV: Understanding Television in the Post-Broadcast Era* (London: Routledge, 2009).

Glossary of key terms

180-degree rule the convention that cameras are positioned only on one side of an imaginary line drawn to connect two performers in a scene. This produces a coherent sense of space for the viewer.

active audience television audiences regarded not as passive consumers of meanings, but as negotiating meanings for themselves that are often resistant to those meanings that are intended or that are discovered by close analysis.

actuality footage television pictures representing an event that was filmed live. The term usually refers to pictures of news events.

adaptation transferring a novel, theatre play, poem, etc. from its original medium into another medium such as television.

aesthetic a specific artistic form. Aesthetics means the study of art and beauty.

affiliates local television stations (normally in the USA) that have made agreements (affiliations) with a network to broadcast programmes offered by that network rather than another.

analogue broadcasting signals in waves of varying frequency. Analogue signals require greater space or 'bandwidth' than digital signals, and do not allow inter-active response from viewers.

Annan Committee a committee reporting in 1977 to government on the future of broadcasting. It supported public service broadcasting, the funding of the BBC by licence fee, and the planned introduction of a fourth television channel.

anthropology the study of humankind, including the evolution of humans and the different kinds of human society existing in different times and places.

audience share the percentage of viewers estimated to have watched one channel as opposed to another channel broadcasting at the same time.

authorship the question of who an author is, the role of the author as creator and the significance of the author's input into the material being studied.

avant-garde work aiming to challenge the norms and conventions of its medium, and the group of people making such work.

back lighting lighting the subject of a shot from behind to provide depth by separating the subject from the background.

balance the requirement in television news and current affairs to present both sides of an argument or issue.

BARB (Broadcasters Audience Research Bureau) the independent body that gathers and reports viewing statistics on behalf of UK television institutions.

binary opposition two contrasting terms, ideas or concepts, such as inside/outside, masculine/feminine or culture/nature.

blooper a mistake by a performer in a programme, or a technical error. The term often refers to humorous mistakes.

bourgeoisie the middle class, who are owners of property and businesses.

brand recognition the ability of audiences to recognise the distinctive identity of a product, service or institution and the values and meanings associated with it.

broadcasting the transmission of signals from a central source which can be received by dispersed receivers over a large geographical area.

budget the money allocated to the making of a particular programme or series of programmes, which is controlled by the producer.

cable television originally called Community Antenna Television (CATV). Transmission of television signals along cables in the ground.

capitalism the organisation of an economy around the private ownership of accumulated wealth, involving the exploitation of labour to produce profit that creates such wealth.

censorship the omission of sensitive, prohibited or disturbing material at any stage in the production process from the initial idea to its transmission.

class a section of society defined by their relationship to economic activity, whether as workers (the working class) or possessors of economic power (the bourgeoisie), for example.

classic serial the dramatisation in serial form of literature written in the past, most often in the nineteenth and early twentieth centuries, where the literary source already has high cultural status.

close-up a camera shot where the frame is filled by the face of a person or a detail of a face. Close-ups may also show details of an object or place.

closed-circuit television a small-scale television system where the images and sound are not intended for broadcast, for example a network of security cameras.

CNN Cable News Network, the first international satellite news channel, operating from the United States.

code in semiotics, a system or set of rules that shapes how signs can be used, and therefore how meanings can be made and understood.

commercial television television funded by the sale of advertising time or sponsorship of programmes.

commissioning the process by which an idea for a programme is selected to go into production.

committed a term used in the study of the politics of culture, implying that a person or a text has a commitment to positive and progressive social change.

commodity a raw material or product whose economic value is established by market price rather than the intrinsic qualities or usefulness of the material or product itself.

computer generated imaging (CGI) the creation of images by programming computers with mathematical equations that can generate realistic two-dimensional pictures.

connotations the term used in semiotic analysis for the meanings that are associated with a particular sign or combination of signs.

consensus a shared and accepted opinion or attitude among a certain group of people.

conventions the frameworks and procedures used to make or interpret texts.

convergence the process whereby previously separate media technologies merge together. For example, computers can now send faxes, show DVD films and play music.

copyright the legal right of ownership over written, visual or aural material, including the prohibition on copying this material without permission from its owner.

couch potatoes a derogatory term for television viewers supposedly sitting motionless at home watching television passively and indiscriminately.

cultural imperialism the critical argument that powerful nations and regions (especially those of the Western world) dominate less developed nations and regions by exporting values and ideologies.

Cultural Studies the academic discipline devoted to studying culture, involving work on texts, institutions, audiences and economic contexts.

culture the shared attitudes, ways of life and assumptions of a group of people.

cut the moment at which one camera shot ceases and another begins, where no transitional visual effect (such as a fade or a dissolve) is used.

cutaway in fictional dialogue or interviews, shots that do not include people speaking. Cutaways often consist of details of the setting or of interviewees (such as hands).

demography the study of population, and the groupings of people (demographic groups) within the whole population.

denotation in semiotics, the function of signs to portray or refer to something in the real world.

deregulation the removal of legal restrictions or guidelines that regulate the economics of the television industry or the standards which programmes must adhere to.

dialectic a term associated especially with Marxist theories, meaning a struggle between two opposing ideas.

diegesis the telling of events as narrative. Diegetic sound is sound emanating from the represented environment, and extra-diegetic sound comes from outside that environment.

digital television television pictures and sound encoded into the ones and zeros of electronic data. Digital signals can also be sent back down cables by viewers, making possible interaction with television programmes.

director the person responsible for the creative process of turning a script or idea into a finished programme, by working with a technical crew, performers and an editor.

discourse a particular use of language for a certain purpose in a certain context (such as academic discourse or poetic discourse), and similarly in television, a particular usage of television's audio-visual 'language' (news programme discourse or nature documentary discourse, for instance).

documentary a form aiming to record actual events, often with an explanatory purpose or to analyse and debate an issue.

docusoap a television form combining documentary's depiction of non-actors in ordinary situations with soap opera's continuing narratives about selected characters.

dolly a wheeled camera platform. A 'dolly shot' is a camera shot where the camera is moved forward or back using this platform.

drama-documentary a television form combining dramatised storytelling with the 'objective' informational techniques of documentary. Abbreviated as 'dramadoc' or 'docudrama'.

dubbing replacing the original speech in a programme, advertisement, etc. with speech added later, often to translate speech in a foreign language.

dumbing-down the notion that television has reduced in quality as compared to an earlier period, showing programmes that are more 'dumb' or stupid and addressing its audience as if they were stupid.

effects measurable outcomes produced by watching television, such as becoming more violent or adopting a certain opinion.

electronic newsgathering (ENG) the use of lightweight cameras and digital technology such as portable satellite transmission dishes to record and transmit news pictures and sound.

ethnicity membership of a group with a specific identity based on a sense of belonging, such as British Asian or Italian-American, for example.

ethnography the detailed study of how people live, conducted by observing behaviour and talking to selected individuals about their attitudes and activities.

fan culture the activities of groups of fans, as distinct from 'ordinary' viewers.

Federal Communications Commission (FCC) the government body in the USA which regulates the operations and output of television companies and other broadcasters.

feminine having characteristics associated with the cultural role of women and not men.

feminism the political and theoretical thinking which in different ways considers the roles of women and femininity in society and culture, often with the aim of critiquing current roles and changing them for the better.

final cut the final edited version of a programme that is delivered to the television institution for broadcast.

flashback a television sequence marked as representing events that happened in a time previous to the programme's present.

flow the ways in which programmes, advertisements, etc. follow one another in an unbroken sequence across the day or part of the day, and the experience of watching the sequence of programmes, advertisements, trailers, etc.

focus groups small groups of selected people representing larger social groupings such as people of a certain age group, gender or economic status, who take part in discussions about a topic chosen for investigation.

format the blueprint for a programme, including its setting, main characters, genre, form and main themes.

franchise the right to broadcast on the terrestrial ITV channel for a set number of years, secured by paying a fee to government.

Frankfurt School a group of theorists in the mid twentieth century who worked on theories of contemporary culture from a Marxist perspective. Key members, notably Theodor Adorno and Max Horkheimer, left Nazi Germany in the 1930s to work abroad.

free market a television marketplace where factors such as quotas and regulations do not restrict the free operation of economic 'laws' of supply and demand.

free-to-air television programming for which viewers make no direct payment.

gatekeepers the critical term used for the people and institutions (such as television commissioning producers, or regulatory bodies) who control access to television broadcasting.

gender the social and cultural division of people into masculine or feminine individuals. This is different from sex, which refers to the biological difference between male and female bodies.

genre a kind or type of programme. Programmes of the same genre have shared characteristics.

globalisation the process whereby ownership of television institutions in different nations and regions is concentrated in the hands of international corporations, and whereby programmes and formats are traded between institutions around the world.

green-screen shooting action against a green background so that images from another source can be pasted in to replace the green background.

hegemony a term deriving from Marxist theories of society, meaning a situation where different social classes or groups are persuaded to consent to a political order that may be contrary to their benefit.

hype publicity and public relations effort aiming to raise interest in a television programme or an aspect of one.

iconic sign in semiotics, a sign which resembles its referent. Photographs, for example, contain iconic signs resembling the objects they represent.

identification a term deriving from psychoanalytic theories of cinema, which describes the viewer's conscious or unconscious wish to take the place of someone or something in a television text.

idents the symbols representing production companies, television channels, etc., often comprising graphics or animations.

ideology the set of beliefs, attitudes and assumptions arising from the economic and class divisions in a culture, underlying the ways of life accepted as normal in that culture.

independent production companies businesses making television programmes which can be sold to television networks that transmit and distribute them.

Independent Television Authority (ITA) the first official body set up to regulate commercial television in Britain.

indexical sign in semiotics, a sign which is the result of what it signifies, in the way that smoke is the result of fire.

information society a contemporary highly developed culture (especially Western culture) where the production and exchange of information is more significant than conventional industrial production.

interactive offering the opportunity for viewers to respond to what is broadcast, by sending signals back to the broadcaster (along a cable or phone line, for example).

intertextuality how one text draws on the meanings of another by referring to it, by allusion, quotation or parody, for example.

licence fee an annual payment by all owners of television sets, which is the main source of income for the BBC.

location any place in which television images are shot, except inside a television studio.

long shot a camera shot taking in the whole body of a performer, or more generally a shot with a wide field of vision.

long take an imprecise term denoting a longer than usual uninterrupted camera shot.

market research the collection of information about consumers and their preferences, used to identify products that can be advertised to consumers likely to buy them.

Marxism the political and economic theories associated with the German nineteenth-century theorist Karl Marx, who described and critiqued capitalist societies and proposed Communism as a revolutionary alternative.

masculine having characteristics associated with the cultural role of men and not women.

media imperialism the critical argument that powerful nations and cultures (especially the USA) exert control over other nations and cultures through the media products they export.

media literacy the skills and competence that viewers learn in order to understand easily the audio-visual 'languages' of media texts.

MediaWatch previously the National Viewers' and Listeners' Association, an organisation devoted to monitoring the activities of British broadcasters, with a special interest in upholding standards of taste and decency.

melodrama a form of drama characterised by exaggerated performance, a focus on reversals of fortune and extreme emotional reactions to events.

merchandising the sale of products associated with a television programme, such as toys, books or clothing.

metaphor the carrying-over from something of some of its meanings on to another thing of an apparently different kind. For example, a television narrative about life aboard ship could be a metaphor for British social life (the ship as metaphor for society).

metonymy the substitution of one thing for another, either because one is part of the other or because one is connected with the other. For example, 'the Crown' can be a metonym for the British state.

mise-en-scène literally meaning 'putting on stage', all the elements of a shot or sequence that contribute to its meanings, such as lighting, camera position and setting.

modality the fit between a fictional representation and the conventional understanding of reality. High modality describes a close fit, and weak modality a distant one.

monopoly control over the provision of a service or product by one institution or business.

narration the process of telling a story through image and sound. Narration can also refer to the spoken text accompanying television images.

narrative an ordered sequence of images and sound that tells a fictional or factual story.

natural break a vague term meaning a point at which a programme can be interrupted without causing undue disruption to the ongoing flow of the programme.

naturalism originally having a very specific meaning in literature and drama, this term is now used more loosely to denote television fiction that adopts realistic conventions of character portrayal, linear cause and effect narrative, and a consistent and recognisable fictional world.

negotiated reading a viewer interpretation of a television text where the viewer understands meaning in relation to his or her own knowledge and experience, rather than simply accepting the meaning proposed by the text.

network a television institution that transmits programmes through local or regional broadcasting stations that are owned by or affiliated to that institution.

news agency a media institution that gathers news reports and distributes them to its customers (who include television news broadcasters).

news value the degree of significance attributed to a news story, where items with high news value are deemed most significant to the audience.

niche audiences particular groups of viewers defined by age group, gender or economic status, for example, who may be the target audience for a programme.

noddy shot in television interviews, shots of the interviewer reacting silently (often by nodding) to the interviewee's responses to questions.

observational documentary a documentary form in which the programme-maker aims to observe neutrally what would have happened even if he or she had not been present.

Ofcom the Office of Communications, a government body responsible for regulating television and other communications media in Britain.

off-line editing the first stage of editing a completed programme, where the sequence of shots, sounds and music is established.

online editing the final stage of editing a completed programme, where effects are added and a high-quality version of the programme is produced.

outside broadcast the television transmission of outdoor events such as sport or ceremonial occasions, using equipment set up in advance for the purpose. Abbreviated as OB.

outsourcing obtaining services from an independent business rather than from within a television institution, usually as a means of cutting costs.

outtake a shot or sequence which was omitted from a finished programme, because of a mistake during production or an artistic decision.

pan a shot where the camera is turned to the left or turned to the right. The term derives from the word 'panorama', suggesting the wide visual field that a pan can reveal.

pan-and-scan capturing a section of an image and enlarging it to fill the television frame, a technique used to fit wide film images into the square television screen.

patriarchy a social system in which power is held by men rather than women, and masculine values dominate.

pay-per-view specific television programmes (such as sports events or films) offered to subscribers on payment of a fixed, one-off fee.

people meter a device resembling a television remote control, used in sample households to monitor what viewers watch. Viewers record which channels they watch and for how long.

period drama television fiction set in the past, most often the nineteenth or early twentieth centuries.

personal video recorder (PVR) a device that records digital television onto a microchip for storage and replay, and can automatically record programmes it thinks the viewer will enjoy.

personalities people appearing on television who are recognised by audiences as celebrities with a media image and public status beyond the role they play in a particular programme.

pitch a very short written or spoken outline for a programme, perhaps only a few sentences, often used to persuade a commissioning producer to commission the programme.

point of view shot a camera shot where the camera is placed in, or close to, the position from where a previously seen character might look.

polysemia the quality of having multiple meanings at the same time. Texts like this are called 'polysemic'.

pool system in journalism, grouping journalists together to share information so that not all of them need to be present at a news event.

popular culture the texts created by ordinary people (as opposed to an elite group) or created for them, and the ways these are used.

Postmaster General the person appointed by government to regulate communications institutions such as the Post Office, radio and television.

postmodernism the most recent phase of capitalist culture, the aesthetic forms and styles associated with it, and the theoretical approaches developed to understand it.

preferred reading an interpretation of a text that seems to be the one most encouraged by the text, the 'correct' interpretation.

prime time the part of a day's television schedule when the greatest number of viewers may be watching, normally the mid-evening period.

private sphere the domestic world of the home, family and personal life.

privatisation the policy of placing industries or institutions in the hands of privately owned businesses, rather than state ownership.

producer the person working for a television institution who is responsible for the budget, planning and making of a television programme or series of programmes.

production values the level of investment in a television production, such as the amount spent on costumes, props, effects and sets.

progressive encouraging positive change or progress, usually implying progress towards fairer and more equal ways of organising society.

psychoanalysis the study of human mental life, including not only conscious thoughts, wishes and fears but also unconscious ones. Psychoanalysis is an analytical and theoretical set of ideas as well as a therapeutic treatment.

public service in television, the provision of a mix of programmes that inform, educate and entertain in ways that encourage the betterment of audiences and society in general.

public sphere the world of politics, economic affairs and national and international events, as opposed to the 'private sphere' of domestic life.

public television television funded by government or by private supporters, rather than solely by advertising.

quality in television, kinds of programme that are perceived as more expensively produced and, especially, more culturally worthwhile than other programmes.

quota a proportion of television programming, such as a proportion of programmes made in a particular nation.

ratings the number of viewers estimated to have watched certain programmes, as compared to the numbers watching other programmes.

realism the aim for representations to reproduce reality faithfully, and the ways this is done.

reality TV programmes where the unscripted behaviour of 'ordinary people' is the focus of interest.

reflexivity a text's reflection on its own status as a text, for example drawing attention to generic conventions, or revealing the technologies used to make a programme.

register a term in the study of language for the kinds of speech or writing used to represent a particular kind of idea or to address a certain audience.

regulation the control of television institutions by laws, codes of practice or guidelines.

resistance the ways in which audiences make meaning from television programmes that is counter to the meanings that are thought to be intended, or that are discovered by close analysis.

satellite television television signals beamed from a ground transmitter to a stationary satellite that broadcasts the signal to a specific area (called the 'footprint') below it.

satire a mode of critical commentary about society or an aspect of it, using humour to attack people or ideas.

schedule the arrangement of programmes, advertisements and other material into a sequential order within a certain period of time, such as an evening, day or week.

semiotics the study of signs and their meanings, initially developed for the study of spoken language, and now used also to study the visual and aural 'languages' of other media such as television.

serial a television form where a developing narrative unfolds across a sequence of separate episodes.

series a television form where each programme in the series has a different story or topic, though settings, main characters or performers remain the same.

set-top box the electronic decoding equipment connected to home television sets that allows access to digital television signals.

shooting ratio the number of minutes of film used to film a scene or complete programme as compared to the screen-time of the finished scene or programme.

shot-reverse-shot the convention of alternating a shot of one character and a shot of another character in a scene, producing a back-and-forth movement which represents their interaction visually.

sign in semiotics, something which communicates meaning, such as a word, an image or a sound.

simulation a representation that mirrors an aspect of reality so perfectly that it takes the place of the reality it aims to reproduce.

slot the position in a television schedule where a programme is shown.

soap opera a continuing drama serial involving a large number of characters in a specific location, focusing on relationships, emotions and reversals of fortune.

sociology the academic study of society, aiming to describe and explain aspects of life in that society.

spectacle a fascinating image which draws attention to its immediate surface meanings and offers visual pleasure for its own sake.

spin-off a product, television programme, book, etc. that is created to exploit the reputation, meaning or commercial success of a previous one, often in a different medium from the original.

sponsorship the funding of programmes or channels by businesses, whose name is usually prominently displayed in the programme or channel as a means of advertising.

status quo a Latin term meaning the ways that culture and society are currently organised.

storyboard a sequence of drawn images showing the shots to be used in a programme.

strand a linked series of programmes, sharing a common title.

stripping in television scheduling, placing a programme or genre of programme at the same time on several days of each week.

structure of feeling the assumptions, attitudes and ideas prevalent in a society, arising from the ideologies underpinning that society.

subject in psychoanalysis, the term for the individual self whose identity has both conscious and unconscious components.

subscription payment to a television broadcaster in exchange for the opportunity to view programmes on certain channels that are otherwise blocked.

subtitle written text appearing on the television screen, normally to translate speech in a foreign language.

symbol a representation which condenses many meanings together and can stand for those many meanings in a certain context. For example, a brand-new car could be a symbol of wealth, social status and masculine prowess.

symbolic sign in semiotics, a sign which is connected arbitrarily to its referent rather than because the sign resembles its referent. For example a photograph of a cat resembles it, whereas the word 'cat' does not: the word is a symbolic sign.

syndication the sale of programmes for regional television broadcasters to transmit within their territory.

syntagm in semiotics, a linked sequence of signs existing at a certain point in time. Written or spoken sentences, or television sequences, are examples of syntagms.

taste and decency conformity to the standards of good taste and acceptable language and behaviour represented on television, as required by regulations.

teaser a very short television sequence advertising a forthcoming programme, often puzzling or teasing to viewers because it contains little information and encourages curiosity and interest.

telenovela a fictional continuing melodrama on television that lasts for a specific number of episodes. Telenovelas are particularly associated with South American television.

terrestrial broadcasting from a ground-based transmission system, as opposed to broadcasting via satellite.

text an object such as a television programme, film or poem, considered as a network of meaningful signs that can be analysed and interpreted.

textual analysis a critical approach which seeks to understand a television text's meanings by undertaking detailed analysis of its image and sound components, and the relationships between those components.

title sequence the sequence at the opening of a television programme in which the programme title and performers' names may appear along with other information, accompanied by images, sound and music introducing the programme.

tracking shot a camera shot where the camera is moved along (often on a miniature railway track) parallel to a moving subject of the shot while photographing it.

trailer a short television sequence advertising a forthcoming programme, usually containing selected 'highlights' from the programme.

treatment a short written outline for a programme, usually written for a commissioning producer to read, specifying how the programme will tell its story or address its subject.

uses and gratifications a theoretical approach that assumes people engage in an activity because it provides them with a benefit of some kind.

utopia an ideal society.

variety programmes entertainment programmes containing a mix of material such as songs and comedy sketches.

vertical integration the control by media institutions of all levels of a business, from the production of products to their distribution and means of reception.

voice-over speech accompanying visual images but not presumed to derive from the same place or time as the images.

voyeurism gaining sexual pleasure from looking at someone or something that cannot look back.

watershed the time in the day (conventionally 9.00 p.m.) after which programmes with content that may disturb children can be shown.

whip-pan a very rapid panning shot from one point to another.

zapping hopping rapidly from channel to channel while watching television, using a remote control (a 'zapper').

Select bibliography

Addley, E., 'Why the cameras love us', *The Guardian*, Big Brother supplement, 14 September 2002, pp. 14–16.

Akass, K. and J. McCabe (eds), *Reading Six Feet Under: TV to Die For* (London and New York: I. B. Tauris, 2005).

—— *Reading Sex and the City* (London and New York: I. B. Tauris, 2004).

Allen, J., 'The social matrix of television: invention in the United States', in E. A. Kaplan (ed.), *Regarding Television: Critical Approaches – An Anthology* (Los Angeles: AFI, 1983), pp. 109–19.

Allen, R. (ed.), *Channels of Discourse, Reassembled: Television and Contemporary Criticism* (London: Routledge, 1992a).

—— 'Audience-oriented criticism and television', in R. Allen (ed.), *Channels of Discourse, Reassembled: Television and Contemporary Criticism* (London: Routledge, 1992b), pp. 101–37.

—— *Speaking of Soap Operas* (Chapel Hill, SC: University of South Carolina Press, 1985).

Allen, S., *News Culture*, third edition (Buckingham: Open University Press, 2010).

Allen, S., G. Branston and C. Carter (eds), *News, Gender and Power* (London: Routledge, 1998).

Alleyne, M., *News Revolution: Political and Economic Decisions about Global Information* (Basingstoke: Macmillan, 1997).

Alps, T., 'Is it make or break time for TV ads?, *The Guardian*, Media section, 11 November 2004, p. 8.

Althusser, L., 'Ideology and ideological state apparatuses: notes towards an investigation', in *Lenin and Philosophy* (London: New Left Books, 1971), pp. 121–73.

Altman, R., 'Television sound', in T. Modleski (ed.), *Studies in Entertainment: Critical Approaches to Mass Culture* (Bloomington: Indiana University Press, 1986), pp. 39–54.

Alvarado, M. and J. Thompson (eds), *The Media Reader* (London: BFI, 1990).

Amadiegwu, M., 'Don't shoot this messenger', *The Guardian*, Media section, 3 July 2006, p. 7.

Ang, I., 'Melodramatic identifications: television fiction and women's fantasy', in C. Brunsdon, J. D'Acci and L. Spigel (eds), *Feminist Television Criticism: A Reader* (Oxford: Oxford University Press, 1997), pp. 155–66.

—— *Living Room Wars: Rethinking Audiences for a Postmodern World* (London: Routledge, 1996).

—— *Desperately Seeking the Audience* (London: Routledge, 1991).

—— *Watching Dallas: Soap Operas and the Melodramatic Imagination*, trans. D. Couling, revised edition (London: Routledge, 1989).

Ang, I. and J. Hermes, 'Gender and/in media consumption', in I. Ang, *Living Room Wars: Rethinking Audiences for a Postmodern World* (London: Routledge, 1996), pp. 108–29.

Annan Committee, *Report of the Committee on the Future of Broadcasting* (London: HMSO, 1977).

Arksey, H. and P. Knight, *Interviewing for Social Scientists* (London: Sage, 1999).

Armstrong, S., 'Are two screens better than one?' *The Guardian*, Media section, 22 November 2010, p. 3.

—— 'Go figure: Black viewing', *The Guardian*, Media section, 22 May 2006, p. 9.

Badsey, S., 'The influence of the media on recent British military operations', in I. Stewart and S. Carruthers (eds), *War, Culture and the Media: Representations of the Military in Twentieth-century Britain* (Trowbridge: Flicks Books 1993), pp. 5–21.

Balnaves, M., J. Donald and S. Hemelryk Donald, *The Global Media Atlas* (London: BFI, 2001).

Bandura, A., *Social Learning Theory* (London: Prentice Hall, 1977).

Barker, C., *Global Television: An Introduction* (Oxford: Blackwell, 1997).

Baudrillard, J., 'The reality gulf', *The Guardian*, 11 January 1991, reprinted in P. Brooker and W. Brooker (eds), *Postmodern After-images: A Reader in Film, Television and Video* (London: Arnold, 1997), pp. 165–7.

—— *In the Shadow of the Silent Majorities*, trans. P. Foss, J. Johnson and P. Patton (New York: Semiotext(e), 1983a).

—— *Simulations* (New York: Semiotext(e), 1983b).

Bayes, S., *The Avid Handbook*, third edition (Woburn, Mass.: Butterworth-Heinemann, 2000).

Bazalgette, C. and D. Buckingham (eds), *In Front of the Children: Screen Entertainment and Young Audiences* (London: BFI, 1995).

BBC, *Producers' Guidelines* (London: BBC, 1993).

Benjamin, W., 'The work of art in the age of mechanical reproduction', in *Illuminations*, ed. H. Arendt, trans. H. Zohn (New York: Schocken Books, 1969), pp. 219–54.

Bennett, J., '"Your window on the world": The emergence of red-button interactive television in the UK', *Convergence*, 14:2 (2008), pp. 161–82.

—— 'The public service value of interactive TV', *New Review of Film and Television Studies*, 4:3 (2006), pp. 263–85.

Bennett, J., and N. Strange (eds), *Television as Digital Media* (Durham, NC: Duke University Press, 2011).

—— 'The BBC's second-shift aesthetics: interactive television, multi-platform projects and public service content for a digital era', *Media International Australia*, 126 (2008), pp. 106–19.

Bertens, H., *The Idea of the Postmodern: A History* (London: Routledge, 1995).

Bignell, J., 'The look: style, technology and televisuality in the new *Who*', in A. O'Day (ed.), *Doctor Who: The Eleventh Hour* (London: I. B. Tauris, 2013).

—— 'Docudrama performance: realism, recognition and representation', in C. Cornea (ed.), *Genre and Performance: Film and Television* (Manchester: Manchester University Press, 2010), pp. 59–75.

—— 'The police series', in J. Gibbs and D. Pye (eds), *Close Up 03* (London: Wallflower, 2009), pp. 1–66.

—— 'Seeing and knowing: reflexivity and quality', in J. McCabe and K. Akass (eds), *Quality TV: Contemporary American Television and Beyond* (London: I. B. Tauris, 2007a), pp. 158–70.

—— 'Citing the classics: constructing British television drama history in publishing and pedagogy', in H. Wheatley (ed.), *Re-viewing Television History: Critical Issues in Television Historiography* (London: I. B. Tauris, 2007b), pp. 27–39.

—— *Big Brother: Reality TV in the Twenty-first Century* (Basingstoke: Palgrave Macmillan, 2005).

—— 'Sex, confession and witness', in K. Akass and J. McCabe (eds), *Reading 'Sex and the City'* (London and New York: I. B. Tauris, 2004), pp. 161–76.

—— *Media Semiotics: An Introduction*, second edition (Manchester: Manchester University Press, 2002a).

—— 'Writing the child in media theory', *Yearbook of English Studies*, 32 (2002b), pp. 127–39.

—— *Postmodern Media Culture* (Edinburgh: Edinburgh University Press, 2000a).

—— 'Docudrama as melodrama: representing Princess Diana and Margaret Thatcher', in B. Carson and M. Llewellyn-Jones (eds), *Frames and Fictions on Television: The Politics of Identity within Drama* (Exeter: Intellect, 2000b), pp. 17–26.

Bignell, J. and A. Fickers, 'Introduction: comparative European perspectives on television history', in J. Bignell and A. Fickers (eds), *A European Television History* (New York: Blackwell, 2008), pp. 1–54.

Bignell, J., S. Lacey and M. Macmurraugh-Kavanagh (eds), *British Television Drama: Past, Present and Future* (Basingstoke: Palgrave, 2000).

Billingham, P., *Sensing the City through Television* (Exeter: Intellect, 2000).

Born, G., *Uncertain Vision: Birt, Dyke and the Reinvention of the BBC* (London: Secker & Warburg, 2004).

Boyd-Barrett, O. and T. Rantanen, *The Globalization of News* (London: Sage, 1998).

Boyle, R. and R. Haynes, *Power Play: Sport, the Media and Popular Culture* (Harlow: Pearson, 2000).

Brandt, G. (ed.), *British Television Drama in the 1980s* (Cambridge: Cambridge University Press, 1993).

Brandt, G. (ed.), *British Television Drama* (Cambridge: Cambridge University Press, 1981).

Branston, G. and R. Stafford, *The Media Student's Book*, second edition (London: Routledge, 1999).

Briggs, A. and P. Cobley (eds), *The Media: An Introduction* (Harlow: Addison Wesley Longman, 1998).

Broadcasting Standards Commission, *Codes of Guidance* (London: BSC, 1998).

Brooker, P. and W. Brooker (eds), *Postmodern After-images: A Reader in Film, Television and Video* (London: Arnold, 1997).

Brown, I., 'T.V. in the Englishman's castle', *BBC Year Book 1951* (London: BBC, 1951), pp. 17–19.

Brown, M., 'Swapping success', *The Guardian*, Media section, 4 October 2004a, p. 10.

—— 'The £100m crisis at Channel 4', *The Guardian*, Media section, 11 November 2004b, pp. 8–9.

—— 'Vying for VIPs', *Guardian*, Media section, 5 March 2001, pp. 8–9.

Brown, M. and M. Wells, 'How did it rate?', *Guardian*, Media section, 27 August 2001, pp. 2–3.

Bruhn Jensen, K. (ed.), *News of the World: World Cultures Look at Television News* (London: Routledge, 1998).

Brunsdon, C., 'Is Television Studies history?', *Cinema Journal*, 47:3 (2008), pp. 127–37.

—— *The Feminist, the Housewife, and the Soap Opera* (Oxford: Oxford University Press, 2000).

—— 'Structure of anxiety: recent British television crime fiction', *Screen*, 39:3 (1998a), pp. 223–43.

—— 'What is the television of television studies?', in C. Geraghty and D. Lusted (eds), *The Television Studies Book* (London: Arnold, 1998b), pp. 95–113.

—— 'Problems with quality', *Screen*, 31:1 (1990), pp. 67–90.

—— 'Crossroads – notes on soap opera', *Screen*, 22:4 (1981), pp. 32–7.

Brunsdon, J., J. D'Acci and L. Spigel, 'Introduction', in C. Brunsdon, J. D'Acci, and L. Spigel (eds), *Feminist Television Criticism: A Reader* (Oxford: Oxford University Press, 1997), pp. 1–16.

Bruzzi, S., *The New Documentary: A Critical Introduction* (London: Routledge, 2000).

Bryant, S., *The Television Heritage: Television Archiving Now and in an Uncertain Future* (London: BFI, 1989).

Buckingham, D., *Moving Images: Understanding Children's Emotional Responses to Television* (Manchester: Manchester University Press, 1996).

—— *Children Talking Television: The Making of Television Literacy* (London: Falmer, 1993a).

—— *Reading Audiences: Young People and the Media* (Manchester: Manchester University Press, 1993b).

—— *Public Secrets: EastEnders and its Audience* (London: BFI, 1987).

Bulkley, K., 'A focus on the future', *The Guardian*, Digital Vision supplement, 25 October 2010, p. 1.

Burton, G., *Talking Television: An Introduction to the Study of Television* (London: Arnold, 2000).

Buxton, D., *The Police Series: From The Avengers to Miami Vice* (Manchester: Manchester University Press, 1990).

Calabrese, A., 'The trade in television news', in J. Wasko (ed.), *A Companion to Television* (Malden, Mass. and Oxford: Blackwell, 2005), pp. 270–90.

Caldwell, J. T., *Production Culture: Industrial Reflexivity and Critical Practice in Film and Television* (Durham, NC and London: Duke University Press, 2008).

Campion, M. J., *Look Who's Talking: Cultural Diversity, Public Service Broadcasting and the National Conversation* (Oxford: Nuffield, 2005).

Carson, B. and M. Llewellyn-Jones (eds), *Frames and Fictions on Television: The Politics of Identity within Drama* (Exeter: Intellect, 2000).

Caughie, J., *Television Drama: Realism, Modernism, and British Culture* (Oxford: Oxford University Press, 2000).

—— 'Television criticism: a discourse in search of an object', *Screen*, 25:4–5 (1984), pp. 109–20.

—— 'Progressive television and documentary drama', *Screen*, 21:3 (1980), pp. 9–35.

Clarke, A., '"You're nicked!": television police series and the fictional representation of law and order', in D. Strinati and S. Wagg (eds), *Come on Down? Popular Media Culture in Post-war Britain* (London: Routledge, 1992), pp. 232–53.

Coles, G., 'Docusoap: actuality and the serial format', in B. Carson and M. Llewellyn-Jones (eds), *Frames and Fictions on Television: The Politics of Identity within Drama* (Exeter: Intellect, 2000), pp. 27–39.

Collins, J., 'Postmodernism and television', in R. Allen (ed.), *Channels of Discourse, Reassembled: Television and Contemporary Criticism* (London: Routledge, 1992), pp. 327–53.

Cook, G., *The Discourse of Advertising* (London: Routledge, 1992).

Cooke, L., *British Television Drama: A History* (London: BFI, 2003).

Corner, J., '"A fiction (un)like any other"?', *Critical Studies in Television*, 1:1 (2006), pp. 89–96.

—— 'Performing the real: documentary diversions', *Television and New Media*, 3:3 (2002), pp. 255–69.

—— *Critical Ideas in Television Studies* (Oxford: Clarendon, 1999).

—— *Studying Media: Problems of Theory and Method* (London: Arnold, 1998).

—— *The Art of Record: A Critical Introduction to Documentary* (Manchester: Manchester University Press, 1996).

—— *Television Form and Public Address* (London: Edward Arnold, 1995).

—— 'Presumption as theory: "realism" in Television Studies', *Screen*, 33:1 (1992), pp. 97–102.

—— (ed.), *Popular Television in Britain* (London: BFI, 1991).

Corner, J. and S. Harvey (eds), *Television Times: A Reader* (London: Arnold, 1996).

Corrigan, P., 'On the difficulty of being sociological (historical materialist) in the study of television: the "moment" of English television, 1936–1939', in T. Syvertsen (ed.), *1992 and After: Nordic Television in Transition* (Bergen: University of Bergen, 1990), pp. 130–60.

Cottle, S. (ed.), *Ethnic Minorities and the Media* (Oxford: Oxford University Press, 2000).

Crawford, A., '"Oh Yeah!": *Family Guy* as magical realism?', *Journal of Film and Video*, 61:2 (2009), pp. 52–69.

Creeber, G. (ed.), *The Television Genre Book* (London: BFI, 2001).

Creeber, G., *Serial Television: Big Drama on the Small Screen* (London: BFI, 2005).

Crisell, A., *An Introductory History of British Broadcasting* (London: Routledge, 1997).

Cumberbatch, G., S. Gauntlett and V. Lyne, *Minority Group Representation on British Terrestrial Television: Key Findings, 1993–2003* (London: BBC/Ofcom, 2004).

Curran, J. and J. Seaton (eds), *Power without Responsibility: The Press and Broadcasting in Britain*, fifth edition (London: Routledge, 1997).

Curtin, M., 'From network to neo-network audiences', in M. Hilmes (ed.), *The Television History Book*, (London: British Film Institute, 2003), pp. 122–5.

D'Acci, J., *Defining Women: The Case of Cagney and Lacey* (Chapel Hill: University of South Carolina Press, 1994).

Dahlgren, P., *Television and the Public Sphere* (London: Sage, 1995).

Dajani, N., 'Television in the Arab East', in J. Wasko (ed.), *A Companion to Television* (Malden, Mass. and Oxford: Blackwell, 2005), pp. 580–601.

Deloitte, 'Perspectives on television in words and numbers', 2011, available at http://www.deloitte.com/view/en_GB/uk/industries/tmt/5d44f5fe4e0f1310Vgn VCM2000001b56f00aRCRD.htm.

Dickinson, R., R. Harindranath and O. Linné (eds), *Approaches to Audiences: A Reader* (London: Arnold, 1998).

Dominick, J., B. Sherman and G. Copeland, *Broadcasting/Cable and Beyond: An Introduction to Modern Electronic Media*, third edition (New York: McGraw-Hill, 1996).

Dovey, J., *Freakshow: First Person Media and Factual Television* (Cambridge: Polity, 2000).

Dowell, B., 'Moving on from Lagos', *The Guardian*, Media section, 6 June 2011a, p. 3.

—— 'Channel 4 corners market for fixed-camera observational documentaries', *The Guardian*, Media section, 10 January 2011b, p. 2.

Dowmunt, T. (ed.), *Channels of Resistance: Global Television and Local Empowerment* (London: BFI, 1993).

Drummond, P. and R. Patterson (eds), *Television and its Audience: International Research Perspectives* (London: BFI, 1988).

Dyer, R., *Light Entertainment* (London: BFI, 1973).

Dyer, R., C. Geraghty, M. Jordan, T. Lovell, R. Paterson and J. Stewart, *Coronation Street* (London: BFI, 1981).

Ebbrecht, T., 'Docudramatizing history on TV: German and British docudrama and historical event television in the memorial year 2005', *European Journal of Cultural Studies*, 10:1 (2007), pp. 35–55.

Eco, U., 'Interpreting serials', in *The Limits of Interpretation* (Bloomington: Indiana University Press, 1990), pp. 83–100.

—— 'A guide to the neo-television of the 1980s', *Framework*, 25 (1984), pp. 18–25.

Eden, J., 'Caruso control', *Radio Times*, 5–11 August 2006, pp. 11–12.

Eldridge, J. (ed.), *Glasgow Media Reader Volume 1: News Content, Language and Visuals* (London: Routledge, 1995).

Ellis, J., 'The end of TV? I don't think so', *Critical Studies in Television* blog, 9 January 2012, http://cstonline.tv/end-of-tv-not.

—— 'Scheduling: the last creative act in television', *Media, Culture & Society*, 22:1 (2000a), pp. 25–38.

—— *Seeing Things: Television in the Age of Uncertainty* (London: I. B. Tauris, 2000b).

—— 'Television as working through', in J. Gripsrud (ed.), *Television and Common Knowledge* (London: Routledge, 1999), pp. 55–7.

—— *Visible Fictions: Cinema, Television, Video* (London: Routledge and Kegan Paul, 1982).

Entwistle, G., 'Net gains are mutual benefits', *The Guardian* Media section, 22 August 2011, p. 4.

Eyre, P., 'Taboo television', *The Guardian* Media section, 24 July 2006, p. 2.

Fairclough, N., *Media Discourse* (London: Arnold, 1995).

Feuer, J., 'Quality drama in the US: the new "Golden Age"?', in: M. Hilmes (ed.), *The Television History Book* (London: British Film Institute, 2003), pp. 98–102.

—— 'Genre study and television', in R. Allen (ed.), *Channels of Discourse, Reassembled* (London: Routledge, 1992), pp. 138–60.

—— 'MTM enterprises: an overview', in J. Feuer, P. Kerr and T. Vahimagi (eds), *MTM: 'Quality Television'* (London: British Film Institute, 1984), pp. 1–31.

Fisher, B., 'Behind the scenes at NYPD Blue with Brian J. Reynolds', International Cinematographers Guild, 1996, available at: http://www.cameraguild.com/interviews/chat_reynolds/reynolds_NYPD.htm.

Fiske, J., *Media Matters* (Minneapolis, Minn.: University of Minnesota Press, 1994).

—— *Television Culture* (London: Routledge, 1992a).

—— 'The cultural economy of fandom', in L. Lewis (ed.), *The Adoring Audience: Fan Culture and Popular Media* (London: Routledge, 1992b), pp. 30–49.

—— 'British cultural studies and television', in R. Allen (ed.), *Channels of Discourse, Reassembled: Television and Contemporary Criticism* (London: Routledge, 1992c), pp. 284–326.

—— 'Postmodernism and television', in J. Curran and M. Gurevitch (eds), *Mass Media and Society* (London: Edward Arnold, 1991), pp. 55–67.

—— *Introduction to Communication Studies* (London: Routledge, 1990).

Fiske, J. and J. Hartley, *Reading Television* (London: Methuen, 1978).

Fitzwalter, R., *The Dream that Died: The Rise and Fall of ITV* (Leicester: Matador, 2008).

Flitterman-Lewis, S., 'Psychoanalysis, film, and television', in R. Allen (ed.), *Channels of Discourse, Reassembled: Television and Contemporary Criticism* (London: Routledge, 1992), pp. 203–46.

Franklin, B. (ed.), *British Television Policy: A Reader* (London: Routledge, 2001).

Freedman, L. and E. Karsh, *The Gulf Conflict 1990–1991: Diplomacy and War in the New World Order* (London: Faber, 1993).

Frith, S., 'The black box: The value of television and the future of television research', *Screen*, 41:1 (2000), pp. 33–50.

Frost, V., 'The press toe the line on the Iraq war', *The Guardian*, Media section, 13 November 2006, p. 7.

Galtung, J. and M. Ruge, 'Structuring and selecting news', in S. Cohen and J. Young (eds), *The Manufacture of News: Social Problems, Deviance and the Mass Media* (London: Constable, 1973), pp. 62–72.

Garber, M., J. Matlock and R. Walkowitz (eds), *Media Spectacles* (London: Routledge, 1993).

Garnett, T., 'Contexts', in J. Bignell, S. Lacey and M. Macmurraugh-Kavanagh (eds), *British Television Drama: Past, Present and Future* (Basingstoke: Palgrave, 2000), pp. 11–23.

Geertz, C., *The Interpretation of Cultures: Selected Essays* (London: Fontana, 1967).

Geraghty, C., 'Audiences and "ethnography": questions of practice', in C. Geraghty and D. Lusted (eds), *The Television Studies Book* (London: Arnold, 1998), pp. 141–57.

—— *Women and Soap Opera: A Study of Prime Time Soaps* (Cambridge: Polity Press, 1991).

Geraghty, C. and D. Lusted (eds), *The Television Studies Book* (London: Arnold, 1998).

Gibbs, J., *Mise-en-Scène: Film Style and Interpretation* (London: Wallflower, 2002).

Gibson, O., 'Every year, it's the most extreme ever', *The Guardian*, 5 June 2006, p. 5.

Giddens, A. *The Consequences of Modernity* (Cambridge: Polity, 1990).

Gillespie, M., 'Ambivalent positionings: the Gulf War', in P. Brooker and W. Brooker (eds), *Postmodern After-images: A Reader in Film, Television and Video* (London: Arnold, 1997), pp. 172–81.

Gitlin, T., *Inside Prime Time* (New York: Pantheon, 1983).

Glasgow Media Group, *War and Peace News* (Milton Keynes: Open University Press, 1986).

—— *More Bad News* (London: Routledge and Kegan Paul, 1980).

—— *Bad News* (London: Routledge and Kegan Paul, 1976).

Goodwin, A., 'MTV', in J. Corner and S. Harvey (eds), *Television Times: A Reader* (London: Arnold, 1996), pp. 75–87.

—— *Dancing in the Distraction Factory: Music, Television and Popular Culture* (London: Routledge, 1993).

Goodwin, A. and G. Whannel (eds), *Understanding Television* (London: Routledge, 1990).

Goodwin, P., 'The role of the state', in J. Stokes and A. Reading (eds), *The Media in Britain: Current Debates and Developments* (Basingstoke: Macmillan, 1999), pp. 130–42.

Gray, A., *Video Playtime: The Gendering of a Leisure Technology* (London: Routledge, 1992).

Gray, H., *Watching Race: Television and the Struggle for 'Blackness'* (Minneapolis, Minn.: University of Minnesota Press, 1995).

Gripsrud, J., 'Television, broadcasting, flow: key metaphors in TV theory', in C. Geraghty and D. Lusted (eds), *The Television Studies Book* (London: Arnold, 1998), pp. 17–32.

—— *The Dynasty Years: Hollywood Television and Critical Media Studies* (London: Routledge, 1995).

Grossberg, L., C. Nelson and P. Treichler, with L. Baughman and J. Macgregor Wise (eds), *Cultural Studies* (New York: Routledge, 1992).

Gurevitch, M., 'The globalization of electronic journalism', in J. Curran and M. Gurevitch (eds), *Mass Media and Society* (London: Edward Arnold, 1991), pp. 178–93.

Habermas, J., *The Theory of Communicative Action*, vol. 2: *Lifeworld and System: A Critique of Functionalist Reason* (Cambridge: Polity, 1987).

Hall, S. (ed.), *Representation: Cultural Representations and Signifying Practices* (London: Sage, 1997).

—— 'Black and white television', in D. Morley and K. Chen (eds), *Remote Control: Dilemmas of Black Intervention in British Film and TV* (London: BFI, 1996), pp. 13–28.

—— 'Encoding/decoding', in S. Hall, D. Hobson, A. Lowe and P. Willis (eds), *Culture, Media, Language* (London: Hutchinson, 1980), pp. 128–38.

Hallam, J. and M. Marshment, 'Framing experience: case studies in the reception of *Oranges Are Not the Only Fruit*', *Screen*, 36:1 (1995), pp. 1–15.

Hammond, M. and L. Mazdon (eds), *The Contemporary Television Series* (Edinburgh: Edinburgh University Press, 2005).

Harbord, J. and J. Wright, *Forty Years of British Television* (London: Boxtree, 1992).

Harrison, J., *Terrestrial Television News in Britain: The Culture of Production* (Manchester: Manchester University Press, 2000).

Hart, C., *Television Program Making* (Oxford: Focal Press, 1999).

Hartley, J., *Tele-ology: Studies in Television* (London: Routledge, 1992).

—— *Understanding News* (London: Routledge, 1982).

Harvey, S., 'Channel 4 television from Annan to Grade', in S. Hood (ed.), *Behind the Screens* (London: Lawrence and Wishart, 1994), pp. 102–29.

Havens, T., *Global Television Marketplace* (London: BFI, 2008).

—— '"The biggest show in the world": race and the global popularity of *The Cosby Show*', *Media Culture & Society*, 22:4 (2000), pp. 371–91.

Herman, E. and R. McChesney, *The Global Media: The New Missionaries of Global Capitalism* (London: Cassell, 1997).

Hewlett, S., 'Why the Daily Mail has it in for Ofcom', *The Guardian*, Media section, 13 June 2011, p. 3.

Hill, A., '*Big Brother*: the real audience', *Television and New Media*, 3:3 (2002), pp. 323–41.

—— *Shocking Entertainment: Viewer Response to Violent Movies* (Luton: University of Luton Press, 1997).

Hill, J. and M. McLoone (eds), *Big Picture Small Screen: The Relations between Film and Television* (Luton: University of Luton Press, 1997).

Himmelwhite, H. T. *et al.*, *Television and the Child: An Experimental Study of the Effect of Television on the Young* (London: Nuffield Foundation and Oxford University Press, 1958).

Hobson, D., 'From *Crossroads* to *Wife Swap*: learning from audiences', *Critical Studies in Television*, 1:1 (2006), pp. 121–8.

—— *Crossroads: The Drama of a Soap Opera* (London: Methuen, 1982).

Hollingsworth, M. and R. Norton-Taylor, *Blacklist: The Inside Story of Political Vetting* (London, Hogarth, 1988).

Holmes, S., '"But this time *you* choose!": approaching the "interactive" audience in reality TV', *International Journal of Cultural Studies*, 7:2 (2004), pp. 213–31.

Holmes, S. and D. Jermyn (eds), *Understanding Reality Television* (London: Routledge, 2004).

Holmes, S. and S. Redmond, *Framing Celebrity: New Directions in Celebrity Culture* (London: Routledge, 2006).

Holmwood, L., 'Mipcom showcases the best of British', *The Guardian* Media section, 9 October 2006, p. 2.

Hood, S. (ed.), *Behind the Screens: The Structure of British Television in the Nineties* (London: Lawrence and Wishart, 1994).

Hutcheon, L., 'The politics of postmodernism, parody, and history', *Cultural Critique*, 5 (1986–7), pp. 179–207.

Huyssen, A., *After the Great Divide: Modernism, Mass Culture and Postmodernism* (London: Macmillan, 1986).

Independent Television Commission, *The ITC Programme Code* (London: ITC, 1998).

Jacobs, J., *Body Trauma TV: The New Hospital Dramas* (London: BFI, 2003).

Jacobson, R., *Television Research: A Directory of Conceptual Categories, Topic Suggestions and Selected Sources* (Jefferson: McFarland, 1995).

Jameson, F., *Postmodernism, or The Cultural Logic of Late Capitalism* (London: Verso, 1991).

—— 'Reading without interpretation: postmodernism and the videotext', in D. Attridge and N. Fabb (eds), *The Linguistics of Writing: Arguments between Language and Literature* (Manchester: Manchester University Press, 1987), pp. 199–233.

Jancovich, M. and J. Lyons (eds), *Quality Popular Television: Cult TV, the Industry and the Fans* (London: BFI, 2005).

Jenkins, H., *Convergence Culture: Where Old and New Media Collide* (Cambridge, Mass.: MIT Press, 2006).

—— *Textual Poachers: Television Fans and Participatory Culture* (London: Routledge, 1992).

Jenkins, S., 'Hill Street Blues', in J. Feuer, P. Kerr and T. Vahimagi (eds), *MTM: 'Quality Television'* (London: British Film Institute, 1984), pp. 183–99.

Jermyn, D. and S. Holmes, 'The audience is dead; long live the audience!: Interactivity, "telephilia", and the contemporary television audience', *Critical Studies in Television*, 1:1 (2006), pp. 49–57.

Jhally, S. and J. Lewis, *Enlightened Racism: The Cosby Show, Audiences, and the Myth of the American Dream* (San Francisco, CA: Westview, 1992).

Jhally, S. and B. Livant, 'Watching as working: the valorization of audience consciousness', *Journal of Communication*, 36:2 (1986), pp. 124–43.

Johnson, C., 'Tele-branding in TV III: The network as brand and programme as brand', *New Review of Television Studies*, 5:1 (2007), pp. 5–24.

Johnson, C. and R. Turnock (eds), *ITV Cultures: Independent Television Over Fifty Years* (London: Open University Press, 2005).

Jones, J., 'Emerging platform identities: *Big Brother* UK and interactive multi-platform usage', in E. Mathijs and J. Jones (eds), *Big Brother International: Formats, Critics and Publics* (London: Wallflower, 2004), pp. 210–31.

Juluri, V., 'Music television and the invention of youth culture in India', *Television and New Media*, 3:4 (2002), pp. 367–86.

Kaplan, E. A., *Rocking Around the Clock: Music Television, Postmodernism and Consumer Culture* (London: Methuen, 1987).

Katz, E. and Liebes, T. 'Mutual aid in the decoding of *Dallas*: preliminary notes from a cross-cultural study', in P. Drummond, *Television in Transition* (London: BFI, 1985), pp. 187–98.

—— 'Once upon a time in Dallas', *Intermedia*, 12:3 (1984), pp. 28–32.

Kauffmann, S. and A. Kennedy, *Avid Editing: A Guide for Beginning and Intermediate Users* (Oxford: Focal Press, 2012).

Kellner, D., *Media Culture: Cultural Studies, Identity and Politics Between the Modern and the Postmodern* (London: Routledge, 1995).

Kerr, P., 'Drama at MTM: Lou Grant and Hill Street Blues', in J. Feuer, P. Kerr and T. Vahimagi (eds) *MTM: 'Quality Television'* (London: British Film Institute, 1984), pp. 132–65.

Kidd-Hewitt, D. and R. Osborne (eds), *Crime and the Media: The Postmodern Spectacle* (London: Pluto, 1995).

Kilborn, R. and J. Izod, *An Introduction to Television Documentary: Confronting Reality* (Manchester: Manchester University Press, 1997).

Kinder, M., 'Re-wiring Baltimore: The emotive power of systemics, seriality, and the city', *Film Quarterly*, 62:2 (2008), pp. 50–57.

Kirkham, S., 'Big Brother in trouble over sex shock (again)', *The Guardian*, 4 August 2006, p. 3.

Klein, P., 'The television audience and program mediocrity', in A. Wells (ed.), *Mass Media and Society* (Palo Alto, CA: Mayfield, 1975), pp. 74–7.

Knox, S., 'Reading the ungraspable double-codedness of *The Simpsons*', *Journal of Popular Film and Television*, 34:2 (2006), pp. 72–81.

Kompare, D., 'Publishing flow: DVD box sets and the reconception of television', *Television & New Media*, 7:4 (2006), pp. 335–360.

—— *Rerun Nation: How Repeats Invented American Television* (New York: Routledge, 2005).

Kozloff, S., 'Narrative theory and television', in R. Allen (ed.), *Channels of Discourse, Reassembled: Television and Contemporary Criticism* (London: Routledge, 1992), pp. 67–100.

Lacan, J., 'The mirror stage', in *Ecrits: A Selection*, trans. A. Sheridan (London: Tavistock, 1977), pp. 1–7.

Lacey, N., *Narrative and Genre: Key Concepts in Media Studies* (Basingstoke: Macmillan, 2000).

Lacey, S., *Tony Garnett* (Manchester: Manchester University Press, 2007).

Langer, J., *Tabloid Television: Popular Journalism and 'Other News'* (London: Routledge, 1998).

Leal, O., 'Popular taste and erudite repertoire: the place and space of television in Brazil', *Cultural Studies*, 4:1 (1990), pp. 19–29.

Liebes, T. and E. Katz, *The Export of Meaning: Cross-cultural Readings of 'Dallas'* (New York: Oxford University Press, 1990).

Leverette, M., B. L. Ott and C. L. Buckley (eds), *It's Not TV: Watching HBO in the Post-Television Era* (London and New York: Routledge 2008).

Lewis, J., *The Ideological Octopus: An Exploration of Television and its Audience* (London: Routledge, 1991).

—— 'Decoding television news', in P. Drummond and R. Paterson (eds), *Television in Transition* (London: BFI, 1985), pp. 205–34.

Lewis, L. (ed.), *The Adoring Audience: Fan Culture and Popular Media* (London: Routledge, 1991).

—— *Gender Politics and MTV: Voicing the Difference* (Philadelphia, Pa.: Temple University Press, 1990).

Liebes, T. and Katz, E., *The Export of Meaning: Cross-cultural Readings of 'Dallas'* (New York: Oxford University Press, 1990).

Lindof, T. (ed.), *Natural Audiences: Qualitative Research of Media Uses and Effects* (Norwood: Ablex, 1987).

Lipkin, S., *Real Emotional Logic: Film and Television Docudrama as Persuasive Practice* (Carbondale, IL: Southern Illinois University Press, 2002).

Lister, M. (ed.), *The Photographic Image in Digital Culture* (London: Routledge, 1995).

Livingstone, S. and R. Das, *Public Attitudes, Tastes and Standards: A Review of the Available Empirical Research* (London School of Economics, 2009). Available at http://eprints.lse.ac.uk/25117/1/Public_attitudes_tastes_and_standards.pdf.

Livingston, S. and P. Lunt, *Talk on Television: Audience Participation and Public Debate* (London: Routledge, 1994).

Lorimer, R., with P. Scannell, *Mass Communications: A Comparative Introduction* (Manchester: Manchester University Press, 1994).

Lull, J. (ed.), *World Families Watch Television* (London: Sage, 1988a).

—— 'Critical response: the audience as nuisance', *Critical Studies in Mass Communication*, 5 (1988b), pp. 239–43.

Lunt, P. and S. Livingstone,, 'Rethinking the focus group in media and communication research', *Journal of Communication*, 46:2 (1996), pp. 76–98.

Lury, K., *Interpreting Television* (London: Hodder Arnold, 2005).

Lury, K., *British Youth Television: Cynicism and Enchantment* (Oxford: Oxford University Press, 2001).

Lusted, D., 'The popular culture debate and light entertainment on television', in C. Geraghty and D. Lusted (eds), *The Television Studies Book* (London: Arnold, 1998), pp. 175–90.

Lyotard, J.-F., 'Answering the question: what is postmodernism?', in T. Docherty (ed.), *Postmodernism: A Reader* (Hemel Hempstead: Harvester Wheatsheaf, 1993), pp. 38–46.

—— *The Postmodern Condition*, trans. G. Bennington and B. Massumi (Manchester: Manchester University Press, 1984).

Macdonald, M., *Representing Women: Myths of Femininity in the Popular Media* (London: Arnold, 1995).

MacGregor, B., *Live, Direct and Biased? Making Television News in the Satellite Age* (London: Hodder Headline, 1997).

Mackay, H. and T. O'Sullivan (eds), *The Media Reader: Continuity and Transformation* (London: Sage, 1999).

MacMillan, A. 'Heroism, institutions, and the police procedural', in T. Potter and C. Marshall (eds), *The Wire: Urban Decay and American Television* (New York: Continuum, 2009), pp. 40–63.

Mader, R., 'Globo village: television in Brazil', in T. Dowmunt (ed.), *Channels of Resistance: Global Television and Local Empowerment* (London: BFI, 1993), pp. 67–89.

Marc, D. and R. Thompson, *Prime Time, Prime Movers: From I Love Lucy to L.A. Law – America's Greatest TV Shows and the People Who Created Them* (NY: Syracuse University Press, 1995).

Marris, P. and S. Thornham (eds), *Media Studies: A Reader* (Edinburgh: Edinburgh University Press, 1999).

Marris, P. and S. Thornham (eds), *Peripheral Vision: New Patterns in Global Television* (Oxford: Oxford University Press, 1996).

Masterman, L., *Television Mythologies: Stars, Shows and Signs* (London: Comedia, 1984).

Mathijs, E. and J. Jones (eds), *Big Brother International: Formats, Critics and Publics* (London: Wallflower, 2004)

May, T., *Social Research: Issues, Methods and Process*, third edition (Buckingham: Open University Press, 2001).

McCabe, J., and K. Akass (eds), *Quality TV: Contemporary American Television and Beyond* (London: I. B. Tauris, 2007).

—— *Reading Desperate Housewives: Beyond the White Picket Fence* (London and New York: I. B. Tauris, 2006).

McCracken, E., *Decoding Women's Magazines: From Mademoiselle to Ms.* (Basingstoke: Macmillan, 1993).

McLean, G., 'CSI: Tarantino', *The Guardian*, New Media section, 11 July 2005, p. 12.

—— 'Corner shop to cop shop', *The Guardian*, Media section, 18 February 2002, pp. 8–9.

McLoone, M., 'Boxed in?: the aesthetics of film and television', in J. Hill and M. McLoone (eds), *Big Picture, Small Screen: The Relations between Film and Television* (Luton 1997), pp. 76–106.

McLuhan, M., *Understanding Media: The Extensions of Man* (London: Ark, 1987).

McNair, B., *News and Journalism in the UK: A Textbook* (London: Routledge, 1994).

McQueen, D., *Television: A Media Student's Guide* (London: Arnold, 1998).

Meech, P., 'Advertising', in J. Stokes and A. Reading (eds), *The Media in Britain: Current Debates and Developments* (Basingstoke: Macmillan, 1999), pp. 25–40.

Messenger Davies, M., 'Production studies', *Critical Studies in Television*, 1:1 (2006), pp. 21–30.

Milch, D. and B. Clark, *True Blue: The Real Stories Behind NYPD Blue* (London: Boxtree, 1996).

Millerson, G., *Video Production Handbook*, third edition (Oxford: Focal Press, 2001).

Mills, B., 'Comedy verité: contemporary sitcom form', *Screen*, 45:1 (2004), pp. 63–78.

Mittell, J., 'All in the game: *The Wire*, serial storytelling and procedural logic', in P. Harrigan and N. Wardip-Fruin (eds), *Third Person: Authoring and Exploring Vast Narratives* (Baltimore: MIT Press, 2009), pp. 429–38.

—— 'Narrative complexity in contemporary American television', *The Velvet Light Trap*, 58:1 (2006), pp. 29–40.

—— *Genre and Television: From Cop Shows to Cartoons in American Culture* (London: Routledge, 2004).

Modleski, T., *Loving with a Vengeance* (Hamden, Conn.: Shoe String Press, 1982).

Moores, S., *Interpreting Audiences* (London: Sage, 1993).

Morley, D., *Television, Audiences and Cultural Studies* (London: Routledge, 1992).

—— *The 'Nationwide' Audience* (London: BFI, 1980).

Morris, M., 'Feminism, reading, postmodernism', in T. Docherty (ed.), *Postmodernism: A Reader* (Hemel Hempstead: Harvester Wheatsheaf, 1993), pp. 368–89.

—— 'Banality in cultural studies', *Block*, 14 (1988), pp. 15–25.

Mort, F., *Cultures of Consumption: Masculinities and Social Space in Late Twentieth Century Britain* (London: Routledge, 1996).

Mosely, R., 'Makeover takeover on British television', *Screen*, 41:3 (2000), pp. 299–314.

Moss, S., 'New kids on the block', *Guardian*, Media section, 28 January 2002, pp. 2–3.

Mullan, B., *Consuming Television* (Oxford: Blackwell, 1997).

Mundy, J., *Popular Music on Screen: From Hollywood Musical to Music Video* (Manchester: Manchester University Press, 1999).

Murdoch, G., 'Authorship and organization', *Screen Education*, 35 (1980), pp. 19–34.

Myers, G., *Ad Worlds: Brands, Media, Audiences* (London: Arnold, 1999).

Nannicelli, T., 'It's all connected: televisual narrative complexity', in T. Potter and C. Marshall (eds), *The Wire: Urban Decay and American Television* (New York: Continuum, 2009), pp. 190–202.

Neale, S. and F. Krutnik, *Popular Film and Television Comedy* (London: Routledge, 1990).

Neale, S. and G. Turner, 'Introduction: what is genre?', in G. Creeber (ed.), *The Television Genre Book* (London: BFI, 2001), pp. 1–7.

Nelson, R., *State of Play: Contemporary 'High-End' TV Drama* (Manchester: Manchester University Press, 2007).

Nelson, R., *TV Drama in Transition: Forms, Values and Cultural Change* (Basingstoke: Macmillan, 1997).

Newcomb, H., *TV: The Most Popular Art* (New York: Anchor, 1974).

—— 'The development of television studies', in J. Wasko (ed.), *A Companion to Television* (Malden, Mass. and Oxford: Blackwell, 2005), pp. 15–28.

Newton, D., *Paving the Empire Road: BBC Television and Black Britons* (Manchester: Manchester University Press, 2011).

Nichols, B., *Introduction to Documentary* (Bloomington: Indiana University Press, 2001).

—— *Blurred Boundaries: Questions of Meaning in Contemporary Culture* (Bloomington: Indiana University Press, 1994).

—— *Representing Reality: Issues and Concepts in Documentary* (Bloomington: Indiana University Press, 1991).

Norris, C., '"Postscript": Baudrillard's second Gulf War article', in P. Brooker and W. Brooker (eds), *Postmodern After-images: A Reader in Film, Television and Video* (London: Arnold, 1997), pp. 168–71.

Orlebar, J., *The Television Handbook*, fourth edition (London: Routledge, 2011).

—— *Digital Television Production* (London: Arnold, 2002).

O'Sullivan, T., 'Television, memories and cultures of viewing 1950–65', in J. Corner (ed.), *Popular Television in Britain: Studies in Cultural History* (London: BFI, 1991), pp. 159–81.

O'Sullivan, T., B. Dutton and P. Rayner, *Studying the Media: An Introduction* (London: Edward Arnold, 1994).

Owens, J., and G. Millerson, *Video Production Handbook*, fifth edition (Oxford: Focal Press, 2011).

Paget, D., *No Other Way to Tell It: Docudrama on Film and Television* (Manchester: Manchester University Press, 2011).

—— 'Acting a part: performing docudrama', *Media International Australia*, 104 (2002), pp. 30–41.

—— *No Other Way to Tell It: Dramadoc/Docudrama on Television* (Manchester: Manchester University Press, 1998).

Pearson, R., 'The writer/producer in American television', in M. Hammond and L. Mazdon (eds), *The Contemporary Television Series* (Edinburgh: Edinburgh University Press, 2005), pp. 11–26.

Petley, J., 'The regulation of media content', in J. Stokes and A. Reading (eds), *The Media in Britain: Current Debates and Developments* (Basingstoke: Macmillan, 1999), pp. 143–57.

Petrie, D. and J. Willis (eds), *Television and the Household: Reports from the BFI's Audience Tracking Study* (London: BFI, 1995).

Philips, D., 'Medicated soap: the woman doctor in television medical drama', in B. Carson and M. Llewellyn-Jones (eds), *Frames and Fictions on Television: The Politics of Identity within Drama* (Exeter: Intellect, 2000), pp. 50–61.

Philo, G., 'Missing in action', *The Guardian*, Higher Education section, 16 April (2002), pp. 10–11.

—— (ed.), *Glasgow Media Reader, volume 2: Industry, War, Economy and Politics* (London: Routledge, 1995).

—— 'Whose news?', *Media, Culture & Society*, 9:4 (1987), pp. 397–406.

Piper, H., 'Reality TV, Wife Swap and the drama of banality', *Screen*, 54:4 (2004), pp. 273–86.

Plunkett, J., 'Miranda's dilemma', *The Guardian*, Media section, 29 August 2011, p. 2.

Poster, M., *The Second Media Age* (Cambridge: Polity, 1995).

Potter, T., and C. W. Marshall (eds), *The Wire: Urban Decay and American Television* (New York: Continuum, 2009).

Purser, P., 'Dennis Potter', in G. Brandt (ed.), *British Television Drama* (Cambridge: Cambridge University Press, 1981), pp. 168–93.

Raeside, J., 'Virtual reality', *The Guardian*, Media section, 1 June 2011.

Rixon, P., *TV Critics and Popular Culture* (London: I. B. Tauris, 2011).

——— *American Television on British Screens: A Story of Cultural Interaction* (Basingstoke: Palgrave Macmillan, 2006).

Rolinson, D., *Alan Clarke* (Manchester: Manchester University Press, 2005).

Roscoe, J. and C. Hight, *Faking It: Mock-documentary and the Subversion of Factuality*, Manchester: Manchester University Press, 2001.

Rose, B. (ed.), *TV Genres: A Handbook and Reference Guide* (Westport, Conn.: Greenwood, 1985).

Rose, B. G., 'The Wire', in G. R. Edgerton and J. P. Jones (eds), *The Essential HBO Reader* (Lexington: Kentucky University Press, 2008), pp. 82–91.

Rosenthal, A. (ed.), *Why Docudrama?: Fact-Fiction on Film and TV* (Carbondale, IL: Southern Illinois University Press, 1999).

Ruddock, A., *Understanding Audiences: Theory and Method* (London: Sage, 2001).

Saussure, F. de, *Course in General Linguistics*, ed. C. Bally, A. Sechehaye and A. Riedlinger, trans. W. Baskin (London: Fontana, 1974).

Scannell, P., 'Television and history', in J. Wasko (ed.), *A Companion to Television* (Malden, Mass. and Oxford: Blackwell, 2005), pp. 51–66.

——— 'Public service broadcasting; the history of a concept', in A. Goodwin and G. Whannel (eds), *Understanding Television* (London: Routledge, 1990), pp. 11–29.

Schlesinger, P., *Putting 'Reality' Together: BBC News* (London: Constable, 1978).

Seale, C., *The Quality of Qualitative Research* (London: Sage, 1999).

Sears, J., '*Crimewatch* and the rhetoric of verisimilitude', *Critical Survey*, 7:1 (1995), pp. 51–8.

Seiter, E., 'Semiotics, structuralism, and television', in R. Allen (ed.), *Channels of Discourse, Reassembled: Television and Contemporary Criticism* (London: Routledge, 1992), pp. 31–66.

Seiter, E., H. Borchers, G. Kreutzner and E.-M. Warth (eds), *Remote Control: Television, Audiences and Cultural Power* (London: Routledge, 1989).

Selby, K. and R. Cowdery, *How to Study Television* (Basingstoke: Macmillan,1995).

Shattuc, J., *The Talking Cure: TV Talk Shows and Women* (London: Routledge, 1997).

Sheen, E. and R. Giddings (eds), *The Classic Novel: From Page to Screen* (Manchester: Manchester University Press, 1999).

Shubik, I., *Play for Today: The Evolution of Television Drama* (London: Davis-Poynter, 1975).

Silverstone, R., *Media and Morality: On the rise of the Mediapolis* (Cambridge: Polity, 2007).

Silverstone, R., *Television and Everyday Life* (London: Routledge, 1994).

Simpson, J., 'What comfort zone?', *The Guardian*, Media section, 29 May 2006, p. 6.

Sinclair, J., 'Latin American commercial television: "primitive capitalism"', in J. Wasko (ed.), *A Companion to Television* (Malden, Mass. and Oxford: Blackwell, 2005), pp. 503–20.

Sinclair, J., E. Jacka and S. Cunningham, 'New patterns in global television', in P. Marris and S. Thornham (eds), *The Media Reader* (Edinburgh: Edinburgh University Press, 1999), pp. 170–90.

——— (eds), *Peripheral Vision: New Patterns in Global Television* (Oxford: Oxford University Press, 1996).

Sleight, G., 'The big picture show: Russell T. Davies' writing for *Doctor Who*', in S. Bradshaw, A. Keen and G. Sleight (eds), *The Unsilent Library: Essays on the Russell T. Davies Era of the New Doctor Who* (London: Science Fiction Foundation, 2011), pp. 15–28.

Smith, A., *Television: An International History*, second edition (Oxford: Oxford University Press, 1998).

Sobchack, V., 'Democratic franchise and the electronic frontier', in Z. Sardar and J. Ravetz (eds), *Cyberfutures* (London: Pluto, 1996), pp. 77–89.

Sparks, R., *Television and the Drama of Crime* (Buckingham: Open University Press, 1992).

Spilsbury, T., 'Shooting stars', *Doctor Who Magazine*, 426 (20 October 2010), pp. 26–30.

Sreberny-Mohammadi, A., K. Nordenstreng, R. Stevenson and F. Ugboajah (eds), *Foreign News in the Media: International Reporting in 29 Countries* (Paris: UNESCO, 1985).

Sreberny-Mohammadi, A., D. Winseck, J. McKenna and O. Boyd-Barrett (eds), *Media in Global Context: A Reader* (London: Arnold, 1997).

Staten, G., and S. Bayes, *The Avid Handbook: Advanced Techniques, Strategies, and Survival Information for Avid Editing Systems*, fifth edition (Oxford: Focal Press, 2008).

Stempel, T., *Storytellers to the Nation: A History of American Television Writing* (NY: Syracuse University Press, 1996).

Stewart, I. and S. Carruthers (eds), *War, Culture and the Media: Representations of the Military in 20th Century Britain* (Trowbridge: Flicks Books, 1996).

Stokes, J. and A. Reading (eds), *The Media in Britain: Current Debates and Developments* (Basingstoke: Macmillan, 1999).

Storey, J. *Cultural Consumption and Everyday Life* (London: Arnold, 1999).

Sweeney, M., 'TV advertising still needs an Xtra factor', *The Guardian*, Media section, 30 August 2011, p. 6.

Thomas, J., 'When digital was new: the advanced television technologies of the 1970s and the control of content', in J. Bennett and N. Strange (eds), *Television as Digital Media* (Durham, NC: Duke University Press, 2011), pp. 52–75.

Thompson, R., *Television's Second Golden Age: From Hill Street Blues to ER* (New York: Syracuse University Press, 1997).

Thornham, S. and T. Purvis, *Television Drama: Theories and Identities* (Basingstoke: Palgrave Macmillan, 2005).

Thurman, N., 'Forums for citizen journalists? Adoption of user generated content initiatives by news media', *New Media and Society*, 10:1 (2008), 139–57.

Thussu, K. D. (ed.), *Electronic Empires: Global Media and Local Resistance* (London: Arnold, 1998).

Tolson, A., *Mediations: Text and Discourse in Media Studies* (London: Arnold, 1996).

Troy, P., 'Sixty-minute men and women: writing the hour drama', *Written By*, September, 1997.

Tulloch, J., *Watching Television Audiences: Cultural Theories and Methods* (London: Arnold, 2000).

—— *Television Drama: Agency, Audience and Myth* (London: Routledge, 1990).

Tulloch, J. and H. Jenkins, *Science Fiction Audiences: Watching Doctor Who and Star Trek* (London: Routledge, 1995).

Tunstall, J. (ed.), *Media Occupations and Professions: A Reader* (Oxford: Oxford University Press, 2001).

—— *Television Producers* (London: Routledge, 1993).

—— *The Media in Britain* (London: Constable, 1983).

Turner, G., and J. Tay (eds), *Television Studies after TV: Understanding Television in the Post-Broadcast Era* (London: Routledge, 2009).

Uricchio, W., 'Rituals of reception, patterns of neglect: Nazi television and its postwar representation', *Wide Angle*, 11:1 (1989), pp. 48–66.

Vest, J. P., *The Wire, Deadwood, Homicide and NYPD Blue: Violence is Power* (Oxford: Praeger, 2011).

Wagg, S. (ed.), *Because I Tell a Joke or Two: Comedy, Politics and Social Difference* (London: Routledge, 1998).

Walker, I., 'Desert stories or faith in facts?', in M. Lister (ed.), *The Photographic Image in Digital Culture* (London: Routledge 1995), pp. 236–52.

Wardlaw, C., and A. Williams, 'Beyond user-generated content: a production study examining the ways in which UGC is used at the BBC', *Media Culture and Society*, 32:5 (2010), pp. 781–99.

Wasko, J. (ed.), *A Companion to Television* (Malden, Mass. and Oxford: Blackwell, 2005).

Wayne, M., *Dissident Voices: The Politics of Television and Cultural Change* (London: Pluto, 1998).

Webster, F., *Theories of the Information Society* (London: Routledge, 1995).

Wells, P., *Animation and America* (New Brunswick: Rutgers University Press, 2002).

—— *Understanding Animation* (London: Routledge, 1998).

Whannel, G., *Fields in Vision: Television Sport and Cultural Transformation* (London: Routledge, 1992).

Whitaker, B., 'Same news, different perspective', *The Guardian*, Media section, 6 February 2006, pp. 1–2.

Whitehouse, M., *Cleaning Up TV: From Protest to Participation* (London: Blandford, 1967).

Wicke, J. and M. Ferguson, 'Introduction: feminism and postmodernism; or, the way we live now', in M. Ferguson and J. Wicke (eds), *Feminism and Postmodernism* (London: Duke University Press, 1994), pp. 1–9.

Williams, R., 'A lecture on realism', *Screen*, 18:1 (1977), pp. 61–74.

—— *Television, Technology and Cultural Form* (London: Collins, 1974).

—— *Drama in Performance* (London: C. A. Watts, 1968).

Winship, J., *Inside Women's Magazines* (London: Pandora, 1987).

Winston, B., *Media Technology and Society: A History* (London: Routledge, 1998).

—— *Claiming the Real: The Documentary Film Revisited* (London: BFI, 1995).

Wood, A., and A. M. Todd, '"Are we there yet?" Searching for Springfield and *The Simpsons'* rhetoric of Omnitopia', *Critical Studies in Media Communication*, 22:3 (2005), pp. 207–22.

Woods, T., *Beginning Postmodernism* (Manchester: Manchester University Press, 1999).

Zhou, Y. and Z. Guo, 'Television in China: history, political economy, and ideology', in J. Wasko (ed.), *A Companion to Television* (Malden, Mass. and Oxford: Blackwell, 2005), pp. 521–39.

Index